KT-197-271

MOTIVATING OFFENDERS TO CHANGE

ONE WEEK LOAN

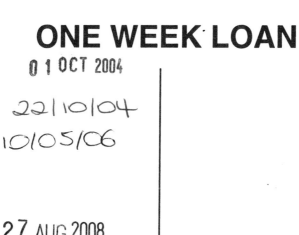

WILEY SERIES IN
FORENSIC CLINICAL PSYCHOLOGY

Edited by

Clive R. Hollin
Centre for Applied Psychology, The University of Leicester, UK

and

Mary McMurran
School of Psychology, Cardiff University, UK

COGNITIVE BEHAVIOURAL TREATMENT OF SEXUAL OFFENDERS
William L Marshall, Dana Anderson and Yolanda Fernandez

VIOLENCE, CRIME AND MENTALLY DISORDERED OFFENDERS:
Concepts and Methods for Effective Treatment and Prevention
Sheilagh Hodgins and Rüdiger Müller-Isberner (*Editors*)

OFFENDER REHABILITATION IN PRACTICE:
Implementing and Evaluating Effective Programs
Gary A. Bernfeld, David P. Farrington and Alan W. Leschied (*Editors*)

MOTIVATING OFFENDERS TO CHANGE:
A Guide to Enhancing Engagement in Therapy
Mary McMurran (*Editor*)

MOTIVATING OFFENDERS TO CHANGE
A Guide to Enhancing Engagement in Therapy

Edited by

Mary McMurran
School of Psychology, Cardiff University, UK

JOHN WILEY & SONS, LTD

Other Wiley Editorial Offices

John Wiley & Sons, Inc., 605 Third Avenue, New York, NY 10158-0012, USA

Jossey-Bass, 989 Market Street, San Francisco, CA 94103-1741, USA

Wiley-VCH Verlag GmbH, Pappelallee 3, D-69469 Weinheim, Germany

John Wiley & Sons Australia, Ltd, 33 Park Road, Milton, Queensland 4064, Australia

John Wiley & Sons (Asia) Pte, Ltd, 2 Clementi Loop #02-01, Jin Xing Distripark, Singapore 129809

John Wiley & Sons (Canada), Ltd, 22 Worcester Road, Etobicoke, Ontario, Canada M9W 1L1

Library of Congress Cataloging-in-Publication Data

British Library Cataloguing in Publication Data

A catalogue record for this book is available from the British Library

ISBN 0-470-84510-4 (cased)
ISBN 0-471-49755-X (paper)

Typeset in 10/12pt Palatino by TechBooks, New Delhi, India
Printed and bound in Great Britain by Antony Rowe Ltd, Chippenham, Wiltshire
This book is printed on acid-free paper responsibly manufactured from sustainable forestry
in which at least two trees are planted for each one used for paper production.

CONTENTS

ABOUT THE EDITOR

Dr Mary McMurran is Senior Baxter Research Fellow in the School of Psychology, Cardiff University, UK, and is funded by the Department of Health's National Programme for Forensic Mental Health Research and Development. She is both a Chartered Clinical Psychologist and a Chartered Forensic Psychologist, and is a Fellow of the British Psychological Society. She has worked with offenders in a young offender's centre, a maximum security psychiatric hospital, a regional secure unit, and in the community. Over the years, she has taken a particular interest in alcohol and crime, a topic on which she has published widely, and in the treatment of personality disordered offenders. She is the author of several structured treatment programmes for such offenders, and these are now widely used in the UK. She is a former Chair of the British Psychological Society's Division of Criminological and Legal Psychology (now the Division of Forensic Psychology), and founding editor of the journal *Legal and Criminological Psychology*.

LIST OF CONTRIBUTORS

Ronald Blackburn

Emeritus Professor of Clinical and Forensic Psychological Studies, Department of Clinical Psychology, University of Liverpool, Liverpool L69 3GB, UK

Christopher Cordess

Professor of Forensic Psychiatry, School of Health and Related Research (ScHARR), University of Sheffield, Regent Court, 30 Regent Street, Sheffield S1 4DA, UK, and Honorary Consultant Forensic Psychiatrist, Rampton Hospital, Retford DN22 0PD, UK

Joel I.D. Ginsburg

Project Officer, Substance Abuse Programs Unit, Correctional Services of Canada, 340 Laurier Avenue West, Ottawa, Ontario, Canada K1A 0P9

Stephen D. Hart

Professor of Psychology, Simon Fraser University, Burnaby, British Columbia, Canada V5A 1S6

James F. Hemphill

Assistant Professor of Psychology, Simon Fraser University, Burnaby, British Columbia, Canada V5A 1S6

John E. Hodge

Director of Psychological Services, Rampton Hospital, Retford DN22 0PD, UK

Clive R. Hollin

Professor of Criminological Psychology, Centre for Applied Psychology, University of Leicester, Leicester LE1 7RB, UK

Lawrence Jones

Consultant Forensic Psychologist, Rampton Hospital, Retford DN22 0PD, UK

D. Richard Laws

South Island Consulting, PO Box 23026, Victoria, British Columbia, V8V 4Z8, Canada

Deborah A. Levesque

Pro-Change Behavior Systems, Inc., PO Box 755, West Kingston, Rhode Island 02892, USA

Vanessa López Viets

Assistant Research Professor, Department of Psychology, University of New Mexico, Center on Alcoholism, Substance Abuse, and Addictions, 2350 Alamo S.E., Albuquerque, New Mexico, 87106, USA

James McGuire

Senior Lecturer in Clinical Psychology, Department of Clinical Psychology, University of Liverpool, Whelan Building, Liverpool L69 3GB, UK

Mary McMurran

Senior Baxter Research Fellow, School of Psychology, Cardiff University, Cardiff CF10 3YG, UK

Ruth Mann

Principal Psychologist, HM Prison Service (England & Wales), Abell House, John Islip Street, London SW1P 4LN, UK

William R. Miller

Distinguished Professor, Departments of Psychology and Psychiatry, University of New Mexico, Center on Alcoholism, Substance Abuse, and Addictions, 2350 Alamo S.E., Albuquerque, New Mexico, 87106, USA

James O. Prochaska

Cancer Prevention Research Center, University of Rhode Island, Kingston, Rhode Island 02881, USA

Stanley J. Renwick

Head of Defence Medical Services Clinical Psychology, Ministry of Defence, The Duchess of Kent's Hospital, Horne Road, Catterick Garrison, DL9 4DF, UK

James Thompson

Leverhulme Special Research Fellow, Centre for Applied Theatre Research, Drama Department, University of Manchester, Manchester M13 9PL, UK

Denise D. Walker

Graduate Student, Department of Psychology, University of New Mexico, Albuquerque, New Mexico, 87131, USA

Glenn D. Walters

Drug Program Coordiator/Clinical Psychologist, Federal Correctional Institute – Schuylkill, PO Box 700, Minersville, Pennsylvania 17954-0700, USA

John R. Weekes

Drug Strategy Coordinator, Correctional Services of Canada, and Adjunct Research Professor of Forensic Addictions, Carleton University, 340 Laurier Avenue West, Ottawa, Ontario, K1A 0P9, Canada

SERIES EDITORS' PREFACE

ABOUT THE SERIES

At the time of writing it is clear that we live in a time, certainly in the UK and other parts of Europe, if perhaps less so in other parts of the world, when there is renewed enthusiasm for constructive approaches to working with offenders to prevent crime. What do we mean by this statement and what basis do we have for making it?

First, by "constructive approaches to working with offenders" we mean bringing the use of effective methods and techniques of behaviour change into work with offenders. Indeed, this might pass as a definition of forensic clinical psychology. Thus, our focus is application of theory and research in order to develop practice aimed at bringing about a change in the offender's functioning. The word *constructive* is important and can be set against approaches to behaviour change that seek to operate by destructive means. Such destructive approaches are typically based on the principles of deterrence and punishment, seeking to suppress the offender's actions through fear and intimidation. A constructive approach, on the other hand, seeks to bring about changes in an offender's functioning that will produce, say, enhanced possibilities of employment, greater levels of self-control, better family functioning or increased awareness of the pain of victims.

A constructive approach faces the criticism of being a "soft" response to damage caused by offenders, neither inflicting pain and punishment nor delivering retribution. This point raises a serious question for those involved in working with offenders. Should advocates of constructive approaches oppose retribution as a goal of the criminal justice systems as incompatible with treatment and rehabilitation? Alternatively, should constructive work with offenders take place within a system given to retribution? We believe that this issue merits serious debate.

However, to return to our starting point, history shows that criminal justice systems are littered with many attempts at constructive work with offenders, not all of which have been successful. In raising the spectre of success, the second part of our opening sentence now merits attention: that is, "constructive approaches to working with offenders to *prevent crime*". In order to achieve the goal of preventing crime, interventions must focus on the right targets for behaviour change. In addressing this crucial point, Andrews and Bonta (1994) have formulated the *need principle*:

> Many offenders, especially high-risk offenders, have a variety of needs. They need places to live and work and/or they need to stop taking drugs. Some have poor self-esteem, chronic headaches or cavities in their teeth. These are all "needs". The need principle draws our attention to the distinction between *criminogenic* and *noncriminogenic* needs. Criminogenic needs are a subset of an offender's risk level. They are dynamic attributes of an offender that, when changed, are associated with changes in the probability of recidivism. Non-criminogenic needs are also dynamic and changeable, but these changes are not necessarily associated with the probability of recidivism. (p. 176).

Thus, successful work with offenders can be judged in terms of bringing about change in noncriminogenic need *or* in terms of bringing about change in criminogenic need. While the former is important and, indeed, may be a necessary precursor to offence-focused work, it is changing criminogenic need that, we argue, should be the touchstone of working with offenders.

While, as noted above, the history of work with offenders is not replete with success, the research base developed since the early 1990's, particularly the meta-analyses (e.g. Lösel, 1995), now strongly supports the position that effective work with offenders to prevent further offending is possible. The parameters of such evidence-based practice have become well established and widely disseminated under the banner of *What Works* (McGuire, 1995).

It is important to state that we are not advocating that there is only one approach to preventing crime. Clearly there are many approaches, with different theoretical underpinnings, that can be applied. Nonetheless, a tangible momentum has grown in the wake of the *What Works* movement as academics, practitioners and policy makers seek to capitalize on the possibilities that this research raises for preventing crime. The task now facing many service agencies lies in turing the research into effective practice.

Our aim in developing this Series in Forensic Clinical Psychology is to produce texts that review research and draw on clinical expertise to advance effective work with offenders. We are both committed to the ideal of evidence-based practice and we will encourage contributors to the Series to follow this approach. Thus, the books published in the Series will not be practice manuals or "cook books": they will offer readers authoritative and critical information through which forensic clinical practice can develop. We are both enthusiastic about the contribution to effective practice that this Series can make and look forward to it developing in the years to come.

ABOUT THIS BOOK

In the early 1990s, Don Andrews identified three key aspects of effective offender treatment—risk, needs and responsivity. Since then, the practice of assessment of risk and the identification of criminogenic needs has advanced apace. The notion of responsivity has, however, received considerably less attention from academics and practitioners. The concept of responsivity is a complex one that incorporates, among other things, an understanding of and a response to the strength (or weakness) of an offender's motivation to change. Motivating offenders to consider change, engage fully in treatment and maintain gains over time is one of the greatest challenges facing the forensic practitioner. Despite this, very little has been written on the topic of motivating offenders to change.

Political support for offender treatment programmes continues to grow, but practitioners and academics must watch that they do not become complacent in the absence of a struggle to promote offender rehabilitation. Work to improve the effectiveness of treatment is a constant endeavour, and it is, perhaps, time to concentrate upon issues of responsivity, including motivation to change. We hope, then, that this book will be a timely prompt to researchers and practitioners in this field.

August 2001   Mary McMurran and Clive Hollin

REFERENCES

Andrews, D. A., & Bonta, J. (1994). *The Psychology of Criminal Conduct*. Cincinnati, OH: Anderson Publishing Co.

Lösel, F. (1995). Increasing consensus in the evaluation of offender rehabilitation? Lessons from recent research synthesis. *Psychology, Crime and Law*, **2**, 19–39.

McGuire, J. (ed.) (1995). *What Works: Reducing Reoffending*, Chichester: John Wiley.

PREFACE

Encouraging offenders to stop offending is a major facet of the role of many professionals in forensic mental health and criminal justice settings. (Mental health professionals may say that their business is to treat the patient's mental disorder, and whether or not that patient offends is nothing to do with them, but this is clearly not the opinion of the public, the media, and the judiciary.) Although not all change is inspired by treatment, this is certainly one way to tackle offending. Interventions of the highest calibre may be on offer, but offenders have to be persuaded to sign up for treatment, be reliable in their attendance, engage in the process, and put into practice the skills and strategies that they are taught.

Some offenders may deny the need for change or resist attempts to help them change. Others may admit the need to change and accept offers of help, but fall short when it comes to putting promises into action. There can be few treatment professionals who have not whiled away an hour when the client did not attend for the session. Indeed, defaulting is so common that the abbreviation "DNA" is widely understood in the world of clinical record keeping to stand for "did not attend". Many professionals actually factor DNA time into their schedules, relying on it for the opportunity to read or clear paperwork. There are also many group workers who have started with a sensible number of clients, only to find somewhere down the line that the number of people turning up scarcely permits the use of the word "group". There are certainly professionals who have asked clients to keep diaries, practise skills, or try new ways of doing things, only to be faced at the next session with blank sheets of paper or excuses.

Recruitment, attendance and compliance are all issues that may be investigated in terms of a client's motivation to change. As soon as we start to think more closely about this, it becomes clear that we need to know what motivation to change is all about, how it may be measured and how therapists can enhance it. Do we know what motivation to change is? If we know what motivation is, can we measure it? If so, should we set a level of motivation that warrants acceptance into treatment? Can we increase a person's level of motivation to change? The notion of altering motivation comes with a warning signal; do we have the right to work on changing people's minds about what they do? These questions are the substance of this text.

The contributing authors are all eminent academics and clinicians, but not all in the same field. Matters relating to motivation to change have been the subject of considerable academic and applied research in the treatment of addictions, and so the expertise of addictions specialists was sought. Many addictions concepts and treatments have been poached and adapted for the understanding and treatment of offenders. The intention here is to continue this useful tradition. Professionals working with offenders, in both mental health services and in prisons, have also been active in working on motivational problems, and here we have the benefit of their wisdom from research and practice.

I am deeply indebted to all authors for their contributions. That so many world-renowned experts have generously made the time to write is gratifying. While editing this book and writing my own chapters, I was employed on a grant from the Department of Health's National Programme for Forensic Mental Health Research and Development, whose support I wish to acknowledge. Thanks also to my host institution—Cardiff University.

As editor, I was in need of a reader to cast a critical eye over my own chapters. I am grateful to Dr Harold Rosenberg of Bowling Green State University, Ohio for tackling this job with all his trademark qualities: intelligence, sensitivity and great good humour.

My hope is that this text will make a difference in practice, helping professionals who work with offenders to develop their treatment programmes. I know for a fact that the book has already succeeded in fulfilling this hope to a degree; it has changed my own thinking and practice. I hope it makes a similar welcome difference to yours.

Mary McMurran

August 2001

Part I

UNDERSTANDING MOTIVATION TO CHANGE

Chapter 1

MOTIVATION TO CHANGE: SELECTION CRITERION OR TREATMENT NEED?

MARY McMURRAN

School of Psychology, Cardiff University, Cardiff, UK

INTRODUCTION

Crime is a matter of perennial public interest and concern, with vast resources poured into the range of activities that contribute to the administration of justice. One aspect of the criminal justice process is dealing with convicted offenders. Broadly speaking, retribution and rehabilitation approaches co-exist in an uncomfortable alliance, while vying with each other for dominance. In recent times, there has been an unprecedented growth in the popularity of offender treatments, with prison and probation services in many countries promoting the development of offender treatment programmes.

In the UK, for example, the Home Office's Crime Reduction Strategy commits considerable financial resources towards developing evidence-based treatment programmes for use in prisons and probation services, ensuring that these programmes are delivered to high standards and evaluating their impact (Colledge et al., 1999; Home Office, 1999a). These programmes tackle offending behaviour per se, as well as mediators of offending, such as sexual deviance, poor problem-solving skills, antisocial beliefs and attitudes, anger problems and substance misuse. The design, implementation and evaluation of programmes is a multidisciplinary endeavour, involving psychologists, probation officers, prison officers, prison managers and researchers.

Treatment no doubt suits the current political and ideological Zeitgeist, but this recent growth in offender treatment is also in large part attributable to the results of meta-analytic studies, commonly called the "What Works" literature. These studies have provided strong evidence that treatment lowers recidivism by at least 10%, which is a modest degree of change but by no means a negligible one (Lipsey, 1995; Lösel, 1995). Meta-analyses have also taught us that the most effective treatments are structured cognitive-behavioural programmes which address offending

Motivating Offenders to Change: A Guide to Enhancing Engagement in Therapy. Edited by M. McMurran.
© 2002 John Wiley & Sons, Ltd.

or mediators of offending, and the greatest effects are with high-risk offenders (Andrews et al., 1990; Lipsey, 1992). Such programmes work best when they are designed to suit offenders' learning styles, operate to high standards of practice, and are conducted in community settings. As a consequence of this knowledge, structured cognitive-behavioural treatment programmes for offenders now abound, targeting a wide range of offending behaviours and mediators of offending. Not only are these programmes used with prisoners and probationers, but professionals working with mentally disordered offenders are also taking them up (Hughes et al., 1997; McMurran et al., 2001).

Despite the apparent effectiveness of structured cognitive-behavioural programmes, not all offenders can be given the advantage of these treatments. Prison and probation personnel do not have the capacity to provide programmes for all offenders within the criminal justice system, even if programmes are reserved only for high-risk offenders, who respond best according to the findings of the meta-analyses. The limited number of programme places has, therefore, to be filled by a selected subgroup of offenders. One common criterion for selecting offenders for such programmes is on their level of motivation to change.

The Scottish Prison Service's programme accreditation criteria, for example, contain the suggestion that programme effectiveness will be ensured if prisoners with the "appropriate" motivation to change are selected, although there is also acknowledgement of the need to take steps to enhance the motivation to change of those who are ambivalent (Scottish Prison Service, 1998). Similarly, guidelines for accreditation of prison and probation offender treatment programmes in England and Wales specify that the offender should be "adequately" motivated to change in order to benefit from the programme (Home Office, 1999b). The possession of "adequate" motivation is a suggested selection criterion, and at the same time motivational enhancement is recommended as an essential component of the treatment.

These criteria reveal that motivation to change is treated partly as a selection criterion and partly as a treatment need. "Appropriate" or "adequate" motivation to change is required for entry to a programme, but thereafter aspects of programme design and delivery ensure that motivation is nurtured, using methods that encourage motivation to flourish. These criteria leave programme designers to judge what "appropriate" or "adequate" motivation might be: the terms come with no definitions or calibrations. The questions that arise are: what kind of motivation is "appropriate" for treatment entry, and how much motivation is deemed "adequate" for treatment entry?

WHAT KIND OF MOTIVATION?

In relation to psychological treatments, Miller (1985) shrewdly observed that "A client tends to be judged as motivated if he or she accepts the therapist's view of the problem (including the need for help and the diagnosis), is distressed, and complies with treatment prescriptions. A client showing the opposite behaviors—disagreement, refusal to accept diagnosis, lack of distress, and rejection of treatment prescriptions—is likely to be perceived as unmotivated, denying, and resistant" (pp. 87–8). Where offenders are concerned, in order to be deemed motivated to change, the professional wants to hear the offender admit to the offence, accept full responsibility for the offence, admit that offending is shameful, express a wish to refrain from offending in future, and own up to needing help from a professional person in order to learn how to refrain from offending. If offenders do not fully admit to the offence, they are denying or minimising culpability; if they do not admit that offending is shameful and express a wish to desist, they are at best anti-social and at worst psychopathic; and if they do not own up to needing the help of a professional, they are considered either arrogant or lacking in insight. In short, an offender is deemed motivated to change as long as he or she agrees with the professional's point of view. A different and potentially more useful perspective is to look at motivation to change from the offender's point of view.

Most human behaviours are considered to be motivated, whether those be-haviours are energetic and appetitive (e.g. running a race to win), or lethargic and avoidant (e.g. watching television because you are too tired for anything else). There are several theories of motivation, with goal-systems or goal-setting theory being one well-founded approach (Karoly, 1993; Locke, 1996). Motivation for most actions can be construed in terms of rational, goal-directed behaviour, and the no-tion of goals is important in understanding human motivation (Karoly, 1993; Locke, 1996). Commitment to a goal is influenced by internal motivators such as values, be-liefs and intrinsic rewards, and by external contingencies, such as material or social rewards and sanctions. Commitment is also influenced by goal attainability, part of which is environmentally determined, but much of which is attributable to the individual's abilities in planning, self-regulation, problem-solving and self-efficacy beliefs. Any volitional behaviour may be examined within this framework, includ-ing motivation to change in therapy (Klinger et al., 1981), and motivation to change offending. Motivation to change offending and motivation to stay the same—that is, to continue offending—are both revealed as positions that represent rational goal choices, based on the individual's characteristics and circumstances.

Motivation to change, defined as commitment to the goal of change, has to be inferred from the person's pre-change behaviours. If one accepts the rational, goal-choice perspective, then the most obvious way to discover what goal the offender intends to pursue is to ask him or her. Does the offender intend to change or not? The problem that now presents itself to the practitioner is how to determine whether an offender's expressed motivation to change is "genuine" or not. Expressed in-tentions are the most readily accessible indicators of motivation to change, and are hence the most commonly used means of assessment.

Although professionals are taught to ask offenders about their motivation to change, they are simultaneously taught to be sceptical about what offenders say, be-lieving them to agree to whatever will have the best outcome for them. An offender may, for example, express a willingness to enter treatment for offending because to do so is likely to attract a more lenient or a non-custodial sentence, rather than be-cause of a genuine desire to change his or her behaviour. In terms of a rational model of motivation, this is a sensible perspective, and if the situational demands are such that promising to change for the better is likely to have a desirable outcome for the offender, then the expressed intention to change must be treated with caution.

However, such scepticism often cuts only one way. When an offender says he or she is *not* motivated to change, this tends to be all too readily believed. Why should professionals, who are so suspicious of an admission of willingness to change, accept unquestioningly the veracity of a statement of lack of motivation to change? There may indeed be reason for an offender to fake willing, and this ought to be checked out, but so may there be reason for an offender to deny any need for or desire to change and this should also be examined more closely.

In addition to what the offender says about his or her intention to change, another commonly used indicator of motivation is previous engagement in and successful response to treatment (Berry et al., 1999). If an offender has taken up offers of treatment in the past, complied with instructions, and shown some improvement, then this is taken as evidence of motivation to change. The return of the compliant offender to the professional offering treatment is not seen as a lack of motivation to change, but more as a temporary lapse or setback in a generally laudable change endeavour. Conversely, if an offender has refused offers of treatment, failed to adhere to treatment protocols, or not improved in treatment, this is taken as an indication of lack of motivation to change. Indeed, as Miller (1985) pointed out, therapists seem inclined to interpret such behaviour not as therapist failure, but as an unmotivated client.

An offender may show no eagerness for treatment, be summarily labelled unmotivated to change, and consequently treatment may be withheld. This is an important decision, often with long-term repercussions, since this assessment of motivation to change may well be taken into account in future assessments, or may even preclude future assessment. It is crucial, then, to consider that perceived motivational failures may, in fact, be failures of the professional, who, in terms of a rational, goal-directed behaviour framework, fails to understand the individual in terms of his or her other life-goals (Karoly, 1993). Looking at some possible alternative interpretations of an offender's denial of culpability, minimisation of harm, unwillingness to stop offending and refusal of help illustrates that there may be rational explanations for apparent lack of motivation to change. Some examples are presented in Table 1.1.

In respect of failure to engage in or respond to treatment, here too there are possible alternative explanations, other than lack of motivation to change. A person who did not attend therapy may have been unable to surmount practical obstacles, or unable to organise his or her chaotic lifestyle sufficiently to attend sessions. There is a logical inconsistency in expecting people with problems to accept help, and

Table 1.1 Alternative interpretations of apparent lack of motivation

"Unmotivated" statement or behaviour	Alternative interpretations
"I didn't do it."	"I'm too ashamed to admit it." "I can't face what will happen next if I admit it."
"It wasn't such a bad thing to do."	"It's the only way I know how to get rewards." "If I admit it was bad, that makes me a bad person."
"I don't want to stop."	"I can't imagine life without this pleasure." "I'd have to change my whole way of life."
"I don't need help."	"I'm scared of what you will ask me to do." "I'll fail and make matters worse."

also expecting them to be capable of overcoming the very problems that besiege them in the first place in order to access that help. If they do not manage to solve this conundrum, they are seen as lacking in motivation to change. A good example of this is in alcohol treatment. A person who has difficulty controlling his or her drinking is deemed to need help. Therapy is offered, but a rule is set that the person should abstain from alcohol in order to access the treatment. If this rule is not adhered to, the offer of therapy is withdrawn. The client's failure to desist from drinking is evidence of a lack of motivation to change his or her drinking problem! Other reasons for failure to comply with therapies are that people may not understand or agree with the goals or methods of treatment, and furthermore, treatment can be a negative experience, apparently aimed at taking away the client's joys in life without constructively building in new sources of rewards.

In short, offenders are mostly rational people, and will therefore sometimes be reluctant to own up to their offending and resistant to admitting the need to change, for a variety of reasons: the desire to keep on with a rewarding behaviour, the desire to avoid feeling ashamed, the fear of embarrassment at being unable to change, and an inability to see how to lead a different life. They may not attend therapy because they experience therapy as aversive, confusing or incomprehensible, or because the very problems for which they have been referred make attendance difficult.

Motivation to change may be understood in the same terms. Offenders want to change for a variety of reasons: they may want to avoid the sanctions and disapproval consequent upon being caught offending, because they feel guilty or ashamed about their behaviour, or because they have acquired or recognised good reasons for leading a different kind of life. They may attend therapy because they agree with the treatment goals, understand the treatment process and because it is convenient to do so. Motivation to change, and lack of it, are rational responses to circumstances. Motivation to change is not a trait that one is born with, to a fixed degree.

These motivational factors may be classified as either: (1) internal—for example, the achievement of a valued goal, or the avoidance of or escape from aversive emotions such as guilt and shame—or (2) external—for example, gaining social acceptance and the avoidance of sanctions and disapproval. It is generally assumed that motivation driven by internal factors is a more reliable predictor of change than motivation that is driven by external factors, and there may be some truth in this, particularly in respect of long-term maintenance of change (Wild et al., 1998). It is also true that goal-directed behaviour is influenced variously by many interacting factors relating to the nature and value of the goal to the individual, the "topography" of the goal (e.g. specificity or ambiguity; ease or difficulty; attainability or otherwise), the cognitive and behavioural skills of the individual in relation to achieving the goal, and the person's perceptions of his or her performance and efficacy (Karoly, 1993; Locke, 1996). In any individual, the number of motivational variables that may be present in various degrees is incalculable, and the effects on motivation to change of treatments targeting any or all of these factors is a question that can only be answered by further research.

In answer to the original question, "What kind of motivation is 'appropriate' for treatment entry?", it might seem that the motivational ideal is for the person to be internally motivated to change, have made a robust decision to change, and have a belief in his or her ability to change. In respect of this ideal, to what degree would a professional expect the offender to be in this state of grace at the first interview? This leads to the second question posed earlier: "How much motivation is 'adequate' for treatment entry?".

HOW MUCH MOTIVATION?

The view that the client must be robustly motivated to change to benefit from treatment is called into question by evidence that compulsory treatment can work. Regarding drug-abuse treatment, Farabee and colleagues (1998) reviewed eleven treatment outcome studies and found that criminal justice referrals did as well as, or better than, voluntary participants in nine of these studies. Similarly, Chick (1998) reviewed mandatory treatments for offenders with alcohol problems, and found that criminal justice referrals had fewer convictions after treatment than did voluntary referrals. Compulsory clients are generally more likely to complete treatment, with completion being a predictor of successful outcome.

Some people believe that those mandated to treatment by the criminal justice system do not have "genuine" motivation to change and hence will do worse than those with autonomous motivation to change (Wild et al., 1998). This view ignores the evidence that many people enter treatment because of external pressure, and even apparent volunteers are there because of ultimatums from family, friends or employers (Polcin & Weisner, 1999). There are, perhaps, fewer differences between volunteers and those mandated to treatment than most people assume. A legal mandate may be an important external motivator for a client to enter treatment and, once there, internal motivation may be enhanced as part of the treatment programme. That is, sanctions and a mandate for treatment may present the opportunity for "softer" approaches to encouraging a client to change his or her goals, such as persuasion, encouragement, enlightenment, empowerment and treatment. Better research is needed, however, to determine whether those who change in mandated treatment intended to change anyway, regardless of the treatment mandate, or if treatment programmes successfully enhance motivation to change in the previously unmotivated—in other words, change a person's goal choice (Farabee et al., 1998).

The issue of compulsory treatment, regardless of intention to change, is likely to become an increasingly important issue in England and Wales, as in other jurisdictions (e.g. LaFond, 2001). Currently, personality disordered offenders can only be compulsorily detained in hospital under mental health legislation if they are considered treatable, with the offender's motivation to change being one key aspect of the determination of treatability or otherwise (Berry et al., 1999; Blackburn, 1993). This is almost certain to change in the near future with a proposed revision of the law to permit the detention, regardless of treatability, of people with severe personality disorder who are deemed dangerous (Department of Health/Home Office, 2000).

Whether in compulsory or voluntary treatment, it seems that the most reliable way to influence behaviour change is through an empathic, empowering approach. In his review of why people change addictive behaviour, Miller (1998) summarised the characteristics of therapists who have most success in changing clients' behaviour. These included the employment of an empathic counselling style and an expectation that the client would succeed in therapy. Motivational interviewing, a set of specific motivational methods, elaborates upon this compassionate therapist style, using techniques that encourage the client to argue for the benefits of change, thus bringing about a robust decision to alter behaviour, where no such decision was present at the outset (Rollnick & Miller, 1995). This approach has worked well in the treatment of addictions, and its author advocates its use in correctional settings (Miller, 1999).

The motivational interviewing approach recognises that most people who engage in problem behaviours are ambivalent about them: they want to change and they want to keep on with the behaviour, both at the same time. An illustration of this with regard to offending is that of a violent offender, who believes that fighting is necessary to maintain a hard image and prevent people taking advantage of him, yet he is growing tired of the legal sanctions and is beginning to think of fighting as a younger man's game. Such a person is ambivalent about his violence, thinking at once that he needs to keep it up and that he ought to be quietening down. Motivational interviewing works on this ambivalence, nudging the person toward the "preferred" outcome, in this case non-violence (Miller, 1996). Motivational interviewing works for people with addictions problems (Miller, 1996), and is being developed with sex offenders (see Chapter 10).

The essence of this section is that treatment can bring about change in people who are apparently unmotivated to receive treatment voluntarily and those who are ambivalent about change. The implication of these findings in relation to using motivation to change as a selection criterion for treatment is that, if motivation to change is not essential for success in treatment, then its use as a selection criterion is dubious. Ceasing to use motivation to change as a selection criterion could be advantageous in that those who are apparently unmotivated to change would not be rejected, as often happens, regardless of risk of reoffending. It has been observed that offenders who are the highest risk for serious recidivism are seen as least motivated to change and may therefore be rejected from treatment (Stewart & Millson, 1995; Thornton & Hogue, 1993), even though offender treatment is most successful when targeted at those who are at high risk of recidivism (Andrews et al., 1990). On the other hand, there are, obviously, ethical implications to both mandatory treatment regardless of the offender's wishes, and "manipulating" motivation to change (see Chapter 4). Some would hold that these activities are defensible in that reducing recidivism is for the greater good of society as a whole (Wild, 1999). Others have concerns about civil liberties, and, furthermore, by spending time on the "unmotivated", we may be taking resources away from those who do want treatment (Farabee et al., 1998), or shifting a burden to health services that ought to be borne by the criminal justice system (Wild, 1999).

SELECTION CRITERION OR TREATMENT NEED?

If professionals are to use motivation to change as a selection criterion, then it is important to be sure that it is a valid selection criterion, in terms of its relationship to treatment outcome. Motivation to change can only be recognised as "genuine"

Table 1.2 Motivational positions

Observed motivation to change	Actual outcome
Motivated to change	Change
Motivated to change	No change
Not motivated to change	Change
Not motivated to change	No change

and robust with any certainty using hindsight. After the fact, we can say that those who ended up changing were genuinely motivated to change at the outset. This tautology highlights the fact that motivation to change is a construct that helps us predict the outcome in which we are interested. Using motivation to change as a predictor of future behaviour, in this case whether the offender will desist from or continue offending, we may derive four motivational positions, as illustrated in Table 1.2: (1) those who are judged motivated to change and who do change; (2) those who are judged motivated to change yet do not change; (3) those who are judged unmotivated to change yet who do change; and (4) those who are judged unmotivated to change and who do not change. At first sight, these four possibilities may be viewed as categorical typologies: (1) the genuinely motivated, (2) the liars, (3) the browbeaten, and (4) the antisocial offenders, with only the genuinely motivated deserving of treatment. One challenge that this offers is that of developing the accuracy of methods of predicting treatment outcome.

Assessing treatability, of which motivation to change is a component, has been likened to assessing dangerousness, but the latter has been the focus of far more attention (Heilbrun et al., 1988; Rogers & Webster, 1989). Motivation to change is one aspect of treatability and is also open to further examination in respect of its relationship to actual outcome. Research in this field first requires a consensus on what is being researched. Motivation to change is a complex construct, whose components need to be unpacked and clarified. In this chapter, a goal-setting perspective has been suggested as one way of clarifying factors influencing change. Valid and reliable research instruments need then to be designed so that these can be related to treatment outcome. The accurate assessment of treatability, whether related to motivation to change or other aspects, is of critical importance, since treatability estimates impact upon where offenders are placed (prison, hospital or community) and how long they stay there. Despite this, there appears to be very little consensus among professionals regarding how treatability is to be judged or assessed (Rogers & Webster, 1989; Quinsey & Maguire, 1983). To summarise, motivation to change needs to be clarified and measured, then tested to see if it predicts who will comply with treatment, who will benefit from treatment, and what effect this has on recidivism (Rogers & Webster, 1989).

We have seen, however, that motivation to change is not essential to achieving the treatment outcome desired by the therapist, and that the client's goals can be changed by therapy. If motivation to change is to be taken to be a treatment need, then we need to be clearer about what factors contribute to motivation to change and how these may be influenced in treatment. In this area, as in others, it behoves all professionals to base their practice on sound knowledge and effective skills.

The practitioner may be best advised to reconsider two common strategies. First, it may not be wise to lament that the offender has turned up with the "wrong" kind of motivation; that is, motivation externally driven. Rejection on this count may be to reject someone who would succeed in therapy. Second, rather than spending time trying to sniff out the truffle of "genuine" motivation, the professional may use the opportunity to help the offender examine the advantages and disadvantages of change, and to inform the offender about those treatments that may be effective in striving towards change. That is, rather than an assessment of motivation, professionals should work on motivational assessment.

CONCLUSION

Can the question posed in the title of this chapter now be answered? Should motivation to change be seen as a selection criterion or a treatment need? The answer is, of course, to incorporate both, as practitioners do now, but using theory-driven, empirically tested probabilistic models of prediction, alongside interventions to enhance motivation to change. As a selection criterion, it is important that we sharpen up knowledge and practice, as has been the case in risk assessments. First, there is scope for clarity and consensus about what "motivation to change" means to practitioners and researchers. Second, valid measures of motivation to change offending need to be developed, based upon a theoretical understanding of motivation and on empirical findings regarding what influences motivation. Third, further work is required to examine the relationship between motivation to change (or lack of it) and treatment outcomes, both offending per se and mediators of offending. Finally, interventions specifically aimed at enhancing motivation to change need to be designed and evaluated. Ethical issues need to be considered in relation to how far one goes in attempting to motivate offenders to change. These activities have, surprisingly, attracted little concerted effort in the field of offender treatment, and it is hoped that this book will enhance the motivation of academics and practitioners to engage in these areas of research.

REFERENCES

Andrews, D.A., Zinger, I., Hoge, R.D., Bonta, J., Gendreau, P., & Cullen, F.T. (1990). Does correctional treatment work? A clinically relevant and psychologically informed meta-analysis. *Criminology*, **28**, 369–404.

Berry, A., Duggan, C., & Larkin, E. (1999). The treatability of psychopathic disorder: how clinicians decide. *Journal of Forensic Psychiatry*, **10**, 710–19.

Blackburn, R. (1993). Clinical programmes with psychopaths. In K. Howells & C.R. Hollin (eds) *Clinical Approaches to the Mentally Disordered Offender*. Chichester: Wiley.

Chick, J. (1998). Treatment of alcoholic violent offenders: ethics and efficacy. *Alcohol and Alcoholism*, **33**, 20–5.

Colledge, M., Collier, P., & Brand, S. (1999). *Programmes for Offenders: Guidance for Evaluators*. London: Home Office, Research, Development and Statistics Directorate.

Department of Health/Home Office (2000). *Reforming the Mental Health Act: Part II High Risk Patients*, Cm 5016-II. Norwich: The Stationery Office.

Farabee, D., Prendergast, M., & Anglin, M.D. (1998). The effectiveness of coerced treatment for drug abusing offenders. *Federal Probation*, **62**, 3–10.

Heilbrun, K., Bennett, W.S., Evans, J.H., Offutt, R.A., Reiff, H.J., & White, A.J. (1988). Assessing treatability in mentally disordered offenders: a conceptual and methodological note. *Behavioral Sciences and the Law*, **6**, 479–86.

Home Office (1999a). *What Works. Reducing Re-offending: Evidence-Based Practice*. London: Home Office, Communications Directorate.

Home Office (1999b). *What Works Initiative Crime Reduction Programme: Joint Prison and Probation Accreditation Criteria*. London: Home Office.

Hughes, G., Hogue, T., Hollin, C., & Champion, H. (1997). First stage evaluation of a treatment programme for personality disordered offenders. *Journal of Forensic Psychiatry*, **8**, 515–27.

Karoly, P. (1993). Goal systems: an organising framework for clinical assessment and treatment planning. *Psychological Assessment*, **5**, 273–80.

Klinger, E., Barta, S.G., & Maxeiner, M.E. (1981). Current concerns: assessing therapeutically relevant motivation. In P.C. Kendall & S.D. Hollon (eds) *Assessment Strategies for Cognitive-Behavioral Interventions*. New York: Academic Press, pp. 161–96.

LaFond, J.Q. (2001). Clinical, legal, and ethical issues for mental health professionals in implementing a sexual predator law in the United States. In D.P. Farrington, C.R. Hollin, & M. McMurran (eds) *Sex and Violence: The Psychology of Crimes and Risk Assessment*. London: Harwood Academic.

Lipsey, M.W. (1992). Juvenile delinquency treatment: a meta-analytic inquiry into the variability of effects. In T.D. Cook, H. Cooper, D.S. Cordray, H. Hartmann, L.V. Hedges, R.J. Light, T.A. Louis, & F. Mosteller (eds) *Meta-Analysis for Explanation: A Casebook*. New York: Russell Sage Foundation.

Lipsey, M.W. (1995). What do we learn from 400 research studies on the effectiveness of treatments with juvenile delinquents? In J. McGuire (ed.) *What Works: Reducing Reoffending*. Chichester: Wiley.

Locke, E.A. (1996). Motivation through conscious goal setting. *Applied and Preventive Psychology*, **5**, 117–24.

Lösel, F. (1995). The efficacy of correctional treatment: a review and synthesis of meta-evaluations. In J. McGuire (ed.) *What Works: Reducing Reoffending*. Chichester: Wiley.

McMurran, M., Charlesworth, P., Duggan, C., & McCarthy, L. (2001). Controlling angry aggression: a pilot group intervention with personality disordered offenders. *Behavioural and Cognitive Psychotherapy*, **29**, 473–84.

Miller, W.R. (1985). Motivation for treatment: a review with special emphasis on alcoholism. *Psychological Bulletin*, **98**, 84–107.

Miller, W.R. (1996). Motivational interviewing: research, practice, and puzzles. *Addictive Behaviors*, **21**, 835–42.

Miller, W.R. (1998). Why do people change addictive behavior? The 1996 H. David Archibald lecture. *Addiction*, **93**, 163–72.

Miller, W.R. (1999). Pros and cons: reflections on motivational interviewing in correctional settings. *Motivational Interviewing Newsletter: Updates, Education, and Training*, **6**, 2–3.

Polcin, D.L., & Weisner, C. (1999). Factors associated with coercion in entering treatment for alcohol problems. *Drug and Alcohol Dependence*, **54**, 63–8.

Quinsey, V.L., & Maguire, A. (1983). Offenders remanded for a psychiatric examination: perceived treatability and disposition. *International Journal of Law and Psychiatry*, **6**, 193–205.

Rogers, R., & Webster, C.D. (1989). Assessing treatability in mentally disordered offenders. *Law and Human Behavior*, **13**, 19–29.

Rollnick, S., & Miller, W.R. (1995). What is motivational interviewing? *Behavioural and Cognitive Psychotherapy*, **23**, 325–34.

Scottish Prison Service (1998). *Prisoner Programme Accreditation Services: Manual of Standards and Accompanying Documentation for Programme and Site Accreditation*, manual no. 082/98. Edinburgh: Scottish Prison Service.

Stewart, L., & Millson, W.A. (1995). Offender motivation for treatment as a responsivity factor. *Forum on Corrections Research*, **7**, 5–7.

Thornton, D., & Hogue, T. (1993). The large-scale provision of programmes for imprisoned sex offenders: issues, dilemmas, and progress. *Criminal Behaviour and Mental Health*, **3**, 371–80.

Wild, T.C. (1999). Compulsory substance-user treatment and harm reduction: a critical analysis. *Substance Use and Misuse*, **34**, 83–102.

Wild, T.C., Cunningham, J., & Hobden, K. (1998). When do people believe that alcohol treatment is effective? The importance of perceived client and therapist motivation. *Psychology of Addictive Behaviors*, **12**, 93–100.

Chapter 2

WHAT IS MOTIVATION TO CHANGE?
A SCIENTIFIC ANALYSIS

Vanessa López Viets, Denise D. Walker and William R. Miller

*Department of Psychology and Center on Alcoholism, Substance Abuse and Addictions
(CASAA), University of New Mexico, Albuquerque, New Mexico USA*

A NEW MOTIVATIONAL PERSPECTIVE

Working with offenders on behavior change issues is both professionally stimulating and challenging. One need not work very long in this field to discover that simply *prescribing or advising* behavior change usually does not work. Neither is it sufficient, in most cases, to guide offenders in *how* they could change. Recidivism and failure to complete or comply with treatment, especially among certain subgroups of offenders, are fairly common outcomes (Firestone et al., 1998; Hanson & Bussiere, 1998), sometimes leading to frustration with offenders' "lack of motivation" for change.

These problems are by no means unique to offender populations. In health care, one of the primary frustrations in treating chronic diseases such as diabetes, hypertension, and heart disease is lack of compliance with prescribed treatment, resulting in life-threatening relapses. Similarly, the management of severe mental illnesses such as schizophrenia and bipolar disorder is plagued by low treatment retention and medication adherence, leading to re-hospitalization. Substance use disorders and other addictive behaviors are characterized by frequent recurrence and a high rate of treatment dropout.

Is Motivation a Trait?

In an attempt to explain such problems, a lack of adherence to treatment requirements and failure to change, are sometimes attributed to the person's "low motivation," "denial," or "hardened" nature. Such language suggests that the problem is something amiss with *the individual*. A variety of hypothesized characteristics

Motivating Offenders to Change: A Guide to Enhancing Engagement in Therapy. Edited by M. McMurran.
© 2002 John Wiley & Sons, Ltd.

are presumed to be responsible. Some have to do with negative character traits (e.g. oppositional, sociopathic), and sometimes such labels are moralistic in tone. Lack of motivation and change may be attributed to impairment of self-regulation, intelligence, or moral development. Stubborn defense mechanisms may be invoked (e.g. denial, rationalization). To be sure, such factors may play a role in motivation, but when used in an explanatory fashion, they have one thing in common: they tend to blame the *person* for not changing. Sometimes the attribution is to volitional processes (being *unmotivated*), and sometimes to the person's *inability* to change. In either case, the problem is seen as residing within the person, and one is left with the impression that there is little anyone else can do to effect change.

This trait conception of motivation can also lead to rather confrontational approaches. When the person is thought to be incapable of seeing reality, or stubbornly unmotivated, or impaired by irrational defense mechanisms, the alternative to inaction can be to turn up the volume in an aggressive attempt to "break him and make him" change. The underlying view seems to be that if one can just make the person feel *bad* enough, change will happen. Various confrontational methods have been tried in an attempt to *force* readiness to change, usually with quite limited success once sanctions are lifted. Thinking of motivation as something like a trait inside the person tends to lead to one of these two approaches: either throwing up one's hands in helpless frustration and waiting for the person to "get serious" and "hit bottom," or trying to override inertia with confrontational and coercive tactics. Sometimes interactions shift back and forth between the two methods.

Motivation as Modifiable

Gradually, a dramatic shift has been occurring in how to think about motivation for change. Research has clearly shown that there are ways to enhance a person's intrinsic motivation for change (Miller, 1999). Clinicians have come to see eliciting client motivation as part of their job. One need not stand by, passively waiting for clients to "get motivated." Indeed, it is not a good idea to do so, for it is a stance that is not particularly effective, and fosters professional frustration and burnout. The better question is not whether clients are motivated, but rather how to enhance their motivation for change. That is, in fact, the subject of this book.

Our task in this chapter is to offer a dynamic framework for understanding what motivation is, and how it changes. This is a starting point, precisely because how one *thinks* about motivation is directly linked to what one *does* (or does not do) to change it. We offer a framework that is well supported by scientific evidence, and is also readily understandable in common-sense everyday language. Interventions, such as motivational interviewing, that are grounded in this perspective have already shown considerable success in promoting positive behavior change in populations often perceived to be difficult or severe (Easton et al., 2000; Garland & Dougher, 1991; Harper & Hardy, 2000; Mann & Rollnick, 1996; Miller, 1983; Saunders et al., 1995). Interventions based on this approach have been found to increase the likelihood of treatment initiation, retention, and adherence as well as positive behavior change. This motivational perspective is applicable to a wide range of problems that appear resistant to change, including addictive and antisocial behaviors.

What are the cornerstones of this new perspective on motivation? We offer these as six key points:

1. Motivation is *modifiable*. Like overt behavior, it can be increased or decreased via lawful principles of human nature.
2. Motivation is a matter of *probabilities*: how *likely* is the person to initiate and persist in a particular action? It is about initiating and directing action (Petri, 1986). Therefore, interventions to influence motivation are those that effectively increase or decrease the probability of an action (Miller, 1985).
3. Motivation is an *interpersonal* phenomenon, something that occurs and changes within the context of human relationships.
4. Motivation is often quite *specific* to a course of action. A person may be unmotivated (low probability) for one type of treatment or change, but quite ready to participate in another. Drug users, for example, are often more motivated to stop or reduce their use of one drug than another.
5. Motivation is *intrinsic* as well as extrinsic. Although it is possible to coerce behavior change when one has control over external contingencies, intrinsically motivated change is more likely to last.
6. Intrinsic motivation for change is engaged by *eliciting it from* rather than installing it in the person.

READY, WILLING, AND ABLE

There is wisdom embedded in everyday language. In English, when a person is particularly motivated to do something, one says that he or she is "ready, willing, and able" to do it. This is a good way to remember the components of motivation, because each of these represents an important precondition for change. One can be willing but not able, or willing and able but not ready to make a change. The more each of these three elements increases, the greater the probability that change will occur. This framework can be helpful not only in conceptualizing motivation, but also in understanding the obstacles to change for a particular individual (Rollnick et al., 1999).

Ready

Some people are willing to change but lack confidence that they can do so. Others are quite confident that they could change, but see little reason to do so. Then there are those who seem to be both willing and able, but still are not ready. Each of these poses different motivational challenges (Miller & Rollnick, 2002).

Priorities

Think of some things that you *could* do, that would be *worthwhile* if you did them and would be consistent with your values, and yet you do not do them. It is quite common, actually, for people to be willing and able to do something, and yet it does not happen. There is something else involved in being fully ready to act.

One common factor here is the importance of a particular act or change relative to others. "Yes, it's important," a person may say, "but it's not the *most* important thing for me right now." Other tasks have a higher priority, and compete for the time and energy required. This is still an issue of importance (willingness) in a way, but in order to understand the situation one must see this particular change through the person's eyes, in the context of other concerns and demands. Of course, if the perceived importance of a certain change increases, then its priority relative to others may also increase, and the person may be ready to pursue it.

Approximations

It is also useful to think of change not as a "cut and dried" affair, but as a process that unfolds over time. Sometimes change does occur as a sudden and dramatic quantum leap (Miller & C'de Baca, 2001), but most behavior change occurs gradually, in small steps, in fits and starts. Recovery from alcohol dependence, for example, does not most often occur as a sudden once-and-for-all decision to abstain, but as successive approximations. Progressively longer periods of time pass between episodes, and periods of excessive drinking become shorter and less severe (Miller, 1996). The immediate establishment of a stable new behavior is more the exception than the rule, and it is helpful to think outside this all-or-none perspective (Prochaska et al., 1992). If a person is not yet ready to commit fully to a particular change, what small step in that direction might the person be willing, able, and ready to take? Each step in turn increases commitment (readiness, willingness, and perceived ability) for the next. Of course, there are certain behaviors, such as sexual offenses, for which there is little tolerance for reoccurrence. This underscores the importance of engaging these offenders in the treatment process to motivate them to change.

Willing

Most social systems, including the legal and correctional systems, hold people at least partially responsible for their own actions. This affirms the role of personal volition, of processes such as choosing, deciding, intending, and willing. Before a change occurs, the person decides that it is important enough to undertake, and forms an intent to do it. In short, the person becomes *willing* to take action and make a change.

Discrepancy

How does this happen? A self-regulation model draws on the metaphor of a thermostat for regulating temperature (Miller & Brown, 1991). An ideal point is set, and around it is a range of acceptability. If room (or body) temperature deviates too far from the ideal, it triggers adjustments (such as turning on a furnace, or sweating) in order to return temperature to within acceptable limits. The same is true of human behavior. A course of action continues until something alerts us that things need to change. In driving, one continues down the road until something triggers a need for change: a red light flashes, an object emerges from the periphery on a collision course, or a road sign indicates that it is time to turn in order to reach a particular destination.

As with the thermostat, the need for change (willingness) is triggered by a perceived *discrepancy* between how things are (status quo) and how things ought to be (goals, desires, values). Consider the simple example of body weight. Most people can specify what they regard to be an ideal body weight for themselves, as well as an acceptable range on either side of that ideal. When the scale indicates that one has exceeded that range, it may trigger action (such as changing diet or exercise) to return to the acceptable range. Why, then, might a person become overweight or anorexic? Perhaps there is no discrepancy for the person, but only in the eye of the beholder. It may also be that current weight is not discrepant with what the person regards to be an acceptable range of body weight. Perhaps there is no reliable feedback that would signal a discrepancy (e.g. the person does not monitor body weight). Under such conditions, the person may see no *reason* to change; it would not seem important enough to trigger efforts to change. Being *willing* to change involves perceiving that the change is important, that there is good reason for change.

Extrinsic and intrinsic motivation

Extrinsic motivation arises from external factors, from conditions outside the person such as social pressures, reinforcement, and punishment. Without question, behavior can often be changed if one has enough control over rewards and penalties. One problem with such extrinsic motivation, however, is that it tends to be short-lived. Usually (though not always) once the control is gone, so is the change. It is even possible to undermine intrinsically motivated behavior by placing it temporarily under the external control of rewards and punishment (Deci & Ryan, 1987).

Intrinsic motivation, by contrast, arises from within the person. Self-regulation has to do with intrinsic motivation (as contrasted with external controls). This type of motivation is positively associated with interest, enjoyment, flexibility, spontaneity, and creativity in the behavior (Deci & Ryan, 1987). Intrinsically motivated behavior is not dependent upon external motivators. Intrinsically motivated change is therefore more likely to persist in the absence of external controls. That is, in fact, one definition of self-regulation. Counseling methods such as motivational interviewing are designed to elicit and enhance intrinsic motivation for change.

Closely linked to intrinsic motivation is the concept of autonomy. Deci and Ryan (1985) postulated that individuals have an inherent desire for freedom to make their own decisions, to be self-determining. When a person perceives an action to be freely chosen and self-determined, it is more likely to occur and persist. The perception of one's behavior as being controlled and manipulated by others is inherently aversive, and tends to undermine persistence, even if the behavior was initially one that had been intrinsically motivated. Moreover, perceived threats to freedom and choice tend to elicit actions (often seen as defiant) that reassert personal freedom, thereby reducing the probability of change, a phenomenon known as psychological *reactance* (Brehm & Brehm, 1981). Behaviors or options that were once of little or no intrinsic value can take on great importance when freedom is threatened. Attempts to control a behavior by punishment can paradoxically increase the extent to which that behavior is valued and practiced. In sum, willingness to change can be enhanced or diminished by efforts to invoke intrinsic or extrinsic motivation.

Able

Self-efficacy

People who are willing to make a change, who see it as worthwhile and important, may nevertheless be stymied if they perceive that they do not have the ability to do so. Such people may say things like, "I would if I could" or "I wish I could"— statements that reflect high willingness but low confidence. In modern psychology, this confidence in one's ability to carry out a specific task is termed *self-efficacy*, which turns out to be a relatively good predictor of whether change will occur and persist. Self-efficacy should not be confused with more generalized constructs such as self-esteem; self-efficacy is specific to each task or change. Nevertheless, there are generalized patterns of perceived powerlessness and hopelessness, often linked to depression or the pattern described by Seligman (1991) as "learned helplessness." People who perceive that their actions in general are unlikely to affect the outcome are unlikely to try to change. The reverse is also true. The likelihood that a person will try (take action) is more driven by perceived ability than by actual current competence.

Hope

It is not only the person's own perceptions of ability or inability that matter. The expectancies of others can also play a powerful role on outcome, yielding positive or negative self-fulfilling prophecies. In one study, psychologists tested patients in alcoholism treatment programs, and identified to staff those who showed particularly high addiction recovery potential (Leake & King, 1977). One year after treatment discharge, the high-potential patients were substantially more likely to be sober, had fewer slips and relapses, and were more likely to be employed. The secret of this study, as you may have guessed, is that these patients had been chosen at random, and did not differ in any way from other patients in the programs, except that the staff believed that they would recover. It is the madness of *The Man of La Mancha*, that seeing the possibilities in another has a way of calling them forth into reality. It is one more example of how motivation for change does not lie solely within the person, but is molded in human relationships.

This phenomenon of hope has obvious implications for work with offenders. The very labels of correctional systems (e.g. prisoner, repeat offender, felon) often invoke in the public mind a pessimistic or cynical set of expectations, which may also be shared by correctional staff. Such perceptions are contagious, and can ultimately be adopted by offenders themselves, who may need to borrow our hope until they can gain their own (Yahne & Miller, 1999). In short, it *matters* how we as professional helpers perceive those with whom we work. Professional burnout that fosters cynicism is hurtful not only to one's ability to help, but to clients as well.

Self-regulation

While it is true that expectations become self-fulfilling, it is also the case that people do differ in their ability to self-regulate their behavior. Individuals with less impulse control are more likely to be pulled by external situations and immediate gratification, with less constraint from long-term values and consequences. Such people do not necessarily lack prosocial values, but do experience greater difficulty in conforming their behavior to long-term goals. When internal controls are more tenuous, self-control can be aided by additional structure, environmental change, and compensatory coping strategies (Miller & Brown, 1991). The need for such external supports tends to be greater in the earlier phases of change (as during a period of probation), and external controls can be faded gradually as self-regulation ability is strengthened.

THE INTERACTIVE NATURE OF MOTIVATION

The perspective we propose here is that motivation for change arises not primarily from within the person, but from interactions and relationships. Rather than being a static phenomenon, motivation is dynamic, fluctuating over time. Interpersonal transactions continually increase or decrease the perceived priority, importance, and confidence for change.

Interpersonal Transactions

Interpersonal influence

The probability that a person will undertake a particular action or change can be influenced by a host of interpersonal factors. Within correctional contexts, the most familiar of these may be the imposition of contingencies (primarily punishment) by a judge, probation officer, or other agent of the courts. There are, however, many other less coercive examples.

- Are you making a referral, and want the client to get there? Making the contact phone call and an appointment while the client is in your office can more than double the chances of the referral being completed (Kogan, 1957).
- Did you just complete an initial session and hope the client will come back? A simple caring phone call or handwritten note shortly after the intake session may double the probability of return (Koumans & Muller, 1965; Koumans et al., 1967).
- Did your client miss a session? Taking the initiative with a letter can halve the chances that the client will drop out (Panepinto & Higgins, 1969).
- Do you want your client to stick with treatment? Offering a single motivational interview beforehand may more than double the number of outpatient sessions

completed, or enhance motivation to work hard during inpatient treatment, and thereby significantly improve outcome (Aubrey, 1998; Brown & Miller, 1993).

- Are you interested in getting your client to attend a twelve-step meeting? In one study, linking clients up with a current AA member who offered support and transportation to the first meeting increased the chances of attending from zero to 100% (Sisson & Mallams, 1981).
- Do you want a client to attend aftercare sessions? Reminder calls or a structured calendar can double the number of aftercare sessions attended (Intagliata, 1976).

Ordinarily one thinks of such things—getting to a referral, attending more sessions, going to AA meetings—as reflecting a client's level of motivation, and so they do. The point here is that even relatively simple actions can substantially impact a client's probability of taking steps toward change.

Interpersonal style

Client motivation is influenced not only by specific actions like those described above, but more generally by the interpersonal style of interaction. Once again, the malleability of motivation is apparent. Consider the following experiment. People with drinking problems were randomly assigned to counselors using one of two styles of counseling. One style was confrontational, challenging them whenever they denied having a problem, and re-emphasizing the hard evidence that they drank too much. The other style was supportive and empathic, relying heavily on reflective listening. Clients assigned to confrontational counseling showed high levels of resistance and denial, and relatively little commitment to change their drinking. Those randomly assigned to a counselor who listened empathically, by contrast, offered far less resistance and evidenced higher levels of commitment to change. More generally, confrontational approaches are relatively ineffective in producing lasting behavior change (Miller et al., 1998). Over the years, treatment programs that once relied heavily upon such tactics have gradually abandoned confrontation in favor of gentler and more effective approaches (e.g. Hazelden Foundation, 1985).

Similarly, professionals who work with sex offenders are finding that confrontational styles are not successful in engaging individuals into treatment. Kear-Colwell and Pollock (1997) conclude that verbal attacks on offenders will impel them to protect their self-image through resistance and disagreement. On the other hand, a motivational approach will elicit from offenders their reasons for wanting to change their behaviors, which will move them into taking responsibility for change. Garland and Dougher (1991) emphasize the crucial task of engaging sex offenders into treatment, because a lack of engagement may lead to poor treatment outcomes and subsequent recidivism. According to these researchers, offenders from community-based and residential treatment programs have benefited from motivational interventions that not only engage them into treatment, but also help them actualize and maintain changes.

Further evidence that interpersonal style influences client outcomes is found in research on the effects of counselor assignment. How well clients fare in the long run can be substantially affected by the counselor to whom they are assigned.

Counselors differ significantly in the rates at which their clients drop out of treatment (Greenwald & Bartmeier, 1963; Raynes & Patch, 1971; Rosenberg & Raynes, 1973; Rosenberg et al., 1976). In one study of nine counselors, success rates of counselors working with problem drinkers ranged from 25% to 100% (Miller et al., 1980). Other studies with random assignment have found large differences among counselors in the rates of relapse and re-arrest within their caseloads (McLellan et al., 1988; Valle, 1981). In fact, the counselor to whom one is assigned may have a larger effect on outcomes than either specific treatment approach or client characteristics (Bergin & Garfield, 1994; Kottler, 1991; Project MATCH Research Group, 1998).

Motivation and Language

Thus far we have emphasized that motivation for change is a product of interpersonal interactions, that it is malleable, and that it is responsive to a counselor's interpersonal style. How does this occur?

One piece of the puzzle is that it is possible to predict, from what clients say during counseling sessions, the likelihood that actual behavior change will occur and endure. In the absence of coercion, higher levels of client resistance during treatment sessions predict that behavior will not change, whereas low levels of resistance are associated with subsequent change (Miller et al., 1993). Psycholinguist Paul Amrhein has similarly reported that behavior change in illicit drug use is predictable from patterns of clients' commitment language during a single counseling session (Amrhein et al., 2000).

What, then, determines whether clients come down on the side of resistance or commitment to change during counseling? Again, counselor style has a major impact. As reported above, clients randomly assigned to a confrontational counselor showed higher rates of resistance and lower rates of commitment (Miller et al., 1993). In this same study, a very specific behavioral outcome—the average weekly amount of alcohol consumption 12 months later—was highly predictable from a single counselor response during a single treatment session: the more the counselor confronted, the more the client drank. In another illustrative study, Patterson and Forgatch (1985) had therapists switch back and forth between directive and empathic counseling styles every twelve minutes within their counseling sessions. Client resistance behavior went up and down in step function. When counselors took a directive and instructional role, resistance was high; when they responded empathically, resistance dropped. Clearly resistance is not an individual characteristic of clients, but is interactive. It takes two to generate resistance, and when it does occur, it can be increased or decreased by counseling style.

Ambivalence

What is going on here? It appears that clients can literally "talk themselves into or out of" change, and their decisions are impacted by the way in which their counselor responds. By the time people walk into the office of a counselor or probation officer, it is a reasonable assumption that they are ambivalent about the target behavior that brought them in. A few may be wholeheartedly committed to their past behavior and see absolutely no disadvantages or problems with it. Some may have had a change of heart and become entirely ready to change. The vast majority, however, lie somewhere in between. They are ambivalent. They have within themselves both sides of the argument: change and status quo.

Now, what happens if you take up one side of the argument with an ambivalent person? The result is rather predictable: he or she will defend the other side. It is an almost automatic response. Tell an ambivalent person that he or she has a real problem and has to change, and he or she is likely to tell you why he or she will not change. Depending on training and orientation, the counselor at this point may conclude that the person is in denial, or out of touch with reality, and thus intensify the argument for change. The response is again predictable: the ambivalent client tends to argue more forcefully against the need for change. If the counselor has some power to enforce consequences, the client may acquiesce instead of going toe-to-toe, but again the likelihood of enduring change is low.

Most people are more inclined to believe what they hear themselves say than what someone else tells them. When a person argues for one course of action, he or she becomes more committed to it. The more forcefully one argues for change in an adversarial context, the stronger the commitment to one's position.

It therefore matters how you manage a counseling session. If you take responsibility for the "good" side of a client's ambivalence, you leave the client only one position. This exchange is what Miller and Rollnick (1991) have termed the *confrontation–denial trap*. The more a counselor confronts, the more the client resists (i.e. argues against change), and thereby becomes more committed to the status quo, even if badgered into submission.

The term "confrontation" usually brings to mind a rather negative, aggressive, aversive interaction, and we have used it thus in the preceding discussion to describe a *style* of communication. However, the linguistic root of "confront" means "to come face to face." Looked at in this way, confrontation is a goal rather than a method, and the question becomes: what is the most effective way to help someone to come face to face with a painful or difficult reality, let it in, and let it change him? Some believe that the best way to achieve this is to "get in the face" of the client or offender, but the evidence, as discussed above, favors a more empathic approach. An empathic style is not passive. In fact, it has been called *active* listening (Gordon, 1970). It can also be used directively, to elicit from clients the arguments for change (Miller & Rollnick, 2002). The style with which one counsels can move people closer to (or further away from) change.

Choice

The above discussion does not diminish offenders' responsibility for their own behavior. While responsibility for change remains with the individual, a motivational perspective also empowers the counselor to influence choices that offenders make (and thereby also places responsibility on us as counselors). A motivational perspective is therefore more optimistic than either a perspective that dismisses offenders as flawed and unmotivated, or one that assumes there is nothing a counselor can do until the offender is motivated.

Do offenders really have a choice? Of course they do. Although the courts can set consequences for various courses of action, offenders nevertheless choose their course of action (and the related consequences). They can and do choose to comply or not comply with what the court wants and requires. Within a motivational perspective, the counselor is interested in understanding what the offender wants, and how his or her choices may advance or detract from those goals. That is, motivation must be understood through the eyes of the offender.

There is a good reason to emphasize offenders' choices rather than their limitations, and it has to do with human nature. When people perceive that they have freely chosen a course of action from among alternatives, they are generally more motivated to carry it out, more likely to persist in it. On the other hand, when people perceive that they are doing something because they are forced to do it and have no choice, they are likely to be resentful and seek to undermine or evade the coercion. Perhaps more importantly, as soon as the perceived coercion is removed, there is a strong tendency to revert to prior patterns of behavior. To be sure, consequences are important in correctional systems, but to emphasize coercion as motivation ("You have to do this. You have no choice.") is to enhance the likelihood of recidivism.

One might expect that when offenders are legally mandated to treatment, they would feel coerced to change and consequently possess little intrinsic motivation. In fact, offenders vary widely in how they perceive their own motivation for seeking treatment, with a substantial proportion reporting little sense of coercion (Wild et al., 1998). This finding is consistent with our own experience in a public substance abuse treatment program in which approximately half of clients are court-referred. We initially assumed that by asking, on our intake form, why people were seeking treatment, we would determine which of them had been court-mandated. Instead, many court-referred clients report that they are coming by their own choice. A skeptical view might be that such clients are simply being deceptive, but in fact we find that many offenders do genuinely perceive that they have chosen to seek treatment. In truth, they have, because others choose not to follow through with treatment and to risk the consequences. A variety of factors, particularly interpersonal ones, play a significant role in how offenders perceive their own motivation for treatment and for change.

This means that offenders' motivation for change is also likely to be influenced by how the counselor perceives it. Consider two extremes in counselor perspective. Counselor A believes that offenders need to be told what to do. If you give them any leeway they will take advantage of it, so you cannot give them any choice. Unless you confront them forcefully with what they have done and firmly direct them in the process of change, no positive change will occur. This perspective places a large amount of responsibility for client change on the clinician. Counseling becomes something that is "given to" clients. The counselor is the authority and expert, and the clients are the reluctant (but ideally submissive) recipients. The counselor knows what is best for offenders, and it is the counselor's job to make them do it. If clients do not follow the counselor's advice and direction, they are noncompliant, resistant, chronic, unmotivated, or not serious about change. This approach is not a particularly pleasant arrangement for the clients, of course, and the psychological principle of reactance would predict resistance to change. The message is clear that the counselor has little faith in the clients' opinions, values, and self-direction. What is often missed is that this is also a rather aversive situation for the counselor, who is cast in an adversarial relationship and whose measure of success is the degree to which clients are obedient to direction. Frustration and anger would be the expected result for both client and counselor.

Counselor B has a different perspective, viewing the clients as the experts with regard to their own life and problems. While taking seriously the responsibilities of her position, Counselor B realizes that people are autonomous and make choices, even under conditions of severe constraint. Because she regards the client intrinsic motivation as the key for change, she is particularly interested in understanding how clients perceive their own behavior and situation. It turns out that as the counselor seeks to understand the clients' thoughts, feelings, and plans, the clients are also caused to reflect on them. As the counselor's understanding increases, so does client self-understanding. In this view, the counselor and clients are collaborators, working together to reflect on the current situation, and what (if anything) the clients want to change. She is especially interested in understanding client desires and values, for these are the engines of change. She believes that every person is capable of change, can choose to change, when the ready, willing, and able components of motivation come together. In her view, the responsibility for change is necessarily left with the clients. It is, of course, not a choice that the counselor can make for clients. Yet the counselor is far from powerless. The counselor's job is to provide the conditions that promote change by enhancing the clients' intrinsic willingness, perceived ability, and readiness to change. The atmosphere is one in which counselor and client think together about possible avenues of change and their consequences, their advantages and disadvantages. Together they think through the short- and long-term consequences of different courses of action. Client autonomy of choice is recognized and affirmed. The goal of the interaction is not to coerce clients to change, but to assist them in thinking about and articulating the reasons for maintaining status quo behavior or making behavior changes.

From Extrinsic to Intrinsic Motivation

Within a motivational perspective, an important task in working with offenders is to move from extrinsic toward intrinsic reasons for change. At first the extrinsic motivators are often quite salient, and the person may resent being coerced, perceiving it as punishment. As discussed above, extrinsically motivated change may last only as long as the extrinsic motivator is in effect. Even with court requirements in place, however, it is possible to move emphasis from extrinsic to intrinsic motivation for change. Sometimes court mandates provide a window of opportunity, bringing people into counseling that they might otherwise not have sought. Within that window, the counselor has an opportunity to foster stable change by exploring and engaging client intrinsic motivation for change. Indeed, research indicates that clients who are court-referred usually show similarly positive outcomes to those who were self-referred to treatment.

Certainly the realities of the person's legal situation need to be acknowledged. The client should have a clear understanding of the consequences that will follow from various courses of action. It is also ethically important for the client to understand the conditions and limits of confidentiality within the counseling relationship, and the extent to which information that is revealed can affect his or her legal outcomes. These are givens, within which the client's choices and options are explored. The more that clients perceive intrinsic reasons for change, and are involved in developing a plan for how best to accomplish it, the more likely they are to show enduring change.

It is here that issues of language are particularly pertinent. Ideally it is the client and not the counselor who should be voicing the arguments for change. As noted above, when a counselor argues for change, the response of an ambivalent client is usually to take up the other side of the argument. To enhance intrinsic motivation, it is the client who should voice the change talk. The counselor carefully avoids eliciting and reinforcing resistance, knowing that it is associated with a lack of change. Instead the counselor elicits the client's own reasons for change, dissatisfactions with the status quo, optimism about change, and stated intentions to change.

ARE OFFENDERS DIFFERENT?

The motivational perspective described in this chapter is based on principles of human psychology, derived from research with a wide range of people, including offenders. The question sometimes arises as to whether these principles of normal human psychology apply to offenders: "Will it work with *my* caseload?"

It is not uncommon to perceive offenders as being different from ordinary people. The very label evokes in the public mind a person who disregards societal norms or lacks a conscience. There is a sense that "those people" need to be treated differently, that they do not respond to ordinary principles of human nature. Aggressive, confrontational tactics that would be ethically unacceptable as treatment for most medical and psychological disorders have sometimes been justified as necessary to "get through" to offenders, as "the only language they understand." In essence, the line between treatment and punishment sometimes blurs, and treatment professionals may inadvertently wind up acting out societal anger at offenders.

Unfortunately, such confrontational tactics tend to decrease rather than increase the probability of behavior change. There is no reason to believe that offenders respond to fundamentally different principles of learning, thinking, and motivation than the rest of humankind. Confrontational approaches to counseling become a self-fulfilling prophecy, engendering evasiveness and resentment while doing nothing to decrease the likelihood of repeat offenses.

Within the psychology of human motivation lie keys for opening the doors of change. People do not respond warmly to being shamed, coerced, berated, or deprived of choice. There is little evidence for the belief that "if you can make them feel *bad* enough, they will change." Instead, approaches that shame and confront tend to diminish the probability of change, fostering in both client and counselor a sense of hopelessness. Change is more likely to be fostered by calling forth the person's own intrinsic motivation, and offering a hopeful and empowering perspective on the possibility of change.

REFERENCES

Amrhein, P. C., Miller, W. R., Yahne, C. E., Palmer, M., & Fulcher, L. (2000). Committing language emergent from a motivational interview predicts behavioral change in drug-addicted clients. Paper presented at the Ninth International Conference on Treatment of Addictive Behaviors, September, Cape Town, South Africa.

Aubrey, L. L. (1998). Motivational enhancement therapy for adolescents with alcohol and drug problems. Paper presented at the Eighth International Conference on Treatment of Addictive Behaviors, January, Santa Fe, NM.

Bergin, A. E., & Garfield, S. L. (1994). *Handbook of Psychotherapy and Behavior Change* (4th edn). New York: Wiley.

Brehm, S. S., & Brehm, J. W. (1981). *Psychological Reactance: A Theory of Freedom and Control.* New York: Academic Press.

Brown, J. M., & Miller, W. R. (1993). Impact of motivational interviewing on participation and outcome in residential alcoholism treatment. *Psychology of Addictive Behaviors, 7,* 211–18.

Deci, E. L., & Ryan, R. M. (1985). *Intrinsic Motivation and Self-Determination on Human Behavior.* New York: Plenum Press.

Deci, E. L., & Ryan, R. M. (1987). The support of autonomy and the control of behavior. *Journal of Personality and Social Psychology, 53,* 1024–37.

Easton, C., Swan, S., & Sinha, R. (2000). Motivation to change substance use among offenders of domestic violence. *Journal of Substance Abuse Treatment, 19,* 1–5.

Firestone, P., Bradford, J. M., McCoy M., Greenberg, D. M., Curry, S., & Larose, M. R. (1998). Recidivism in convicted rapists. *Journal of the American Academy of Psychiatry and the Law, 26,* 185–200.

Garland, R. J., & Dougher, M. J. (1991). Motivational intervention in the treatment of sex offenders. In W. R. Miller & S. Rollnick (eds), *Motivational Interviewing: Preparing People to Change Addictive Behavior* (pp. 303–13). New York: Guilford Press.

Gordon, T. (1970). *Parent Effectiveness Training.* New York: Wyden.

Greenwald, A. F., & Bartmeier, L. H. (1963). Psychiatric discharges against medical advice. *Archives of General Psychiatry, 8,* 117–19.

Hanson, R. K., & Bussiere, M. T. (1998). Predicting relapse: a meta-analysis of sexual offender recidivism studies. *Journal of Consulting and Clinical Psychology, 66,* 348–62.

Harper, R., & Hardy, S. (2000). An evaluation of motivational interviewing as a method of intervention with clients in a probation setting. *British Journal of Social Work, 30,* 393–400.

Hazelden Foundation. (1985). You don't have to tear 'em down to build 'em up. *Hazelden Professional Update, 4,* 2.

Intagliata, J. (1976). A telephone follow-up procedure for increasing the effectiveness of a treatment program for alcoholics. *Journal of Studies on Alcohol, 37,* 1330–5.

Kear-Colwell, J., & Pollock, P. (1997). Motivation or confrontation: which approach to the child sex offender? *Criminal Justice and Behavior, 24,* 20–33.

Kogan, L. S. (1957). The short-term case in a family agency: Part II. Results of study. *Social Casework, 38,* 296–302.

Kottler, J. A. (1991). *The Compleat Therapist.* San Francisco, CA: Jossey-Bass.

Koumans, A. J. R., & Muller, J. J. (1965). Use of letters to increase motivation in alcoholics. *Psychological Reports, 16,* 1152.

Koumans, A. J. R., Muller, J. J., & Miller, C. F. (1967). Use of telephone calls to increase motivation for treatment in alcoholics. *Psychological Reports*, **21**, 327–8.

Leake, G. J., & King, A. S. (1977). Effect of counselor expectations on alcoholic recovery. *Alcohol Health and Research World*, **11**, 16–22.

Mann, R. E., & Rollnick, S. (1996). Motivational interviewing with a sex offender who believed he was innocent. *Behavioural and Cognitive Psychotherapy*, **24**, 127–34.

McLellan, A. T., Woody, G. E., Luborsky, L., & Goehl, L. (1988). Is the counselor an "active ingredient" in substance abuse rehabilitation? An examination of treatment success among four counselors. *Journal of Nervous and Mental Disease*, **176**, 423–30.

Miller, W. R. (1983). Motivational interviewing with problem drinkers. *Behavioural Psychotherapy*, **1**, 147–72.

Miller, W. R. (1985). Motivation for treatment: a review with special emphasis on alcoholism. *Psychological Bulletin*, **98**, 84–107.

Miller, W. R. (1996). What is a relapse? Fifty ways to leave the wagon. *Addiction*, **91** (suppl), S15–S27.

Miller, W. R. (ed.) (1999). *Enhancing Motivation for Change in Substance Abuse Treatment*. Treatment Improvement Protocol (TIP) Series, no. 35. Rockville, MD: Center for Substance Abuse Treatment.

Miller, W. R., Andrews, N. R., Wilbourne, P., & Bennett, M. E. (1998). A wealth of alternatives: effective treatments for alcohol problems. In W. R. Miller & N. Heather (eds), *Treating Addictive Behaviors: Processes of Change*, 2nd edn (pp. 203–16). New York: Plenum Press.

Miller, W. R., Benefield, R. G., & Tonigan, J. S. (1993). Enhancing motivation for change in problem drinking: a controlled comparison of two therapist styles. *Journal of Consulting and Clinical Psychology*, **61**, 455–61.

Miller, W. R., & Brown, J. M. (1991). Self-regulation as a conceptual basis for the prevention and treatment of addictive behaviors. In N. Heather, W. R. Miller, & J. Greeley (eds), *Self-Control and the Addictive Behaviours* (pp. 3–79). Sydney: Maxwell Macmillan.

Miller, W. R., & C'de Baca, J. (2001). *Quantum Change: When Epiphanies and Sudden Insights Transform Ordinary Lives*. New York: Guilford Press.

Miller, W. R., & Rollnick S. (1991). *Motivational Interviewing: Preparing People to Change Addictive Behavior*. New York: Guilford Press.

Miller, W. R., & Rollnick, S. (2002). *Motivational Interviewing: Preparing People to Change*, 2nd edn. New York: Guilford Press.

Miller, W. R., Taylor, C. A., & West, J. C. (1980). Focused versus broad-spectrum behavior therapy for problem drinkers. *Journal of Consulting and Clinical Psychology*, **48**, 590–601.

Panepinto, W. C., & Higgins, M. J. (1969). Keeping alcoholics in treatment: effective follow-through procedures. *Quarterly Journal of Studies on Alcohol*, **30**, 414–19.

Patterson, G. R., & Forgatch, M. S. (1985). Therapist behavior as a determinant for client noncompliance: a paradox for the behavior modifier. *Journal of Consulting and Clinical Psychology*, **53**, 846–51.

Petri, H. L. (1986). *Motivation: Theory and Research*. Belmont, CA: Wadsworth.

Prochaska, J. O., DiClemente, C. C., & Norcross, J. C. (1992). In search of how people change: applications to addictive behaviors. *American Psychologist*, **47**, 1102–14.

Project MATCH Research Group (1998). Therapist effects in three treatments for alcohol problems. *Psychotherapy Research*, **8**, 455–74.

Raynes, A. E., & Patch, V. D. (1971). Distinguishing features of patients who discharge themselves from psychiatric wards. *Comprehensive Psychiatry*, **12**, 473–9.

Rollnick, S., Mason, P., & Butler, C. (1999). *Health Behavior Change: A Guide for Practitioners*. New York: Churchill Livingstone.

Rosenberg, C. M., Gerrein, J. R., Manohar, V., & Liftik, J. (1976). Evaluation of training of alcoholism counselors. *Journal of Studies on Alcohol*, **37**, 1236–46.

Rosenberg, C. M., & Raynes, A. E. (1973). Dropouts from treatment. *Canadian Psychiatric Association Journal*, **18**, 229–33.

Saunders, B., Wilkinson, C., & Phillips, M. (1995). The impact of a brief motivational intervention with opiate users attending a methadone programme. *Addiction*, **90**, 415–24.

Seligman, M. E. P. (1991). *Learned Optimism*. New York: Knopf.

Sisson, R. W., & Mallams, J. H. (1981). The use of systematic encouragement and community access procedures to increase attendance at Alcoholics Anonymous and Al-Anon meetings. *American Journal of Drug and Alcohol Abuse*, **8**, 371–6.

Valle, S. (1981). Interpersonal functioning of alcoholism counselors and treatment outcome. *Journal of Studies on Alcohol*, **42**, 783–90.

Wild, T. C., Newton-Taylor, B., & Alletto, R. (1998). Perceived coercion among clients entering substance abuse treatment: structural and psychological determinants. *Addictive Behaviors*, **23**, 81–95.

Yahne, C. E., & Miller, W. R. (1999). Evoking hope. In W. R. Miller (ed.), *Integrating Spirituality into Treatment: Resources for Practitioners* (pp. 217–33). Washington, DC: American Psychological Association.

Chapter 3

AN INDIVIDUAL CASE FORMULATION APPROACH TO THE ASSESSMENT OF MOTIVATION

LAWRENCE JONES

Rampton Hospital, Retford, UK

Historically, motivation has been seen as a selection criterion for treatment and was assessed informally using criteria such as "agreement with the therapist, acceptance of diagnosis, expressed desire for help, apparent distress and compliance with advice" (Miller and Rollnick, 1991), which, they observe, "with the exception of compliance with advice . . . are of little value in predicting change" (p. 95). This passive approach to motivation and its assessment has been replaced by a more active interventionist stance, where non-engagement is seen as a challenge for the practitioner's assessment and intervention skills. The concept of "untreatability", whereby the client is blamed for not engaging and left ultimately to his or her own devices, has been supplanted by the notion that the therapist, or the therapy team, are responsible for *creating the contingencies* under which engagement can take place. While the client's right to refuse to engage needs to be acknowledged, "failure" to engage needs also to be seen as failure to formulate accurately or intervene effectively. The ability to accurately formulate the kinds of processes that generate, obstruct, interrupt or maintain engagement behaviours, in a collaborative manner, is central to this approach.

The primary aim in assessing motivation is to develop a working formulation that can inform any intervention(s) identified as being useful, make predictions about engagement problems, and contribute to risk appraisal and management. While ideally this should be a collaborative exercise, with the client and practitioner moving towards a shared view of what drives that individual's motivation, in reality, assessment may result in the clinician being unable to agree with the client about some aspects of the formulation. Ethically it is important, at the outset, to spell out the potential outcomes of the assessment and how the information is going to be used.

Motivating Offenders to Change: A Guide to Enhancing Engagement in Therapy. Edited by M. McMurran.
© 2002 John Wiley & Sons, Ltd.

The assessment model advocated in this chapter is an *individual case formulation approach* (Bruch & Bond, 1998; Kohlenberg & Tsai, 1994; Persons, 1989; Turkat, 1979, 1985, 1990; Turkat & Maisto, 1983). Essentially, this model focuses on developing an individually tailored account of the behaviour being examined using a combination of functional analysis and model development through hypothesis testing. Using this approach with an offender population necessitates extensive use of clinical interviewing and information from custodians and carers. Briggs (1994) emphasises the importance of the clinical interview when he writes "our preference in assessing motivation is . . . to exploit the personal interaction of the interviewer and interviewee" in order to capture "the subtleties of attitude and values" (p. 55) necessary to evaluate motivation.

PRACTICE ALGORITHM

A useful strategy for any practitioner making complex judgements and decisions that have ultimately to be clinically defensible is to map out a practice algorithm, describing the criteria employed in making these judgements and decisions. Clinical expertise is as much the ability to formulate a heuristic for effectively *selecting*, *sequencing* and *combining* assessments and interventions from a variety of different approaches as it is the ability to deliver and evaluate those interventions. Most practitioners have an implicit algorithm that they use from memory; mapping this out can be a useful way of stepping back from the implicit model and testing it out. A practice algorithm needs to be continually updated in the light of changing experience, peer review and assimilation of relevant literature. This chapter is an account of one such algorithm (Figure 3.1).

STAGE 1: ASSESSING CONTEXTUAL
AND SITUATIONAL VARIABLES

The practice algorithm starts with an analysis of contextual and situational variables in order to facilitate the interpretation of information obtained later in the assessment. Without this information, it is difficult to tease out what aspects of the individual's behaviour are being driven by their learning history and what by current contingencies. It is surprising how often situational variables are ignored in the analysis of engagement behaviours (Mischel, 1973). Perhaps this is due to the emphasis in offender interventions on taking personal responsibility for change, rather than blaming some external agency, yet even the best designed and conducted interventions can be significantly undermined by conducting them in contexts which in various ways contradict the message of the intervention. Examples include anger management programmes in settings where staff are bullying inmates, or sex offender programmes in contexts where non-treatment staff exhibit misogynistic attitudes. Assessing the context will help the practitioner to evaluate the person–situation interaction.

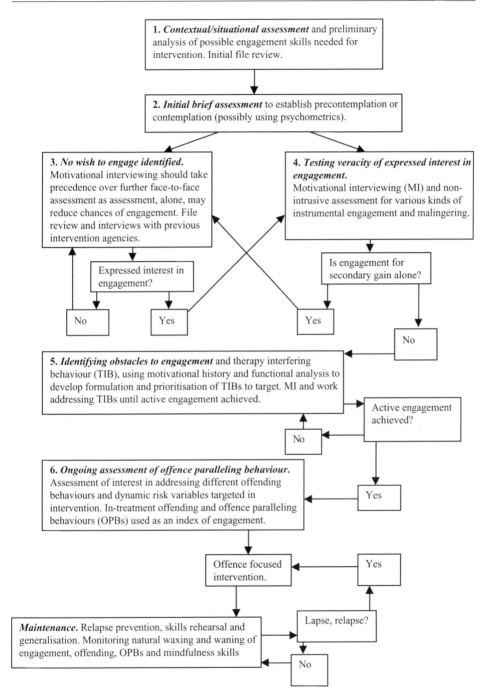

Figure 3.1 Practice algorithm for assessment of motivation

Basic Needs

Maslow (1970) argued that engaging in treatment will have little priority until basic human needs for things like food, shelter, personal safety and belonging have been met. The extent to which safety and belonging needs are met in custodial populations is critical to the capacity to engage. There is a considerable literature on the impact on staff of working with offender populations; little attention has been paid, however, to the impact on fellow inmates. Clinical experience highlights the significance of threats to personal safety and problems with maintaining significant relationships in generating ruptures in the therapeutic alliance or other aspects of engagement behaviour. Often situational variables are compounded by personal vulnerabilities. If many resources need to be marshalled in order to execute safety manoeuvres, addressing real or perceived threats to physical or psychological safety and dignity, then it is unlikely that much will be left to address other issues.

Regime

It is important to gauge how often fights, assaults, substance abuse, weapons finds and other indices of offending behaviour are evident among peers in the residential setting. This can be a good index of the kinds of pressure that might be placed on an individual. A related area to assess is the level of structure in the regime that the individual is living in. It is useful to identify what activities are available to the individual and to what extent the individual has made use of these. Besides the obvious management issue of more structure/activity scheduling being necessary for more disorganised and difficult clients (Ostapiuk & Westwood, 1986), it can be useful to identify what kind of niche the individual finds within the organisation and how they make use of it. Peer pressure, particularly in prison settings, to "run with the pack", get involved in substance abuse, euphoric recall of "the ones we got away with", and to bully-or-be-bullied can be difficult to counter. Evidence of doing this, even if done falteringly, can be an important indicator of a need to change. Examples might include seeking out education, religious activities, or jobs that involve being taken away from the delinquent ethos.

Staff Variables

In most settings, there will be staff in therapeutic and non-therapeutic roles who will influence the client's motivation in different ways. Assessment of situational variables should examine the impact of staff on engagement behaviour. Overly authoritarian behaviour, for example, may provoke disengagement; overly collusive staff behaviour may lead to entrenchment and intervention-engendered commitment to change being defused. Gillis and colleagues (1999) report evidence that leadership style can impact on offender motivation; they found that productivity and punctuality were greater when leaders had credibility and a "transformational"

Table 3.1   Engagement behaviour shaped by the organisational context

Organisational contingencies	Behaviour most likely to achieve freedom
1985 Little treatment available, parole contingent on "good" custodial behaviour	Keep "head down", minimise offending. If on normal location pretend not to be a sex offender. Normalise offending
1990 Sex offender treatment programme optional	Motivated individuals engage, otherwise as above
1993 Sex Offender Treatment Programme (SOTP) established	Increased pressure to engage, increased instrumental engagement, release conditional on successful completion of programme
Late 1990s SOTP required in order to get parole Enhanced thinking skills and extended SOTP programmes established	Sense of the goalposts being moved, instrumental engagement more difficult to maintain as intervention time increases, increasing litigation as criteria for establishing manageable risk become increasingly stringent

leadership style characterised by pushing people to achieve their best by changing attitudes, beliefs, values and needs. Asking questions like "What kinds of therapist have you responded well to in the past?" can also help to clarify the kinds of interpersonal style the individual responds to best.

Organisational Contingencies

A critical situational variable is the kind of information, formal and informal, that the individual has about how to be released and the relevance of engaging in treatment to this process. In recent years what is expected of an individual in order to be released has been changing at a significant pace. If we take, as an example, sex offender treatment in the prison context from the 1980s to the present day, there have been big changes in the kinds of engagement behaviour shaped by the organisational context (see Table 3.1).

Demands Placed by Interventions

Before conducting an assessment with the individual, the practitioner needs to think about the kinds of demands the various types of interventions will place on the individual. This is particularly true in settings where there is a limited range of interventions and where the offender is required to complete specific interventions in order to be considered for release. If, for instance, the intervention requires the ability to work in a group, then it will be particularly important to assess their ability to tolerate being in a group and make intimate disclosures in a group context. Offenders with poor ability to trust and with a tendency to think that

Table 3.2   Focusing assessment on the demands made by engaging in specific interventions

Intervention method	Client obstacles to overcome	Assessment areas and strategy
Addressing lack of remorse	Need to avoid negative emotion	History of evasion Distress tolerance skills
Exploring offending behaviour in groups with peers	Need to maintain peer acceptance as "good offender", "tough guy" etc.	Extent of reliance on criminogenic peers for esteem enhancement
Exploring new ways of thinking and new behaviours	Reluctance to admit: (a) Lack of knowledge (b) Somebody else "knows better" Feeling "dominated" or "controlled". Fear of affective reaction to re-evaluating past behaviour	Learning history Tolerance of not knowing Experience of learning from others Clients' anticipation of affective reaction to re-evaluating past behaviour
Rehearsal of new skills	Picture of self as "competent" and able not to offend; erroneous equation of knowing about skill with having the skill	Knowledge of difference between knowing about and doing
Disclosure of aspects of the offence and personal past in functional analysis	Fear of: (a) Disclosure being used as evidence of seriousness of risk (b) Being disbelieved or misinterpreted (c) Being judged or ridiculed (shame) (d) Ostracism from peers (e) Others being upset by disclosure content (f) Feeling guilt	Perception of positive and negative consequences of disclosure Suspiciousness, history of being misconstrued. Extent of fear of being judged, laughed at, or offending others Previous reaction to shame/guilt
Taking responsibility for actions past, present and future	Negative affect associated with past avoidance of responsibility	Capacity to manage negative affect without avoiding or acting out
Brainstorming/solution generation exercises	Poor concentration, distractibility, self-consciousness	Cognitive functioning Self-consciousness
Role playing	Self-consciousness, social anxiety, distrust	Self-consciousness, social anxiety, "paranoid" suspiciousness in group settings
Exploring past offence-related problems	Interest in current problems	Offender's implicit model of change

others are being judgemental or exploitative often find group-based interventions too distressing and consequently disengage. Some other examples of intervention demands and relevant assessment strategies (to be used when the individual has begun to engage at stages 3 and 4 in the algorithm) are shown in Table 3.2.

Initially examining situational variables enables the practitioner to make sense of later information about the offender's orientation towards treatment.

STAGE 2: INITIAL BRIEF ASSESSMENT OF INTEREST IN CHANGE

Once the contextual and situational analysis has been completed, the practice algorithm moves on to a quick assessment of apparent interest in engagement in treatment. The timing of this assessment needs careful consideration. The process of assessment is often alienating for the person being assessed. Consequently, the extent to which assessment is mixed with intervention may depend on the clinician's initial judgement of the client's *capacity to tolerate* the assessment process. If it is obvious that the initial task should be getting a motivational foothold, then extensive structured interviewing and form filling is futile. There is a danger that this client group, particularly those who are uninterested or actively opposed to engaging in treatment, construe the assessment process as invasive or as "not listening to their real concerns" and thus become less willing to engage. It is important not to alienate them and to begin motivational interviewing and alliance building as early as possible. Miller and Rollnick (1991), on the other hand, highlight the positive potential of the process of assessing motivation as a way of *generating* motivation. Indeed, much of the motivational interviewing method they espouse involves an implicit assessment component.

The initial assessment is designed to establish if the offender is contemplating change. If they are, then more detailed assessment can take place. If they are not, then the emphasis should be on motivational interviewing and alliance building. Out of session, file reviews and interviews with previous intervention agents focusing on what has worked and what has not, help to complete a motivational picture of the client.

Competing Goals

It is also useful to take an inventory of the client's current goals and concerns and to ask him or her to rank order them, to ascertain the extent to which resources allocated to engaging in treatment are competing with other goals. This is particularly useful when interventions may have to compete for time with other activities. Interpersonal theorists such as Blackburn (1990) typically identify two significant dimensions of interpersonal behaviour—status (dominance versus submission) and affiliation (friendly versus hostile). For assessment purposes, it is useful to see people as being interested in specific *interpersonal projects*—coherent goal-oriented behaviours—linked with each of these dimensions. Offenders are often preoccupied with managing the disturbances they experience in relationships as a consequence of incarceration. It is therefore useful to assess at what stage the client is in his or her various relationship "projects". Is he or she seeking a relationship, forming a relationship, going through a honeymoon period, maintaining a long-term relationship, becoming estranged in a relationship, grieving a lost relationship, or avoiding relationships altogether? Absence of any current relationship "projects" is also significant.

If visits are regular and relationships are stable, there is little chance that this will affect engagement. Unstable relationships, however, can seriously impinge on engagement—especially if the initial establishing contingencies had involved interpersonal motivators. Letters and visits are very important features of an offender's emotional world. Any disruption in their delivery in a predictable manner will often significantly affect mood and engagement. It is likely that a large amount of an individual's personal resources will be allocated to managing relationship ruptures of any kind, often at the expense of interventions. This emotional survival strategy should not be misconstrued as "lack of motivation". Asking about how the individual deals with these eventualities can help in gauging how resilient engagement will be to interpersonal uncertainty.

Similarly, it is useful to investigate current status "projects". Is the client seeking status, defending newly acquired status, bullying, reorienting to lost status or being bullied, maintaining status, forming strategic alliances, reacting to authority or deferring to authority? Offenders spend a significant amount of time and effort managing status. If the dominance hierarchy is in a state of flux, then little time or energy is going to be left for engagement in interventions.

Brown (1997) describes the development of what he terms a "motivational monopoly" or "reward specialism" in addictions to behaviour. Addictive behaviours are those that become increasingly rewarding for an individual. The features to identify in assessment are salience, conflict over cessation, apparent loss of control, relief from states associated with withdrawal, low self-esteem, and relapse and reinstatement. Any behaviour that has addiction status for an individual, whether this is substance abuse, offending, or obsessional compulsive behaviour, will seriously affect resources available for engagement.

Other competing goals include education and work. Erez (1987) surveyed North American offenders' views of where their needs originated and found that two thirds felt their needs came from a lack of education and employment skills. The tendency of some offenders to go to work rather than "attend group" may be a reflection of this perceived priority; to interpret this as avoidance or laziness may be unjustified. Assessment of outcome expectancies for going to education and work is therefore useful.

Exploring the offender's beliefs about release can prove useful in formulating why they are engaging. Some offenders may not want to be released and see their futures as being inside. An analysis of why this is the case for this individual is then important.

Assessing Readiness to Change

Miller and Rollnick (1991) and Miller (1985) advocate two approaches to the direct assessment of motivation; (1) exploring the client's self-acknowledged readiness to change, and (2) cost–benefit analysis for continuation of the behaviour(s). Most current assessment falls loosely into one or other of these approaches. Miller and Rollnick (1991) highlight four aspects of readiness to change: (1) the person's judgement of a need to change, (2) the perceived possibility of changes occurring,

(3) the individual's self-efficacy for change, and (4) the person's stated intention to change within a particular time frame

Judgement of a need to change

The most commonly used strategy for assessing the individual's judgement of a need to change is to use Prochaska and DiClemente's (1982) stages of change paradigm. This model marked a significant step forward in the conceptualisation of motivation, and was developed as part of a broader "transtheoretical model" (TTM) of change aimed at matching different types of intervention to different "levels" of problem and different stages of change. The "levels" at which a problem can be targeted, they argue, are symptomatic, situational, interpersonal, intrapersonal and systemic. The model also identifies five stages in a typical change process: precontemplation, contemplation, preparation, action and maintenance. The most frequently used assessment instrument for identifying an individual's motivation is the Stages of Change Questionnaire, often called URICA (University of Rhode Island Change Assessment) (McConnaughy et al., 1983, 1989) or questionnaires based on this (Rollnick et al., 1992; McMurran et al., 1998).

There are, however, problems with the psychometric assessment of the stages of change model. First, there is little recognition of the complicating factor of faking good for various instrumental gains, a factor that is particularly pervasive in assessments in custodial settings where the incentive to fake motivation is high. Following Rothfleisch (1997), DiClemente and Prochaska (1998) argue that in situations such as these "there are demand characteristics that make affirmation of unwillingness to change or of ambivalence about change problematic for most clients". Second, there is no assessment of what specifically the individual is being asked to think about changing and by what method the individual is being asked to contemplate change. One recently developed instrument incorporating aspects of the transtheoretical model is Wong and Gordon's (1999) Violence Risk Scale version 2 (VRS). This instrument has the advantages of being based on observation, as opposed to self-report, and being about specific behaviours, thereby recognising the possibility that an individual can be at *different* stages of the change process for *different* behaviours. Third, there is no means of assessing active opposition to change as contrasted to passive lack of interest in changing. Fourth, there is no explicit theoretical model of engagement in treatment. Other models, such as the theory of reasoned action, or planned behaviour (Ajzen, 1988, 1991; Ajzen & Fishbein, 1980) have a much clearer theoretical basis. Finally, there is little evidence supporting the model. A recent review by Sutton (2001) argued that the evidence for the model was meagre and inconsistent. Nonetheless, the model is useful for *describing* some aspects of the change process, and has never claimed to *explain* engagement behaviour. As for the empirical validity, more research into the predictive validity of this kind of model is needed to see if it can tell us something about the progress of offenders in treatment programmes (McMurran et al., 1998).

In addition to using psychometric assessment, a brief interview exploring the individual's interest in change in various areas is essential. A strategy to use in this initial interview is to ask about the costs and benefits of changing. Miller and

Rollnick (1991), in their development of the decisional balance model of Janis and Mann (1977) and Appel (1986), suggest that an assessment of perceived costs and benefits of a particular behaviour would establish whether the individual is motivated to change that behaviour. Motivation in this context is defined as a state in which the costs outweigh the benefits. Essentially this is a form of functional analysis focusing on the consequences. At this stage of the practice algorithm, this should only involve basic direct questioning without extensive probing. If some degree of interest in change is established, even in a circumscribed area, then further assessment of instrumental engagement and malingering can be started.

The perceived possibility of changes occurring

Assessment of the individual's perception of the possibility of change is critical. One strategy for doing this is to ask about people's beliefs in the possibility that *others* can change (Jones & Brown, 1998). This enables the practitioner to tap beliefs about what change involves.

Assessing the client's model of change is critical to this endeavour. Miller and Rollnick (1991) point out that often refusal to engage, or disengagement, is due to a mismatch between the client's model of change and the therapist's model of change. Jones and Brown (1998) reported some of the "folk" psychological models of change encountered in a population of personality disordered offender patients.

The "kick up the backside" model

The client believes that the only way to bring about change is through punishment. This may link in with their offence-related belief in violence as an effective way of bringing about behavioural change in others.

The "willpower" model

Essentially this model holds that change is brought about by an internal agency that is construed as either "weak" or "strong". Few people have any sense of what makes their "will" weak or strong, tending more towards a fatalistic formulation.

The "faith" model

The client sees change as being reliant on faith, in self or some external agency. This model resembles the construct of self-efficacy, but, as with the willpower model, tends to be more fatalistic.

The "old bad" self versus the "new good" self

The self is seen as being completely dysfunctional in the past and completely functional in the present or after treatment. The process of change is about disposing of the former and building up the latter. The old self is something that needs to be "got rid of" in an almost physical sense, like rubbish.

Change means not enjoying yourself anymore

The client sees change as a series of sacrifices of enjoyable activities without replacing them. They picture themselves becoming increasingly depressed and lonely.

Passive change

The client construes change as something *done to* them by others, not involving any effort themselves. Quick results are expected. Often the client has a medical model of the problem and sees medication as the solution.

Change means working on having been abused

The client sees the intervention as ridding themselves of distressing memories and helping them to avoid the distressing feelings that go with them. Offending behaviour is not recognised as a target.

Outcome expectancies for the kinds of intervention that are being offered need to be assessed. Questions such as "What do you expect to get out of this kind of treatment?" tap this domain. If the expectations are high and unrealistic, for instance expecting to stop having thoughts of offending, or to be able to control strong urges or cravings after two or three sessions, then the chances of disengaging after an initial "honeymoon period" may be high.

The individual's self-efficacy for change

McMurran et al. (1998) report the measurement of self-efficacy using the 17-item general self-efficacy subscale of Sherer et al.'s (1982) self-efficacy scale. They found a significant correlation between this measure and the action subscale of the Stages of Change questionnaire. They indicate that the relationship between self-efficacy and stage of change is not a simple one, citing the finding of DiClemente and Hughes (1990) that in a sample of problem drinkers precontemplators rated high on self-efficacy. They interpreted this as denial and minimisation. This complex association between self-efficacy and stages of change can be better understood if criminogenic self-efficacy (or addiction-related self-efficacy in the case of substance abuse) is differentiated from non-criminogenic self-efficacy. If efficacy enhancement and esteem enhancement are linked with offending behaviour, then one would expect a correlation between self-efficacy and precontemplation; change would be seen as inflicting a loss of self-esteem and self-efficacy. Conversely, if efficacy enhancement and esteem enhancement were linked with prosocial behaviours and values then one would expect a correlation with action and maintenance of change. Differentiating between types of self-efficacy and self-esteem (i.e. criminogenic versus non-criminogenic) is suggested also by Bandura's (1977) original model of situation-specific self-efficacy.

The person's stated intention to change within a particular time frame

Procrastination is a familiar feature of change processes. In behavioural terms, procrastination is reinforcing in that it is both avoiding the distress of the withdrawal of something rewarding and, at the same time, enjoying the feeling that something is going to be done about the problem behaviour. Contemplators and individuals embarking on the action phase often procrastinate. Exploration of proposed timetabling for change is critical. Putting off addressing certain criminogenic beliefs, emotional difficulties or behaviours is an important issue to identify. We are all familiar with the individual who attempts to barter with treatment agents; offering, for example, to attend a group addressing offending behaviour, but asking if they can continue to have deviant fantasies—even though they recognise that they are contributing to their offending behaviour.

The Miller and Rollnick (1991) schema outlined here has much in common with the recent theory of planned behaviour (TOPB) advocated by Ajzen and Fishbein (1980) and Ajzen (1988, 1991), which emphasises the role of "intention" in predicting social behaviour. One significant difference is the additional emphasis in TOPB on "subjective norms", i.e. beliefs about how specified others would view the behaviour—in this case engagement in treatment—along with one's motivation to comply with those views. Asking about the clients' perception of respected others' views on change and engagement is thus an additional useful strategy.

STAGE 3: PARALLEL ASSESSMENT AND INTERVENTION FOR THOSE WHO DO NOT WISH TO ENGAGE

For those in whom no interest in change is identified, the algorithm indicates that motivational interviewing (Miller & Rollnick, 1991) should take precedence over further assessment until the clinician deems the client capable of tolerating further direct assessment. Assessment with these individuals is essentially dynamic and based on the practitioner's ongoing in-session formulation and reformulation of the issues. Before this, however, it is useful to contact professionals who have previously intervened with the client in order to establish what has worked and what has failed to work for the individual (see later).

STAGE 4: TESTING VERACITY OF EXPRESSED INTEREST IN ENGAGEMENT

For those where some indication of an interest in change is identified, the algorithm highlights the importance of testing the nature of this engagement. Jones (1997) suggests a framework for assessing types of engagement, adapted from one originally developed by Woods (1979) for educational settings. This looks at both attitudes to the goals of change and attitudes to the means of change. For either the goals or the means, the individual can take any one of the following attitudinal stances:

Table 3.3   Modes of adaptation to intervention (adapted from Woods, 1979)

Attitude to MEANS of changing	Attitude to GOALS of intervention					
	Indifference	Indulgence	Identification	Rejection without replacement	Ambivalence	Rejection with replacement
Indifference	Retreatism			Retreatism		
Indulgence		Ingratiation	Ingratiation			
Identification	Ritualism	**Compliance**	Compliance			
Rejection without replacement	Retreatism			Retreatism		
Ambivalence	*Colonisation*				**Opportunism**	
Rejection with replacement	*Intransigence*					Rebellion

Note: Modes in bold are the most frequent, those in italic the least frequent.

(1) indifference, (2) indulgence, (3) identification, (4) rejection without replacement, (5) ambivalence or (6) rejection with replacement.

This model provides a way of exploring types of adaptation that are often encountered in organisational settings, not just forensic populations. Different combinations of attitudes to the goals and means of change produce a variety of characteristic modes of adaptation (Table 3.3).

There are several modes of adaptation to treatment. Two types of *compliance* are identified: (1) optimistic compliance, where the individual takes on the aims of the intervention in an air of expectant hope or belief in a "quick fix", and (2) instrumental compliance, where the individual complies for reasons such as to impress the parole board. *Ingratiation* is where the individual aims to maximise benefits by earning the favour of treatment agents and those in power. *Ambivalence or opportunism* is characterised by ambivalence towards both the intervention goals and the means of achieving them. The individual reacts against early optimism—after initial "honeymoon" engagement—with less consistent application to intervention and frequent but momentary and often opportunistic experimentation with more "deviant" modes of adaptation. *Ritual participation* is where the individual "goes through the motions" of change with little investment in it, saying the "right things" but not demonstrating change in action. *Intransigence* is evidenced by preoccupation with issues relating to autonomy. This individual rejects the therapeutic means and is generally cynical about or indifferent to its ends. *Rebellion* is when the individual actively opposes both the means and goals of intervention. Such individuals often also actively subvert others' engagement. *Colonisation* is when the individual tries to maximise available gratification by "working the system", maybe complying only when the programme is enjoyable and disengaging when it gets demanding. *Retreatism* is when the individual is not committed but has no alternative motivation either. This strategy involves truanting either literally or psychologically by withdrawing. Typically, the individual is seen as moving between different adaptive modes as he or she goes through a treatment process. Recognising the variety of qualitatively different types of engagement is essential to formulating the kind of engagement an individual is likely to exhibit.

STAGE 5: IDENTIFYING OBSTACLES TO ENGAGEMENT

Once it is established that the individual is actively interested in change and is capable of tolerating further assessment, the next task identified in the algorithm is to focus on potential therapy interfering behaviours (Jones 1997; Linehan 1993) that might disrupt the maintenance of engagement behaviour.

Motivational History Taking

If we see motivation as a set of specific treatment engagement behaviours—overt and covert—that facilitate desired change in behaviour, then the assumption that there is some internal entity called "motivation" is not necessary. Examples of engagement behaviours include attending sessions, attending to session content, accepting the utility of change, feeling open to new ways of looking at things and tolerating distress associated with dissonance. The aim of taking a motivational history is then to develop a working formulation for which skill deficits, attitudinal changes and obstacles to engagement may benefit directly from intervention, or may help to structure an intervention tailored for that particular individual. In addition, the aim is to make specific informed predictions about the probable character of an individual's engagement behaviours over the course of an intervention—not simply at the front end of an intervention. Based on both the formulation and the consequent predictions of probable future behaviour, recommendations for future strategies for addressing needs and/or testing the veracity of the formulation can be made.

A useful starting point for conducting these functional analyses is to identify establishing contingencies, i.e. the contingencies that lead to the onset of specific engagement relevant behaviours.

Establishing contingencies

Walters (1998) argues that "change begins with a crisis". He defines a "crisis" as "the point at which a client becomes aware of a discrepancy between his or her stated goals and current behaviour". The exploration of the establishing contingencies, for a specific motivational stance, allows for the identification of a much wider range of possible factors contributing to a change in engagement behaviours. Jones and Brown (1998) suggested that functional analysis, looking at the various establishing contingencies at critical engagement and disengagement turning points, is a useful assessment strategy. This involves identifying *turning points* in engagement for an individual and then attempting to pinpoint what change(s) in contingencies brought about this change. Bandura's (1977, 1986) social learning theory approach suggests three types of motivational establishing contingencies: external, vicarious

Table 3.4   Examples of establishing contingencies for engagement in treatment

Establishing contingency	Interpersonal (external or vicarious)	Intrapersonal (cognitive and affective)
Aversive	Loss of freedom, loss or threat of loss of critical relationships with family or friends	Onset of: low self-esteem, boredom, restlessness, depression, cognitive processing of offence related material
Reinforcing	Encouragement from significant others, seeing others benefit from change	Pleasure in anticipating release, pleasure in feeling "in control"

and self-reinforcement. Jones and Brown (1998) identified examples of aversive and reinforcing interpersonal and intrapersonal establishing contingencies for motivational turning points in a sample of personality disordered offender patients in a special hospital (Table 3.4).

The social and interpersonal nature of many establishing contingencies needs to be recognised and understood in the context of the analysis of relationship projects and status projects outlined previously. Engagement is then contingent upon a perception that "treatment", however the individual construes that, will make things less aversive. Similarly, maintaining reinforcing contingencies such as support from significant others can drive the onset of engagement behaviour.

Clearly, the kind of engagement eventually obtained in the therapeutic process is going to be dependent on the kind of establishing contingencies that instigate and maintain the individual's engagement behaviours. Engagement driven by trying to get out of a custodial setting will appear very different from engagement driven by remorse. A mismatch between the establishing contingencies and the kind of engagement in treatment may be evidence of malingering, malingered engagement having a very different set of establishing contingencies from non-malingered engagement. This is not to say, however, that engagement for secondary gain may not change over time under the influence of the new contingencies brought to bear during the intervention to become more change oriented.

This assessment involves three stages: (1) taking a motivational history, including an account of the onset of the current engagement behaviour, (2) monitoring and interviewing staff about current engagement behaviour, and (3) functional analysis of engagement behaviours and examination of the match between establishing contingencies and current behaviour.

Identifying repeating pattern of engagement/disengagement

Even for those who are most actively engaged in treatment, commitment to change can vacillate. Proponents of the stages of change model argue that people typically cycle through the different stages of change (Prochaska et al., 1992). Assessment can usefully focus on this in order to develop *pre-emptive strategies* to prevent therapy interfering behaviours (Jones 1997, Linehan 1993). Following the basic behavioural tenet that past behaviour, is the best predictor of future behaviour, it is conceptually useful to think of each individual as having a motivational "signature", not unlike the "relapse signature" identified by Birchwood and colleagues (1989) in psychotic patients. This is a repeating pattern of both engagement and disengagement over time. This should not be confused with trait models of motivation: what we are dealing with is a history of learned engagement and disengagement behaviours. A feature of people with histories of offending behaviour is their tendency to repeatedly rupture relationships with intervention agents and agencies (Safran et al., 1996); formulation of the motivational "signature" is a way of identifying this pattern of repeated ruptures. Through sequential functional analysis (Gresswell, 1994) of previous engagement and disengagement behaviours, a model of this process can be developed. Information for this analysis comes from careful focused interviewing of current and past intervention agents.

Previous history of treatment dropout (Jones, 1997) or superficial engagement provides critical information for this kind of analysis. Jones and Brown (1998) and Hogue and Jones (1999) argue that people who have had repeated experiences of therapy not impacting on reconviction or levels of personal distress are likely to develop a cynical view of the possibility of change. Jones and Brown (1998) describe this as a "serial abstinence violation effect, leading to conditioned disbelief in change" and a tendency "to talk in a 'motivated' way whilst continuing to behave in an 'unmotivated' way".

Two models can be useful for pinpointing critical or sensitive periods for possible disengagement. Firstly, the Power and Dalgleish (1997) Schematic, Propositional, Associative and Analogical Representation Systems (SPAARS) model gives a framework for thinking about different and parallel types of cognitive processing. It is not possible to do justice to this model in this chapter, but it is useful to mention here the fact that individuals are potentially processing information in contradictory ways at the same time. A conceptualisation of the conflict between automatic learned behaviour and consciously developed intentions is useful in that so often clients describe an experience of a deliberating or controlled self being overwhelmed by the pressure of overlearned automatic behaviour (see also Baumeister & Heatherton, 1996, on self-regulation failure and misregulation). Each person will have an extensive history of a relationship between these aspects of their functioning. If they have been motivated to change and have repeatedly been unsuccessful, then this relationship is likely to be fractious. A formulation of the kinds of problems the client experiences in this relationship is useful. Some of the possible points of tension in the typical change process are mapped out in Table 3.5.

The second model is the Stiles et al. (1992) assimilation model of change during psychotherapy. The assimilation model (AM) derives from Piaget's (1962, 1970) work on assimilation and proposes that schema gradually develop and change during therapy as new, often distressing, information is assimilated. The stages of assimilation are, they argue, predictable, accompanied by specific affective processes and follow the sequence outlined in Table 3.5.

Dropout from treatment is often due to distress tolerance problems in the initial stages of assimilation and change. Identification of the actual material that was being dealt with at the time of previous treatment dropout(s), as well as an assessment of the client's affective response to the treatment, can help to highlight specific affect tolerance vulnerabilities. This dropout from treatment is often at a critical stage of withdrawal of reinforcement when a behavioural burst (the characteristic

Table 3.5 Stages of change linked with assimilation model of change, behavioural change processes and SPAARS model

Stages of change	Stages of assimilation	Typical affective and cognitive processes	Typical behavioural process	SPAARS model
Precontemplation	1. No recognition of need to change, denial	Minimal distress if problem actively denied, otherwise vague negative affect, minimisation	Avoidance	Automatic unchanged, controlled unchanged
Contemplation	2. Unwanted thoughts about change, initially actively avoided	Strong unfocused negative feelings, connection with content of cognitions not always recognised	Avoidance, exposure (to dissonance or discrepancy)	Automatic unchanged, controlled changing
Contemplation	3. Vague awareness and recognition of seriousness of problem	Acute psychological pain or panic associated with the problematic thoughts and experiences being assimilated. Difficulty formulating problem	Exposure, desensitisation, behavioural bursting	
Action	4. Problem statement/clarification	Clear sense of problem associated with less intensity of negative affect	Exposure, desensitisation	Automatic changing, controlled changed
Action	5. Understanding/insight	Problem experience incorporated into a schema, affect less negative and increasingly positive	Exposure, skills acquisition	
Action	6. Application/working through	New schema used to address problems. Positive affect	Rehearsal	
Action, maintenance	7. Problem solution	Successful solution of specific problem accompanied by increased feelings of self-efficacy	Rehearsal	
Maintenance	8. Mastery	New schema used in other contexts, automatic processing increases and affect becomes more neutral	Rehearsal, generalisation	Automatic changed, controlled changed

increase in frequency and intensity of a behaviour following the withdrawal of reinforcement) has not subsided. This initial increase in problem behaviours can lead to premature termination and a consequent need for a longer period of exposure in future interventions. Assessment of the style of intervention, gauging the extent to which it was confrontational and/or failed to take into account the kinds of distress, confusion and increase in offending behaviour, often associated with changing behaviour and cognition, is also useful. Related to this is the Dunmore et al. (1997) and Ehlers et al. (1998) notion of "mental defeat". Ehlers found that not submitting psychologically to the abuser or perpetrator was a protective factor for recovery from interpersonally induced post-traumatic stress disorder (PTSD). For offenders who have been abused, not submitting psychologically may have been a significant survival strategy; for these people intervention may be experienced as a form of mental defeat that may trigger a defensive reaction.

Individuals at the second stage may not necessarily acknowledge the extent to which their off-session behaviour was being driven by session content. Negative affect may result in "acting out" behaviour not attributed by the client to session content. Information about sensitivities is best gleaned from people who have previously intervened with the individual. Care needs to be taken in exploring this kind of issue with the client as, if it has been a repeating pattern of treatment dropout, this may in itself precipitate a crisis.

For offenders with multiple problems it is difficult sometimes to cope with serial exposure to dissonance or discrepancy as each problem is dealt with. People often get stuck between treatment targets and argue that they have changed now and do not need any more help. It is easier to see oneself as having changed than it is to see oneself as still needing to change. Effectively staying in the action stage requires the individual to tolerate the discrepancy without either jumping into premature closure or giving up. This perhaps reflects a natural inability to be learning new things and assimilating others at the same time, and may account for the motivational cycling described by Prochaska et al. (1992).

In addition to looking at engagement behaviours in previous therapeutic endeavours, it is useful to look at *other* situations that may have required similar engagement and commitment behaviours, such as relationships, educational engagements and work engagements.

Engagement Skills

If "motivation" is seen as a combination of engagement skills and active incentive to use those skills, then assessment needs to take an audit of what skills are available to the client. All too often, absence of engagement skills is misconstrued as absence of willingness to engage. Examples of the kinds of skills required for most interventions are:

1. An ability to form a relationship with therapist(s), through session attendance skills, relationship forming skills, trusting the therapist as a person and as a professional, trusting that therapy will bring about beneficial change (treatment efficacy beliefs), relationship maintenance skills, and relationship rupture repair skills.

2. An ability to identify and tolerate feelings associated with change, such as the ability to identify feelings, tolerance of feelings of interpersonal vulnerability, tolerating distress associated with dissonance (discrepancy, in motivational interviewing terms), tolerating loss of face, shame and betrayal associated with disengaging from criminogenic peer network, the capacity to relinquish old sources of reinforcement in the absence of anything but the promise of new sources of reinforcement, and the capacity to accept a new identity incorporating the newly acquired behaviours, often against a background of having an unstable sense of self.
3. An ability to employ those cognitive skills necessary for change, such as the ability to problem solve, generate dissonance, initiate thought process and carry it through, resolve dissonance, establish and maintain attention, and remember session content.

STAGE 6: ONGOING ASSESSMENT OF OFFENCE PARALLELING BEHAVIOUR AND RISK

Once the initial obstacles to engagement have been identified and targeted and the intervention is under way, it is necessary to monitor the ongoing behavioural evidence for motivation. Assessment of motivation to change and maintain change is an essential part of risk assessment. It is not good enough to demonstrate that an individual has acquired new skills in a treatment programme; it is necessary to identify the probability that the individual will be motivated to mobilise those skills in the new settings they find themselves in after release.

Offending and Offence Paralleling Behaviour as an Index of Quality of Engagement

As well as analysing the situational and contextual variables potentially affecting engagement, it is useful to analyse the extent to which the individual demonstrates cross-situational consistency in his or her behaviour (Table 3.6). Careful monitoring of sequences or cycles of behaviour exhibited by an offender in the custodial setting, that either repeat or resemble (functionally) index offences or other offending targeted in intervention, is a useful way of assessing the kind of engagement an individual is demonstrating. For offenders in the community, information, ideally from collateral sources, about behaviour in the residential (e.g. home or hostel) setting can be used in a similar way. Jones (1997, 2000, 2001) has termed this kind of behavioural sequence or cycle *offence paralleling behaviour* (OPB). On its own OPB is not an index of engagement. It needs to be interpreted against the background of other factors such as length of time in treatment, congruence with behaviour in other settings, e.g. congruence between behaviour during treatment sessions and on the ward, and evidence of ineffective or misguided attempts to manage behaviour.

If the engagement is plausible, then engagement behaviours will be reinforcing to the extent that they are seen as a means of achieving a goal of living a non-offending lifestyle. If this has some real value to the individual, this goal should also be evident

Table 3.6 Formulating cross-situational behavioural congruence and incongruence

	Behaves impeccably in non-treatment settings	Behaves in a uninterested way in non-treatment settings	Offence paralleling behaviour in non-treatment settings
Behaves impeccably during intervention	Congruence 1. Client behaviour is "too good to be true" 2. Either self-deception or malingering 3. May be evidence of change	1. Client malingering with intervention agents, does not perceive a need to malinger on ward 2. Client responding to different situational contingencies, e.g. more structure during sessions	1. Client malingering in session but unable to inhibit OPB on ward 2. Client engaged but unable to implement new skills yet 3. Intervention not targeting relevant offending behaviour 4. Client responding to different situational contingencies, e.g. more structure during sessions
Behaves in a uninterested way during intervention	1. Client feels that they do not need to change any more 2. Client responding to different situational contingencies, e.g. more structure in non-treatment settings than in session	Congruence 1. Client depressed or mentally ill 2. Alternative interests monopolising motivation	Apparent lack of interest may be a consequence of allocating significant resources to managing behaviour in session
Actively disrupts intervention sessions	Client finds content or process of intervention disturbing	Client finds content or process of intervention disturbing	Congruence Offence paralleling behaviour not being inhibited, little incentive to engage.

in arenas other than treatment sessions. Cross-situational behavioural congruence, then, provides a useful source of information for analysing the plausibility and or generalisability of an individual's engagement. When in-session behaviour is better than out-of-session behaviour, it can indicate that the quality of engagement is not substantial. In order to conclude this, it is necessary to exclude other possible explanations such as poor relationships with staff or peers affecting the individual's behaviour in these contexts.

If an audit of OPBs and behavioural congruence is taken at the end of an intervention and there is evidence of incongruence, then the veracity of the observed changes should be questioned, assuming, that is, that it is only possible to malinger for brief periods and that behavioural leakage will inevitably occur. As a measure of engagement, this is probably better than relying on in-session "good" behaviour. Clinical experience indicates that often individuals who make the most change do so after going through various crises and that during these crises their presentation is cross-situationally congruent.

The extent to which dynamic factors are assessed to impact on reconviction or reoffending must take into account this kind of motivational assessment. Indeed, it is theoretically possible that an individual can learn, through the course of an intervention, how to be less conspicuous in their offending and more able to evade detection. Monitoring cross-situational behavioural congruence, offence paralleling behaviour and prosocial non-offending activities can aid in testing the hypothesis that the intervention is inadvertently shaping detection evasion skills.

The colloquial expression "he's talking the talk but he's not walking the walk" describes one way in which engagement might not be having the desired impact. The critical question, for an assessment of motivation is *why* there is a mismatch between what the offender is saying and what they are doing. Are they complying superficially with treatment? Superficial compliance can take several forms. Are they not able to respond to the content of the programme? Have they not had enough time to demonstrate the change? Do they enjoy deceiving intervention agents (so called "duping delight")? Is the therapist shaping up deception behaviour in session as opposed to genuine change?

CONCLUSION

All too often motivation has been seen as a single variable, when the reality is that it involves a variety of different intrapersonal, interpersonal and contextual variables interacting with each other. Engagement behaviour is a complex phenomenon and needs to be assessed in a variety of different ways. Assessment cannot be done without considering the impact that the process of assessment may have on the client; the practitioner has to be aware, at every stage of the assessment, of the client's potential reaction to the assessment process. Forming a good working relationship with the client and pre-empting any interference with this should be the primary objective. The assessment of motivation comes as a secondary goal. Hopefully, this chapter has demonstrated the importance of developing a detailed formulation of engagement behaviours based on analysis of long-term and proximal antecedents. The utility of multiple sources of information for assessing the validity of formulation has also been demonstrated. As psychologists and forensic practitioners, we can all too easily fall back on questionnaires, just because they are there, and not get our hands dirty trying to think about what the issues are for this individual. Whatever strategy we employ, using a practice algorithm may be one way of making explicit the kinds of decisions we are making and the evidence we have for making them in the way we do.

Psychometric assessment in this area is still in its infancy. More work needs to be done developing standardised, valid and reliable assessment instruments that focus on contextual variables, engagement as a set of skills, offence paralleling behaviour, patient therapist matching, individuals' attitudes to and beliefs about the means and goals of change, and developmental cycling through different stages of change. Ultimately these can be judged by their ability to predict engagement and engagement problems.

1. ACKNOWLEDGEMENTS

Thanks to Todd Hogue and Jason Davies for comments on earlier drafts of this chapter.

REFERENCES

Ajzen, I. (1988). *Attitudes, Personality and Behaviour.* Milton Keynes: Open University Press.

Ajzen, I. (1991). The theory of planned behaviour. *Organizational Behavior and Human Decision Processes*, **50**, 179–211.

Ajzen, I. & Fishbein M. (1980). *Understanding Attitudes and Predicting Social Behaviour.* Englewood Cliffs, NJ: Prentice Hall.

Appel, C.P. (1986). From contemplation to determination: contributions from cognitive psychology. In W.R. Miller & N. Heather (eds) *Treating Addictive Behaviours: Processes of Change* (pp. 59–89). New York: Plenum Press.

Bandura, A. (1977). *Social Learning Theory.* New York: Prentice Hall.

Bandura, A. (1986). *Social Foundations of Thought and Action: A Social Cognitive Theory.* Englewood Cliffs, NJ: Prentice Hall.

Baumeister, R.F. & Heatherton, T.F. (1996). Self-regulation failure: an overview. *Psychological Inquiry*, **7**, 1–15.

Birchwood, M., Smith, J., MacMillan, F., Hogg, B., Prasad, R., Harvey, C., & Bering, S. (1989). Predicting relapse in schizophrenia: the development and implementation of an early signs monitoring system using patients and families as observers. *Psychological Medicine*, **19**, 649–56.

Blackburn, R. (1990). Treatment of the psychopathic offender. In K. Howells & C.R. Hollin (eds) *Clinical Approaches to Working with Mentally Disordered and Sexual Offenders.* Issues in Criminological and Legal Psychology, no. 16 (pp. 54–66). Leicester: British Psychological Society.

Briggs, D. (1994). Assessment of sexual offenders. In M. McMurran & J.E. Hodge (eds) *The Assessment of Criminal Behaviours of Clients in Secure Settings.* London: Jessica Kingsley.

Brown, I. (1997). A theoretical model of the behavioural addictions—applied to offending. In J.E. Hodge, M. McMurran, & C.R. Hollin (eds) *Addicted to Crime?* Chichester: Wiley.

Bruch, M. & Bond, F.W. (1998). *Beyond Diagnosis: Case Formulation Approaches in CBT.* Chichester: Wiley.

DiClemente, C.C. & Hughes, S.O. (1990). Stages of change profiles in alcoholism treatment. *Journal of Substance Abuse*, **2**, 217–35.

DiClemente, C.C. & Prochaska, J.O. (1998). Towards a comprehensive, transtheoretical model of change; stages of change and addictive behaviors. In W.R. Miller & N. Heather (eds) *Treating Addictive Behaviours*, 2nd edn. New York: Plenum Press.

Dunmore, E., Clark, D.M., & Ehlers, A. (1997). Cognitive factors in persistent versus recovered post-traumatic stress disorder after physical or sexual assault: a pilot study. *Behavioural and Cognitive Psychotherapy*, **25**, 147–59.

Ehlers, A., Clark, D.M., Dunmore, E., Jaycox, L., Meadows, E., & Foa, E.B. (1998). Predicting response to exposure treatment in PTSD: the role of mental defeat and alienation. *Journal of Traumatic Stress*, **11**, 457–71.

Erez, E. (1987). Rehabilitation in justice: the prisoner's perspective. *Journal of Offender Counselling, Services and Rehabilitation*, **11**, 5–19.

Gillis, C., Getkate, M., Robinson, D., & Porporino, F. (1999). *Correctional Work Supervisor Leadership and Credibility: The Influence on Offender Work Motivation.* Correctional Service Canada. http://www.csc-scc.gc.ca/text/pblct/forum/e073/e073e.shtml.

Gresswell, D.M. (1994). Multiple murder in England and Wales 1982–1991: An analysis. Phd thesis, School of Psychology, University of Birmingham, UK.

Hogue, T.E. & Jones, L. (1999). Personality disorder attrition rates: Comparisons and suggestions. Poster presented at the 5th Anglo-Dutch Conference on Personality Disorder and Forensic Psychiatry, Amsterdam.

Janis, I.L. & Mann, L. (1977). *Decision Making: A Psychological Analysis of Conflict, Choice and Commitment.* New York: Free Press.

Jones, L. (1997). Developing models for managing treatment integrity and efficacy in a prison based TC: the Max Glatt Centre. In E. Cullen, L. Jones, & R Woodward (eds) *Therapeutic Communities for Offenders.* Chichester: Wiley.

Jones, L. (2000). Identifying and working with clinically relevant offence paralleling be- haviour. Paper presented at Division of Clinical Psychology, Forensic Special Interest Group, Nottinghamshire, UK.

Jones, L. (2001). Anticipating offence paralleling behaviour. Paper presented at Division of Forensic Psychology Conference, Birmingham, UK.

Jones, L. & Brown, V. (1998). Motivation and motivational assessment of personality disordered offenders. Paper presented at Division of Forensic Psychology Conference, Durham UK.

Kohlenberg, R.J. & Tsai, M. (1994). Functional analytic psychotherapy: a radical behav- ioral approach to treatment and integration. *Journal of Psychotherapy Integration*, **4**, 175– 201.

Linehan, M.M. (1993). *Cognitive Behavioural Treatment of Borderline Personality Disorder*. New York: Guilford Press.

McConnaughy, E.A., Prochaska, J.O., & Velicer, W.F. (1983). Stages of change in psychother- apy: measurement and sample profiles. *Psychotherapy Theory, Research and Practice*, **20**, 368–75.

McConnaughy, E.A., DiClemente, C.C., Prochaska, J.O., and Velicer, W.F. (1989). Stages of change in psychotherapy: a follow up report. *Psychotherapy*, **26**, 494–503.

McMurran, M., Tyler, P., Hogue, T., Cooper, K., Dunseath, W., & McDaid, D. (1998). Measur- ing motivation to change in offenders. *Psychology, Crime and Law*, **4**, 43–50.

Maslow, A.H. (1970). *Motivation and Personality*, 2nd edn. New York: Harper & Row.

Miller, W.R. (1985). Motivation for treatment: a review with special emphasis on alcoholism. *Psychological Bulletin*, **98**, 84–107.

Miller, W.R. & Rollnick, S. (1991). *Motivational Interviewing: Preparing People to Change Addictive Behaviour*. New York: Guilford.

Mischel, W. (1973). Towards a cognitive social learning reconceptualisation of personality. *Psychological Review*, **80**, 319–24.

Ostapiuk, E.B. & Westwood, S. (1986). Glenthorne youth treatment centre: working with ado- lescents in graduations of security. In C.R. Hollin & K. Howells (eds) *Clinical Approaches to Criminal Behaviour*, Issues in Criminological and Legal Psychology, no. 9. Leicester: British Psychological Society.

Persons, J. (1989). *Cognitive Therapy in Practice. A Case Formulation Approach*. New York: Norton.

Piaget, J. (1962). *Play Dreams and Imitation in Childhood*. New York: Norton.

Piaget, J. (1970). Piaget's theory. In P.H. Mussen (ed.) *Carmichael's Manual of Child Psychology*, vol. 1. 3rd edn (pp 703–32). New York: Wiley.

Power, M.J. & Dalgleish, T. (1997). *Cognition and Emotion: From Order to Disorder*. Hove: Psychology Press.

Prochaska, J.O. & DiClemente, C.C. (1982). Transtheoretical therapy: towards a more inte- grative model of change. *Psychotherapy: Theory, Research and Practice*, **19**, 276–88.

Prochaska, J.O., DiClemente, C.C., & Norcross, J.C. (1992). In search of how people change: applications to addictive behaviors. *American Psychologist*, **47**, 1102–14.

Rollnick, S., Heather, N., Gold, R., & Hall, W. (1992). Development of a short readiness to change questionnaire for use in brief opportunistic interventions amongst excessive drinkers. *British Journal of Addiction*, **87**, 743–54.

Rothfleisch, J. (1997). Assessing different measures of stages of change with cocaine depen- dent clients. Doctoral dissertation, University of Houston, TX .

Safran, J., Muran, D., & Christopher, J. (1996). The resolution of ruptures in the therapeutic alliance. *Journal of Consulting and Clinical Psychology*, **64**, 447–58.

Sherer, M., Maddux, J.E., Mercandante, B., Prentice-Dunn, S., Jacobs, B., & Rogers, R.W. (1982). The self-efficacy scale: construction and validation. *Psychological Reports*, **51**, 663–71.

Stiles W.B., Meshot C.M., Anderson, T.M., & Sloan, J.R. (1992). Assimilation of problematic experiences: the case of John Jones. *Psychotherapy Research*, **2**, 81–101.

Sutton, S. (2001) Back to the drawing board? A review of applications of the transtheoretical model to substance use. *Addiction*, **96**, 175–86.

Turkat, I. (1979). The behaviour analysis matrix. *Scandinavian Journal of Behaviour Therapy*, **8**, 187–9.

Turkat, I. (1985). *Behavioural Case Formulation*. New York: Plenum.

Turkat, I. (1990). *The Personality Disorders: A Psychological Approach to Clinical Management*. New York: Pergamon.

Turkat, I. & Maisto, S.A. (1983) Functions of and differences between psychiatric diagnosis and case formulation. *The Behaviour Therapist*, **6**, 184–5.

Walters, G.D. (1998) *Changing Lives of Crime and Drugs: Intervening with Substance Abusing Offenders*. Chichester: Wiley.

Wong, S. & Gordon, A. (1999). Violence risk scale (Version 2), manual. Regional Psychiatric Centre (Prairies), Correctional Services of Canada.

Woods, P. (1979). *The Divided School*. London: Routledge & Kegan Paul.

Part II

MOTIVATIONAL ENHANCEMENT IN PRACTICE

Chapter 4

ENHANCING MOTIVATION OF OFFENDERS AT EACH STAGE OF CHANGE AND PHASE OF THERAPY

JAMES O. PROCHASKA* AND DEBORAH A. LEVESQUE[†]
*Cancer Prevention Research Center, University of Rhode Island, Kingston, USA
[†]Pro-Change Behavior Systems, Inc., Kingston, USA

What moves people to take action? The answer to this key question depends on what type of action is to be taken. What moves people to start therapy? What moves them to continue? What moves people to progress in therapy? And what moves them to continue to progress after therapy has terminated? Answers to these questions can provide guidance as we struggle with one of the field's most pressing concerns: what types of programs can have the greatest impact on an entire population of criminal offenders, even those who are unmotivated to change?

What motivates offenders to change? The answer to this question depends in part on where they are at in the change process. What motivates people to begin thinking about changing can be different from what motivates them to begin preparing to take action. Once action is taken, still different forces can motivate people to maintain action or, conversely, to move backwards and relapse back to criminal behaviors. Fortunately, the answers to these complex questions may be quite simple if we approach interventions systematically using the Transtheoretical Model (Prochaska & DiClemente, 1983; Prochaska et al., 1992a, 1994a).

Twenty years of research on the addictions and other types of behaviors have found that change is a process that unfolds over time through a series of stages: precontemplation, contemplation, preparation, action, maintenance, and termination. *Precontemplation* is the stage in which people are not intending to take action in the foreseeable future, usually operationally defined as the next six months. People may be in this stage because they are uninformed or under-informed about the consequences of their behavior. Or they may be demoralized because they tried to change several times and failed. Both groups tend to avoid reading, talking or

Motivating Offenders to Change: A Guide to Enhancing Engagement in Therapy. Edited by M. McMurran.
© 2002 John Wiley & Sons, Ltd.

thinking about their high-risk behaviors. They tend to underestimate the benefits of changing and overestimate the costs. Unaware that they are making such mistakes, it can be difficult for them to change. Many people remain stuck in the precontemplation stage for years, doing considerable damage to others and themselves.

Other theories may characterize these clients as resistant or unmotivated, or as not ready for therapy or rehabilitative programs. The fact is most traditional treatment programs are not ready for such individuals and are not motivated to match their needs.

We have identified two major forces that can move people to progress. The first is developmental events. In our research the mean age of smokers reaching longer-term maintenance is 39. Those of us who have gone through age 39 know that it is a mean age. It is an age when we reevaluate how we have been living and whether we want to enhance the quality and quantity of the second half of our lives. With criminal behavior, age is a powerful change agent. Keep offenders alive long enough and most will "age out" of their criminal lifestyles and adopt a more mature way of living.

The other naturally occurring force is environmental events. One of our favorite examples is a couple that we followed who were both heavy smokers. Their dog of many years died of lung cancer. This eventually moved the wife to quit smoking. The husband bought a new dog. So even the same event can be processed differently by different people. There are other examples: the hit man for the mob who begins to seriously think about changing when his wife leaves him to protect their son from a similar lifestyle; or the domestic violence offender who decides to seek help when he learns that his own daughter has been physically abused by her husband.

Do we have to wait helplessly for offenders to age, or to hit bottom or suffer significant losses? There is a third force that can help offenders in the precontemplation stage to progress. It is called planned interventions.

Contemplation is the stage in which people are intending to take action in the next six months. They are more aware of the pros of changing but are also acutely aware of the cons. When offenders begin to seriously contemplate giving up crime, their awareness of the costs of changing can increase. There is no free change. This ambivalence, or love–hate relationship with a criminal lifestyle, can keep offenders stuck in the contemplation stage for years. We often characterize this phenomenon as chronic contemplation or behavioral procrastination. These folks are not ready for traditional action-oriented programs. That hit man became torn between his love of his family and the fear of "the family."

Preparation is the stage in which people are intending to take action in the immediate future, usually measured as the next month. People in preparation typically have taken some significant steps in the past year. These individuals have a plan of action, such as going to a recovery group, consulting a counselor, talking to a pastor, buying a self-help book or relying on a self-change approach. These are the people we should recruit for action-oriented rehabilitative programs.

Action is the stage in which people have made specific overt modifications in their lifestyles within the past six months. Since action is observable, behavior change often has been equated with action. (Unfortunately, we tend to overlook important behavioral changes that occur in the earlier stages and lead to stage progression). To be in the action stage, people must attain a certain behavioral criterion that scientists and professionals agree is sufficient to reduce the risk of harm to others or the self. In smoking, for example, only total abstinence counts. With alcoholism and alcohol abuse, many believe that only total abstinence can be effective, while others accept controlled drinking as effective action. With criminal offenders, zero tolerance is the official policy of the criminal justice system.

Maintenance is the stage in which people are working to prevent relapse but they do not apply change processes as frequently as people in the action stage do. They are less tempted to relapse and increasingly more confident that they can sustain their changes. Based on temptation and self-efficacy data, we estimated that maintenance lasts from six months to about five years.

One of the common reasons that people relapse in the action stage is that they are not well prepared for the prolonged effort needed to progress to maintenance. Many think the worst will be over in a few weeks or a few months. If they ease up on their efforts too early, they are at great risk of relapse.

To prepare people for what is to come, we encourage them to think of making permanent changes as a marathon, rather than a sprint. Individuals with little or no preparation would not enter the Boston marathon because they know they would not succeed. If they had done some preparation, they might make it for several miles before dropping out. Only those who are well prepared could maintain their effort mile after mile. People familiar with the Boston marathon know they have to be well prepared to survive Heartbreak Hill at about the 20-mile mark. What is the behavioral equivalent of Heartbreak Hill for offenders? Across the dozens of chronic behaviors we have studied, we have found that the majority of relapses occur during times of emotional distress. We are at our emotional and psychological weakest when depressed, anxious, angry, bored, lonely, stressed and distressed. We cannot prevent emotional distress from occurring. But we can help offenders prevent relapse by preparing them to cope with distress without falling back to criminal lifestyles and other self-defeating and destructive behaviors.

Termination is the stage in which individuals have zero temptation and 100% self-efficacy. They are confident they will not return to their old habits, no matter how much emotional distress they experience. It is as if they had never acquired the habit in the first place. In a study of former smokers and alcoholics we found that less than 20% of each group had reached the criterion of no temptation and total self-efficacy (Snow et al., 1992). While the ideal goal is to be totally "cured" or rehabilitated, we recognize that for many offenders the best they can achieve is a lifetime of maintenance.

ASSESSING STAGE OF CHANGE

Stage of change can be assessed using two self-report methods. In the first, a classification algorithm is used to place individuals in one of five mutually exclusive stage categories based on their responses to a few questions about past behavior, present behavior, and their intentions (DiClemente et al., 1991). Alternatively, change can be assessed using continuous measures that represent the degree to which individuals' attitudes and behaviors characterize each of the different stages. Although subjects progress from one stage to another, they may have attitudes and exhibit behaviors that characterize more than one stage at the same time. Their profiles or patterns of scores on the various measures characterize their readiness to change (Levesque et al., 2000a; McConnaughy et al., 1983, 1989).

PHASES OF PLANNED INTERVENTIONS

Let us apply the stages of change model to see how we can motivate more offenders at each phase of planned interventions to change their lifestyles and desist from crime. The five phases are:

1. Recruitment
2. Retention
3. Progress
4. Process
5. Outcomes

Recruitment

Too few studies have paid attention to one of the skeletons in the closet of professional treatment programs for most problem behaviors. The fact is these programs recruit or reach only a small minority of individuals with the problem. Less than 25% of populations with DSM-IV diagnoses ever enter professional therapy programs (Veroff et al., 1981a, b). With smoking, the most deadly of addictions, less than 10% participate in professional programs (US Department of Health and Human Services, 1990). We can assume that a similarly small percentage of criminal offenders would enter rehabilitative programs if they were not mandated by the criminal justice system.

Given the enormous costs of violence and other criminal behaviors to perpetrators, their families, friends, employers, communities, and healthcare systems, we must motivate many more offenders to participate in appropriate programs. Some governments and health care systems are seeking to treat such costly conditions on a population basis. But when they turn to the biggest and best clinical trials treating recalcitrant behaviors like addictions on a population basis, what do they discover? Trial after trial reports troubling outcomes (e.g. COMMIT, 1995; Ennett et al., 1994; Glasgow et al., 1995; Luepker et al., 1994). Whether the trials were done with work sites, schools or entire communities, the results are remarkably similar: no significant effects compared to the control conditions.

If we examine more closely one of these trials, the Minnesota Heart Health Study, we can find hints of what went wrong (Lando et al., 1995). About 90% of individuals in the treatment and control communities reported seeing media stories about smoking, one of the study's targeted behaviors. However, only about 4% of smokers in the study reported participating in one of our most powerful behavior change interventions—clinics, classes and counseling. If managed care offers free state-of-the-science smoking cessation clinics, only 1% of smokers are recruited

(Lichtenstein & Hollis, 1992). We simply cannot have much impact on the health and mental health of our nation if our best programs reach so few people.

How do we motivate many more offenders to seek and benefit from appropriate help? By changing our paradigms and our practices. There are two paradigms that we need to consider changing. The first is an action-oriented paradigm that construes behavior change as an event that occurs quickly, immediately, discretely and dramatically. Treatment programs that are designed to have people immediately stop offending are implicitly or explicitly designed for the portion of the population who are in the preparation stage.

Research comparing stage distributions across behaviors and populations finds that about 40% of pre-action individuals are in precontemplation, 40% in contemplation, and only 20% in preparation (Laforge et al., 1999; Velicer et al., 1995). These data suggest that if we offer action-oriented interventions to all offenders, we are targeting less than 20% of the at-risk population. If we are to meet the needs of all offenders, we must design interventions for the 40% in precontemplation and the 40% in contemplation.

The second paradigm change that this approach requires is a shift from a passive–reactive to a proactive approach to recruitment. Most professionals have been trained to be passive–reactive—to passively wait for patients to seek services and then react. The biggest problem with this approach is that the majority of people with problems never seek services.

Offering stage-matched interventions and applying proactive or outreach recruitment methods, we have been able to motivate 80–90% of smokers to enter our treatment programs in six large-scale clinical trials (Prochaska et al., 2001 a, b). This is a quantum increase over the 1–4% participation rates found in other studies.

There are regions of the National Health Service in the United Kingdom that are training health professionals in these new paradigms. Over 6000 physicians, nurses, counselors and health educators have been trained to proactively interact at each stage of change with their entire patient populations who smoke, or abuse alcohol, drugs or food. If we are to have a serious impact on violence and other crime, we must learn to reach out to the entire population of offenders and offer stage-matched therapies.

What happens if professionals change only one paradigm and proactively recruit entire populations without stage-matching? This experiment has been tried in one of the largest managed care organizations in the United States (Lichtenstein & Hollis, 1992). Physicians spent time with all smokers to recruit them for a state-of-the-art, action-oriented clinic-based smoking cessation program. If that didn't work, nurses spent up to 10 minutes to get them to sign up, followed by 12 minutes of health education and a counselor call to the home. This intensive recruitment protocol motivated 35% of smokers in the precontemplation stage to sign up. But only 3% showed up, 2% finished up and 0% ended up better off. Of individuals in the contemplation and preparation stages, 65% signed up; 15% showed up, 11% finished up and some small percentage ended up better off.

In important ways our legal systems can be seen as proactively delivering people to action-oriented behavior change programs. But do offenders show up for counseling, probation or other behavior change programs? Do they show up physically, mentally and emotionally? Do they finish up? Do they end up better off? A recent meta-analysis of published and unpublished outcome research found no overall effect for batterer treatment across studies relying on partner reports of recidivism, and a fairly small effect across studies relying on police reports and court records (Levesque & Gelles, 1998). We can blame offenders for not showing up, finishing up or ending up better off, or we can look to alternatives to action-oriented programs.

In a study of illegal drug users, we examined whether people were in therapy out of coercion versus choice. We compared participants in each stage of change and to our surprise we found that people in precontemplation were no more likely to be mandated or coerced into treatment by the criminal justice system, employers, spouses, or social service agencies; however, they perceived themselves as being in treatment more because of coercion than choice. Participants in later stages of change perceived therapy participation more as a function of choice than coercion. The implications of these data are clear: transforming coercion into choice requires that we help people progress out of precontemplation. The more people progress, the more they are likely to perceive proactive interventions as sources of positive social influence that can help them become free from destructive and self-defeating lifestyles, and the less they have to resist and react against counselors who are trying to help them make changes.

What can move a majority of offenders to participate in treatment? Given the growing research evidence, we believe that the answer is professionals who are motivated and prepared to proactively reach out and offer interventions that match offenders' stage of change.

Retention

What motivates people to continue in therapy? Or conversely, what moves clients to terminate counseling quickly and prematurely? A meta-analysis of 125 studies found that nearly 50% of clients drop out of treatment (Wierzbicki & Pekarik, 1993). Across studies, there were few consistent predictors of premature termination, except substance abuse, minority status and lower education. While important, these variables did not account for much of the variance.

One excellent predictor of premature dropout and poor outcome from therapy is the stage of change of the client at intake (Beitman et al., 1994; Brogan et al., 1999; Levesque & Chell, 1999). We should not treat offenders in the precontemplation stage as if they were in the action stage and expect them to continue in therapy, but we do. We try to pressure them to take action when they are not prepared, driving them away and then blaming them for not being motivated enough for our action-oriented programs.

With clients who enter therapy in the action stage, relapse prevention strategies are appropriate. But would relapse prevention make any sense with the 40% of clients in precontemplation? What might be a good match here? We could recommend a dropout prevention approach, since we know these patients are likely to leave early if we do not help them to continue.

With clients who enter therapy in the precontemplation stage, you could share your key concerns: "I'm concerned that therapy may not have a chance to make a significant difference in your life because you may be tempted to leave early." You could then explore whether they have been pressured to enter therapy. How do they react when someone tries to pressure or coerce them into changing when they are not ready? Can they let you know if they feel that you are trying to pressure or coerce them? You want to help them, but can't force them to change; you can only encourage them to take steps where they are most likely to succeed.

We now have three studies that examine program retention rates of individuals receiving stage-matched interventions (Prochaska et al., 1993; 2001a, b). What is clear is that when treatment is matched to stage of change, people in precontemplation continue at the same high rates as those who start in preparation. This result held when participants were recruited proactively (we reached out to them to offer help), and when they were recruited reactively (they called us for help). Unfortunately, these studies have been conducted only with smokers. But if they hold up across problems, we will be able to offer a practical answer to the question: what motivates people to continue in therapy? Stage-matched interventions can increase retention.

Progress

What moves people to progress in therapy and to continue to progress after therapy has ended? The *stage effect* predicts that the amount of successful action taken during treatment and after treatment is directly related to the stage people are in at the start of treatment (Prochaska et al., 1992a). Smokers in preparation are twice as likely to be abstinent at one month post-treatment than contemplators, who in turn are twice as likely to be abstinent than precontemplators. The pattern continues at six months post-treatment (DiClemente et al., 1991). A single brief intervention that helps individuals advance only one stage will double their chances of taking effective action in the near future (Prochaska et al., 1992a).

The stage effect has been found across a variety of problems and populations including rehabilitative success for brain injury and recovery from anxiety and panic disorders following random assignment to placebo or effective medication (Beitman et al., 1994; Lam et al., 1988). In the latter study, the psychiatrist leading the trial concluded that patients should be assessed for their stage of readiness to benefit from such medication and helped through the stages so they are well prepared before being placed on the medication.

We have already seen that if we try to move all people with problems to immediate action we are likely to miss a majority of them because they do not show up, or do not finish up. A more realistic goal, especially in brief therapy, is to use stage-matched interventions to help clients progress one stage. For clients who move relatively quickly, we can aim for two stages. Understandably, therapists who work with offenders experience a sense of urgency: violence and other criminal behaviors must stop immediately to protect others from harm. However, based on the stage effect we know that if we can help individuals progress one stage in one month, we can about double their chances of taking effective action by six months. If we help them progress two stages, we can triple or quadruple their chances of taking effective action (Prochaska et al., 2001b). Setting such realistic goals can enable many more offenders to enter therapy, continue in therapy, progress in therapy and continue to progress after therapy.

The 6000 British health professionals who were trained in the stage approach experienced a dramatic increase in morale. They were able to see progress with the majority of their patients where they once saw failure when immediate action was the only criterion of success. They were much more confident that they could match the needs of all their patients rather than just the 20% or so who were prepared to take immediate action.

The models of therapy that we choose should be good for our mental health as well as the mental health of our clients. After all, we are involved in therapy for a lifetime, whereas most of our clients are involved for only a brief time. If our pressure to produce immediate results is transferred to offenders who are not prepared for such action, we will repeat the past: we will not reach them and we will not retain them. We can help many more offenders to progress but only if we set realistic goals for them and for us. Otherwise we risk demoralizing and demotivating both them and ourselves.

Process

If we are to help motivate offenders to progress from one stage to the next, we will need to know principles and processes of change that can produce such progress.

Principle 1: The pros of changing must increase for people to progress from precontemplation

We found that in 12 out of 12 studies the pros were higher in contemplation than in precontemplation (Prochaska et al., 1994b). This pattern held true across 12 problem behaviors: quitting cocaine, delinquency, consistent condom use, safer sex, sedentary lifestyles, high-fat diets, obesity, sun exposure, smoking, radon testing, mammography screening, and physicians practicing behavioral medicine.

Here is a technique for raising the pros. Ask offenders in precontemplation to tell you all the benefits or pros of ending the violence or ending other criminal behavior. They typically can list four or five. Let them know that there are 10 to 12 times that number. Challenge them to double or triple their list for your next meeting. As their list grows to include pros like more peace of mind, more self-respect, and better relationships with family members, they will be more motivated to begin to seriously contemplate changing.

Principle 2: The cons of changing must decrease for people to progress from contemplation to action

In 12 out of 12 studies we found that the cons of changing were lower in action than in contemplation (Prochaska et al., 1994b).

Principle 3: The pros must outweigh the cons for people to be prepared to take action

In 12 out of 12 studies the cons of changing were higher than the pros in precontemplation but in 11 out of 12 the pros were higher than the cons in the action stage.

The one exception was quitting cocaine among addicts, the only group consisting largely of inpatients. For individuals in inpatient programs (or prisons), taking action may be more under the social controls of residential care than under self-control. Elevated cons relative to the pros would not bode well for immediate discharge. A major challenge for offenders is to help them transform social coercion into social influence, and social controls into self-control.

Here is a research example of how such transformation can occur. In the United States, the Air Force coerces all cadets to quit smoking for the six weeks of boot camp. This compliance is documented by regular blood cotinine testing. The consequence of breaking this rule is severe: the cadets have to repeat boot camp. Violations of this rule are rare under such social coercion and control.

But after six weeks of total abstinence what is the recidivism rate for smoking at 12-month follow-up? Well over 100%, since many enlisted people learn to smoke in the service. These data suggest that the Air Force is a major risk factor for smoking. Similarly, being in prison is a major risk factor for learning more criminal behavior.

The military wanted to become smoke free but was concerned that coercion could make things worse. So they asked a group of colleagues to create what they called a relapse prevention program. Their brief, 45-minute session during boot camp focused primarily on all the pros of not returning to smoking, such as saving the equivalent of one month's salary and being more likely to be promoted (Klesges et al., 1999).

A year later this brief intervention had no overall effects on the 30 000 randomly selected treated cadets compared to an untreated control group. But the results were remarkable with the subgroup of smokers in precontemplation—that is, individuals who were in action because of coercion and intended to return to smoking as soon as their forced abstinence was over. A year later, three times as many of the treated precontemplators were not smoking compared to those who were untreated. Among enlisted African-Americans, four times as many treated cadets were not smoking. These results show how interventions appropriate for a given stage (like increasing the pros among precontemplators) can be highly effective when administered to the subgroup of individuals in that stage, and ineffective when administered in a one-size-fits-all fashion to all individuals. Messages matched to individuals who are most at risk for recidivism, namely those in precontemplation, can dramatically increase the odds of bringing high-risk behaviors under self-control after social controls are removed.

It should be noted that if we used raw scores to assess these patterns, we would often find that the pros of changing are higher than the cons, even for people in precontemplation. It is only when we use standardized scores that we find that the cons of changing are always higher than the pros among precontemplators. This means that compared to their peers in other stages, people in precontemplation underestimate the pros and overestimate the cons. They are probably not particularly conscious that they are making these mistakes, since they do not know how they compare to their peers.

Principle 4: The *strong principle* of progress holds that in order to progress from precontemplation to effective action, the pros of changing must increase one standard deviation (Prochaska, 1994).

Table 4.1 Stages by Processes of change

Precontemplation	Contemplation	Preparation	Action	Maintenance
Consciousness raising				
Dramatic relief				
Environmental reevaluation				
	Self-reevaluation			
		Self-liberation		
			Helping relationships	
			Contingency management	
			Counter-conditioning	
			Stimulus control	

Principle 5: The *weak principle* of progress holds that in order to progress from contemplation to effective action, the cons of changing must decrease one half standard deviation.

Since the pros of changing must increase twice as much as the cons decrease, we place twice as much emphasis on the benefits of changing than on the costs. We believe we may have discovered mathematical principles for how much positive motivations must increase and how much negative motivations must decrease. Sensitive assessments of the pros and cons can guide interventions, giving us and our clients feedback on whether our therapeutic efforts are producing progress and when they are failing. Together we can modify our methods if we are not seeing the movement needed to become adequately prepared for action.

Principle 6: We need to match particular processes of change to specific stages of change.

Table 4.1 presents the empirical integration that we have found between processes and stages of change. Guided by this integration, we would apply the following processes with patients in precontemplation:

1. *Consciousness raising* involves increasing awareness about the causes, consequences, and cures for a particular problem. Interventions that can increase awareness include observations, mild confrontations, interpretations, feedback, and education, like bibliotherapy. Often one of the first phenomena we have to make more conscious is how offenders defend themselves when they feel pressured or coerced into taking action. Withdrawing, getting angry, denying, blaming, or threatening are some of the common defenses offenders use to defeat attempts to make them act in ways they are not prepared to act. Some techniques, like confrontation, can increase treatment resistance and dropout. Instead, we recommend motivational enhancement methods like providing personal feedback about the current and long-term consequences of continuing their destructive or self-defeating behavior. Increasing the cons of not changing is the corollary of raising the pros of changing. Clearly, consciousness-raising techniques are designed in part to increase the pros of changing.

2. *Dramatic relief* involves emotional arousal about one's current behavior and relief that can come from changing. Fear, inspiration, guilt, and hope are some of the emotions that can move people to contemplate changing. Psychodrama, role playing, grieving, and personal testimonies are examples of techniques that can move people emotionally.

We should note that earlier behavior change literature concluded that interventions like education and fear arousal did not motivate behavior change. Unfortunately, many interventions were evaluated by their ability to move people to immediate action. Processes like consciousness raising and dramatic relief are intended to move people to contemplation, not immediate action. Therefore, we should assess their effectiveness by whether they produce the progress they are expected to produce. Fortunately, the field never stopped believing that education and emotion can move people, in spite of what some studies said.

3. *Environmental reevaluation* combines both affective and cognitive assessments of how a destructive behavior affects one's social environment and how changing would impact on that environment. Empathy training, value clarification, and family or network interventions can facilitate such reevaluation.

We may believe that offenders do not care about the impact of their behavior on others. In a study of prostitutes, intravenous drug users, and street youth, what was the most important pro for them to consistently use condoms? HIV and AIDs prevention was number two. Prevention of other sexually transmitted diseases was number three. Pregnancy prevention was not in their top ten. Their number one pro was, "I would be a more responsible human being." This was true across four different subpopulations. The lesson learned? Do not stereotype populations. And do not assume that we know what will and will not motivate people to break out of high-risk behaviors.

Here is a brief media intervention in California aimed at smokers in precontemplation. A man clearly in grief says, "I always feared that my smoking would lead to an early death. I always worried that my smoking would cause lung cancer. But I never imagined it would happen to my wife." Beneath his grieving face appears this statistic: "50 000 deaths per year are caused by passive smoking, the California Department of Health."

In 30 seconds we have consciousness raising, dramatic relief and environmental reevaluation. No wonder such media interventions have been evaluated to be an important part of California's successful reduction of smoking.

4. *Self-reevaluation* combines both cognitive and affective assessments of one's self-image free from a long-standing lifestyle. Imagery, healthier role models, value clarification, and self-narratives are techniques that can move people to reevaluate who they were, who they are, and who they want to be. In his study of British ex-convicts who ended up "making good," Maruna (2000) found that "to desist from crime, ex-offenders need to develop a coherent, prosocial identity for themselves. As such, they need to account for and understand their criminal pasts (why they did what they did), and they also need to understand why they are now 'not like that anymore'" (p. 7). As offenders progress into preparation, they begin to develop more of a future focus as they imagine how their life will be free from destructive and self-defeating behaviors.

5. *Self-liberation* is both the belief that one can change and the commitment and re-commitment to act on that belief. Techniques that can enhance such willpower include contracts and other public rather than private commitments. Motivational research also suggests that if people only have one choice they are not as motivated as if they have two choices (Miller, 1985). Three is even better but four does not seem to enhance motivation. Wherever possible, we try to provide people with three of the best choices for applying each process. With smoking cessation, for example, we used to believe there was only one way to commit to changing, and that was to quit cold turkey. We now know there are at least three good choices: (a) cold turkey, (b) nicotine replacement, and (c) nicotine fading. Asking clients to choose which alternative they believe would be most effective for them, and which they would be most committed to can enhance their motivation and self-liberation. This approach stands in stark contrast to the doctor or probation officer ordering a person to attend a particular program, such as AA.

6. *Helping relationships* combine caring, openness, trust, and acceptance, as well as support for changing. Rapport building, a therapeutic alliance, counselor calls, buddy systems, sponsors and self-help groups can be excellent sources of social support. If people become dependent on such support for maintaining change, we need to be careful to fade out such support lest termination of therapy become a condition for relapsing.

7. *Contingency management* involves the systematic use of reinforcements and punishments for taking steps in a particular direction. Since we find that successful self-changers rely much more on reinforcement, than punishment, we emphasize reinforcements, for progressing rather than punishments for regressing. Contingency contracts, overt and covert reinforcements, and group recognition are strategies for increasing reinforcement and incentives that increase the probability that healthier responses will be repeated.

   To prepare people for the longer term, we teach them to rely more on self-reinforcements than social reinforcements. We find clinically that many clients expect much more external reinforcement and recognition than others actually provide. Relatives and friends can take action for granted too quickly. Acquaintances typically generate only a couple of positive consequences early in action. Self-reinforcements are much more under self-control and can be given more quickly and consistently when temptations to lapse or relapse are resisted.

8. *Counter-conditioning* requires the learning of healthier behaviors that can substitute for problem behaviors. We just discussed three healthy alternatives to smoking. Counter-conditioning techniques tend to be quite specific to a particular behavior and include desensitization, assertion, and cognitive counters to irrational self-statements that can elicit anger, anxiety, outrage, or distress.

9. *Stimulus control* involves modifying the environment to increase cues that prompt healthier responses and decrease cues that are tempting. Avoidance and environmental re-engineering like avoiding criminal peers, removing addictive substances and paraphernalia, and attending self-help groups can provide stimuli that elicit healthier responses and reduce risks for relapse.

10. *Social liberation* involves society creating more alternatives for people, such as more job training and job opportunities, rehabilitative programs, and community-based halfway houses. These alternatives can help liberate offenders from chronic criminal patterns by providing more prosocial choices. This change process has not been found to be as stage-specific as others are, in part because it depends more on social change than on self-change.

Competing theories of therapy have implicitly or explicitly advocated alternative processes of enhancing motivation for change. Which moves people more, cognitions or emotions? Or is it values, decisions, or dedication? Are we ruled by contingencies, or by environmental conditions or conditioned habits? Or is it the therapeutic relationship that is the common healer across all therapeutic modalities?

Our answer to the last of these questions is yes. Our integrative answer is that therapeutic processes originating from competing theories can be compatible when they are combined in a stage-matched paradigm. With patients in earlier stages of change, we can enhance motivation through more experiential processes that produce healthier cognitions, emotions, evaluations, decisions, and commitments. In later stages we seek to build on such solid preparation and motivation by emphasizing more behavioral processes that can help condition positive habits, reinforce these habits, and provide physical and social environments that support constructive lifestyles freer from destructive and self-defeating patterns.

WHAT ARE YOUR FAVORITE PROCESSES OF CHANGE?

In your own work, which processes of change do you use? We recently conducted a detailed review of five published domestic violence treatment guides in order to assess the extent to which recommended interventions are geared toward readiness to change and to identify processes of change that may be under- or overutilized (Levesque et al., 2000b).

Four of the five treatment guides examined relied most heavily on consciousness raising, followed by counter-conditioning. In fact, the general pattern was to introduce a topic (e.g. assertiveness) and then introduce a related skill that serves as an alternative to violence (e.g. making assertive requests), and then to introduce another new topic, and other new skill, and so on. The one exception to this rule, the manual outlining the Duluth model (Pence & Paymar, 1993), relied very little on counter-conditioning, which is not surprising given the authors' assumption that skill building cannot change the underlying patriarchal attitude structures that support violence against women. Their efforts to sensitize men to societal efforts to protect women are represented in their relatively high use of social liberation.

The manuals seem to pay little attention to readiness to change, and tend to underutilize several processes that are potentially powerful motivators early in the change process, including dramatic relief, environmental reevaluation, and self-reevaluation. Programs also underutilize more behaviorally oriented strategies that are important in relapse prevention, including reinforcement management and helping relationships.

Which process of change do you use? Which do you overutilize? Underutilize? How can you match your interventions more closely to clients' stage of change?

Outcomes and impacts

What happens when we combine all of these principles and processes of change to help entire populations to move toward action on their problems? We will examine several clinical trials applying stage-matched interventions to smoking cessation to see what lessons we might learn about the future of behavior change generally and treatment of criminal offenders specifically.

In our first large-scale clinical trial, we randomly assigned 739 reactively recruited smokers (they called us) to one of the following four treatment conditions (Prochaska et al., 1993).

1. Standardized: one of the best home-based, action-oriented cessation programs.
2. Individualized: stage-matched manuals.
3. Interactive: expert system computer reports plus manuals.
4. Personalized: counselors plus computers and manuals.

All participants completed by mail or telephone a 40-item survey that assessed stage of change, decisional balance, self-efficacy, and the processes of change. In the individualized condition, participants received stage-matched manuals that teach users about the general principles of behavior change, their particular stage of change, and the processes they can use to progress to the next stage.

In the interactive condition, participants received stage-matched manuals and computer-generated feedback reports that provided information about their stage of change, their pros and cons of changing, their most tempting situations, and their use of change processes appropriate to their stages. At baseline, participants were given positive feedback on what they were doing correctly and guidance on which principles and processes of change they needed to apply more in order to progress. The report referred participants to the manuals, which provided more stage-matched exercises and strategies for change. In two additional progress reports delivered over the next six months, participants also received positive feedback on any improvement they had made on any of the variables important to their progress. Demoralized and defensive smokers could begin progressing without having to quit and without having to work too hard. Smokers in the contemplation stage could take small steps like delaying their first cigarette in the morning to increase their self-efficacy and better prepare them for quitting.

In the personalized condition, smokers received three expert system feedback reports, the stage-matched manuals, and four proactive counselor calls over the six-month intervention period. Three of the calls were based on the computer reports. In the call without a report, both clients and counselors had a hard time telling whether any significant progress had occurred since their last interaction.

The four treatment groups were followed over 18 months: during the 6-month intervention period and for 12 months thereafter. The two self-help (standardized and individualized) manual conditions paralleled each other for 12 months. At 18 months, however, the stage-matched manuals moved ahead. This is an example of a *delayed action effect*, which we often observe with stage-matched programs. It takes time for participants in the early stages to progress all the way to action. As a result, some treatment effects based on action-oriented criteria are observed only after considerable delay. But it is encouraging to find treatments producing therapeutic effects months and even years after treatment ended.

The computer (interactive) and counselor (personalized) conditions outper-formed the manual only (individualized) condition. The computer and counselor conditions paralleled each other for 12 months. Then, the effects of the counselor condition flattened out while the computer condition effects continued to increase. We can only speculate as to the differences between these two conditions at longer-term follow-up. Participants in the personalized condition may have become some-what dependent on the social support and social control of the counselor calling during the 6-month intervention period. Termination of the counselors may have resulted in no further progress because of the loss of this social control and support.

The next test was to demonstrate the efficacy of the expert system when applied to an entire population of smokers recruited proactively (we called them). Over 80% of 5170 smokers contacted by phone agreed to participate in the study, even though less than 20% were in the preparation stage. The expert system outper-formed assessment alone at the 6-month follow-up, and this benefit increased at each follow-up during the subsequent 18 months (Prochaska et al., 2001b). The im-plications here are that expert system interventions in a population can continue to demonstrate benefits long after the intervention has ended.

We then showed remarkable replication of the expert system's efficacy in a Health Maintenance Organization (HMO) population of 4000 smokers with 85% partici-pation (Prochaska et al., 2001a). In the first population-based study using proactive recruitment, the expert system was 34% more effective than assessment alone; in the second it was 31% more effective. These differences are both clinically and sta-tistically significant. While working on a population basis, we were able to achieve a level of success normally found only in intense clinic-based programs that serve more highly motivated smokers. The implication is that by using a stage-matched approach to treat all offenders—whether or not they are motivated to take action— we might be able to achieve the kind of success rates we would find if we had the luxury of working primarily with more highly motivated clients.

In our HMO study, counselors plus expert system computers were outperform-ing the expert systems alone at 12 months, but then by 18 months began to decline while the computers alone increased. Once again, it appears that when the social support and control offered by the counselors are offered and then withdrawn, people do worse. The expert system computers, on the other hand, may maximize self-reliance.

In a more recent clinical trial, we faded out counselors over time as a method for dealing with dependency on the counselor. Fading was effective and has im-plications for how counseling should be terminated: gradually, over time, rather than suddenly. We believe that the most powerful change programs will combine the personalized benefits of counselors and consultants with the individualized, interactive and data-based benefits of expert system computers. We are currently developing stage-based manuals, a multimedia expert system, and counselor protocols for domestic violence offenders at each stage of change.

If these results continue to be replicated, therapeutic programs for offenders will be able to produce unprecedented impacts. However, to produce these impacts requires the following shifts in thinking and practice:

1) from an action paradigm to a stage paradigm;
2) from a reactive to a proactive approach to intervention;
3) from expecting participants to match the needs of our programs to having our programs match their needs;
4) from clinic-based to population-based programs that still apply the field's most powerful individualized and interactive intervention strategies.

REFERENCES

Beitman, B.D., Beck, N.C., Deuser, W.E., Carter, C.S., Davidson, J.R.T., & Maddock, R. J. (1994). Patient stage of change predicts outcome in a panic disorder medication trial. *Anxiety*, **1**, 64–9.

Brogan, M.M., Prochaska, J.O., & Prochaska, J.M. (1999). Predicting termination and continuation status in psychotherapy using the transtheroretical model. *Psychotherapy*, **36**, 105–13.

COMMIT Research Group (1995). Community Intervention Trial for Smoking Cessation (COMMMIT): I. Cohort results from a four-year community intervention. *American Journal of Public Health*, **85**, 183–92.

DiClemente, C.C., Prochaska, J.O., Fairhurst, S.K., Velicer, W.F., Velasquez, M.M., & Rossi, J.S. (1991). The process of smoking cessation: an analysis of precontemplation, contemplation, and preparation stages of change. *Journal of Consulting and Clinical Psychology*, **59**, 295–304.

Ennett, S.T., Tobler, N.S., Ringwalt, C.L., & Flewelling, R.L. (1994). How effective is drug abuse resistance education? A meta-analysis of Project DARE outcome evaluations. *American Journal of Public Health*, **84**, 1394–1401.

Glasgow, R.E., Terborg, J.R., Hollis, J.F., Severson, H.H., & Boles, S.M. (1995). Take Heart: results from the initial phase of a work-site wellness program. *American Journal of Public Health*, **85**, 209–16.

Klesges, R.C., Haddock, C.K., Lando, H., & Talcott, G.W. (1999). Efficacy of forced smoking cessation and an adjunctive behavioral treatment on long-term smoking rates. *Journal of Consulting and Clinical Psychology*, **67**, 952–8.

Laforge, R.G., Velicer, W.F., Richmond, R.L., & Owen, N. (1999). Stage distributions for five health behaviors in the United States and Australia. *Preventive Medicine*, **28**, 61–74.

Lam, C.S., McMahon, B.T., Priddy, D.A., & Gehred-Schultz, A. (1988). Deficit awareness and treatment performance among traumatic head injury adults. *Brain Injury*, **2**, 235–42.

Lando, H.A., Pechacek, T.F., Pirie, P.L., Murray, D.M., Mittelmark, M.B., Lichtenstein, E., Nothwehr, F., & Gray, C. (1995). Changes in adult cigarette smoking in the Minnesota Heart Health Program. *American Journal of Public Health*, **85**, 201–8.

Levesque, D.A., & Chell, D. (1999). Stages of change and attrition from batterer treatment. Paper presented at the 51st Annual Meeting of the American Society of Criminology, November, Toronto, Canada.

Levesque, D.A., & Gelles, R.J. (1998). Does treatment reduce recidivism in men who batter? Meta-analytic evaluation of treatment outcome research. Paper presented at Program Evaluation and Family Violence Research: An International Conference, July, Durham, NH.

Levesque, D.A., Gelles, R.J., & Velicer, W.F. (2000a). Development and validation of a stages of change measure for men in batterer treatment. *Cognitive Therapy and Research*, **24**, 175–99.

Levesque, D.A., Driskell, M.M., & Prochaska, J.A. (2000b). Transtheoretical model of change processes used in batterer intervention programs, unpublished manuscript.

Lichtenstein, E. & Hollis, J. (1992). Patient referral to smoking cessation programs: who follows through? *Journal of Family Practice*, **34**, 739–44.

Luepker, R.V., Murray, D.M., Jacobs, D.R., et al. (1994). Community education for cardio-vascular disease prevention: risk factor changes in the Minnesota Heart Health Program. *American Journal of Public Health*, **84**, 1383–93.

Maruna, S. (2000). *Making Good: How Ex-Convicts Reform and Rebuild their Lives*. Washington, DC: American Psychological Association.

McConnaughy, E.A., Prochaska, J.O., & Velicer, W.F. (1983). Stages of change in psychother-apy: measurement and sample profiles. *Psychotherapy: Theory, Research and Practice*, **20**, 368–75.

McConnaughy, E.A., DiClemente, C.C., Prochaska, J.O., & Velicer, W.F. (1989). Stages of change in psychotherapy: a follow-up report. *Psychotherapy*, **26**, 494–503.

Miller, W.R. (1985). Motivation for treatment: a review with special emphasis on alcoholism. *Psychological Bulletin*, **98**, 84–107.

Pence, E., & Paymar, M. (1993). *Education Groups for Men who Batter: The Duluth Model*. New York: Springer-Verlag.

Prochaska, J.O. (1994). Strong and weak principles for progressing from precontemplation to action based on twelve problem behaviors. *Health Psychology*, **13**, 47–51.

Prochaska, J.O., & DiClemente, C.C. (1983). Stages and processes of self-change of smoking: toward an integrative model of change. *Journal of Consulting and Clinical Psychology*, **51**, 390–5.

Prochaska, J.O., DiClemente, C.C., & Norcross, J.C. (1992a). In search of how people change: applications to the addictive behaviors. *American Psychologist*, **47**, 1102–14.

Prochaska, J.O., Norcross, J.C., Fowler, J.L., Follick, M.J., & Abrams, D.B. (1992b). Attendance and outcome in a work-site weight control program: processes and stages of change as process and predictor variables. *Addictive Behaviors*, **17**, 35–45.

Prochaska, J.O., DiClemente, C.C., Velicer, W.F., & Rossi, J.S. (1993). Standardized, individ-ualized, interactive and personalized self-help programs for smoking cessation. *Health Psychology*, **12**, 399–405.

Prochaska, J.O., Norcross, J.C. & DiClemente, C.C. (1994a). *Changing for Good*. New York: William Morrow.

Prochaska, J.O., Velicer, W.F., Rossi, J.S., Goldstein, M.G., Marcus, B.H., Rakowski, W., Fiore, C., Harlow, L., Redding, C.A., Rosenbloom, D., & Rossi, S.R. (1994b). Stages of change and decisional balance for twelve problem behaviors. *Health Psychology*, **13**, 39–46.

Prochaska, J.O., Velicer, W.F., Fava, J.L., Ruggiero, L., Laforge, R.G., Rossi, J.S., Johnson, S.S., & Lee, P.A. (2001a). Counselor and stimulus control enhancements of a stage-matched expert system for smokers in a managed care setting. *Preventive Medicine*, **32**, 23–32.

Prochaska, J.O., Velicer, W.F., Fava, J.L., Rossi, J.S., & Tsoh, J. (2001b). Evaluating a population-based recruitment approach and a stage-based expert system intervention for smoking cessation. *Addictive Behaviors*, **26**, 583–602.

Snow, M.G., Prochaska, J.O., & Rossi, J.S. (1992). Stages of change for smoking cessation among former problem drinkers: a cross-sectional analysis. *Journal of Substance Abuse*, **4**, 107–16.

US Department of Health and Human Services (1990). *The Health Benefits of Smoking Cessation: A Report of the Surgeon General*, DHHS Publication no. CDC 90-8416. Washington, DC: US Government Printing Office.

Velicer, W.F., Fava, J.L., Prochaska, J.O., Abrams, D.B., Emmons, K.M., & Pierce, J.P. (1995). Distribution of smokers by stage in three representative samples. *Preventive Medicine*, **24**, 401–11.

Veroff, J., Douvan, E., & Kulka, R.A. (1981a). *The Inner America*. New York: Basic.

Veroff, J., Douvan, E., & Kulka, R.A. (1981b). *Mental Health in America*. New York: Basic.

Wierzbicki, M., & Pekarik, G. (1993). A meta-analysis of psychotherapy dropout. *Professional Psychology: Research and Practice*, **29**, 190–5.

Chapter 5

BUILDING AND NURTURING A THERAPEUTIC ALLIANCE WITH OFFENDERS

CHRISTOPHER CORDESS

School of Health and Related Research (ScHARR), The University of Sheffield, UK

INTRODUCTION

Motivation for patients or clients to enter into and persist within a therapeutic alliance—or treatment relationship—is problematic for anyone, including ourselves, at the best of times. There are numerous circumstances in which the resistance to entering into a therapeutic relationship overcomes the desire for help and for possible change. Equally, there are many occasions when the temptation to sever the treatment relationship are just too inviting, compared with the demands of continuing to work on that most refractory of entities, the "self", and its habits and wilful behaviours. There is a wealth of contemporary psychological literature from a cognitive perspective, especially on motivational interviewing, which is central to this subject. This chapter, however, will examine the *psychodynamic* body of knowledge concerning the therapeutic alliance, with particular reference to offenders and to the special vulnerability and fragility of that relationship for the majority of offender patients or clients.

The most rewarding and moving experiences of my professional life in forensic psychiatry and psychotherapy have been those of getting to know and to be trusted by patients and clients. Put into professional terms, this may be described as "building and nurturing" a therapeutic alliance; it takes many forms. It may, for example, involve the negotiation of sullen and silent first meetings with an alienated adolescent, with the later breakthrough into feeling trusted and being allowed truly "alongside" that young person. It may be the eventual outcome of a coercive and resisted detention and treatment by a person suffering from psychosis under the Mental Health Act, which slowly—possibly over years—evolves into a working relationship of mutual trust and respect. I have reported elsewhere on a

Motivating Offenders to Change: A Guide to Enhancing Engagement in Therapy. Edited by M. McMurran.
© 2002 John Wiley & Sons, Ltd.

not untypical case: a patient was compulsorily admitted to hospital from prison in a florid psychotic state after the attempted murder of his parents. He was initially aggressively antagonistic to treatment and then for about a year was opposed to therapeutic interventions, including family therapy. Five years on, he lived in his own flat and had close relationships with members of the multidisciplinary team (MDT) as well as with his consultant psychiatrist. He became a voluntary patient, gained stability, established his life independently—and subsequently complained that I did not see him often enough (Cordess, 1996)! Whatever form it takes, it has—as with friendship—to be *earned*, and is certainly not merely a given, nor can it entirely be taught, although some helpful pointers will hopefully be shared in what follows in this chapter.

It is fundamental to the therapeutic alliance that a patient or client should feel listened to and understood. Frequently it has been my experience that offenders, say in prison, cannot believe that a professional is willing to spend an hour or two getting to know them and listening in an informed way. This is the case especially in Young Offender Institutions (YOI), where it appears that being listened to, and heard, has just not been part of the life experience of many wayward youngsters. Equally, for some, such a listening stance will increase an already lively sense of suspiciousness or "paranoia". This may be the consequence of the threat of the unknown or unexpected, or it may be heavily loaded by previous experience of relationships and environments which have been mistrustful, coercive, abusive or bullying. Whereas there is much to be said for the description of the psychodynamic psychotherapeutic mode as that of the "talking treatment", to this should be added, too, the "listening treatment", for it is both. A Dr Barnardo's poster of some years ago made the point well: under the picture of a sad looking, disadvantaged child, the caption ran "What this boy needs is a good *listening* to". The contrast was with that mode of dealing with the marginal of our society—including offenders—which has increasing currency: that of doing things *to* people, whether it be by new legislation, e.g. people with Dangerous and Severe Personality Disorder (D&SPD), or by increasingly operationalised "packages" of care which take into account little of the individual's particular history and world view. It has been well said, by a patient, that "madness begins when other people stop trying to understand you". This is the predicament of increasing numbers of those who are socially excluded from—or fail within—the current mainstreams of our increasingly competitive society.

Only infrequently is a "treatment contract" and alliance set up in forensic clinical practice in the (relatively) straightforward way that, for example, the prototypic psychotherapeutic referral and contract is made in private practice. Rather, a referral and a therapeutic alliance may *emerge*—for example, as part of an assessment for the court of an inmate in prison or a YOI, or in the course of multidisciplinary work. The therapeutic relationship of forensic psychotherapy is an applied psychodynamic one, and some of the usual rules need to be adapted. Because of this need for such adaptation and flexibility, there also needs to be particular caution against "wild analysis", a gross form of "acting out of the counter-transference" or other essentially unhelpful and potentially dangerous practices. These terms will be explained and expanded later in the text.

It seems to me that all voluntary approaches and engagements in treatment are ambivalent, with at least one component being a deep-seated wish *not* to change, but rather to preserve the status quo—which, after all, is one's current "identity". Countering this universal conservatism there may be varying degrees of desire for change, springing from innate, personal motivation or from degrees of ulterior motivation or frank coercion. For example, there may be pressure—subtle or otherwise—from family members, spouse or society; there may be a coercive "choice", e.g. the alternative of probation "with a condition of treatment" to a prison sentence, or there may be frank coercion, e.g. treatment within a secure hospital under the Mental Health Act.

THE CONTEMPORARY CONTEXT

A problem in much contemporary clinical practice, but especially in work with offenders, i.e. in "forensic practice", is that we currently work within a societal and political system—in England and Wales at least—that aims to address and reduce offending behaviour by increasingly coercive methods. Our political system and policies for dealing with offenders has moved from one of a predominantly rehabilitative ethos, which obtained roughly up until the early 1970s, to one of authoritarianism. Garland (2001, p. 176) writes:

> where rehabilitative interventions are undertaken today their character is rather different than before. They focus more upon issues of crime control than upon individual welfare, and are more "offence centred" than "client-centred". The offence is no longer taken to be a superficial presenting symptom; it is instead the thing itself, the central problem to be addressed. Where once the individual's personality or social relations formed the object of transformative efforts, that object is now offence behaviour and the habits most closely associated with it. The immediate point is no longer to improve the offender's self-esteem, develop insight, or deliver client centred services, but instead to impose restrictions, reduce crime, and protect the public. These shifts in practice prompt treatment programmes to hold themselves out as being for the benefit of future victims rather than for the benefit of the offender. It is future victims who are now "rescued" by rehabilitative work, rather than the offenders themselves.

Part of this change is the consequence of the loss of faith in the possible rehabilitation of offenders—the "nothing works" mythology of the 1970s and 1980s. This "failure model" (Rothman, 1974), influenced by negative research reports, increasing crime rates and a general sense of disillusionment, caused dismantling of prison-based treatments, probation and social programmes as well as clinical treatments. It is also the consequence of a culture which has become averse to just about any level of risk. "The practice of rehabilitation," writes Garland (2001), "is increasingly inscribed in a framework of risk rather than a framework of welfare. Offenders can only be 'treated' (in drug-abuse programmes, anger-management groups, offence-reduction programmes, etc.) to the extent that such treatment is deemed to be capable of protecting the public, reducing risk, and being more cost-effective than simple, unadorned punishment" (p. 176).

The proposed new Mental Health Act (outlined in the now withdrawn White Paper *Reforming the Mental Health Act*, 2000), proposed new legislation for (1) compulsory "care and treatment" outside hospital, for non-offenders, and (2) much increased powers for the "compulsory care and treatment" for mentally disordered offenders. The introduction of the term Dangerous and Severe Personality Disorder (D&SPD), along with proposals for special new units in which to detain such people, was the most crude evidence for this shift towards coercion and compulsion. The use of the terms "care and treatment" is actually obfuscating in this context; this mental health legislation apparently unashamedly puts public protection before the patient's "best interest" and his or her primary right to care and treatment. It is my submission that the word and the activity of "treatment" has been hijacked—indeed, perverted in this context—so that building and nurturing a therapeutic alliance becomes contaminated. Put another way, there is ever decreasing "therapeutic space" in which mutually and freely to interact (an essential of all proper treatment, or indeed education). Draconian policies of risk reduction might be justifiable—whatever one personally thinks of them—within the criminal justice system. Present policy, and these proposals in particular, however, seek to implicate psychiatrists and other mental health professions in the cause of public (third party) protection, with only secondary concern for the best interests of the individual client or patient. Such policy may be seen as the "hybridisation" of agencies, roles and professions (Fennell, 2000) so that inter-agency and multi-agency working will include mental health professionals working alongside, and sharing information with, law enforcement agencies, e.g. the police, as well as with agencies and professions which do not share the professional ethics of the health professions (see below).

One response therefore in the light of my title is that a culture of authoritarianism and unconsidered intolerance has replaced the concepts of "building and nurturing" in the response of our society to the offender population. This is no subtle departure from previously accepted and observed boundaries: the White Paper *Reforming the Mental Health Act*—incredibly—includes the following proposal: "In the new legislation there will be a new (statutory) duty covering the disclosure of information about patients suffering from mental disorder between health and social services agencies and other agencies, for example housing agencies or criminal justice agencies" (Part I (Section 2.3.1) and Part II (Section 5.2)).

An authentic therapeutic alliance requires that a therapeutic space be preserved within the appropriate boundaries: It aims to achieve a safe setting in which there can be the greatest freedom of expression and exploration of thoughts, feelings and fantasies (and phantasies; see below). Although some degree of "acting out"—*agieren*, in the original German description by Freud—is inevitable, the therapeutic alliance is based upon the notion of talking rather than acting precipitately. Freud (1914) wrote of the phenomenon, "the patient does not remember anything of what he has forgotten or repressed but acts it out. He reproduces it not as a memory but as an action; he repeats it, without, of course, knowing that he is repeating it . . . for instance, the patient does not say that he remembers that he used to be defiant and critical towards his parents' authority; instead he behaves in that way to the therapist" (p. 150).

In this chapter, however, I emphasise not these dangers so much as their direct opposite—the breaking of the boundaries of the therapeutic setting by outside forces. This may be specific, as in new proposals by government for more coercive practices, or for obligatory sharing of hitherto private information with an ever increasing number of individuals and agencies, or it may be part of the Zeitgeist of a culture in which the *perception* of mental health professionals is that they are primarily agents of social control. As a parent of a young woman charged with an offence and referred to me wrote, "Perhaps she sees all psychiatrists merely as extensions of the law, and as implicitly critical. If someone could establish a therapeutic relationship with her which I believe is possible, then I believe she could be helped".

The dangers for therapeutic potency of this new culture of surveillance, coercion and control can be illustrated by comparing different cultures within the prison system. The mainstream prisons are generally dominated by a culture of fear and mistrust, thereby reinforcing mental defences, "paranoid" thinking, dissembling and 'denial'. Within the therapeutic prison of HMP Grendon Underwood, by contrast, there is the identified task of creating and nurturing a culture of maximum trust and open engagement—of authenticity—in which therapeutic alliances can occur. In technical terms, following Melanie Klein, one major difference is that of the system which relies on "paranoid-schizoid" mechanisms of fear and coercion—in both inmates and staff—which is effectively nihilistic, and, on the other hand, one which encourages and supports that psychological state described as the "depressive position"—of mutual concern, therapeutic alliance and possible reparation (Hinshelwood, 1989).

In this climate, what is it to speak of "building and nurturing a therapeutic alliance", when the prospects for all of those in treatment—whether offenders or not—are that there will be increased coercion exerted upon them to engage and remain in "treatment", for the benefit not of themselves but of others, and that hitherto confidential information will be freely shared with other agencies? For offenders, there is the much increased danger that, should they be so unguarded (or ill) within their "treatment" as to reveal aspects of potential risk, they will be treated coercively and punitively for their failure to be able to "play the system". This Zeitgeist of zero tolerance of risk and a massively increased ethos of coercion and control create fundamental problems for all mental health professionals, but psychotherapists, and more centrally, forensic psychotherapists, are especially well placed to understand the folly of these intended policies in a particular way. We know that in so far as "treatment" is coercive, it is likely to be ineffective, inducing merely compliance at best, or defiance of the system at worst. In clinical, psychodynamic, terms we know that therapeutic potency requires us to struggle to avoid being identified with the "internal policeman" or punitive super-ego which forensic patients so readily project into the therapist and the system in which they act. It is our task to understand and interpret such forces and not to act them out. It is also necessary to add that some treatments for the severely mentally ill or disordered, whether they are offenders or not, need to be started under coercion; in so far as they are creative and effective, however, they need to move—however gradually—towards voluntariness and self-motivation.

I believe that it is our duty to oppose these serious erosions of therapeutic possibility which will sabotage clinically effective therapeutic relationships in the short term, and do untold damage to perceptions of our role (increasingly as enforcers), to our effectiveness, and thereby to patients in the longer term.

Essentially, these policies require that the client, if he is to preserve his best interests and is capable of doing so, should be continually on his guard, allow only partial self-revelation, avoiding a full therapeutic alliance, and allow only limited degrees of "trust" (which, effectively, is no trust at all). In short he should aim at being "economical with the truth", and aim for *in*authenticity, rather than authenticity, in order not to fall foul of these new powers of the State. These policies, in my view, represent a full frontal attack on the necessary integrity of the patient–therapist therapeutic alliance.

EMPIRICAL DATA ON DROPPING OUT OF THERAPY

A number of studies have shown that dropout from psychotherapy is common, especially for patients with borderline personality disorder (Gunderson et al., 1989; Skodol et al., 1983). Shea et al. (1990) demonstrated differential rates of dropout from psychotherapy of patients with personality disorders belonging to different clusters in DSM-III-R. Cluster A, which includes paranoid, schizoid and schizo-typal subtypes, and Cluster B, which includes antisocial, borderline, histrionic and narcissistic subtypes of personality disorder, both of which are common to offender populations, showed dropout rates of 36% and 40% respectively. Cluster C patients, which refers to avoidant dependent, obsessive-compulsive subtypes, by contrast, only showed a rate of 28%.

There is a growing weight of evidence that dropout rates are higher for group therapy (Perry & Bond, 2000), which argues for the availability of individual treatments to be made available alongside group programmes.

Also, treatments of shorter duration have been found to have a mean lower percentage of dropouts than those of longer duration, and this argument is often used in their favour, but clearly this is to be expected, since those patients in longer duration treatments have greater opportunity for dropping out. Also, such evidence should not be used to justify shorter treatments (or "treatment packages") where the offender population is often available—either at Her Majesty's pleasure or in detention under the Mental Health Act—for long or indefinite periods of time.

Gunderson et al. (1989) studied the immediate causes of early discontinuation of psychotherapy in a group of sixty newly hospitalised inpatients suffering from bor-derline personality disorder: the most common causes were "covert opposition", "familial resistance" or "angry dissatisfaction" with treatment. It is my own clinical impression, which needs studying empirically, that overt and covert family influ-ences are frequently the significant controlling influence on many patients held in secure hospitals. It is as if the identified patient, with whom one is trying to make a treatment alliance, is the "puppet" who is controlled by the various "strings" of the family who exist outside. Prototypically this may involve a young man or woman and a vulnerable but authoritarian parent. In these cases an attempt must be made to engage the family in the treatment programme, preferably working with them together with the patient in an (albeit adapted) form of family therapy (Cordess, 1992).

Frequently this is difficult to achieve because the family system will have settled around the status quo of the identified patient as scapegoat, and will resist any challenges to this state of affairs. In this author's view, the next phase of develop-ment of psychological treatment offered to offenders should be that of well-trained staff offering sophisticated family interventions.

The establishment of an initial positive therapeutic alliance early in the thera-peutic relationship is the single most important factor in predicting good outcome (Horvarth & Luborsky, 1993). This is said to be true whatever the type of treatment offered. To my knowledge, the cultural and political context (e.g. statutory report-ing laws) within which the therapeutic alliance is attempted has not been studied for its effect upon seeking therapy or dropout rates.

There is also empirical evidence that the presence of depression may indicate the ability to form attachments and to develop a positive therapeutic alliance (Woody et al., 1985). Clearly attachment theory and the qualitative and quantitative assess-ment of adult attachment status by the Adult Attachment Interview (AAI) (Main & Hesse, 1992) should be extremely helpful in predicting attachment capacity to form a therapeutic alliance. To date, there are no studies which specifically address this issue.

PSYCHODYNAMIC ASPECTS OF THE THERAPEUTIC ALLIANCE

At the core of the forensic psychotherapy enterprise is the (rather unremarkable) theoretical assumption that behaviour (and, therefore, action) is suffused with per-sonal meaning through the agency of individual thought processes and intimately entwined emotional states. Offender patients frequently have only restricted ac-cess and ability to reflect upon their subjective mental states: rather, they are more prone to "act out" or enact impulsively. While psychodynamacists acknowledge some (restricted) place for behaviour theory and therapy, and a far greater place for cognitive-behavioural and systemic approaches, they place their stall in the realm of not only conscious mental events, but also of *pre*conscious and *un*conscious men-tal activity, including unconscious phantasy. The convention is used here of using the different spellings of *fantasy* and *phantasy* for conscious and unconscious phe-nomena, respectively. In this context, unconscious phantasy refers to the sublimi-nal mental representation which accompanies all action. Using another discourse, it is partly made up of implicit (or procedural) memory, as opposed to autobio-graphical (event) or explicit memory. Psychodynamic psychotherapeutic practice distinguishes itself by its concerns with these unconscious mental events (as well as conscious events), as they appear within the patient–therapist interaction (the transference/counter-transference relationship). The aim is the gaining of *affective* as well as *cognitive* understanding. The forensic psychotherapist, in addition, pays particular attention to this interaction in the light of possible re-enactment of as-pects of the offensive behaviour (or related palimpsests of the behaviour) within the professional relationship. The theoretical stance is taken that by addressing different elements of the way of being, feeling and thinking within a therapeutic relationship, greater self-understanding and capacity for "reflective self function" (Fonagy et al., 1997), and empathy, will thereby be achieved, and provide alterna-tive coping strategies to those of the offending behaviours.

In psychodynamic psychotherapy that aspect of the interaction and conversation with the patient that is, classically, regarded as mutative (i.e. productive of change) entails *interpretation*, which includes, too, the senses conveyed by *clarification* and *explanation*, in a trusting, secure and empathic relationship. Interpretation is the procedure whereby, by means of analytic investigation (listening with a "third ear"), an understanding is reached of the latent meaning of what the patient says and does and is communicated verbally to the patient. It reveals the defensive conflicts of the patient and its ultimate aim is to identify the wish, anxiety or fear that is expressed by every product of the unconscious as well as the conscious. It is a mutual exercise requiring at least intermittent motivation from both therapist and patient. However, no therapeutic relationship can consist only of interpretation, unless it is to become a fearsome caricature of itself. Bateman and Holmes (1995, p. 168). write that "the overvaluation of interpretation in the transference as the main curative factor [in psychotherapy] has led to the neglect of other factors such as affirmation, validation and even praise and support". They give the view that "whatever the [psychotherapist's] theoretical allegiance, he/she must work in a flexible way as the balance between interpretive work at one extreme, and supportive interventions on the other, shifts back and forth throughout treatment". (p. 168). These authors give a useful list of the spectrum of therapeutic interventions that maintain any therapeutic alliance: support, affirmation, reassurance, empathy, encouragement, elaboration, clarification, confrontation, interpretation. In general, they state "the closer the intervention is to the interpretative pole of the continuum, the more psychodynamic the treatment" (p. 168).

Such a therapeutic stance stands in stark contrast to "packaged" treatments, which have become popular within offender treatment in prisons and now in hospitals, which—at their worst—have affinities with the application of Blu-Tack to a wall. These therapies—like the Sex Offender Treatment Programme (SOTP), for which so far we have no outcome evidence—apply a treatment package to an individual, irrespective of his personal or clinical condition. In the case of the SOTP one merely needs to be regarded as a sex offender—which may often be disputed, e.g. when a violent offence has an apparent sexual flavour. The treatment programme is stuck on to the person and there is a hope that it will "stick". It is essentially directive and didactic (at best) and applied onto the client, rather than explanatory or individualised.

Central to the practice of psychoanalytic psychotherapy are the concepts of transference and counter-transference, both of which, too, are intimately entwined within the therapeutic (treatment) alliance. Transference is characterised by the recreation, unconsciously, of past forms of relationship—"facsimiles" (typically those with the parents)—in the therapeutic alliance with the therapist. Clearly, this recreation may have positive elements (e.g. love, generosity and reparative wishes)—the "positive transference"—and negative elements (e.g. aggression, hate, sadism etc.)—the "negative transference". In most people, most of the time, there will be an intermingling and mixture of both, but especially in offender patients, whose biological predisposition may be towards excessive aggression, and whose environmental influences will usually have been largely depriving or destructive, the negative transference will predominate.

Conversely, counter-transference encompasses the whole of the therapist's unconscious reactions to the individual patient, and especially his or her reaction to the patient's transference. The high degree of underlying disturbance—which is defended against in delinquent and perverse acting out in some offenders—will be drawn into the therapeutic relationship and will be projected in the transference. Temple (1996) writes that:

> in some offenders there will be a tendency for more paranoid processes to be evident which will test the therapist's capacity to contain and understand this in the counter-transference. The therapist is likely to be treated as a dangerous and persecuting figure who needs to be "controlled". Inexperienced therapists find this difficult when their conscious intention is to be helpful. A recognition of this state will allow the therapist to be cautious in not interpreting too quickly or forcefully and not demanding too great an intensity of contact which may provoke uncontrolled reactions. The capacity to tolerate the counter-transference as described by Carpy (1989) will be important, particularly in the early stages of the treatment, when a treatment alliance is being established. The treatment alliance will have to become sufficiently strong to contain the negative disturbed aspects of the transference.

Put another way, many offender patients are interpersonally "offensive" at times, if one is to be in an intimate relationship with them: this is axiomatic for those with antisocial or dissocial personality disorder, who are characterised by their "acting out" harmfully against others. It is for this reason that the family, social and occupational lives of many forensic patients or clients are often chaotic and disrupted, replete with separations, losses jealousies, and sometimes interpersonal or sexual violence. It is the task of the therapeutic relationship, by achieving a therapeutic alliance, to understand this propensity to destructive acting out, and to be able to get it into words and to discuss it rather than it needing to be endlessly actually repeated. It is also the case that many offender patients find talking rather than acting either different or quite beyond their capacities. There may be relative degrees of incapacity to symbolise and a "concretisation" of thought. In these cases the arts therapies—whether art, music or drama—may be particularly helpful in allowing a therapeutic alliance to grow "without words".

One of the aims of the psychotherapeutic process is to release the patient from the "prescriptions" he feels he must follow, according to his early family patterns and other internalised habits and structures.

It is commonplace in forensic clinical practice to come up against, for example, the deep conservatism of the young delinquent in a YOI. He may tell you that he was abused by his father and elder brothers; he may tell you that they are either in prison or in secure hospitals; he may acknowledge that he seems to be following closely in their footsteps. You will ask if there is anything you can do to halt and prevent this inexorable family "tradition", graduating from residential home to YOI to prison or secure hospital. More than likely he will reply no; either reluctantly or fatefully, his identifications and expectations control him and he feels that he has little autonomous choice. The task of building and nurturing a therapeutic alliance with such a young person will aim to free him from his script, and to do so by being yourself—interpreting the pressure upon you to be like his father or his brother—yet in an understanding and sympathetic way that lets him know that you are aware of his predicament.

Another familiar scenario is that of the failing, and sometimes offender, parent who tells you (truthfully) "I want to give my kids what I didn't have: I want them to have the best". Although this is the honourable intention, it is commonplace that you, and they, will be witnesses to the repetition for their own children of exactly what they wished to avoid. That is, there is a terrible transgenerational mirroring which can only be stopped by powerful therapeutic intervention.

Norton (1996, p. 406), from the perspective of the therapeutic community, makes the general point:

> Forensic patients' addiction to action and concrete solutions to their emotional conflicts and also their ambivalence and mistrust often compromises their treatment, whether as in-patients or out-patients, and this means that they experience little or no actual time to really question their own or others' attitudes and behaviour in the face of emotional conflict. Because of this there is difficulty in creating and maintaining a treatment alliance, which may require of the patient or resident delayed gratification of needs, especially during out-patient treatment, which necessarily requires survival between treatment sessions. The result is a strong, and sometimes overwhelming, tendency to pervert, challenge, distort or neutralize potentially therapeutic structures and processes so as to maintain the belief that genuine (i.e. depressive position) care does not exist. This is evident at every stage of treatment.

In all treatments there may be what appears to be a paradoxical effect of phases of improvement, either in symptoms or in sense of well-being, followed by phases of deterioration and negativism. Such a pattern may be part of the so-called negative therapeutic reaction (NTR), which appears paradoxical, since it does not appear to serve the best interests of the client or patient. Rather it is a destructive force undoing and sabotaging his or her improvement and apparent best interests. There is much to be said about this phenomenon, since it is especially common among offender patients. However, the reader is referred to specialised texts for a full account. Essentially, the NTR is the product of the patients'—usually unconscious—wish not to get "better" and this may be for a number of reasons. Mostly it is considered that guilt plays a large part, i.e. the patient feels that he or she does not deserve to get better. Since low self-esteem is common in offenders, this is a frequently found phenomenon. Also, envy of the therapist may play a part—as if the patient were saying "I do not want you to think that you can make me better". These negative reactions need to be described and interpreted to patients in order for them to have the opportunity not to undermine their own improvements.

It would, however, be wrong to assume that psychoanalytic psychotherapy is entirely non-coercive, and totally voluntary—even outside of the forensic setting—although that is what it aims to be, or aims to achieve as nearly as possible. Hinshelwood (1997) writes of the cultivation by early psychoanalysts of the positive transference, to the exclusion of the negative, as a way of overcoming the patient's resistance to forming a creative treatment alliance. He comments that the manipulation of the patient by encouraging the positive transference—as we all do in our own ways—especially with offender patients, "cannot really represent autonomous consent, [which] in this sense is not 'informed consent' " (Hinshelwood, 1997). He rejects the attractive, but simplistic, solution that the therapeutic alliance involves conscious consent, and that transference, by contrast, represents unconscious phenomena that are not relevant to the notion of consent, as put forward first by Zetzel (1956). Such a distinction relies on the notion that conscious and unconscious are separate states and phenomena existing independently of each other. This is clearly not the case. The unconscious, and therefore the transference, intrudes into all of our decision making to a more or less obvious extent.

CONCLUSION

The therapeutic alliance is essential for all effective and lasting treatment interventions. Even those interventions which begin coercively need to aim for mutuality and consent, and genuine motivation, for greatest long-term benefit and change. The present "culture of control" (Garland, 2001) within the wider community, within the criminal justice system and increasingly within mental health provision, is regressive in therapeutic terms. It compromises or negates the necessary therapeutic alliance and thereby undermines the rehabilitative and health seeking initiatives of individuals, organisations (like mental health services) and society.

Mental health professionals need to be vigilant concerning the protection of conditions which allow the development of the therapeutic alliance, as well as achieving training in its detailed clinical aspects. The alternative of joining in the control society is anti-therapeutic, and best left to those for whom it is their proper professional role.

REFERENCES

Bateman, A. & Holmes, J. (1995). *Introduction to Psychoanalysis: Contemporary Theory and Practice*. London: Routledge.

Carpy, D.V. (1989). Tolerating the counter transference: a mutative process. *International Journal of Psychoanalysis*, **70**: 287.

Cordess, C. (1992). Family therapy with psychotic offenders and family victims in a forensic psychiatric service unit. In Proceedings of the 17th Congress of the International Academy of Law and Mental Health (pp. 366–80). Leuven, Belgium.

Cordess, C. (1996). The multidisciplinary team. In C. Cordess & M. Cox (eds) *Forensic Psychotherapy: Crime, Psychodynamics and the Offender patient*. London:Jessica Kingsley.

Fennell, P. (2000). Stigmatising care in the community: community care and risk management. In *Every Family in the Land*, Chapter 6, The Law and Mental Illness. *www.stigma.org*

Fonagy, P., Target, M., Steele, H., Steele, M., Leigh, T., Levinson, A. & Kennedy, R. (1997). Morality, disruptive behaviour, borderline personality disorder, crime and their relationship to security of attachment. In L. Atkinson & K. Zucker (eds) *Attachment and Psychopathology*. New York: Guildford.

Freud, S. (1914). Remembering, repeating and working through. *The Standard Edition of the Complete Psychological Works of Sigmund Freud*, vol 12. London: Hogarth Press.

Garland, D. (2001). *The Culture of Control*. Oxford: Oxford University Press.

Gunderson, G.J., Frank, A.F. & Ronningstam, E.F. (1989). Early discontinuance of borderline patients from psychotherapy. *Journal of Nervous and Mental Disease*, **177**: 38–42.

Hinshelwood, R.D. (1989). *A Dictionary of Kleinian Thought*. London: Free Association.

Hinshelwood, R.D. (1997). *Therapy or Coercion. Does Psychoanalysis Differ from Brainwashing?* London: Karnac.

Horvath, A.O. & Luborsky L. (1993). The role of therapeutic alliance in psychotherapy. *Journal of Consulting and Clinical Psychology*, **61**: 561–73.

Main, M. & Hesse, E. (1992). Disorganised/disoriented behaviour in the strange situation, lapses in the monitoring of reasoning and discourse during the parent's adult attachment interview, and dissociative states. In M. Ammanati & D. Stern (eds) *Attachment and Psychoanalysis*. Rome: Guis, Laterza & Figli.

Norton, K. (1996). The personality disordered forensic patient. In *Forensic Psychotherapy. Crime Psychodynamics and the Offender Patient*. London: Jessica Kingsley.

Perry, C. & Bond, M. (2000). Empirical studies of psychotherapy for personality disorders. In J. Gunderson & G. Gabband (eds) *Psychotherapy for Personality Disorders*. Washington, DC: American Psychiatric Press.

Rothman, D. (1974). Prisons: the failure model. *The Nation*, 21st December, 657.

Shea, M.T., Pilkonis, P.A. & Beckham, E.(1990). Personality disorders and treatment outcome in the NIMH Treatment of Depression Collaborative Research Programme. *American Journal of Psychiatry*, **147**: 711–18.

Skodol, A.E., Buckley, P., Charles, E. (1983). Is there a characteristic pattern to the treatment history of clinic outpatients with borderline personality? *Journal of Nervous and Mental Disease*, **171**: 405–10.

Temple, N. (1996). Transference and countertransference: general and forensic aspects. In C. Cordess & M. Cox (eds) *Forensic Psychotherapy: Crime, Psychodynamics and the Offender Patient*. London: Jessica Kingsley.

Woody, G.E., McLellan, T. & Luborsky, L.L. (1985). Sociopathy and psychotherapy outcome. *Archives of General Psychiatry*, **42**: 1081–86.

Zetzel, E. (1956). Current concepts of transference. *International Journal of Psycho-Analysis*, **37**: 369–76.

Chapter 6

MOTIVATIONAL INTERVIEWING WITH OFFENDERS*

RUTH E. MANN,[†] JOEL I. D. GINSBURG[‡] AND JOHN R. WEEKES[§ ‡]

[†] HM Prison Service, England & Wales, London, UK
[‡] Correctional Service of Canada, Ottawa, Canada
[§] Carleton University, Ottawa, Canada

INTRODUCTION

Some criminal offenders are distressed by their antisocial behaviours and intend to become law-abiding citizens in the future. Others see their crimes as rational or rewarding, and argue that in their circumstances, or because of their histories, repetition is inevitable or desirable or both. Still others appear that they fully intend to change, but in fact their intentions are weak, their impulses are strong and their prospects of rehabilitation are poor. In these ways, criminal offenders can be likened to persons addicted to substances such as alcohol, nicotine or other drugs. The behaviour is labelled by some as antisocial, self-harming or illegal, but to the individual engaging in the behaviour, it seems rewarding, relaxing or simply necessary to cope with life's demands. Labelling a behaviour as a "problem" is a value judgement and it should never be assumed that a criminal offender sees his or her behaviour to be as much of a problem as the rehabilitation professional does.

Motivational interviewing (MI) acknowledges and addresses the issue that a "problem behaviour" as defined by a criminal justice agency might not be seen as such by a client. MI was developed initially as a procedure to help alcohol abusers think about whether they wanted to change (Miller, 1983). Over the past 20 years, MI has been accepted enthusiastically by health professionals who were attracted to a treatment approach that worked with clients rather than against them, that stressed the importance of empathy and respect for clients, and which seemed to work. Although the majority of reported applications of MI have continued to

---

* The views and opinions expressed in this chapter are those of the authors and do not necessarily represent those of Her Majesty's Prison Service, the Correctional Service of Canada, or the Solicitor General of Canada.

Motivating Offenders to Change: A Guide to Enhancing Engagement in Therapy. Edited by M. McMurran.
© 2002 John Wiley & Sons, Ltd.

focus on problem drinkers, MI has also been practised with an increasingly diverse range of clients, including opiate abusers (Saunders et al., 1995), smokers (Rollnick et al., 1997), individuals with eating disorders (Killick & Allen, 1997; Treasure & Ward, 1997), diabetics (Trigwell et al., 1997), obese individuals (Smith et al., 1997) and patients with health problems (Rollnick et al., 1999).

This chapter will explain the principles and techniques of MI and their applications with offenders. Until now, there have been few published reports of the use of MI with offenders. We will argue that there are sound theoretical and clinical reasons why MI should be adopted as part of any rehabilitative strategy with offenders.

THE DEVELOPMENT OF MI

MI can be defined as "a directive, client-centered counseling style for eliciting behaviour change by helping clients to explore and resolve ambivalence" (Rollnick & Miller, 1995). MI was conceived as an alternative to the traditional model of motivation in problem drinkers, which conceptualised lack of motivation as a personality trait. In his first published account of MI, Miller (1983) suggested instead that motivation should more correctly be understood as a *state*, a product of the interaction between the health professional and the client. Put another way, the suggestion was that the traditional style of dealing with problem drinkers (i.e. labelling, shaming, assuming clients will be resistant) was producing resistance or counter-motivational behaviour. Miller suggested that all problem drinkers experience an internal "motivational struggle" and are capable of recognising the negative aspects of their drinking, as long as they are not being pushed to accept the label "alcoholic." Later, Miller (1985) summarised empirical research indicating that therapists tend to assume a client is motivated only if he or she accepts the therapist's diagnosis, seems distressed by his or her behaviour, and complies with the therapist's treatment prescriptions. Miller's review concluded that these indicators are unreliable; in fact, clients do better when they initiate their own action towards recovery, when their self-efficacy is supported, and when they are able to choose between various treatment alternatives.

Theoretical and clinical accounts of MI were developed over the next 10 years. Miller and colleagues (1988) reviewed the theoretical context of MI, and summarised the three essential components of a motivational intervention as *affirmation*, *awareness* and *alternatives*. Miller and Rollnick (1991) produced a full-length textbook which describes the clinical practice of MI in considerable detail and which has become the mainstay handbook of the approach. The follow-up handbook (Miller & Rollnick, 2002) is likely to prove equally popular. Rollnick and colleagues (1992) developed some brief MI strategies that could be used by health professionals who only have very short-term contact with clients (e.g. physicians, hospital staff, etc.). The ethics of MI, and in particular the question of whether MI is "manipulative", given that it may develop an intention to change through processes of which clients are unaware, were considered by Miller (1994). In this discussion, Miller pointed out that MI should not (if practised properly) engage any values that the client does not already hold. MI does not impose the therapist's values on the client, but

Table 6.1   Principles of motivational interviewing

1. Motivation to change is elicited from the client and not imposed from without.
2. It is the client's task, not the counsellor's, to articulate and resolve his or her ambivalence.
3. Direct persuasion is not an effective method for resolving ambivalence.
4. The counselling style is generally a quiet and eliciting one.
5. The counsellor is directive in helping the client to examine and resolve ambivalence.
6. Readiness to change is not a client trait, but a fluctuating product of interpersonal interaction.
7. The therapeutic relationship is more like a partnership or companionship than expert/passive recipient roles.

Source: Adapted from Rollnick & Miller (1995).

aims to increase the client's recognition of his or her own values, and the tension between these values and the problem behaviour.

MAJOR PRINCIPLES OF MI

MI is based on the notion that many clients with problem behaviours have some underlying concerns about their behaviour, but may find it difficult to recognise, acknowledge, verbalise or examine their ambivalence. Some clients ("precontemplators") may not have any conscious concerns, but may realise some ambivalence if enabled to examine their behaviour in a supportive, non-judgemental context. The intention of MI is to provide a context within which the client feels accepted and comfortable enough to face his or her problem behaviour and any accompanying ambivalence about change. The MI counsellor, then, encourages clients to examine their behaviour in the light of their values, beliefs and goals, and supports them through any experience of cognitive dissonance produced by this self-examination. Only when the client has verbalised discomfort with his or her behaviour, does the MI counsellor begin to explore the possibility of behaviour change. Throughout the intervention, "the client's situation is understood as one of being stuck through understandable psychological principles" (Miller & Rollnick, 1991, p. 56).

Rollnick and Miller (1995) emphasise that MI is more than just a set of techniques; it has a "spirit" which, if not present, would render the techniques empty. They list seven major principles, which are reproduced in Table 6.1.

It is usually difficult for a therapist to adopt the MI spirit unless he or she has read about and reflected on these principles. It is only when the therapist is fully able to empathise with the client, and can match his or her interventions to the client's level of readiness to change, that he or she can avoid rushing the client towards behaviour change.

MAJOR TECHNIQUES OF MI

Although MI has been described as an approach that is characterised by a "spirit" or style of interaction, it also includes some specific techniques. The style of the approach is of primary importance—in a sense, one could view the style as the "glue" that holds the approach and its techniques together. As a full discussion of the style and techniques used in MI and which characterise the approach is beyond the scope of this chapter, readers are referred to Miller and Rollnick (1991, 2002) for a full account.

The general approach of MI (Miller & Rollnick, 1991) includes the following components:

1. Express empathy. This is the hallmark of the style or spirit of the approach. Reflective listening is the main way through which empathy is achieved and expressed.
2. Develop discrepancy. This refers to building a discrepancy between the target behaviour (e.g. substance abusing behaviour) and the individual's values, beliefs, and goals.
3. Avoid argumentation. Arguing is always counterproductive. It produces resistance and defensiveness, making open exploration of ambivalence less likely.
4. Roll with resistance. The path of least resistance is not always straight ahead. Trying to fight or obstruct resistance will usually lead you to "butt heads" with the client. Using the MI approach, it is better to be flexible and use the client's momentum to your advantage. For example, express empathy by listening to and affirming the client's position and then invite him or her to entertain a new perspective by using a technique like reframing.
5. Elicit self-motivational statements. The goal is to have the client present arguments for change. Self-motivational statements are statements made by the client that indicate acknowledgement or recognition of a problem, intention to change or optimism about change.
6. Emphasise choice. People feel more committed to courses of action that they have freely chosen, rather than those they take because they feel under pressure to do so. MI guidelines stress the importance of offering choices to clients, so that they can select from a menu of options rather than feel forced onto the only path available.

Specific MI techniques or micro-skills which are used to achieve these aims include:

- *Asking open-ended questions*. When used judiciously, this counsellor technique encourages the client to continue communicating. Further, use of this technique can aid the counsellor in gathering key information. Open-ended questions should always be followed by *reflective listening*. This ensures that the counsellor follows the client's meaning rather than imposing his or her own structure on the dialogue, and therefore enables the client to build on his thinking
- *Affirming*. The counsellor explicitly states his or her appreciation of the client's strengths. This helps the counsellor convey a sense of acceptance and understanding toward the client. It also strengthens the client's sense of self-efficacy, which is an important foundation for sustaining change.
- *Summarising*. This technique helps the counsellor and client keep track of the content of the session. It also allows the counsellor to selectively reinforce key

information presented by the client. When the client hears his own view presented back to him, he may decide that it is not entirely logical or balanced after all.

- *Decisional balance.* This technique is used to look at the good things and the not-so-good things about the target behaviour. These pros and cons can be contrasted with the good things and the not-so-good things about change (new behaviour).
- *Exploring goals* and *asking evocative questions* are other examples of techniques that can be used with offenders to elicit self-motivational statements.

REASONS TO USE MI WITH OFFENDERS

There are several reasons why MI is applicable to working with offenders. First, and as noted earlier, offending has been conceptualised as being similar in many important ways to addictive behaviours such as substance abuse (George & Marlatt, 1989). For example, like substance abuse, offending produces emotional gratification (e.g. excitement, relief, success etc.) for the offender, who may have difficulty achieving such positive emotional states through other means. This is not to say that we conceptualise offending as an addictive behaviour, but simply that in a pragmatic sense treatment interventions developed in the addictive field could potentially also work with offenders. This has certainly been the case with relapse prevention, for example, which was originally developed for use with substance misusers (Marlatt & Gordon, 1985) and which has been enthusiastically adopted in the sexual offender treatment field (Laws, 1989; Laws et al., 2000). The value of MI with offenders should be considered optimistically for this reason.

Second, offending is a behaviour which elicits negative evaluations and stigmatising labels, in some cases to even more of an extent than alcoholism or drug abuse. If, as Miller contends, stigmatisation and labelling can damage motivation to change, then it is hardly surprising that offenders are resistant when invited to address their offending. Labels such as *psychopath, antisocial* and *deviant* are often used in the criminal justice system. Even more derogatory labels, such as *monster, pervert* and *villain,* are used in the media. A humanistic approach like MI can be used to counteract the motivational damage caused by labelling.

Third, as noted earlier, offending usually brings rewards to the offender as well as punishment. Many offenders could be viewed as having made a rational choice to offend, weighing up the potential positive consequences (e.g. financial gain) against the negative (e.g. imprisonment). Criminal offenders often do not see themselves as being in need of "treatment" or do not regard their behaviour as problematic. Thus, from a therapist's perspective, they typically present as unmotivated to change. This is especially likely to be found by therapists who, as described by Miller (1985), only judge motivation to be present if the client agrees with the therapist's diagnosis, shows distress, and accepts the treatment prescription. Such offenders are often written off as untreatable because of their lack of apparent motivation to change. The MI approach provides therapists with an alternative way of conceptualising client motivation and working with adjudicated clients. It allows offenders to reconsider the positive and negative consequences of their behaviour more thoroughly and to relate their behaviour to their value system. Many offenders respond well to this approach and realise that they had omitted or wrongly weighted certain negative consequences in their original balancing exercise.

Fourth, MI is also thought to be particularly appropriate for extrinsically motivated individuals (Miller, 1987) like many offenders. Ryan and colleagues (1995) examined the initial motivations for alcohol treatment among a group of alcoholics and found that individuals exhibiting high levels of external and internal motivation demonstrated favourable treatment attendance and treatment retention. With offenders, external motivation is provided by societal agents such as the courts and parole boards. Internal motivation, or motivation that is initiated and sustained by the individual's own actions, may not be as readily available or observable in offenders. MI might provide an effective "boost" to the offender's internal motivation or natural change processes (Miller et al., 1988) so that an optimal balance between external and internal motivation can be achieved, thus resulting in enhanced treatment participation and outcome. In the past, the traditional approach to motivating offenders to change has been mainly coercive. Indeed, the whole notion of imprisonment as a deterrent could be said to be based on the idea that extrinsic motivations will stop people offending. Miller compares this mindset with that of counsellors who advocated using confrontational approaches with alcoholics in the recent past. Perhaps offenders, like the previously misunderstood alcoholics, will respond much better to MI than to confrontation or coercion (Miller, 1999).

Fifth, existing evidence that brief motivational interventions with problem drinkers can increase the effectiveness of subsequent treatment (Bien et al., 1993a; Brown & Miller, 1993) suggests that further investigations in different settings and with different client groups are warranted. MI is a brief intervention that can be used with offenders. In many jurisdictions, intensive rehabilitation programmes are available for correcting criminal thinking and behaviour. MI has potential as an adjunctive intervention to these programmes.

Sixth, it should be noted that a substantial proportion of offenders have serious substance abuse problems which are often associated with their offending behaviour (Walters, 1998). Even if MI is not found to be useful with offending behaviour rehabilitation, it has already proved itself to be useful in substance abuse interventions. Substance abuse programmes in correctional settings face the same client motivation challenges as programmes in health care settings, and therefore MI is particularly warranted as a component of these programmes.

Finally, we see the use of MI and its humanistic approach for interacting with offenders as having the potential to contribute significantly toward cultural change within corrections and the broader criminal justice system. Traditionally, corrections has been seen as a harsh, dehumanising regime with a raison d'être to punish law-breakers. It could be argued that the remnants of this approach are alive and well in many jurisdictions today, either explicitly or implictly. The introduction of MI within correctional settings is an alternate way of conceptualising and working with offenders that is supportive, non-judgemental, and fundamentally humanistic. Anecdotal reports by offenders who have participated in MI interventions indicate that the experience can be profoundly positive because few, if any, individuals have ever treated them with such support and respect. For perhaps the first time, they were treated as if they were capable of making "good" decisions and setting reasonable goals.

RECOMMENDATIONS FOR MI WITH OFFENDERS

Given the varied reasons for piloting MI with offenders, it is perhaps surprising that so little has been written about using MI in correctional settings. A few authors have recommended using MI with forensic populations. For example McMurran and Hollin (1993) suggested using MI with alcohol abusing young offenders, and Garland and Dougher (1991) advocated the use of MI with sexual offenders. These latter authors described some of the factors that undermine motivation to change in this population (e.g. environmental barriers, labelling) and concluded that "motivation enhancing strategies are absolutely critical in working with this population" (Garland & Dougher, 1991, p. 313). Further, they believe that motivation for change is the most important determinant of treatment outcome in offender populations, thus motivational interventions could occupy a crucial role in correctional treatment programmes.

Annis and Chan (1983) indirectly recommended MI by questioning the value of highly intensive and confrontational group treatment of offenders with alcohol and drug problems. Murphy and Baxter (1997) noted that many treatment programmes for domestic abuse perpetrators are confrontational in philosophy and implementation. They discussed the dangers of confrontational approaches, especially the risk that they reinforce the belief held by some domestic violence perpetrators that relationships are based on coercive influence. MI was recommended as a viable treatment alternative to such confrontational approaches.

Kear-Colwell and Pollack (1997) examined the merits of an MI approach with sexual offenders compared to the traditional confrontational approach. They noted the likelihood that clients will respond with resistance and disagreement to formulations of their behaviour as "sexual problems". They described how this resistance is viewed by therapists as "denial" and liken the whole pattern to the "confrontation–denial trap" described by Miller and Rollnick (1991, p. 66). Kear-Colwell and Pollack noted how the confrontational approach has often been viewed as the only way to work with sexual offenders, despite the absence of empirical support for this approach. They suggested that MI would work successfully in partnership with relapse prevention to produce an intervention that is not like a "win–lose battle". (Kear-Colwell & Pollack, 1997, p. 31). Further, Kear-Colwell and Pollock (1997) observed that confrontational approaches disempower offenders by removing responsibility for change and encouraging self-labelling. The conclusion is that motivational approaches like MI provide a more positive influence on the change process.

The appearance over the past few years of MI within corrections has not gone unnoticed by its proponents. Miller (1999) writes of a "recent surge of interest" in MI from the criminal justice field in North America. He likens the traditional dehumanising stance towards prisoners to the "punitive, moralistic and arrogant" stance found in the addictions field 20 years ago. He speculates that we may be seeing a sea change in our attitude towards "the last major group in our society whom it is generally acceptable to abuse" (Miller, 1999). Miller (1999) endorses using MI in correctional systems because it is brief, inexpensive, and can be of significant benefit in treating addictive behaviours and is therefore potentially applicable to offenders. Miller (1999) strongly supports using MI throughout the phases of an offender's contact with the criminal justice system, from arrest to warrant expiry.

Due to the absence of empirical evidence, using MI in correctional settings is still pioneering. Offenders typically show a range of characteristics that are negatively associated with treatment outcome, such as personality disorder, impulsivity, aggressiveness and poor emotional control. These characteristics mean that the criminal population is potentially more pathological than many of the samples described in the MI literature. This means that while there are indications that MI could be very valuable with offenders, it should not be embarked upon without evaluation procedures in place.

ACCOUNTS OF MI WITH OFFENDERS

Mann and Rollnick (1996) described a case study in which MI was used with a sex offender who believed he was innocent. The client admitted to having had intercourse with his victim and stated that he believed that she had consented. Mann and Rollnick discussed the question of how to respond motivationally to such a statement. The traditional approach would be for the therapist to assume that the client was in denial, in fact that he was lying. The MI formulation in this case was to view the client as being in an "internal struggle" about his responsibility for the offence. The spirit and some of the techniques of MI such as giving assessment feedback were used with the client. The client responded to the intervention by acknowledging that he had committed a rape, and went on to successfully engage in a cognitive-behavioural treatment programme.

Mann (1996) describes two further case studies of MI with sexual offenders. In the first of these, Mr G, MI was applied with a high-risk sexual offender who wished to drop out of a cognitive-behavioural treatment programme. Use of simple, amplified and double-sided reflection (Miller & Rollnick, 1991) allowed the therapist to realise that Mr G was resisting being labelled as a sex offender. The case was then formulated as a resistance issue, caused by Mr G being forced into a treatment programme when he was still ambivalent about the idea of change. When the issue of labelling was firmly de-emphasised, and Mr G was offered the opportunity to freely choose his next course of action, he decided to continue with treatment.

In another case, MI was applied when Mr B, a child molester, showed a lack of understanding that his release plan (buying a sweet shop) might place him in high-risk situations. In this case, the MI technique of affirming, to strengthen self-efficacy, was used by specifically acknowledging Mr B's progress in treatment. An MI decisional balance strategy known as "good things/less good things" (Rollnick et al., 1992) was followed, allowing Mr B to think through the advantages and disadvantages of his plan, without the therapist making any judgements. Mr B ultimately decided that his plan was inappropriate.

Ginsburg (2000) implemented an MI intervention with offenders with drinking problems. In his intervention, an MI typically lasting from 90 to 120 minutes was conducted with 42 participants. The interview consisted of motivational feedback of assessment information (Miller & Rollnick, 1991, chapter 7), the Typical Day procedure (Rollnick et al., 1992), development of discrepancy, a decisional balance exercise (Sobell et al., 1996), and an emphasis on the participant's responsibility and self-efficacy. Comparison of those participating in the MI intervention with a random-allocation control group found that the use of MI enhanced problem recognition and increased thinking about the possibility of change (Ginsburg, 2000).

OTHER SUGGESTED APPLICATIONS OF MI WITH OFFENDERS

Collaborative Risk Assessment

The science of risk assessment—predicting recidivism using static and dynamic factors—is fast growing in popularity. Some static risk scales, e.g. Static-99 for sexual offenders (Hanson & Thornton, 2000), are completed on the basis of simple file information, whereas other more general risk assessment instruments (e.g. the Psychopathy Checklist—Revised; Hare, 1991) involve the use of interviews and comprehensive file reviews. Thornton's Structured Risk Assessment procedure for sexual offenders (Thornton, 2002) and Hanson's Sex Offender Needs Assessment Rating (Hanson & Harris, 2001) are examples of the most recent static-plus-dynamic type of risk assessment scale. These procedures modify actuarial assessments of risk by adding in clinical information about the presence and strength of empirically determined dynamic risk factors (such as intimacy deficits, distorted attitudes supporting offending, poor self-management skills).

Many clinicians working with offenders have experienced discomfort with the idea of completing such risk assessment procedures without any client involvement and then presenting the results as a *fait accompli* to the client. Miller and Rollnick (1991) caution against making evaluations of clients without their involvement and note that assessment is sometimes seen as an obstacle or hurdle by client and therapist alike. Instead, Miller and Rollnick (1991) recommend that assessment be made more motivational by involving the client. The client can be asked to evaluate, add to and/or correct the therapist's assessment.

These guidelines can be applied successfully to risk assessment (Mann & Shingler, 2001). First, it is important to frame the purpose of risk assessment as defining collaboratively why the problem behaviour (i.e. the offence) occurred. Often offenders are eager to participate in such a discussion, perhaps because it demonstrates that the assessor sees them as an individual with a personal explanation. Then, dynamic risk factors can be presented in the following way: "Some things have been established by research to often figure in someone's offending. We have found that typically about five or six of these things figure strongly as reasons for a particular offence, with a few more figuring mildly. The aim of this procedure is to work out which things from this list figured in *your* offending". This introduction is followed by a collaborative investigation of the presence or absence of each risk factor in the individual's life at the time he or she offended.

The Correctional Service of Canada (CSC), in its national sex offender programme (Yates et al., 2000), has incorporated collaborative risk assessment into its group programme, in a way that is very consistent with MI principles. In this programme, dynamic risk factors are explained to the group early in treatment. Group members are then invited to discuss factors relevant to their respective cases. According to the programme manual, "the intent of the exercises is to assist in beginning to build a collaborative therapeutic relationship between the therapist and clients by being transparent about the nature of risk... By increasing clients' awareness about their risk to offend sexually, this exercise also serves as a motivational enhancement technique" (Yates et al., 2000, p. 45). Again, the principle is that the client knows him/herself best and can participate actively in the formulation of his or her treatment needs.

Pre-treatment Readiness Training

One obvious use of MI would be as preparation for a cognitive-behavioural or skills training programme. If motivation for behaviour change is maximised before a change-oriented programme begins, then participation in, and benefit from, the programme is likely to increase. Brief pre-treatment preparations, such as MI, which impact on motivation to change should enhance natural change processes (Bien et al., 1993a). Many accounts of MI with non-criminal populations involve MI sessions preceding treatment sessions (e.g. Brown & Miller, 1993). In the forensic literature, the case study described by Mann and Rollnick (1996) also involved MI sessions prior to initiating treatment. This was done to assist a sex offender in partial denial to decide whether to undertake a cognitive-behavioural treatment programme. Bien et al., (1993a) note that providing a brief MI intervention prior to a full-length treatment programme reduces pressure on the treatment delivery system to provide immediate treatment.

The Correctional Service of Canada's women offenders' substance abuse programme, like other CSC programmes, makes use of a pre-programme semi-structured interview to develop rapport, explore key substance abuse issues, and determine the candidate's suitability for treatment. Moser and Ginsburg (1999) modified this interview to ensure that it complied with the MI approach and enhanced the quality of the interaction between interviewer and offender.

Miller and Rollnick (1991) noted that most cognitive-behavioural therapy assumes that the client is motivated and therefore does not include a motivational component. The focus of cognitive-behavioural rehabilitation programmes is usually to teach the "how" of change whereas MI addresses the "why" of change. This highlights how MI can complement existing treatment programmes by providing a motivational foundation (Bien et al., 1993a; Miller & Rollnick, 1991).

In-treatment Motivational Exercises

Correctional programming is becoming increasingly popular in many countries. For example, the CSC, Her Majesty's Prison Service (England and Wales), and the Scottish Prison Service all offer a range of national treatment programmes aimed at assisting offenders to become law-abiding citizens. MI can be incorporated into groupwork programme design as well as being offered as a pre-treatment intervention. In fact, the accreditation procedures for correctional programmes in both England and Canada require motivational components to be designed into treatment. Dempsey (1996) provided an account of a group programme that incorporates MI exercises into its curriculum. In one exercise, group members (sex offenders) wrote down and then discussed good and bad things about not abusing. When group members complained about the terminology of the exercise, group leaders rolled with the resistance and agreed to try the exercise using different terminology—gains and losses. Dempsey noted that one further benefit of this exercise was that it identified different stages of readiness to change. Group members who were embracing change were more prepared to talk about the bad things about not abusing (e.g. loss of sexual excitement).

The CSC's women offenders' substance abuse programme is specifically designed to enhance treatment readiness and preparedness through the use of various intervention techniques and exercises, including MI (Kerr, 1997). The programme is divided into two phases, with the focus of Phase 1 being to prepare women offenders with substance abuse problems for treatment. They then transition to Phase 2, which commences the process of instilling new skills and knowledge within a relapse prevention framework.

EVALUATING MI

Evaluating MI is not straightforward, because as an intervention it can be difficult to guarantee that people are conducting MI properly. A therapist may be following MI strategies, but if he or she is not adopting the MI style or spirit, then the intervention is not MI. Tappin et al. (2000) describe the lengths to which it is necessary to go to be sure than an evaluation is true to the spirit and techniques of MI. Their intention was to evaluate the effectiveness of MI with pregnant smokers. The careful strategies used by these authors included audiotaping all counselling interviews (171 in all), transcribing interviews with 25% of the intervention clients, and then scoring each interview three times, using a rating scale provided by Miller (Tappin et al., 2000).

The first "pass" through the interview involved allocating global scores on twelve dimensions involving therapist attributes (e.g. empathy, genuineness), client attributes (e.g. affect, cooperation) and completing interaction scales (e.g. collaboration). The second pass involved classifying therapist verbal behaviour into one of eight categories, four of which were defined as MI consistent (e.g. affirmation, emphasis on control) and four which were defined as MI inconsistent (e.g. confronting, warning). Client responses were also categorised into motivational statements or resistance statements. The third pass measured the percentage of time spent talking by the client. Before any of these ratings could be completed, raters were trained as a group using nine interviews, and then they independently rated 32 interviews to assess inter-rater reliability. These measures may seem excessive, but given that MI is defined as much by its spirit or style as by its content, any less stringent methodology could risk misclassifying non-motivational work as MI.

EVALUATIONS WITH NON-OFFENDERS

Most empirical studies of the effectiveness of MI have involved clients with alcohol or substance abuse problems. With problem drinkers, MI is related to an improved response to treatment, at least in the short-term (e.g. Bien et al., 1993b; Brown & Miller, 1993). It was also shown to be more effective in reducing alcohol consumption than skills training with heavy drinkers, particularly those who showed poor problem recognition before the intervention (Heather et al., 1996). MI is certainly better than confrontational feedback, which can lead to increased drinking (Miller et al., 1993). With young male drinkers, MI has been found to have a lower dropout rate than classroom-style intervention or bibliotherapy via a self-help manual (Baer et al., 1992).

The first published randomised trial of MI was conducted by Saunders and colleagues (1995). Opiate users attending a methadone programme were randomly assigned to a brief motivational intervention or an educational placebo control group. Those participants receiving a motivational interview demonstrated more contemplation of change, better treatment compliance, and fewer opiate-related problems. At a three-month follow-up, many of the MI group were observed to be in the action stage of change, while many of the control group remained in the precontemplation stage. However, there was no difference in the severity of dependence between the two groups at a six-month follow-up.

Finally, it should be noted that MI is cost-effective. Miller et al. (1995) demonstrated that it was an inexpensive intervention to deliver, especially because the time required to deliver an MI intervention is usually only between 25 minutes and 2 hours (Holder et al., 1991).

EVALUATIONS WITH OFFENDERS

The only empirical study of the use of MI with offenders to date was conducted by Ginsburg (2000). This experimental study (n = 83) used MI to enhance treatment readiness in a group of inmates who exhibited symptoms of alcohol dependence. Relative to randomly-allocated control group participants (n = 41), the inmates who participated in a motivational interview (n = 42) showed increases in problem recognition and contemplation related to their drinking behaviour. These findings show positive outcomes of using MI with substance abusing clients, and they were interpreted as providing preliminary support for continued investigation of the use of MI with incarcerated offenders. Ginsburg also addressed the issue of ensuring his intervention was "truly MI". Two prominent MI scientist/practitioners reviewed his intervention and a random sample of MI session audiotapes was reviewed by a member of the Motivational Interviewing Network of Trainers.

FUTURE DIRECTIONS FOR MOTIVATIONAL INTERVIEWING WITH OFFENDERS

Hopefully, the overview of MI that we have provided in this chapter supports its use with offenders. Recent research and theorising in corrections suggests that significant reductions in future criminal offending can be achieved when well-designed intervention programmes that target key criminogenic factors are provided to offenders (e.g. Andrews et al., 1990; Lipsey, 1995; Losel, 1995). It is our observation that more and more correctional jurisdictions are incorporating correctional pro-grammes as a fundamental element of the way in which they do business. But, it is insufficient for offenders to fulfil their correctional treatment plans simply by at-tending prescribed programming. We need them to benefit from their programme experience by learning, if not mastering, critical new skills that will lessen the like-lihood that they will relapse and reoffend. When we consider some of the more simplistic and traditional ways of fostering offender involvement in programmes that we see so often in use, we can only conclude that we need new ways of preparing and engaging offenders to receive intervention services. For us, the hu-mane, respectful, and non-judgemental approach offered by MI holds considerable promise for introduction into the corrections and criminal justice contexts.

As helping professionals working within two large correctional bureaucracies, we feel that a number of issues need to be emphasised. First, we should resist the temptation that happens so often in large organisations to turn an approach like MI into a panacea or "magic bullet" on which all kinds of unrealistic expectations and claims are founded (Gendreau et al., 2000). Clearly, MI is no "cure-all". But it is an approach that has real value in guiding the way in which we think about and attempt to work with offenders. Second, we also need to resist the cynics who will be tempted to compartmentalise and minimise the approach as simply the flavour of the month with a short half-life that will soon fizzle out and die. It is critical to develop solid positioning and implementation strategies to carefully weave MI into existing correctional operations and treatment practices. Third, MI is not an approach for bleeding hearts who wish to run so-called "hug-a-thug" programmes. On the contrary, MI is a subtle and relatively sophisticated approach to behaviour change in which the interpersonal interaction between the counsellor and client is key to assisting clients in challenging themselves by examining their behaviour. Finally, there is the challenge of implementing an approach like MI that might naively be seen as "soft" within a bureaucratic environment that can be politically charged with "get tough" rhetoric for dealing with offenders. As researchers and practitioners committed to assisting offenders in reducing their risk to reoffend, we must persevere to provide treatment services with demonstrated efficacy in facilitating behaviour change.

From our perspective, it would be unfortunate if MI is used piecemeal with offenders. To maximise its contribution to, and utilisation within, corrections, we see the potential for MI to be used in multiple and potentially interrelated ways. As we described earlier, the application of MI to correctional treatment can occur either as a pre-treatment "primer" to prepare offenders for treatment, or MI can be used to sustain offender treatment motivation throughout other phases of treatment. We see significant value in providing MI training to case management, parole and probation officers, and others who have ongoing direct involvement with offenders. These front-line individuals have primary responsibility for managing offenders' correctional treatment plans and monitoring correctional treatment. By virtue of their role, they attempt to engage the offender in discussions about the details of their offending and, in turn, extract from those discussions areas that the offender needs to address through treatment.

Finally, training correctional/prison officers (or *all* correctional staff for that matter) to use MI and other communication and interview tools has the potential to influence the culture and atmosphere within institutions. This should also enhance the quality and nature of officers' overall approach to thinking about and working with offenders. Obviously, this is a long-term goal that is ambitious, expensive, and even somewhat grandiose, but we believe that MI, blended with other staff training and education, has the potential to improve our correctional results and contribute to the evolution of modern rehabilitative corrections.

1. ACKNOWLEDGMENTS

The authors wish to thank Richard Clair and Marc Brideau for their helpful comments on an earlier version of this chapter.

REFERENCES

Andrews, D. A., Zinger I., Hoge R. D., Bonta J., Gendreau, P. & Cullen, F. T. (1990). Does correctional treatment work? A clinically-relevant and psychologically-informed meta-analysis. *Criminology*, **28**, 369–404.

Annis, H. M. & Chan, D. (1983). The differential treatment model. Empirical evidence from a personality typology of adult offenders. *Criminal Justice and Behavior*, **10**, 159–73.

Baer, J. S., Marlatt, G. A., Kivlahan, D. R., Fromme, K., Larimer, M. E. & Williams, E. (1992). An experimental test of three methods of alcohol risk reduction with young adults. *Journal of Consulting and Clinical Psychology*, **60**, 974–9.

Bien, T. H., Miller, W. R. & Boroughs, J. M. (1993b). Motivational interviewing with alcohol outpatients. *Behavioural Psychotherapy*, **21**, 347–56.

Bien, T. H., Miller, W. R. & Tonigan, J. S. (1993a). Brief interventions for alcohol problems: a review. *Addiction*, **88**, 315–35.

Brown, J. M. & Miller, W. R. (1993). Impact of motivational interviewing on participation and treatment outcome in residential alcoholism treatment. *Psychology of Addictive Behaviors*, **7**, 211–18.

Dempsey, R. (1996). Using motivational interviewing techniques in a prison setting and in the community with a partner. In R. Mann (ed.) *Motivational Interviewing with Sex Offenders*. NOTA, PO Box 508, Hull, UK.

Garland, R. J. & Dougher, M. J. (1991). Motivational intervention in the treatment of sex offenders. In W. R. Miller & S. Rollnick (eds) *Motivational Interviewing: Preparing People to Change Addictive Behavior*. New York: Guilford.

Gendreau, P., Goggin, C. & Smith, P. (2000). Generating rational correctional policies: an introduction to advances in cumulating knowledge. *Corrections Management Quarterly*, **4**, 52–60.

George, W. H. & Marlatt, G. A. (1989). Introduction. In D. R. Laws (ed.) *Relapse Prevention with Sex Offenders*. New York: Guilford.

Ginsburg, J. I. D. (2000). Using motivational interviewing to enhance treatment readiness in offenders with symptoms of alcohol dependence. PhD thesis, Carleton University, Ottawa, Ontario, Canada.

Hanson, R. K. & Harris, A. (2001). The Sex Offender Need Assessment Rating (SONAR): a method for measuring change in risk levels 2000–1, Corrections Research Department of the Solicitor General of Canada.

Hanson, R. K. & Thornton, D. (2000). Improving risk assessment for sex offenders: a comparison of three actuarial scales. *Law and Human Behaviour*, **24**, 119–36.

Hare, R. (1991). *The Hare Psychopathy Checklist Revised*. Toronto, Ontario: Multi-health Systems.

Heather, N., Rollnick, S., Bell, A. & Richmond, R. (1996). Effects of brief counselling among heavy drinkers identified on general hospital wards. *Drug and Alcohol Review*, **15**, 29–38.

Holder, H., Longabaugh, R., Miller, W. R. & Rubonis, A.V. (1991). The cost effectiveness of treatment for alcoholism: a first approximation. *Journal of Studies on Alcohol*, **52**, 517–40.

Kear-Colwell, J. & Pollack, P. (1997). Motivation or confrontation: which approach to the child sex offender? *Criminal Justice and Behavior*, **24**, 20–33.

Kerr, D. (1997). *The Women's Substance Abuse Program*. Ottawa: Reintegration Programs, Correctional Service of Canada.

Killick, S. & Allen, C. (1997). Shifting the balance: motivational interviewing to help behavior change in people with bulimia nervosa. *European Eating Disorders Review*, **5**, 33–41.

Laws, D. R. (ed.) (1989). *Relapse Prevention with Sex Offenders*. New York: Guilford.

Laws, D. R., Hudson, S. M. & Ward, T. (eds) (2000). *Remaking Relapse Prevention with Sex Offenders*. London: Sage.

Lipsey, M. W. (1995). What do we learn from 400 research studies on the effectiveness of treatment with juvenile delinquents? In J. McGuire (ed.) *What Works: Reducing Reoffending*. Chichester: Wiley.

Losel, F. (1995). The efficacy of correctional treatment: a review and synthesis of meta-evaluations. In J. McGuire (ed.) *What Works: Reducing Reoffending*. Chichester: Wiley.

Mann, R. E. (ed.) (1996). *Motivational Interviewing with Sex Offenders: A Practice Manual*. NOTA, PO Box 508, Hull, UK.

Mann, R. E. & Rollnick, S. (1996). Motivational interviewing with a sex offender who believed he was innocent. *Behavioural and Cognitive Psychotherapy*, **24**, 127–34.

Mann, R. E. & Shingler, J. (2001). Collaborative risk assessment. Paper presented at the annual conference of the National Organisation for the Treatment of Abusers, September, Cardiff, Wales.

Marlatt, G. A. & Gordon, J. R. (eds) (1985). *Relapse Prevention*. New York: Guilford.

McMurran, M. & Hollin, C. R. (1993). Motivational interviewing. In *Young Offenders and Alcohol Related Crime: A Practitioner's Guidebook*. Chichester: Wiley.

Miller, W. R. (1983). Motivational interviewing with problem drinkers. *Behavioural Psychotherapy*, **11**, 147–72.

Miller, W. R. (1985). Motivation for treatment: a review with special emphasis on alcoholism. *Psychological Bulletin*, **98** (1), 84–107.

Miller, W. R. (1987). Techniques to modify hazardous drinking patterns. In M. Galanter (ed.) *Recent Developments in Alcoholism*. New York: Plenum Press.

Miller, W. R. (1994). Motivational interviewing III: On the ethics of motivational intervention. *Behavioural and Cognitive Psychotherapy*, **22**, 111–23.

Miller, W. R. (1999). Pros and cons: reflections on motivational interviewing in correctional settings. *MINUET (Motivational Interviewing Newsletter: updates, Education and Training)*, **6** (1), 2–3 Available from http//www.motivationalinterview.org/clinical/prosandcons.htm

Miller, W. R. & Rollnick, S. (eds) (1991). *Motivational Interviewing: Preparing People to Change Addictive Behavior*. New York: Guilford.

Miller, W. R. & Rollnick, S. (eds) (2002). *Motivational Interviewing*, 2nd edn. New York: Guilford.

Miller, W. R., Sovereign, R. G. & Krege, B. (1988). Motivational interviewing with problem drinkers: II. The drinker's check-up as preventive intervention. *Behavioural Psychotherapy*, **16**, 251–68.

Miller, W. R., Benefield, R. G. & Tonigan, J. S. (1993). Enhancing motivation to change in problem drinking: a controlled comparison of two therapist styles. *Journal of Consulting and Clinical Psychology*, **61**, 455–61.

Miller, W. R., Brown, J. M., Simpson, T. L., Handmaker, N. S., Bien, T. H., Luckie, L. F., Montgomery, H. A., Hester, R. K. & Tonigan, J. S. (1995). What works? A methodological analysis of the alcohol treatment outcome literature. In R. K. Hester & W. R. Miller (eds) *Handbook of Alcoholism Treatment Approaches. Effective Alternatives*, 2nd edn. Boston: Allyn & Bacon.

Moser, A. E. & Ginsburg, J. I. D. (1999). *Pre-Program Semi-Structured Interview for the Women Offenders' Substance Abuse Program*. Ottawa: Reintegration Programs, Correctional Service of Canada.

Murphy, C. M. & Baxter, V. A. (1997). Motivating batterers to change in the treatment context. *Journal of Interpersonal Violence*, **12**, 607–19.

Rollnick, S. & Miller, W. R. (1995). What is motivational interviewing? *Behavioural and Cognitive Psychotherapy*, **23**, 325–34.

Rollnick, S., Heather, N. & Bell, A. (1992). Negotiating behaviour change in medical settings: the development of brief motivational interviewing. *Journal of Mental Health*, **1**, 25–37.

Rollnick, S., Butler, C. & Stott, N. (1997). Helping smokers make decisions: the enhancement of brief intervention for general medical practice. *Patient Education and Counselling*, **31**, 191–203.

Rollnick, S., Mason, P. & Butler, C. (1999). *Health Behavior Change: A Guide for Practitioners*. New York: Churchill Livingstone.

Ryan, R. M., Plant, R. W. & O'Malley, S. (1995). Initial motivations for alcohol treatment: relations with patient characteristics, treatment involvement, and dropout. *Addictive Behaviours*, **20**, 279–97.

Saunders, B., Wilkinson, C. & Phillips, M. (1995). The impact of a brief motivational intervention with opiate users attending a methadone programme. *Addiction*, **90**, 415–24.

Smith, D. E., Heckemeyer, C. M., Kratt, P. P. & Mason, D. A. (1997). Motivational interviewing to improve adherence to a behavioural weight-control program for older obese women with NIDDM: a pilot study. *Diabetes Care*, **20**, 53–4.

Sobell, L. C., Cunningham, J. A., Sobell, M. B., Agarwell, S., Gavin, D. R., Leo, G. I. & Singh, K. N. (1996). Fostering self-change among problem drinkers: a proactive community intervention. *Addictive Behaviours*, **21**, 817–33.

Tappin, D. M., McKay, C., McIntyre, D., Gilmour, W. H., Cowan, S., Crawford, F., Currie, F. & Lumsdon, M. (2000). A practical instrument to document the process of motivational interviewing. *Behavioural and Cognitive Psychotherapy*, **28**, 17–32.

Thornton, D. (2002). Constructing and testing a framework for dynamic risk assessment. *Sexual Abuse: A Journal of Research and Treatment*, in press.

Treasure, J. & Ward, A. (1997). A practical guide to the use of motivational interviewing in anorexia nervosa. *European Eating Disorders Review*, **5**, 102–14.

Trigwell, P., Grant, P. J. & House, A. (1997). Motivation and glycemic control in diabetes mellitus. *Journal of Psychosomatic Research*, **43**, 307–15.

Walters, G. D. (1998). *Changing Lives of Crime and Drugs: Intervening with Substance-Abusing Offenders*. Chichester: Wiley.

Yates, P. M., Goguen, B. C. & Nicholaichuk, T. P. (2000). *National Sex Offender Treatment*, vol. II: *Moderate Intensity Program*. Ottawa: Correctional Service of Canada.

Chapter 7

MOTIVATING OFFENDERS TO CHANGE THROUGH PARTICIPATORY THEATRE

JAMES THOMPSON

University of Manchester, Manchester, UK

INTRODUCTION

This chapter aims to examine the role of participatory theatre in offender treatment initiatives. This does not refer to the "putting on of plays" for these groups, but rather the use of theatre exercises, games, role-plays and dramatic metaphor as part of offender rehabilitation programmes. The contention of this chapter is that these techniques are a valuable part of these programmes and that they play a useful role in the motivation of participants. Offenders can suffer from hyperactivity, be impulsive and can have poor attention spans. In addition, they may have had bad experiences at school, leaving them unresponsive to conventional or didactic methods of education. By offering offenders active, participatory and thought-provoking exercises, theatre methods potentially do much to enhance engagement in programmes and motivation to change. Their use aims to meet the need for programmes to be responsive to the capabilities and learning styles of the clients.

While the chapter will concentrate on the use of these techniques when they are implemented with the explicit recognition that they derive from theatre, it also recognises that many quasi-theatrical techniques are used as part of programmes without them necessarily identifying themselves as "theatre-based". Behaviour rehearsal, role play and simulation exercises have for a long time been tools used by various therapeutic traditions (see Goldstein & Glick, 1994; Rose 1998 for examples relating to offender rehabilitation programmes). The fields of dramatherapy and pyschodrama have specifically developed in this meeting point seeking to generate disciplines that build on experience of various therapeutic/theatre practices (Jennings, 1987; Moreno, 1983).

The writing here is based, however, first and foremost on my experience as a theatre practitioner who has sought to *apply* his skills to a particular field. I bring theatre exercises and a theatre practice that has for many criminal justice

Motivating Offenders to Change: A Guide to Enhancing Engagement in Therapy. Edited by M. McMurran.
© 2002 John Wiley & Sons, Ltd.

staff provided a valuable addition and at times complete methodology for their offender rehabilitation practice (Thompson, 1999). This is not to say that exercises can be mechanically taken from one tradition and placed within the boundaries of another. The process of the *application* is complex and must be done with care. However, my experience of developing these programmes with colleagues from a number of criminal justice agencies has demonstrated that there is considerable potential for a fruitful dialogue to be developed in practice.

The chapter will outline my background as a practitioner and developer of theatre-based offending behaviour programmes. It will then describe in detail six different component exercises that have been used as part of these programmes. Each exercise will be explained in detail, an example will be given of how it functions in practice, and finally the assumptions about the motivational characteristic of each exercise will be discussed. I am writing this article directed at the non-theatre reader who has an expertise in offender treatment or wider offender rehabilitation matters. What I am asking is that in reading these exercises you contemplate how they might be adapted to support or enhance your programme's motivational aspects. In the process of applying theatre, the theatre person offers the techniques and starts a debate about how they might be adapted. Importantly, however, this process requires that the experts in the host context consciously translate this material into possible practical approaches for their own field.

BACKGROUND

During the course of 1990 and 1991 I had been running drama workshops in probation centres across the Greater Manchester region. These were usually weekly sessions as part of regular probation groups. I involved the clients in a few theatre games and then different role-play exercises, which when working well led to the creation of small scenes to be shown to others in the centre or to be recorded on video. The rationale for these workshops was that they were a positive recreational activity for the groups and that in the creation of the final product they gave them some increased confidence and heightened self-esteem. While the intention was not for the work to be offence focused, the topics covered in the role-plays and subsequent videos were nearly always related to drugs, theft, violence and car crime.

These workshops were sponsored by Greater Manchester Probation Service Practice Development Unit (PDU) as a pilot scheme to examine what potential drama had to become a part of core probation centre programmes. Although there was no detailed study made, the anecdotal evidence from the centres was that the work was well received. Two main reasons were cited. First, the staff felt that the innovative approach of the drama workshop was refreshing and helped them see their clients in a new light. Second, they reported that drama had engaged clients and held their attention in ways that other group work had not. This feedback led the PDU to commission myself and a colleague to create a workshop for their clients that, rather than unintentionally creating stories from clients' views of crime, intentionally became offence focused. We were still developing this workshop a year later when we set up the Theatre in Prisons and Probation (TIPP) Centre and the final product, the Blagg! workshop, became this organisation's first project.

The Blagg! workshop has been discussed in detail elsewhere (Thompson, 1996, 1999), but it is worth describing here briefly. It was a day-long event that could be fitted into other programmes and would generate a debate on whatever "criminal behaviour" a particular group chose for it. Through a series of drama exercises, the thinking behind a certain offence was explored, the consequences examined and strategies for avoiding the offence in the future were practised. The actual exercises used were not specific exercises for offending behaviour work, but very basic drama techniques structured and ordered for a particular purpose. Although the workshop has been described as an offending behaviour workshop, in fact it only becomes an "offending behaviour" workshop when it is used with an offender group in the context of a treatment programme. When it was framed as that and the issues placed into the structure were offending related, it functioned as an extended offending behaviour exercise. When done with schoolchildren it is different—it can transform into a workshop on bullying, for example. When done with drama students it can be an exercise to develop plot and storyline. Blagg! is thus drama workshop first and in application it is translated into offender rehabilitation. I seek to repeat this process here by offering drama exercises for the reader to translate to what they understand of rehabilitation programmes.

The TIPP Centre's second programme was a full eight-session anger management programme, again commissioned by the PDU. This programme is now the core court ordered programme for men convicted of violence who are under supervision by Greater Manchester Probation Service. Although this programme uses much anger management terminology in the description and structure of the exercises, again it must be viewed as a set of drama exercises which are translated in the context of work with violent offenders into a rehabilitation programme. Drama work does not possess the automatic quality of managing people's anger or examining their behaviour. It is wrong to see it as any type of panacea, as it can have any range of effects, both positive and negative. The series of drama exercises in the Pump! programme was carefully constructed within the framework of anger management, but only functioned as that in the specific translations the staff using the course made of each moment. Their anger management expertise became translated and exercised through the techniques we brought.

The TIPP Centre continues to develop programmes for vulnerable groups. These include various offender populations, young people at risk and people suffering from mental ill health. Since I left the Centre in 1999 I have both taught in this area and developed programmes for many different contexts. After the first commission and the development of the Blagg! project, I believed that it was the task of a person who applied their theatre to different contexts to be fully literate in each new context. Subsequently I have changed my approach to where I now feel that we as theatre people should trust our techniques more and work closely with our partners in the other disciplines so that they are able to understand our intentions and translate with us. This chapter is thus an attempt to try this process in writing.

The rest of this chapter will explain six different "drama" exercises. They are called drama exercises because it is from a theatre workshop context that I originally encountered them. This does not mean that they are not perhaps familiar to other groupwork contexts. Each exercise is explained, and an example of the application of the exercise in a broadly criminal justice setting is given, followed by a discussion of the assumptions that the exercise makes about how it motivates offenders to change.

EXERCISE 1: FRUIT BOWL

This exercise is often played as a first warm-up or ice-breaking exercise. Sitting in a circle of chairs, each member of the group is given alternately the name of one fruit—apple, orange or pear. In a small group, you might chose to use only two fruits so there are always at least three people per item. The groupwork leader then stands in the middle having taken their own chair away and calls out one of those fruits. If it is their fruit, the participants have to get up and try to sit in another empty chair. The person in the middle will try to sit down as well. This will leave one person over in the middle, who then repeats the exercise, calling out the same or another fruit. If the person in the middle says "fruit bowl" everybody has to change chairs.

The exercise can be adapted so that the person in the middle might ask a question that the group have to respond to by moving. It might be about something that they are wearing, that they like or have eaten that day. If the answer is affirmative, the group member must change chairs. For example, the person in the middle could ask: "Anybody who has had a cup of coffee this morning?", "Anybody wearing the colour black?", "Anybody who did not want to come here this morning?".

Obviously, the questioning can get too personal. If this happens it should be emphasised that participants do not have to get up and therefore they do not have to give their response to an over-personal question. Questions about the programme, their experiences and their lives are not automatically out of bounds, however.

The Experience: Wigan Car Crime Group

As part of an offending behaviour group being run in Wigan, Greater Manchester for young men convicted of car crime, Fruit bowl was run as the first exercise of one particular session. The first impression on entering the probation centre room was a group of men who were physically very committed to staying in their seats. There were about ten participants, all in their late teens or early twenties.

When each person was given their fruit to remember they returned some very bemused looks. Once the next stage was explained and the first fruit was called out the game started and they moved from chair to chair. They only really understood the game once it was played. One member of the group did not want to move and stayed firmly in his seat. However, very soon another member of the group went right up to him and persuaded him to move because he wanted his chair. He shuffled and moaned but did slide across to another chair. From then on, although he still moved slower than the rest, he changed chairs when required. He reluctantly joined in, but maintained the performance of a person "not enjoying himself". All the others were enthusiastically jumping up, running across the circle and diving onto chairs.

At the beginning of the session, the group was split into small knots of friends. There were clearly the high status mixed with the less confident, with allegiances between individuals marked by the positions of their chairs and their bodies. However imperfect the circle at the beginning of the exercise, it developed into a more or less perfect one by the end. In addition, the organisation of the mini-groupings was disturbed by the rush they all made to find any free seat in the room. The order of the circle, clearly prescribed at the beginning of the session according to the alliances and power relations within the group, was now reordered in a random way.

The Assumptions and Questions

The first assumption is that by creating a physical activity the group will be more prepared to undertake and concentrate on the session. What is often noticed after running this game is that at its end, you are left with a group of people all leaning forward in their chairs, breathing deeply and closely observing you the leader. Their physical engagement with the exercise has made them more mentally ready to listen to your next instruction, or the next exercise. The behaviour in the room before a session starts might look like "lounging" or people doing nothing but it is important to remember that it is a physical activity. The group will be thinking about their attitude to being in the group, but they are also displaying that attitude in their bodies. If you only ask their minds to start concentrating on what is often difficult material, you will not have challenged the "thinking" that is made evident through their bodies.

An exercise like this, therefore, is a challenge to the routine that is displayed through the body, and that routine is minutely connected to their cognitive processing of the groupwork. Making people move around in ways that to them are unfamiliar will prepare them to move their thoughts in similar unfamiliar patterns. That final state of sitting and looking, because it contains an element of exhaustion, is more of a neutral state on to which work can be built. They will be more open and ready to consider new ways of behaving from that position rather than being forced to adapt the lounging attitudes with which they entered the room.

This whole exercise hints at the central assumption about the role of drama in motivating offenders to change. It is based on the belief that changing behaviour cannot be achieved without accepting that behaviour is an emotional, cognitive *and physically* driven process. To examine and thus challenge behaviour, the physical script and processes that are involved in its creation must be linked to the thinking.

EXERCISE 2: THE CONTINUUM

The continuum can be done as one of the first exercises in a session. The group leader explains that there is an invisible diagonal line that divides the room from one corner to the other. This line measures a continuum that moves from agreement to disagreement. At one end, right in the corner, is strongly agree and at the other end is completely disagree. The group leader explains that he or she is going to make a statement and the group members then have to stand on the line, positioning themselves according to their response. If they agree with the statement they go to one end, if they disagree they move to the other. If, however, they are in only partial agreement, they must stand on the scale at that point that they think best illustrates their opinion. All are asked to stand and the first statement is spoken aloud. The first can be light-hearted to get the group familiar with the exercise. As it progresses increasingly difficult and controversial subjects can be tackled.

Once the group has lined up, the groupwork leader can approach different people and ask them questions. These are never about their opinions on the subject, but instead about their position: "Why are you standing there?", "Why are you a few feet away from the end and not right at the end?", "What would it take for you to move in that direction?".

If there is clearly great disagreement with clusters of participants around certain points, the varying positions can be questioned. Rather than the workshop leader arguing with the participant, he or she can go to the other end of the line to find an alternative view. If there is a co-worker he or she can participate and therefore offer a different view as part of the exercise.

The Experience: Brazil Prison AIDS Workshop

As part of an HIV/AIDS and sexually transmitted diseases education programme in the state of São Paulo prison system, this exercise is used to assess understanding of risk behaviours and to examine increased awareness at the end of the programme. During the first workshops the exercise is explained and a number of questions about AIDS/HIV transmission are asked. These start with general queries on transmission and move to the more complex issues around safe behaviour. This is done in both men's and women's prisons, and the groups are very soon moving across the room to position themselves according to their opinion. Arguments do occur but they are framed as criticism of where a person is standing. A participant is asked by another group member to "move over here" rather than being told that they are wrong.

Gradually the technique of the exercise is handed over to the group. They then use it to make statements to each other, both to test the group's understanding but also to open up questions where they have doubt. For example, questions have been asked about sharing nail cutters (a common activity among male and female prisoners in Brazil), female to female sex, and whether a person who is HIV positive needs to practise safe sex if having sex with another HIV positive person. Debates are strong and people shift their opinion visually as they shuffle up or down the continuum during the discussion. The group leaders offer their expertise where necessary but also respect the knowledge that is held within the group.

The exercise is often repeated at the beginning of each session when people have new questions that have occurred to them during the period between workshops. At the end of the programme, the exercise is repeated with the same statements that were made in the first session. With the help of the group, the workshop leaders note down the differences in the responses. They monitor the exercise by noting for example: "Do people all move to one particular position?", "Are people more confident in where they place themselves?", "Has anybody changed their place since the exercise was first played?".

These notes are used as part of the monitoring of the project, with a visual record made on a drawn "continuum line" to illustrate the different positions of participants. The final statements that are made to the group are in relation to the programme as a whole. The group are asked to position themselves according to how successful, appropriate, enjoyable and useful they have found the course. While acknowledging that any public act of evaluation will be problematic, their responses provide one form of feedback on the programme.

The Assumptions and Questions

This exercise assumes that a physical response to a statement will be easier for some groups than a verbal one. By literally making a stand, placing your body, you will display the affective response to a question rather than a more carefully considered one. This is often useful material for the groupwork leader. In addition, as the exercise progresses, you can witness cognitive processes as people have to speak or justify their position, or by the fact that during a discussion some will start to shift from where they have been standing. The physical jump to one place becomes tempered and adapted by their thinking. Besides triggering a discussion on the issue raised by the question, the exercise leads to questions about the relation between actions and subsequent justifications.

The exercise is based on the premise that non-direct questioning is less threatening to certain offender groups. It asks people to comment on their physical position ("why are you there?"), not on their personal opinion. It therefore challenges thinking without confronting it. It also visually displays positions that are often hidden if groups are only asked for verbal responses. Asking someone directly for their opinion on, for example, violence can lead to nervous prevarication or denial. People often move and justify afterwards. This exercise plays on this tendency, but adds the need for people to speak up for an action they have already taken.

Different groups have varying means of expressing their opinions and contrasting learning styles. This exercise complements the verbal exercises in a programme by allowing a space for people who are more physically "articulate". This should not be allowed to supersede the discursive, but the language of the body is as complex and dynamic for some as words and conversation are for others.

Observing changes in a group is hard, especially during drawn-out conversations about sensitive subjects. This exercise, by placing those debates on their feet, allows the groupwork leader to see the shifts that people are making. A person will often happily shuffle down a line when they would not admit verbally that they are wrong or they wished to change their opinion. This offers a language of movement in place of a language of agreement or disagreement that will be less threatening for participants, and allow them to shift without directly having to speak out.

EXERCISE 3: HYPNOSIS

Group members are asked to stand up and find a partner. Standing in pairs, they then have to label themselves *A* and *B*. *A* must then put their arm horizontally in front of them with their palm facing outwards as though they were trying to stop someone. *B* must then place their nose a few centimetres away from the centre of their partner's palm. Once noses are facing palms, *A*s can then move slowly around the room. *B*s, however, must maintain exactly the same distance from the palm at all times. *A*s can move their partners gently wherever they want to in the room. They can move up high or take them down across the floor. The exercise should be done in silence and individuals should be encouraged to test their partners but not make it dangerous or impossible for them. Sudden or very fast movements make it unlikely that the follower will maintain the distance at all times.

After a short while *A* and *B* swap over, with *B* becoming the leader and *A* the led. The exercise is then repeated, now with *B* leading *A*. The final stage is that *A* and *B* must hold out their arms, and each one must keep their nose close to the other's palm. This simultaneous version can be played out for a short while, before the whole group are asked to feedback on what they liked or did not like about the exercise.

The Experience: Child Soldiers

This exercise was used as part of a programme for "child soldier" detainees in prison rehabilitation camp in Sri Lanka. Twenty-four young men between the ages of 13 and 24 were participating in the programme.* The camp's aim was to run a range of educational and vocational programmes with the young men so that after one year they could return to their families and communities without returning to the armed rebel group and the war. Although perhaps strictly speaking they might not be considered "offenders", they were seen as that in this context, they were in a secure setting and the authorities planned and executed various rehabilitation programmes with them.

Hypnosis was one of the first exercises on the first morning of work. They very easily found partners and space around the room. Some started the exercise by tearing around the room, some by rapidly jerking their arms up and down, others by moving their arms in slow careful sweeps. The more the instructions were clarified and repeated, the quieter and more controlled the group became. Gradually the loud and excited chattering, and the exuberant energy displayed by this group, became focused on taking their partners into all corners and possible positions in the room.

The exercise became slower and slower with the entire group by the end moving as if to some kind of inaudible music. Although some occasionally did break down and laugh or lose the quiet concentration, the majority stayed focused until the end. When the exercise was brought to a close, the group were asked which they preferred, the "leader" or the "led". The majority answered that they felt more comfortable being the leader. A few said they preferred being the led and then explained why. A discussion was developed about the exercise, about the

---

* Although the government stated that the Centre was for "Child soldiers", there were many detainees over 18. Since writing this chapter, on 25 October 2000 at least 27 inmates were killed in a massacre, a disturbing reminder that all rehabilitation programmes need a supportive social and political context in which to operate if they are to be able to succeed.

roles involved and about what responsibilities came with each task they had been given.

The Assumptions and Questions

This exercise, as with the others, relies on purely physical actions to elicit responses from the group. The exercise thus works as a physical metaphor that the group will fill with their interpretations. It does not have a right or wrong response, but it will open a series of meanings from which the group will discuss some powerful issues. That discussion will be based on an immediate emotional memory triggered by the exercise, and therefore very quickly you will be debating at the level of feeling rather than simply "thinking".

Power, control and responsibility are crucial areas of debate for offender groups. However, conceptually they are somewhat difficult both to describe and to grasp. If discussion on these terms remains at the level of verbal question and response, the debate will remain detached. The group will speak "theoretically" and easily be able to distance themselves from any difficult implications. By conducting a physical exercise that will practically enact a situation of power, control and responsibility in the room, the group will discuss from an immediate and "real" experience. The group leader will be able to ask direct questions about what it feels like to be led by different people and in different ways. He or she will be able to ask why certain people chose to make it very hard for their partner and why others took it slowly. The evidence will be there in the room. The group will not be talking about what they do externally to the session, with all the risk of justification and minimisation that occurs, but about what has actually taken place and how they feel about it. The group workers can question from what they have seen, not from what they assume. They can challenge an abuse of power, for example, from inside the structure of an exercise that does not require them directly to attack an incident in someone's life.

The final assumption is that the difficult physical movement is useful in itself. People in their daily lives not only develop very rigid patterns of thought, but also very rigid patterns of movement. Both these together lead to repeated patterns of behaviour. When a person is following a palm, their body will have to twist and turn into positions that are unfamiliar. They will have to use muscles that have not been tested for a long time. As our bodies are as much conditioned and adapted to the lives we lead as our thoughts are, it is important to stretch and use the unused parts in a process that seeks to promote personal change.

EXERCISE 4: WHAT'S THE STORY?

Two volunteers are taken from the group. The first is asked to stand just in front of the "audience" and the second to stand several metres further to the back. The second should be behind but slightly to one side of the other. Those in the audience, looking straight on, should be able to see them both. The groupwork leader then asks the audience "what's the story?". What, to them, does this scene represent? It is important that the two people standing hold themselves as neutrally as possible.

Any suggestion that the group offers is then repeated back by the group leader. If it is of particular interest or the idea seems unusual, a further question can be asked to clarify the story. Detail can be asked for, to expand or develop an interesting idea. The question—"what's the story?"—should be repeated frequently to push the group to come up with as many readings as possible.

Once it seems the group have exhausted their ideas, the volunteer at the back is asked to take one step forward. Then the question is repeated—what is the story now? New readings are taken, being careful to accept all and insist that none is the final or correct answer. This is then repeated, with each step forward resulting in new readings. The final point is reached when the person at the back moves alongside and then in front of the other volunteer.

Once the final readings have been offered, the group is asked to choose their favourite from all the different stories. They must decide upon one that they would like to see brought to life. Obviously, a consensus needs to be arrived at and negotiated carefully to avoid the volunteers being asked to demonstrate a scene that ridicules them. Strange, entertaining or amusing scenes should be allowed as long as the volunteers are happy to perform them. The group are then asked to choose one line for each actor in the story they have selected. Once the lines (one each) have been agreed upon and the volunteers have been asked if they are content with them, the groupwork leader calls "action" and the two lines are spoken by the volunteers. At the end of the mini-scene, the groupwork leader encourages applause for what is often the first piece of role-play in the session.

The Experience: Bolton Offending Behaviour Group

In Bolton probation office, Greater Manchester, this exercise was run at the beginning of a session midway through an offending behaviour programme. The group had been told that they were going to do some drama in this particular meeting. They were playing pool and grumbling about what exactly that meant right up to the moment of the start of the session. After a short introduction, two volunteers were requested. They jumped up quickly because it was explained that they were going to have to do less than the audience. The first leant at the back against the pool table. The other stood right at the front, practically on top of the other men on the course.

The first question of "what's the story?" was met with a complete silence. After a little while, however, one person seemed to understand the exercise. He pointed at the person at the back and said that he was a mugger about to rob the innocent person at the front. A further question was asked—"who is this person at the front?". The group explained who he was and what he was doing. From this point onwards the group offered ideas fairly easily. The next story was that these were two people queuing in the bank, with the one at the back looking nervous because he was about to rob it. Then they were two people in a queue in an unemployment office. Then they were a dad and a son who had had an argument. Then a staff member suggested, to much amusement from the group and some shuffling from the volunteers, that they were a woman and a man who had just had a row and were now not talking to each other.

The group came up with numerous suggestions, some deliberately mocking the exercise and each other, some directly connected to crime and others with no apparent connection to them or their circumstances. All were welcomed as positive ideas. If anyone offered particularly interesting characters (the dad and son, for example), they would be asked for more detail. Finally, the group agreed very rapidly to see the scene between the man and woman. The volunteers, who had in fact been subtly changing the way they stood after each suggestion, maintained that they were quite happy now to take on these roles. After much discussion from the audience, two lines were given. They were spoken with much ham passion from the volunteers and the watching group broke out into applause. Both volunteers bowed, milking the mock adoration from the rest of the group.

The Assumptions and Questions

Any group that is told that role play is a component of the course they are about to undertake will be very nervous and understandably apprehensive about what this entails. On a very basic level, this exercise is about allaying those fears and demonstrating that role-play is a simple, non-threatening activity of which anybody is capable. This exercise emphasises that role-play should be as much about the work of the audience suggesting and directing the action as it is about those who have volunteered to act.

However, this exercise is about much more than introducing acting and dispelling the fears of participants. This exercise comes from the very heart of theatre practice, because it is about encouraging people to look and to see. In examining different stories closely in the neutral image of two standing people, a group starts to exercise their capacity to have insight into the world around them. I would suggest that this is vital for offending rehabilitation programmes. It is the way we read or interpret what we see in the world around us that leads to our responses in action. This exercise initially therefore is about getting people to practise looking hard at what is in front of them. Too often groups of people, not only offenders, assume what they have seen rather than look closely at what is there. This exercise is thus a practical way of encouraging people to really examine situations, and be aware of the minute differences in meaning that can arise from the subtlest physical changes in position.

In encouraging close observation, this exercise is also demonstrating that what is seen at first can change on closer inspection. If on the initial reading a group member saw one story, after further concentrated looking they can often see another. If it was at first two people waiting for a bus, it then becomes two people about to run a race. Rarely, however, do offenders look twice. Action and some offending are a rapid response to an immediate, often unfounded, reading of an event. "What's the story?" explicitly shows the rewards of looking at a situation hard and noting that there is more than one possible interpretation.

The next assumption is that this exercise is valuable because it ensures that there is no one correct reading. All interpretations are accepted by the groupwork leader. A multitude of perspectives on one simple image are shown to be possible and legitimate. The exercise encourages the group to develop their own perspective taking abilities, but it also requires each member to listen to and respect the differing perspectives of each other. The assumption is that in offering a practical demonstration in which the group have been personally involved, these important discussions and debates within offender treatment programmes will be easier to engage in. It is hard to persuade a violent offender that what happened during their particular offence might have relied on his or her misreading of the situation. Verbal challenges to the accuracy of the report offered by a client can simply be rebuffed. This exercise, however, gives a concrete example of how the same moment can be interpreted in many different ways by the group, and how therefore this must be possible in the far more complex images thrown up in everyday life. This exercise aims to spread doubt about what we think we have seen, and force us to take a second look.

EXERCISE 5: THREE IMAGES OF A STORY

The previous exercise involved creating an image out of the bodies of the participants. Exercise 5 extends this but now with the deliberate intention of creating images of moments, stories or incidents. The group are split into teams of three or four. They are then asked to create a frozen image using each other's bodies that shows a key moment relating to the topic they have been discussing. The exact instruction will depend on the focus of that particular group. If, for example, it was a car crime group, they might be asked to create an image of the moment of breaking into a car. If it were a drug users group, they might show an image of dealing drugs or committing a robbery to obtain money. However, the image does not have to be crime focused. It might be necessary to show an image of a couple in mid-argument or a domestic scene between a young person and their parent. The first image that the group create will simply be a central moment that indicates a problem, dilemma or crisis situation related to the groupwork theme.

All members of the group should be in the image, it should be presented completely still and they should be given only a few minutes to complete it. Once all groups are ready, each one is shown and read, much like the "What's the story?" exercise above. The group leader will encourage multiple readings and direct the focus of the group to follow the objectives of the session. If the groupwork is particularly concerned with victim empathy and there is a victim portrayed in the image, the leader can ask questions specifically about his or her situation: "What are they feeling?", "What will they do after this moment?". The image should be a springboard for enquiry into areas that are not normally witnessed or thought about by a group.

After a thorough reading of each image, the leader instructs the groups to create two more scenes relating to the first one. Exactly what these scenes are to represent depends on the issues and images that have already been demonstrated. The instructions should, however, direct the group into places that are unfamiliar. So, for example, one group might be asked to present two images that happened before the image they created that show how and why the moment occurred. Another group might be asked to create two images from the perspective of one particular character in the first image that show what happened in his or her future. Another group might be asked to show one real consequence of the moment and one ideal.

Each instruction aims to develop the narrative of the original scene, focusing on areas that are important for the groupwork and the issues that are being discussed.

Finally, each group presents their three images in chronological order. So one might present their two new images from the past and then end with their original. Another group might start with their original and then show the next two images of a particular future. Each image series can be shown a number of times to allow the audience proper space to look closely and read what they think is happening. Once all readings have taken place, a group can discuss what they were trying to portray. The differences between the readings and the actual intentions can then be discussed.

The Experience: Salford Anger Management

This exercise was used as part of a court-ordered anger management programme for violent offenders in Salford, Greater Manchester. The group were asked to create an image of the moment of violence. There were only seven men so this was done in one group of three and one group of four. One member of staff worked with each group. Very quickly they decided on basic elements of setting, situation and the characters involved. They had been using images in all sessions of this programme and were therefore familiar with this technique.

The group of four showed an image of two men with two more looking on. One man was holding the neck of the other, while he reached for some kind of object behind him. The man whose neck was being held appeared to be backed against a wall. The two onlookers were rising up out of their seats. The group watching this scene immediately read it as a pub. They disagreed about what the man was reaching for, however. One said a pool cue, another said a glass and the other said he was not reaching but about to swing his fist. The group leader asked what the man was thinking at that moment. The group very quickly offered a list of expletives and feelings linked to anger. The direction was then turned towards the man against the wall: "What was he thinking?". The group had different opinions. One said that it was pure fear, another said it was violent resentment and desire for revenge. The focus was also shifted to the onlookers, and their impressions and thoughts on the incident were asked for. Finally, the group presenting the image were asked to return and create new images that represented two moments that led up to this incident.

The next group presented an image of a man standing leaning over to slap a seated woman (played by a probation officer), while another client was on the floor with his head in his hands. The third client was not in the image, and sat out. The group read the scene and then the group leader directed their attention to the character on the floor. It was agreed that this was a child. A discussion quickly developed about the child's thoughts and feeling at this moment. Then the focus was directed to the woman. The group were asked to suggest what she was thinking at this moment. At this stage, the exercise was changed slightly. The woman probation officer was asked to take up the position of the man, and the man doing the slapping was asked to be the woman in the chair. They were then asked to express what they thought the characters were feeling. Once all comments from those observing this image were taken, this group was asked to create two images of the future, one that represented the future for the child, and one for the future of the woman.

Each group then presented their three images in sequence. The first group showed a man apparently knocking into another, then an image of one remonstrating with the person who had stumbled, and then finally the original image of the man with his hands around the neck of the other. The focus of the questioning was to examine what thoughts had gone through the head of the attacker from the moment he was knocked until the point where he grabs. The group came up with a list of different interpretations that he had made, which justified how he behaved. They also questioned the amount of alcohol he had drunk. The thoughts of the man doing the knocking in the first scene were also discussed. This showed that he could have stumbled into the assailant in an act of deliberate provocation or completely innocently. The possibility of each made it easy to point out the inappropriateness of the violent response.

The next group showed one image of a woman holding a bag and opening a door and a second image of the person who originally played the child in a still moment of hitting the participant who had not taken part in the original image. The group were very clear about the scene with the woman. She was leaving and taking the child with her. The group debated how this would affect the man, and how likely it was that it could happen. They were less clear about the third image, however. Several different opinions were suggested. The most persuasive was that this was the child several years later beating up someone else. This led to an intense debate about the relation between violent upbringings and violent futures.

The Assumptions and Questions

This exercise works with many of the assumptions already outlined for the "What's the Story?" exercise. Its premise is that the presence of three-dimensional cases in the groupwork room will make issue debate easier. There is material to reflect upon which does not require the group leader to ask the client to speak only from their personal experience. The clients' experiences are portrayed in the images that they create, or are projected onto the images that they observe. The leader uses these reflections to direct the discussion. This provides a less threatening and more concrete way for the opinions and justifications of groups members to be explored or challenged.

The second important assumption behind this exercise is that people create very strict narratives to explain their actions and their lives. With many client groups these narratives are extremely fixed and will rarely have any central character other than the offender themselves. One point of this exercise is to shift the narrative with which the group are familiar to focus on new central characters. The women, the victims, the children and the onlookers thus become the major focus. This encourages the group to examine another person's story or perspective. In addition, people's narratives have very clear cause and effect chains, and this exercise seeks to disturb the beliefs behind these certainties. It asks for several possible futures; it asks for reasons why things happened. It plays with time, and permits a group to explore possibilities rather than assume that results are inevitable.

Linked to this desire to play with narrative structure is the assumption that in creating still images, a pause will be allowed in a process that is usually very fast. The stillness allows the group leader to explore the thinking in a moment, when often the client will insist that it "just happened". This exercise allows thoughts to be placed at each moment, and different thoughts to be suggested. The exercise can be developed to show how an alternative thought at a particular still moment could lead to a different image afterwards. It is thus a visual demonstration of the idea of offenders stopping and thinking before they act. A role-play in real time, particularly of violence, can lead to purely affective responses. At worst, role-plays can lead to a heightened pleasure from the recreation of emotional moments. This acts to reinforce behaviour rather than challenge it. The use of still images ensures that it is the thinking of characters that is central to the session. It is also an important principle of this work that people shift between roles in any use of theatre in group work. An over-identification with a certain negative role in a session can do as much to maintain behaviours as any exercise can do to challenge them.

EXERCISE 6: SMALL SCENES

This exercise would be done only after the group have done a considerable amount of work using the still image type exercises outlined above. It is assumed that the group have been working on a particular incident or crime, and this next exercise is further exploration of that moment. The group are asked to consider up to four incidents in the life of an offender prior to the crime that they have been discussing. This "offender" is not a real member of the group but a fictional person who has committed a crime that is similar to those committed by a number of people present. The four incidents are, for example, one hour, one day, one week and one month before the actual offence. These moments cannot be general (he or she was unemployed) but must be specific incidents (he or she goes to a job interview). Volunteers are asked to role-play each of these scenes and the audience give them their opening lines. This time, however, they continue the scene, demonstrating what it was at that moment that propelled the central character to commit the offence.

Once the scenes have been acted, the group are then asked to return to the first scene that they created. Those that performed it the first time are asked to repeat it exactly as they did before. The audience, however, now has the task of trying to prevent their character from reaching the moment of the crime. They must try to stop the scene before it is too late. If they have an idea for what their central character could have done that would have prevented them committing the crime later they shout stop, and then replace the central character. They then have to continue the scene but this time trying to do it in such a way that the outcome is changed. The scene can be repeated several times, so that different options and interventions are tried. Eventually all the four scenes are revisited in this way so that a variety of alternative strategies have been suggested and practised. It is vital that an audience member does not shout out their idea from the luxury of their seat. If they have a suggestion for changing the direction of a scene, they must be encouraged to try it out. It is easy to talk about doing something; trying it is always much harder. Finally, the alternatives that have been attempted are discussed and related to the real lives of the participants.

The Experience: Manchester Bail Hostel

This exercise was done as part of a life skills course for a mixed male and female group in a Manchester Probation Bail Hostel. The crime that the group had been concentrating on was a case of cheque book fraud by a fictional young women client. They were asked to create several scenes of the moments that led up to this offence. There were three suggestions. The first was that the previous day her boyfriend had brought her a stolen cheque book and credit card and persuaded her to take them. The second was that a week before a loan shark had arrived at the door and given her an ultimatum about the payment of a debt. The final suggestion was that about six months previously she had accompanied her friend on a shopping trip when her friend had successfully used a stolen card. Each of these moments was acted out. A particularly enthusiastic participant played the central character and three other participants played the boyfriend, loan shark and friend.

The first scene that was examined again was the one in which the boyfriend appeared with the stolen cheque book and card. The scene was repeated and a chorus of "stops" were offered almost as soon as the boyfriend's knock on the door was heard. The first person let the boyfriend in but when he showed her the stolen cheque book, she very clearly told him to leave. To much amusement from the group, she physically removed him from her "house". The strategy was debated and the degree to which it was positive or possible was discussed. The next intervention was less physical. This person tried to argue with the boyfriend, that if he really cared for her he would be bringing money, not stolen goods. The group liked this, but some thought that she would be too intimidated by him to speak that freely. The third intervention was done by a man. His tactic was simple. He did not answer the door. He sat there silently and did not respond to the knocks. While the group felt that perhaps this was unrealistic in the circumstances, it was agreed that at times ignoring, blanking or simply avoiding situations is a suitable or appropriate way out.

The Assumptions and Questions

The first assumption that this exercise makes is that fictional stories are a useful way of developing inclusive groupwork discussions. While the real offences of a group will at times be vital material for any offending behaviour course, by creating a relevant fictional structure you can create a point of reference to which all have an equal relationship. It allows group members to take up the position of commentator and reflector, and means that they are able to talk without having to directly justify. The fictional account will also allow a point of comparison between their lives and that of another. It will allow them to suggest changes in behaviour. The group leader can make very critical judgements of the behaviour of a fictional character which, while implicating the participants, might not alienate them in the same way that a direct personal confrontation would.

This exercise's primary use, however, is as an active method for eliciting strategies for change and then practising them. It presents a problem or dilemma that questions the group's problem solving abilities. It asks them what they would or could do in similar circumstances. However, rather than remaining in the realm of discussion, it insists that the participants actually try out these alternatives. This exercise is thus a form of behaviour rehearsal that rather than encouraging the group to practise one form of ideal behavioural response, asks them instead to search physically for different solutions. As with all the exercises presented here, this technique assumes that by trying out a strategy physically a person will learn more than by simply speaking about it.

CONCLUSION

This chapter has outlined a range of different theatre-based exercises which, I have argued, have certain motivational characteristics. It has examined core components of a "drama workshop" that if adapted and carefully implemented can become valuable tools for a probation or prison groupwork team. Many techniques like these already form a regular part of groupwork programmes. However, there are many programmes that use very few interactive or participatory approaches. The task is to convince staff and programme designers that these exercises are not only accessible to the clients but also easily used by group workers.

While I make no apologies that this account has been based on a series of anecdotes, I would argue that these exercises do correspond with research into programme effectiveness. The assumptions are based on both experience and the guides to good practice that can be found in the literature (see, for example, Chapman & Hough, 1998; Goldstein & Glick, 1994; Harland, 1996; Hollin, 1990; McGuire, 1995; Rose, 1998). There has been direct evaluation of theatre-based programmes (Chandler, 1973), but this type of study has been less influential in developing the work than the reports from group workers who have used the techniques within existing programmes. Their accounts of how theatre techniques have been beneficial in supporting existing groupwork objectives have inspired service managers to develop further training in and use of these approaches. This means that in several groupwork programmes participatory theatre exercises have become a core and standard teaching method, not an extra session in need of separate evaluation or justification. This chapter aims to be part of a debate that encourages these developments. It is in a sense the elaboration of a hypothesis on which further serious and credible evaluation needs to be built.

REFERENCES

Chandler, M. (1973). Egocentrism and antisocial behavior: the assessment and training of social perspective taking skills. *Developmental Psychology*, **44**, 326–33.
Chapman, T. & Hough, M. (1998). *Evidence Based Practice*. London: HMIP, HMSO.
Harland, A.T. (ed.) (1996). *Choosing Correctional Options that Work*. London: Sage.
Goldstein, A. & Glick, B. (1994). *The Pro-Social Gang: Implementing Aggression Replacement Training*. Thousand Oaks, CA: Sage

Hollin, C.R. (1990). *Cognitive-Behavioural Interventions with Young Offenders*. New York: Pergamon Press

Jennings, S. (ed.) (1987). *Dramatherapy, Theory and Practice for Teachers and Clinicians*, vol. 1. London: Routledge.

McGuire, J. (ed.) (1995). *What Works: Reducing Reoffending*. Chichester: Wiley.

Moreno, J.L. (1983). *The Theatre of Spontaneity*. New York: Beacon House.

Rose, S. (1998). *Group Therapy with Troubled Youth: A Cognitive-Behavioural Interactive Approach*. London: Sage.

Thompson, J. (1999). *Drama Workshops for Anger Management and Offending Behaviour*. London: Jessica Kingsley.

Thompson, J. (1996). Blagg! Rehearsing for change. *Probation Journal*, December, 190–4.

Chapter 8

MAINTAINING MOTIVATION FOR CHANGE USING RESOURCES AVAILABLE IN AN OFFENDER'S NATURAL ENVIRONMENT*

GLENN D. WALTERS

Federal Correctional Institution-Schuylkill, Pennsylvania, USA

One of the more widely accepted "facts" in the field of criminology is the robust relationship that surfaces when past criminal conduct and future criminal outcomes are compared. In a review of 16 studies addressing the early aggression/later criminality hypothesis, Olweus (1979) calculated a mean correlation of 0.68 between early childhood aggression and subsequent criminality. Recidivism data also show that one of the best predictors of future criminality is the severity and frequency of past criminality (Gendreau et al., 1996). However, there is little consensus and a great deal of debate over how this relationship should be interpreted. Criminologists adopting an epiphenomenal perspective on the early–later criminality connection allege that early and later criminality are linked by a common association with one or more "third" variables; two of the more popular candidate "third" variables in this regard are low self-control (Gottfredson & Hirschi, 1990) and a genetically-based set of personality traits (Wilson & Herrnstein, 1985). Termed the population heterogeneity position because a certain portion of the population is seen as crime-prone, this perspective emphasizes the stability and continuity of criminal behavior over time.

A second group of theoreticians contend that early criminality is causally connected to later criminality by virtue of the fact that early delinquency expands opportunities for future criminal involvement while reducing opportunities for participation in non-criminal activities and relationships. Proponents of this model,

---

* The assertions and opinions contained herein are the private views of the author and should not be construed as official or as reflecting the views of the Federal Bureau of Prisons or United States Department of Justice. Correspondence concerning this chapter should be directed to Glenn D. Walters, Psychology Services, Federal Correctional Institution-Schuylkill, P.O. Box 700, Minersville, PA 17954–0700, USA.

Motivating Offenders to Change: A Guide to Enhancing Engagement in Therapy. Edited by M. McMurran.
© 2002 John Wiley & Sons, Ltd.

coined the state-dependent perspective on the early–later criminality association, maintain that crime trajectories are sensitive to outside influences and that crime is a dynamic process (Loeber & LeBlanc, 1990; Laub & Sampson, 1993). In stark contrast to the population heterogeneity model, which argues for continuity in crime trajectories, advocates of the state-dependent position emphasize change and transition. Other theoreticians have taken a third or intermediate position by proposing a typology of trajectories. The two most popular crime typologies are Moffitt's (1993) persistent- and adolescent-limited approach and Patterson's (1993) early- and late-starter dichotomy.

Paternoster and colleagues (1997) tested all three models in a group of 838 young adults 4–6 years after their release from the North Carolina Division of Youth Services. The results of this study drafted modest support for both the population heterogeneity and state-dependent positions but failed to confirm the typological approach, leading the authors to conclude that both continuity and change contribute to the early–later criminality correlation. Although support for the population heterogeneity model can be found in other studies as well (Hirschi & Gottfredson, 1995), the state-dependent view that life circumstances significantly influence criminal conduct cannot be denied. Research indicates that changes in drug use patterns (Horney et al., 1995), employment (Farrington et al., 1986), family constellation (Mednick et al., 1990), marital adjustment (Laub et al., 1998), peer relations (Ullman & Newcomb, 1999), and place of residence (Osborn, 1980) can exert a profound effect on future criminal outcomes independent of measurable individual differences in criminal propensity.

Developmental events are of cardinal significance in initiating, maintaining, and terminating criminal involvement according to proponents of the state-dependent perspective. Embedded within the developmental trajectories of a person's life are transitions that stimulate change in criminal conduct and other patterns. The well-documented relationship between age and crime (Hirschi & Gottfredson, 1983) may, in fact, be a function of these life transitions. Crucial transitional events like marriage and childbirth (Gove, 1985) as well as age- and experience-relevant changes that invite a re-evaluation of life goals and growing dissatisfaction with the natural consequences of the criminal lifestyle (Shover & Thompson, 1992) imbue the accounts of people who have desisted from crime on their own. The purpose of this chapter is to illustrate how the natural environment can be used to motivate a transition in criminal trajectories leading to long-term maintenance of crime desistance. It therefore makes sense to begin with a brief review of research on people who have desisted from crime without the services of a mental health professional or formal treatment program.

NATURAL DESISTANCE FROM CRIME

Walters (2000c), in a review of the literature on natural recovery from substance abuse, places the prevalence of self-remission from alcohol, tobacco, and illicit drug abuse at 26.2% when a broad definition of recovery is employed and 18.2% when a narrow definition of recovery is utilized in follow-ups averaging 5.3 years. Besides noting the predominance of natural recovery over treatment-assisted change, Walters also comments that recovery is frequently initiated by personal crises (health concerns, pressure from family and friends, extraordinary events) and maintained by social support, willpower, and identity transformation. While there are no data currently available with which to calculate the overall rate of natural desistance from crime, studies show that recidivism in offenders released from state prison stands at two-thirds after three years (Beck & Shipley, 1989). What is sometimes overlooked is that many of those who avoid reincarceration within three years are never reincarcerated, a feat normally accomplished without professional assistance (Walters, 1992). It may well be that natural desistance from crime is as common as natural recovery from substance abuse.

In an effort to identify, catalogue, and decipher the factors responsible for natural desistance from crime, John Irwin (1970), a former convict himself, interviewed 15 individuals with extensive histories of criminal involvement who had been crime-free for a number of years. The reasons given by these individuals for desisting from crime touched on both the initiation—fear of future incarceration, reduction in sexual and financial expectations—and maintenance—development of a satisfying relationship with a woman, regular involvement in extravocational and extradomestic activities like sports and hobbies—phases of desistance. The initiation–maintenance breakdown has also been employed by other investigators looking to solve the natural desistance from crime conundrum.

Sommers and colleagues (1994) discovered that the decision to change in 30 criminally involved adult females was preceded by a sense of despair ignited by the natural consequences of criminal activity. These women used their despair to temporarily arrest the lifestyle and begin questioning their criminally oriented views of themselves and the world. Mulvey and La Rosa (1986) observed a similar pattern in a group of 10 male juvenile offenders who had been crime-free for at least two years. Like the women in the Sommers et al. (1994) investigation, 9 out of 10 adolescents made a conscious decision to desist from crime and lead a better life. It would seem that the decision to change, rather than being a single transition, is actually a series of transitions in a criminal trajectory that gradually culminate in desistance. The role of the decision-making process in many of these individuals' eventual desistance from crime suggests that a change in cognition often predates a change in behavior.

Crises leading to despair include the shock of seeing a crime partner killed or coming close to death oneself (Cusson & Pinsonneault, 1986), the cumulative effects of aging (Sommers et al., 1994), a growing fear of incarceration (Hughes, 1998), and the perception that one's criminal life has been unsuccessful (Jolin & Gibbons, 1987). However, positive events and experiences can also serve as crises, e.g. a growing respect and concern for children (Hughes, 1998), the desire to do something productive with one's life (Shover, 1996), and the assumption of adult responsibilities in the form of marriage or an occupation (Jolin & Gibbons, 1987). Desistance was also initiated by a change in expectancies, which research shows are potent mediators of crime (McMurran, 1997), to the extent that desistance is often accompanied by a reduction in the perceived benefits of crime (Hughes, 1998) and a corresponding increase in the anticipated costs of crime (Cusson & Pinsonneault, 1986).

Once initiated, change must be reinforced and maintained to continue. In research on natural desistance from crime there is evidence that disassociating oneself from those who remain in the criminal lifestyle and constructing a non-criminal social group are critical in maintaining initial desistance from crime (Adler, 1993; Mulvey & La Rosa, 1986; Sommers et al., 1994). A sense of connection to the conventional social order helped participants in the Sommers et al. (1994) study maintain their new way of life by giving them a stake in conformity. A change in identity or self-view was observed not only in this study but in several other investigations on self-desistance from crime as well (Hughes, 1998; Shover, 1996). Affirmation of one's identity as a non-criminal by respected non-criminals in the community may also be of central significance in maintaining desistance from crime (Meisenhelder, 1977; Sommers et al., 1994). These various outcomes suggest that the initiation and maintenance of criminal desistance can be as protracted and complex as the initiation and maintenance of the criminal involvements from which one is attempting to desist.

A WORD ABOUT MOTIVATION

Therapists affiliated with traditional schools of psychotherapy often assume that difficult clients—in other words, clients who do not go along with the prescribed intervention—are unmotivated for change. Such resistance is then used to justify termination of a therapeutic relationship the clinician finds unpleasant. From the standpoint of the model on which the present chapter is based, however, motivation is an interactive construct that has as much to do with the helper and the client–helper relationship as it does the client. Motivation, according to this model, is a complex and dynamic process that interacts on several planes. It may therefore be more accurate to say that "difficult" clients are often ambivalent about change because of conflicting motivations. The nature of these conflicting motivations is the topic of discussion in this section and is grounded in Walters' (1990, 2000b) belief that crime can be understood as a lifestyle.

According to lifestyle theory, all living organisms possess a life or survival instinct. This life instinct is believed to interact with a constantly changing environment to create a condition of apprehension and threat known as existential fear (Walters, 1999c). There are two general classes of reaction to existential fear: defensive, in the form of withdrawal, aggression, immobilization, and appeasement/submission (Marks, 1987), and constructive, in the form of affiliation, control/predictability, and status (Walters, 1999c). The dualistic nature of threat reactions mirrors the dualism found in motivation (approach/avoid novel and familiar stimuli) and outcome (change/continuity). Because a lifestyle is grounded in defensive strategies, novelty avoidance, and continuity, an effective program of assisted change must emphasize constructive strategies, the value of approaching novelty, and the necessity, possibility, and efficacy of change toward an eventual goal of achieving dynamic balance.

By virtue of being an open system the human organism actively exchanges energy with its environment. This process, commonly referred to as self-organization (Walters, 1999b), fosters organismic growth and complexity because the forms created through self-organization are more complex than the ones they replace. In addition, continuity makes one's life more orderly and stable. The balancing of these two opposing outcomes, continuity and change, and their corollary motivational states—novelty-avoidance and novelty-approach, respectively—is the essence of adaptive living. When one of these two opposing motivation–outcome composites predominates problems arise. In the case of continuity/novelty-avoidance the result is stagnation; in the case of change/novelty-approach the upshot is psychological chaos. Given the role of continuity/novelty-avoidance in maintaining a lifestyle, a balance can most easily be struck by advocating the change/novelty-approach conglomerate through self-organization.

MOTIVATING CLIENTS TO MAINTAIN CHANGE

Formal intervention is neither a necessary nor a sufficient condition for change. In fact, as the results reviewed in an earlier section of this chapter imply, natural desistance is probably more common than professionally assisted change. For this reason, formal or professional efforts to facilitate natural desistance can be made more efficient by considering the reports of those who have desisted without professional help. The present discussion construes crime as a lifestyle characterized by four principal styles of interaction (Table 8.1). Although everyone engages in these four interactive styles from time to time, the criminal lifestyle is marked by regular and habitual enactment of each style. Accordingly, the criminal lifestyle is conceptualized as a relative construct that falls along a continuum rather than an absolute construct that forms a pure dichotomy. The human capacity for change or self-organization, on the other hand, is viewed to be a natural consequence of our status as open systems capable of exchanging energy with the external environment.

A criminal lifestyle is defined by the interactive styles a person pursues. However, belief systems are what drive a lifestyle. The self- and world-views are two particularly important belief systems with respect to explaining the continuity and change of delinquency and adult criminal conduct. Those who desist from crime typically do so by altering one or both of these belief systems. It is important to understand that lifestyles evolve in phases, initiation followed by maintenance (Walters, 1998). During lifestyle initiation the novice is socialized into the lifestyle through actual or symbolic interaction with those already involved in the pattern. The socialization

Table 8.1   Interactive styles observed in a criminal lifestyle

Interactive style	Definition
Irresponsibility	Poor accountability and a general unwillingness to meet personal obligations to self and others
Self-indulgence	Pursuit of immediate gratification irrespective of the negative long-term consequences
Interpersonal intrusiveness	Violation of other people's rights, privacy, dignity or personal space
Social rule breaking	Unwillingness to abide by the rules of society and specific authority figures (e.g. parents, teachers, work supervisors)

process fosters change in a person's self- and world-views, changes that are reinforced and preserved during the maintenance phase. Desistance also creates change in a person's belief systems through resocialization, a process that includes both an initiation and maintenance phase. Although both the initiation and maintenance of desistance are important topics of discussion, the present section will restrict itself to the subject of providing helpers with suggestions on how to motivate clients to maintenance desistance by changing their involvements, commitments, and identifications.

Changing Involvements

Involvements are the activities people prefer and the social groups with whom they interact. A change in involvements is frequently cited as pivotal in promoting change maintenance in persons desisting from crime without professional assistance (Adler, 1993; Hughes, 1998; Irwin, 1970; Jolin & Gibbons, 1987; Sommers et al., 1994). Substitution and the construction of social support networks are two ways clients can maintain desistance from crime by altering their involvements.

Substitution

One of the attractions of a criminal lifestyle is that it helps structure people's time, which, in turn, minimizes the decisions people must make and their perceived responsibility for these decisions. A lifestyle also makes life more predictable, giving the individual a greater sense of control over his or her environment. Time structuring and predictability are key linchpins of lifestyle maintenance (Walters, 1999c). Criminal involvements center around preparing, planning, and committing crimes, celebrating after a successful crime, hanging out with other criminals, and justifying one's criminal activity by resorting to various cognitive maneuvers and distortions such as the ones outlined in Table 8.2. Eliminating criminal involvements in someone committed to a criminal lifestyle will typically create a void that the person will undoubtedly fill with whatever was there before (criminal lifestyle) if a suitable substitute is not found. The goal of substitution is to motivate change maintenance by assisting the client with the development of non-criminal alternative involvements in work, school, family, sports, hobbies, and other interests.

Effective facilitation of the substitution process takes place in three steps or stages. The first step of the substitution process is to identify the wants and aspirations being met by the criminal lifestyle. This can be accomplished by having clients list the experiences and outcomes they believe they would miss were they to completely disassociate themselves from a criminal lifestyle. Once a list of missed experiences and outcomes has been assembled the next step is to identify alternative activities designed to achieve these experiences and outcomes in ways that do not bring the person into conflict with the law. The third and final step of the substitution process is to encourage implementation of these alternative activities. By contracting with clients to engage in a specified number of substitute activities according to a predetermined schedule the helper can motivate the client to achieve effective substitution.

Table 8.2 Definitions and examples of the eight thinking styles that support a criminal lifestyle

Thinking style	Definition	Example
Mollification	Justifying and rationalizing one's actions based on a consideration of external circumstances	"If I hadn't grown up in a poor home then I wouldn't have been forced into a life of crime."
Cutoff	Rapid elimination of common deterrents to crime	"Damn it, if they want something to get worked up over I'll give it to them."
Entitlement	Sense of ownership or privilege; misidentification of wants as needs	"They kept me locked up for six years, now I'm going to get mine. After all, they owe me."
Power orientation	Exerting power and control over other people, the nonsocial environment, or one's own mood	"Give me the money or I'll blow your freaken head off!"
Sentimentality	Seeking to minimize the negative repercussions of a criminal lifestyle by performing various good deeds	"I may be a drug dealer but I'm also a nice guy; I make it a point to give a young fella a dollar or two each time I return to the old neighborhood in my new Mercedes."
Superoptimism	Deceiving oneself into believing that the negative consequences of a criminal lifestyle can somehow be indefinitely postponed	"There's no way the police are going to catch me, because I'm too smart and they're too stupid."
Cognitive indolence	Lazy, uncritical thinking marked by shortcuts and a lack of critical reasoning	"It makes no sense working for a paycheck when I can can get everything I want from burglarizing homes."
Discontinuity	Lack of consistency or congruence in one's thinking over time; can give rise to a "Jekyll and Hyde" persona	"Each time I leave prison I start out with the best of intentions but within several weeks I am right back into the 'game,' as if I'd never even gone to prison."

Note: The reader should consult Walters (1990, 1998) for more information on these thinking styles.

Social support networks

Social support was found to be a powerful predictor of future substance abuse and criminal outcomes in questionnaires completed by 210 young licit and illicit drug users (Hammersley et al., 1990). However, social support can be a double-edged sword with the power to either maintain change or stimulate relapse. If the source of one's social support is a criminal associate or gang then the support is likely to lead back to a criminal lifestyle. Enabling an offender's antisocial behavior by providing a buffer between the offender and the natural consequences of his or her criminal involvement illustrates how family members, friends, and even mental health professionals, particularly those who offer clients responsibility-easing excuses—often in the form of a psychiatric diagnosis or attribution of disease—for their rule-violating actions and decisions, can encourage criminal relapse. Helpers can best assist their clients by supplying them with the skills that will help them steer clear of relapse-promoting relationships, even if this means avoiding family members who may be involved in illegal activities or who, through enabling, shield a client from the negative consequences of his or her actions.

Positive social support can be incorporated into a client's social network by encouraging clients to surround themselves with people who make them feel good about leading a law-abiding life. The helper can assist clients with the construction of a positive social support group by furnishing them with social skills training and sage advice. Social skills training supplies clients with interactive skills that expand their options in social situations. Clients must seek out and develop noncriminal friendships with the understanding that gaining other people's trust will take time and that they must be patient and prepare themselves for periodic setbacks. Helpers can further motivate change maintenance in currently desisting clients by providing them with advice on how to meet people. Work is often a good place to start in developing a positive social support network, but there are a number of other settings where friendships can be initiated and nurtured, from church, to community groups for singles or parents without partners, to social clubs and bars, assuming, of course, that the bar is not frequented by antisocial types or the client is not trying to overcome a drinking problem in addition to a crime problem.

Changing Commitments

Commitments are the goals and values that guide a person's decisions. Altered commitments have been observed in a number of individuals who have desisted from crime without benefit of professional treatment (Cusson & Pinsonneault, 1986; Jolin & Gibbons, 1987; Mulvey & La Rosa, 1986; Shover, 1983). Helpers can assist clients in maintaining change by focusing on two primary avenues of commitment generation and motivation: goals and values.

Expectancies and goals

Outcome expectancies, in the handful of studies that have explored this issue, appear to play a principal role in initiating and maintaining criminal conduct (McMurran, 1997; Slaby & Guerra, 1988). In a recent study on outcome expectancies and crime, Walters (2000a) uncovered a complex relationship between expectancies for crime and existential fear that may explain why expectancies exert such a powerful influence on a person's actions and decisions. A criminal lifestyle, in addition to structuring a person's time, promises relief from fear, but as many long-term convicts can attest, the promise is empty. Ultimately the person grows increasingly dependent on the lifestyle to cope with the problems of everyday living and the fear engendered by changes that threaten the lifestyle's existence. The paradox that a lifestyle presents is that people begin to place greater value on continuing the pattern than on protecting their own safety and well-being because they equate survival of the lifestyle with survival of the self (Walters, 1999c). This may be why people who demonstrate commitment to a criminal lifestyle are willing to risk their lives and freedom for the opportunity to participate in lifestyle activities.

Trained helpers can motivate clients to maintain initial desistance from crime by assisting them in the modification of crime-related outcome expectancies. Anecdotal evidence from the author's own clinical work with adult offenders insinuates that increased appreciation and anticipation of the long-term negative consequences of crime often accompany change. Positive outcome expectancies for crime, on the other hand, often do not change as a result of effective programming. This observation is corroborated by empirical research on assisted recovery from alcohol abuse (Jones & McMahon, 1994) and aggressive behavior (McDougall & Boddis, 1991). A review of life lessons with clients, where the natural negative consequences of criminal activity and thinking are identified, outlined, and defined, is a strategy capable of raising the salience of negative outcome expectancies for crime in the minds of those expressing an interest in change. An additional tactic for motivating change maintenance vis-à-vis expectancies and goals is to engage clients in discussions designed to highlight the benefits of non-crime and intensify positive outcome expectancies for such activities given the fact that dismissing the positive aspects of conventional life is one way people maintain a criminal lifestyle.

Values and priorities

Values are the general standards people follow in evaluating the significance of sundry life events. Priorities are behavioral manifestations of these values. Lifestyle theory proposes four general value clusters: social (value of interpersonal interaction), work (value of energy output, exertion, and performance), visceral (value of immediate experience), and intellectual (value of knowledge and understanding). It is argued that no single cluster is more important than the other three and that the intent of an adaptive response is to dynamically balance all four clusters so that a person's decisions can have equal access to all four classes of value. The criminal lifestyle, by contrast, is dominated by visceral values because of its emphasis on immediate gratification, which then increases value system imbalance (Walters, 1998). The goal of maintenance phase desistance is not the elimination of visceral values but the realization of balance between the four value clusters.

Trained helpers can assist clients in maintaining change by asking them to demarcate and clarify their value commitments. It does not take long for a criminal lifestyle to rearrange a person's priorities in life because the short-term hedonistic value of criminal outcomes has a tendency to constrict a person's time horizon (Wilson & Herrnstein, 1985) so that short-term gain is pursued with little apparent regard for the long-term negative consequences of one's actions. Clinicians can help clients balance their goals by encouraging them to consider both the short- and long-term ramifications of their actions. Values can be balanced in a similar manner by having the individual compare his or her values in life (e.g. social or work values in which family relations and career aspirations are highlighted) with what he or she has actually achieved (e.g. in and out of prison, hospitalization, loss of family or job). Using a procedure such as value clarification clients can begin the process of reconstructing their belief systems through reconciliation of the discrepancies that exist between their stated values and what they have actually accomplished in life. In situations where a criminal lifestyle surfaces at such an early age that it interferes with development of a client's value skills, a more intensive program of assisted change may be necessary (see Walters, 1998).

Changing Identifications

Identifications are the attributes, roles, and experiences a person employs in constructing his or her self-view. Of those who desist from crime without formal assistance, a change in identity is often cited as instrumental in maintaining desistance (Fagan, 1989; Meisenhelder, 1977; Shover, 1996; Sommers et al., 1994). There are two primary pathways by which helpers motivate change maintenance in their clients' identifications: encouraging clients to resist labels and helping them transform their identities.

Resisting labels

Labeling is an everyday occurrence. In fact, labeling allows us to organize our experience into manageable units so that we are in a position to comprehend and act on our world. Problems arise, however, when people become the target of our labeling efforts. Labeling people robs them of their individuality and humanity because people are too complex to be summed up in a single word, phrase, or diagnosis. If the individual accepts the label as valid, then the overgeneralized thinking upon which this label is based will restrict the person's options in life to where the label can actually become a self-fulfilling prophecy (Walters, 1999a). Research indicates that resilience in high-risk children corresponds with increased confidence and cognitive complexity, both of which can be used to combat the labels that are often thoughtlessly assigned to high-risk children (Garmezy, 1993). Confidence can be instilled by supplying clients with skills training and affording them the opportunity to successfully implement these skills (Bandura, 1997). Promoting increased cognitive complexity in clients is another way helpers can motivate change maintenance, and is a topic to which we now turn our attention.

Identity transformation

The search for an identity can lead to lifestyle initiation, which once established can act to maintain the lifestyle. An early study in which marijuana use increased in jurisdictions where the penalties for possession were more severe illustrates how the search for an identity might initiate a drug or criminal lifestyle (Stuart et al., 1976). The lifestyle maintaining features of a criminal identity are revealed in a study by Oyserman and Markus (1990), where it was ascertained that highly delinquent youth possess possible selves organized almost exclusively around crime and minimally around doing well in school, whereas less delinquent youth molded their possible selves around school, work, and relationships with non-deviant peers. The self, according to Gold (1994), is an active agentic process capable of conferring purpose, meaning, and direction in life. As such, identity plays as vital a role in crime desistance as it does in crime initiation and maintenance.

Identity transformation is of prime significance when it comes to motivating change maintenance, and, like substitution, can be broken down into three steps or stages. The first step of the identity transformation process is to encourage clients to reject all labels as descriptive of themselves since no single phrase, term, or epithet could possibly capture the complexity or uniqueness of the individual human being. Instead, clients should strive to see themselves as people who have had problems with crime in the past but who can choose to behave differently in the present and future. This is followed by the second step of the identity transformation process, in which the purpose is to broaden, incite, and intensify the client's cognitive complexity skills by playing devil's advocate, engaging the client in Socratic dialogues, and highlighting incongruencies between a client's observable conduct and stated self-view in order to create cognitive dissonance designed to stimulate the client's natural self-organization abilities. Integration of the emerging polarities and dualities that surface in a client's thinking during step two is the principal goal of step three. The dialectic method (thesis–antithesis–synthesis) is of critical importance in realizing the objectives of the third and final stage of the identity transformation process.

A CASE EXAMPLE

Mike is a 53-year-old white male who served $8\frac{1}{2}$ years of a 13-year sentence for possession of cocaine, with intent to distribute. His case was first presented in 1990 as part of a discussion on criminal development (Walters, 1990, pp. 187–8). The author first met Mike in 1988 when the latter enrolled in a criminal lifestyle class the author was holding for inmates in a maximum-security Federal penitentiary. Five years later Mike transferred to a medium-security institution where the author had relocated two years earlier. Between the two institutions Mike and the author had met in weekly individual or group sessions for a period of nearly four years and Mike completed all phases of the author's Lifestyle Change Program (Walters, 1999d). Although Mike was released from custody in 1995 he has kept in contact with the author through periodic telephone calls and letters.

Mike, being an individual of above-average intelligence who began his criminal career at relatively late age (32), appreciated the importance of staying away from old drug and criminal associates as a means of preventing relapse back to a criminal lifestyle. He indicated that he had met a woman while in prison through a religious organization, and while most such relationships tend to dissolve once the individual is released from prison, after 6 years Mike is still living with this woman and has adopted her two children. He attributes his new-found freedom and desistance from crime to the fact that he spends the majority of his time either at work or with his family and has found substitutes for crime in his work, participation in physical exercise, and interest in hobbies like ceramics and woodworking.

In terms of changing his commitments, Mike states that he began sacrificing immediate gratification for more long-term satisfaction while in prison and adds that he has maintained and further developed this change in commitment while in the community. Family activities and his business have replaced Mike's prior preoccupation with drugs and crime. Now, rather than distributing drugs he distributes newspapers to a growing number of retail customers across a large metropolitan area in the mid-Atlantic region of the United States. During one of their phone conversations, Mike shared with the author his belief that the "straight life really isn't all that bad once you get used to it." It would seem that by elevating the salience of positive outcome expectancies for non-criminal activity and boosting his negative outcome expectancies for drug use and crime, Mike has taken a gigantic step toward meaningful and lasting change.

One of the steepest hurdles Mike had to clear in resocializing himself to a new way of life was discarding his old criminal identity. It was clear from watching Mike interact with other inmates that he relished the opportunity to speak about his criminal exploits and the reputation he had created for himself in the community. By the same token, he understood that he had to abandon this identity and find a new way of viewing himself if he was to remain crime-free in the community. Mike advised that he found a new sense of purpose and identity in his roles as husband, father, health advocate, and businessman. He also was more willing to allow himself to fit into conventional society and was no longer obsessed with the idea of rebelling in order to bring attention to himself. The meaning and satisfaction he derived from his new-found identity as family man and honest worker were enough to keep him from reverting back to his old gangster self-image. To further maintain these changes and reinforce his new way of life, Mike will need to continue developing his sense of self through increased cognitive complexity.

CONCLUSION

In searching for ways to motivate clients to maintain lifestyle desistance our efforts are more apt to meet with success if we make use of natural resources available in a client's home environment than if we ignore the environment in which the client must function. It is imperative that we remain humble when discussing our helping skills and therapeutic "successes" for the sobering fact is that there is nothing a helper can do to match, let alone exceed, the power of the natural environment to impact and modify a person's actions. There is no doubt that helpers are in a position to provide clients with the opportunity to learn essential skills; however, clients must be able to make effective use of these skills in real-life situations if the helper's efforts are to bear fruit. It should also be pointed out that successful application of these skills encourages growth beyond the client–helper relationship to realization of the ultimate goal of assisted change—namely, self-reliance. A helper operating out of the present framework is working towards his or her eventual obsolescence, if not for all clients, then for clients with whom he or she interacts as a means of stimulating the natural self-organization process that motivates change initiation and maintenance in people previously committed to a criminal lifestyle.

Helpers can facilitate the self-organization process believed to exist in all living beings by furnishing clients with information on how to maintain and facilitate the natural change process. Lifestyle theory proposes four key elements of self-organization—responsibility, meaning, community, and confidence—that not only initiate change but maintain it as well (Walters, 2000b). By keeping these four elements clearly in mind and using them as criteria against which one's actions and decisions can be assessed for adaptability, the client has in his or her possession a skill that can be of great practical assistance in managing the problems of everyday life. It is critical, nevertheless, that a client appreciate the perpetual nature of the change process and understand that transitions and new trajectories are as vital to change maintenance as is continuity. Before the client–helper relationship is terminated and the client and helper move on to bigger and better things, the client should be advised to remain vigilant in the face of adversity for today's adaptation can become tomorrow's lifestyle if one comes to depend on the pattern to manage problems in living. After all, every lifestyle, long before becoming a pattern, began as an adaptation.

REFERENCES

Adler, P. (1993). *Wheeling and Dealing: An Ethnography of an Upper-Level Drug Dealing and Smuggling Community*, (2nd edn). New York: Columbia University Press.

Bandura, A. (1997). *Self-Efficacy*. New York: Freeman.

Beck, A. J., & Shipley, B. E. (1989). Recidivism of prisoners released in 1983. *Bureau of Justice Statistics Special Report* (NCJ-116261). Washington, DC: Bureau of Justice Statistics.

Cusson, M., & Pinsonneault, H. P. (1986). The decision to give up crime. In D. B. Cornish & R. V. Clarke (eds) *The Reasoning Criminal: Rational Choice Perspectives on Offending* (pp. 72–82). New York: Springer-Verlag.

Fagan, J. (1989). Cessation of family violence: deterrence and dissuasion. In L. Ohlin & M. Tonry (eds) *Family Violence. Crime and Justice: A Review of Research*, vol. 11 (pp. 377–425). Chicago, IL: University of Chicago Press.

Farrington, D. P., Gallagher, B., Morley, L., St. Ledger, R. J., & West, D. J. (1986). Unemployment, school leaving, and crime. *British Journal of Criminology*, **26**, 335–56.

Garmezy, N. (1993). Vulnerability and resilience. In D. C. Funder, R. D. Parke, C. Tomlinson-Keasey, & K. Widaman (eds) *Studying Lives through Time: Personality and Development* (pp. 377–98). Washington, DC: American Psychological Association.

Gendreau, P., Little, T., & Goggin, C. (1996). A meta-analysis of the predictors of adult offender recidivism: what works! *Criminology*, **34**, 401–33.

Gold, M. (1994). Changing the delinquent self. In T. M. Brinthaupt & R. P. Lipka (eds) *Changing the Self: Philosophies, Techniques, and Experiences* (pp. 89–108). Albany, NY: State University of New York Press.

Gottfredson, M., & Hirschi, T. (1990). *A General Theory of Crime*. Stanford, CA: Stanford University Press.

Gove, W. R. (1985). The effect of age and gender on deviant behavior: a biopsychosocial perspective. In A. S. Rossi (ed.) *Gender and the Life Course* (pp. 115–44). New York: Aldine.

Hammersley, R., Forsyth, A., & Lavelle, T. (1990). The criminality of new drug users in Glasgow. *British Journal of Addiction*, **85**, 1583–94.

Hirschi, T., & Gottfredson, M. (1983). Age and the explanation of crime. *American Journal of Sociology*, **89**, 552–84.

Hirschi, T., & Gottfredson, M. (1995). Control theory and the life-course perspective. *Studies on Crime and Crime Prevention Biannual Review*, **4**, 131–42.

Horney, J., Osgood, D. W., & Marshall, I. (1995). Criminal careers in the short term: intra-individual variability in crime and its relation to local life circumstances. *American Sociological Review*, **60**, 655–73.

Hughes, M. (1998). Turning points in the lives of young inner-city men forgoing destructive criminal behaviors: a qualitative study. *Social Work Research*, **22**, 143–51.

Irwin, J. (1970). *The Felon*. Englewood Cliffs, NJ: Prentice Hall.

Jolin, A., & Gibbons, D. C. (1987). Age patterns in criminal involvement. *International Journal of Offender Therapy and Comparative Criminology*, **31**, 237–60.

Jones, B. T., & McMahon, J. (1994). Negative alcohol expectancy predicts post-treatment abstinence survivorship: the whether, when, and why of relapse to a first drink. *Addiction*, **89**, 1653–65.

Laub, J., & Sampson, R. (1993). Turning points in the life course: why change matters to the study of crime. *Criminology*, **31**, 301–26.

Laub, J. H., Nagin, D. S., & Sampson, R. J. (1998). Trajectories of change in criminal offending: good marriages and the desistance process. *American Sociological Review*, **63**, 225–38.

Loeber, R., & LeBlanc, M. (1990). Toward a developmental criminology. In M. Tonry & N. Morris (eds) *Crime and Justice: An Annual Review of Research*, vol. 12 (pp. 375–437). Chicago, IL: University of Chicago Press.

Marks, I. M. (1987). *Fears, Phobias, and Rituals: Panic, Anxiety, and their Disorders*. New York: Oxford University Press.

McDougall, C., & Boddis, S. (1991). Discriminations between anger and aggression: implications for treatment. *Issues in Criminological and Legal Psychology*, **2**(17), 101–6.

McMurran, M. (1997). Outcome expectancies: an important link between substance use and crime? In S. Redondo, V. Garrido, & R. Barbaret (eds) *Advances in Psychology and Law: International Contributions* (pp. 312–21). Berlin: Walter de Gruyter.

Mednick, B. R., Baker, R. L., & Carothers, L. E. (1990). Patterns of family instability and crime: the association of timing of the family's disruption with subsequent adolescent and young adult criminality. *Journal of Youth and Adolescence*, **19**, 201–20.

Meisenhelder, T. (1977). An exploratory study of exiting from criminal careers. *Criminology*, **15**, 319–34.

Moffitt, T. (1993). Adolescent-limited and life-course persistent antisocial behavior: a developmental taxonomy. *Psychological Review*, **100**, 674–701.

Mulvey, E. P., & La Rosa, J. F. (1986). Delinquency cessation and adolescent development: preliminary data. *American Journal of Orthopsychiatry*, **56**, 212–24.

Olweus, D. (1979). Stability of aggressive reaction patterns in males: a review. *Psychological Bulletin*, **86**, 852–75.

Osborn, S. G. (1980). Moving home, leaving London, and delinquent trends. *British Journal of Criminology*, **20**, 54–61.

Oyserman, D., & Markus, H. R. (1990). Possible selves and delinquency. *Journal of Personality and Social Psychology*, **59**, 112–25.

Paternoster, R., Dean, C. W., Piquero, A., Mazerolle, P., & Brame, R. (1997). Generality, continuity, and change in offending. *Journal of Quantitative Criminology*, **13**, 231–66.

Patterson, G. (1993). Orderly change in a stable world: the antisocial trait as a chimera. *Journal of Consulting and Clinical Psychology*, **61**, 911–19.

Shover, N. (1983). The latter stages of ordinary property offenders' careers. *Social Problems*, **31**, 208–18.

Shover, N. (1996). *Great Pretenders: Pursuits and Careers of Persistent Thieves*. Boulder, CO: Westview.

Shover, N., & Thompson, C. (1992). Age, differential expectations, and crime desistance. *Criminology*, **30**, 89–104.

Slaby, R. G., & Guerra, N. G. (1988). Cognitive mediators of aggression in adolescent offenders: I. Assessment. *Developmental Psychology*, **24**, 580–88.

Sommers, I., Baskin, D. R., & Fagan, J. (1994). Getting out of the life: crime desistance by female street offenders. *Deviant Behavior*, **15**, 125–49.

Stuart, R. B., Quire, K., & Krell, M. (1976). Penalty for the possession of marijuana: an analysis of some of its concomitants. *Contemporary Drug Problems*, **5**, 553–63.

Ullman, J. B., & Newcomb, M. D. (1999). The transition from adolescent to adult: a time of change in general and specific deviance. *Criminal Behaviour and Mental Health*, **9**, 74–90.

Walters, G. D. (1990). *The Criminal Lifestyle: Patterns of Serious Criminal Conduct*. Newbury Park, CA: Sage.

Walters, G. D. (1992). *Foundations of Criminal Science*, vol. II: *The Use of Knowledge.* New York: Praeger.

Walters, G. D. (1998). *Changing Lives of Crime and Drugs: Intervening with Substance-Abusing Offenders.* Chichester: Wiley.

Walters, G. D. (1999a). *The Addiction Concept: Working Hypothesis or Self-Fulfilling Prophecy?* Boston, MA: Allyn & Bacon.

Walters, G. D. (1999b). Crime and chaos: applying nonlinear dynamical principles to problems in criminology. *International Journal of Offender Therapy and Comparative Criminology,* **43**, 134–53.

Walters, G. D. (1999c). Human survival and the self-destruction paradox: an integrated theoretical model. *Journal of Mind and Behavior,* **20**, 57–78.

Walters, G. D. (1999d). Short-term outcome of inmates participating in the Lifestyle Change Program. *Criminal Justice and Behavior,* **26**, 322–37.

Walters, G. D. (2000a). Outcome expectancies for crime: their relationship to fear and the negative consequences of criminal involvement. *Legal and Criminological Psychology,* **5**, 261–72.

Walters, G. D. (2000b). *The Self-Altering Process: Exploring the Dynamic Nature of Lifestyle Development and Change.* Westport, CT: Praeger.

Walters, G. D. (2000c). Spontaneous remission from alcohol, tobacco, and other drug abuse: seeking quantitative answers to qualitative questions. *American Journal of Drug and Alcohol Abuse,* **26**, 443–60.

Wilson, J., & Herrnstein, R. (1985). *Crime and Human Nature.* New York: Simon & Schuster.

Part III

SPECIAL ISSUES

Chapter 9

ETHICAL ISSUES IN MOTIVATING OFFENDERS TO CHANGE

RONALD BLACKBURN

University of Liverpool, Liverpool, UK

INTRODUCTION

Questions about what is the right, good, or proper course of action arise whenever people have power to influence the lives of others, and the need for ethical justification of psychologists' decision making has been increasingly emphasised in recent decades (Bersoff, 1999; Francis, 1999). Because the interests and rights of professionals, their clients, their employing organisations, and society at large do not always coincide, asserting the rights of one party may often entail violation of the rights of others. Recognition of professional obligations in the light of these competing claims is necessary to avoid harm and exploitation.

Awareness of the potential of psychological treatment methods to harm disadvantaged clients increased during the 1970s as evidence emerged that mental health practices sometimes violated the rights of detained people. For example, the token economy provided one of the earliest systematic attempts to motivate change in prisoners and institutionalised patients, but some programmes entailed deprivation of food, clothing, or other resources which were then used as reinforcers. These programmes were suspended in the United States following court rulings that this was an unwarranted deprivation of human rights (Wexler, 1973). Support for the development of behaviour modification programmes in prisons was also withdrawn following reports of the coercive use of aversive methods to motivate institutional compliance (Erwin, 1978; Stolz et al., 1975).

Recent approaches to motivating offenders to change, such as motivational interviewing (Miller, 1994; Miller & Rollnick, 1991), are more sensitive to clients' rights. Nevertheless, they raise ethical questions that apply to any attempts by helping professionals to intervene in the lives of offenders. For example, can change be justifiably imposed? Do offenders have the right not to be changed? Why should mental health practitioners seek to change offenders in the first place? These issues are

Motivating Offenders to Change: A Guide to Enhancing Engagement in Therapy. Edited by M. McMurran.
© 2002 John Wiley & Sons, Ltd.

considered here from a psychological perspective. However, because the answers to such questions come from an ethical rather than a psychological orientation, this chapter first examines the nature of ethical justification.

ETHICAL JUSTIFICATION AND CLINICAL PRACTICE

Ethical justification for an action entails compliance with standards defined by moral values about what ought or ought not to be done. However, some psychological perspectives question the wisdom of the professional applications of ethical standards. Radical behaviourists construe values in terms of the practices that are reinforcing in a group or culture, which have evolved because of their ultimate survival value (Plaud & Vogeltanz, 1994; Skinner, 1953). Some behaviour therapists therefore suggest that ethical principles are subjective and relative to situations (Feldman & Peay, 1982).

R. F. Kitchener (1980) points out that one consequence of this relativism is the "dangerous belief" that moral decisions in therapy do not have to be justified because they cannot be justified. However, he notes that in practice, therapists who take the relativist position are inconsistent and typically appeal to some general ethical principle to guide therapeutic practices that is neither subjective nor relative, such as "maximising benefit". Kitchener argues that while it may be true that what is valued or reinforcing varies between individuals and cultures, it does not follow that what *ought* to be valued is subject to the same variability. The relativist view therefore commits the "naturalist fallacy" in failing to distinguish between what is actually valued and what is valuable, i.e. between the realms of fact and value.

Despite some attempts to bridge the gap between facts and values (Waterman, 1989), the prevailing view is that these remain distinct realms of knowledge, and that we cannot logically move from "is" to "ought" (Kendler, 1993). The empirical fact that a psychological intervention "works" in terms of effectiveness is not, then, in itself sufficient to claim that it *ought* to be applied. All treatment additionally requires an ethical justification. What this might be is not immediately obvious. However, the basis for ethical clinical decision-making has been developed in several analyses by moral philosophers (Beauchamp & Childress, 1979; Hare, 1981; K. S. Kitchener, 1984). Kitchener's analysis offers a useful framework for examining the ethics of attempts to change offenders.

A Hierarchical Model of Ethical Thinking

Kitchener's model distinguishes the intuitive and the critical-evaluative levels of ethical reasoning. The *intuitive level* is the immediate, pre-reflective response to specific situations based on the observed facts and acquired ethical beliefs. Feelings of "should" and "should not" form the basis for most everyday moral judgements, and are also the most common basis on which psychologists resolve ethical dilemmas (Thelen et al., 1994). However, moral intuition is frequently insufficient to resolve a dilemma, and may fail to take account of wider implications.

K.S. Kitchener argues that to evaluate or justify moral decisions, we need to move to the reflective *critical-evaluative level*, which has three tiers. The first is to appeal to *moral rules*, clearest examples being the injunctions of professional codes of conduct. For example, the *Code of Conduct, Ethical Principles and Guidelines* of the BPS (British Psychological Society, 2000) and the *Ethical Principles and Code of Conduct* of the APA (American Psychological Association, 1992) provide basic rules of professional behaviour which members of these bodies are expected to observe. However, professional codes evolved to protect professions from regulation by outside agencies, and provide only minimal general guidelines (Hare-Mustin et al., 1979).

The limitations of professional codes may be resolved by appeal to more general *ethical principles*. Professional codes are at least implicitly derived from general principles, and the APA's *Ethical Principles* is, in fact, divided into General Principles, which are aspirational ideals (competence, integrity, professional and scientific responsibility, respect for people's rights and dignity, concern for others' welfare, and social responsibility), and Ethical Standards, which are enforceable rules of conduct. Although there is no exhaustive set of principles, Kitchener identifies autonomy, beneficence, nonmaleficence, justice, and fidelity as the most definitive principles in clinical settings.

Autonomy refers to the right of people to be treated as self-determining agents who are free to choose their own courses of action, provided that this does not violate the autonomy of others. Exceptions arise when the capacity for free choice is impaired. For example, medicine and the law generally accept the paternalistic principle that others may make decisions on behalf of an individual whose competence is impaired by mental illness. Paternalism, it should be noted, is a justification under certain conditions but not a valued ideal, and many argue that it should be limited to the prevention of self-harm.

Beneficence specifies the duty to do good. This is implicit in the notion of "helping professions", which underlines an obligation to benefit clients. The principle of *nonmaleficence* asserts a duty to avoid doing harm, and is as fundamental to applied psychology as it is to medicine. In a moral context, *justice* is generally equated with "fairness", and implies that equal persons should be treated equally. Finally, *fidelity* involves faithfulness, promise keeping and loyalty, which are basic to any trusting relationship. Therapists' obligations and clients' rights follow from these principles. For example, ethical requirements for informed consent observe the principle of autonomy, while beneficence and nonmaleficence underlie the requirement that professionals should be competent to provide the services they undertake.

Ethical theories form the highest level of the hierarchy, two contrasting positions being identified in moral philosophy. *Deontological theories*, associated particularly with Kant, hold that there are certain moral rules which it is always our duty to obey, and that the morality of actions derives from their intrinsic rightness or wrongness. In contrast, *consequentialist theories* argue that actions should be judged right or wrong purely on the basis of their consequences rather than their conformity to any absolute moral rule. The main paradigm is the utilitarianism of Bentham and Mill, which defines morality in terms of maximising the greatest happiness or welfare of the greatest number. These theories can lead to conflicting prescriptions in applying ethical principles. For example, deontology gives primacy to autonomy and justice, and implies that the first consideration of clinicians is the rights of the individual client. Utilitarianism, however, implies that the welfare of the community takes precedence over individual rights.

Because philosophers continue to disagree about these theories, Kitchener suggests that they are of limited utility in resolving ethical dilemmas. Ethical principles provide the appropriate level in ethical decision making and their relevance should always be considered. These principles are neither absolute nor relative, but have *prima facie* validity, and should be considered binding unless they can be overturned by stronger moral obligations.

An unresolved problem is that there is no agreed ordering of the priority of these principles when they conflict. If autonomy always had precedence over beneficence, it would never be ethical for clinicians to intervene in the life of an offender against their will. Again, if there is a choice between harming someone and benefiting others, many would argue that nonmaleficence is the stronger obligation. However, short-term harm can be justified by preventing more serious harm or by longer-term benefits, and how much harm to an individual can be tolerated in the service of wider benefits is a frequent source of ethical dilemmas in dealing with offenders. Kitchener argues that when principles lead to conflicting judgements, decisions need to be examined in terms of the balance of harms and benefits. This does not avoid the problems of indeterminacy in ethical standards, but applying these principles in practice may sharpen both our moral intuitions and the way in which we apply the rules of our professional codes.

Autonomy and Determinism

The principle of autonomy is crucial to the ethics of both clinical practice and research. Therapists of all persuasions appear to subscribe to this principle, claiming that their practice increases the ability of their clients to avail themselves of wider options (Jensen & Bergin, 1988; Kazdin, 1975; Strupp, 1971). Miller and Rollnick (1991) suggest that motivational interviewing similarly respects client autonomy, advising therapists that "clients are at liberty to do whatever they wish to do, and it is not your job to convince them otherwise" (p. 129).

However, there is a fundamental conflict between acceptance of autonomy and the commitment of psychology to determinism. If all behaviour is caused, respect for autonomy rests on assumptions of freedom which are unrealistic and unattainable, and we cannot justifiably expect free choices when offering a client the possibility of change. As Davison (1976) observed, "if we are to take the basic deterministic dictum of science seriously, we must come to grips with the conditions surrounding even those decisions in therapy which have hitherto been termed voluntary or free" (p. 157).

Therapists have as yet failed to get to grips with this issue. Some avoid the determinism/free will debate, and accept that "it is exceedingly important for individuals to feel free independently of whether in fact they are" (Kazdin, 1975, p. 234). Alternatively, soft determinism maintains that all human behaviour is caused, but still allows for the existence of free choice. For example, while dismissing the traditional notion of autonomy, Bandura (1989) views freedom as "the exercise of self-influence", which operates deterministically on behaviour through thought, and which determines personal freedom to avail one's self of many options. People are thus *partial* authors of their situations.

Although these views permit acceptance of the ethical desirability of granting clients the right to choose, no psychologist accepts that human agency entails complete freedom because this would be incompatible with the possibility of psychology as an explanatory science. While both ethics and the law accept that free choice can be constrained by mental disorder, psychologists need to challenge the assumption that absence of disorder implies unconstrained freedom, and therapists should recognise this in ethical justifications of their practice.

WHO IS THE CLIENT?

People convicted of a crime do not thereby forfeit their right to be treated by professionals with respect, whatever suffering their behaviour has caused to others. One of the aspirational ideals of the APA *Ethical Principles* is that "Psychologists accord appropriate respect to the fundamental rights, dignity, and worth of all people". This is as basic to ethical treatment of offenders as to treatment of clients in other settings.

Ethical threats when working with offenders come particularly from the competing demands of the client, the institutional context, the criminal justice system, and the values of the therapist. The BPS *Code of Conduct* enjoins psychologists to "hold the interest and welfare of those in receipt of their services to be paramount at all times". However, psychologists employed by any organisation to provide services to individuals must invariably face the question of "who is the client?". This is a major source of ethical dilemmas and role conflicts for psychologists in the criminal justice system (Monahan, 1980). The dilemmas are particularly acute when treatment services are directed to changing offending behaviour. Because the desistance of offenders from their antisocial acts serves primarily the interests of society, the clinician's usual role as agent of the individual is compromised. Instead, he or she must function as a "double agent", being simultaneously helper and agent of social control (Halleck, 1971).

Attempts to resolve the conflict inherent in these dual roles depend on moral and political beliefs about the relation between society and the individual (Halleck, 1971). The individualistic view, associated with Szasz (1963), is that the helping professions should always give priority to the individual and avoid involvement in coercive treatment. The extreme collectivist view, in contrast, holds that professional responsibilities are always to society as a whole. The implications for ethical practice entailed by adoption of either of these two extremes should be recognised. As employees of agencies whose functions include public protection, clinicians in criminal justice settings cannot avoid their responsibilities for social control, and adoption of an individualist stance at all times would evade their moral obligation to use their skills to help protect society (Halleck, 1987). According priority to society, on the other hand, risks denial of individual welfare and uncritical acceptance of the goals of an imperfect justice system.

The excuse of "just obeying orders", although widespread, is not an ethical defence for clinicians.

Although most psychologists working with offenders probably incline towards the individualistic view, practice frequently displays implicit acceptance of a collectivist position. Treatment in prisons often supports organisational goals to make prisoners compliant and manageable (Brodsky, 1980), and the continued emphasis on recidivism and institutional adjustment as outcome measures of the effectiveness of treatment programmes places treatment in the service of social control. Beneficial effects on the quality of life of offenders remain infrequently documented.

Acceptance of a compliance ideology is similarly suggested by the current preoccupation with risk assessment methods and by the adoption of the title "forensic" by psychologists and other professionals to cover all roles performed within the criminal justice system. Clinical services for offenders and forensic services for the legal system entail incompatible allegiances and ethical obligations (Appelbaum, 1997; Blackburn, 1996; Strasburger et al., 1997). To subsume them under a single heading is morally myopic.

Monahan (1980) argued that both the individual offender and the criminal justice system may be clients but in different roles and with varying priorities. In some roles, such as staff selection or training, the organisation or the wider system is clearly the primary client. However, in providing treatment for an offender, the psychologist must be primarily the agent of the individual. This means making it explicit when the priority is the problems of the offender and when it is the problems the offender causes for others (Feldman & Peay, 1982).

GOALS AND VALUES IN ATTEMPTS TO CHANGE OFFENDERS

Strategies for motivating change assume that the goals cannot be imposed on a client, and focus on exploration and negotiation of goals, including the option of not desisting from the problem behaviour (Miller & Rollnick, 1991). The options for offenders, however, are quite limited, and commitment to change may often entail acceptance not only of society's values but also the values and goals of individual therapists. While some offenders clearly have psychological problems that justify therapeutic intervention, criminal activities are not in themselves dysfunctional, and for many offenders, the only negative consequences of their behaviour come from being caught and convicted. Given that the "problem" may lie in social conditions as much as the offender, therapeutic attempts to move the offender beyond the "precontemplation" stage of change may well reflect the imposition of the therapist's views about the offender's best interests.

There may be times when the interests of offender and society are not incompatible. For example, it may seem self-evident that for persistently violent men to give up their harmful behaviour is in the interests not only of potential future victims, but also of the offenders themselves in terms of avoiding further retributive punishment and loss of liberty. If, however, the offender sees his behaviour as justified and accepts the consequences, attempts at change entail a paternalistic denial of his right to self-determination.

Rehabilitation or Compliance?

In conventional mental health settings, the need for change is determined by the client's complaints of distress or dysfunction, and the goal of change is the promotion of psychological health. In contrast, when the client is an offender, the need for change is instigated by the complaints of others who find the offender's behaviour objectionable, and the goal of change is compliance of the individual with society's rules. The dilemma for therapists is whether this goal is compatible with the ethical principles of autonomy, beneficence and nonmaleficence that justify the helping role.

The traditional justification for the involvement of helping professionals with offenders has been the rehabilitation of the individual. Rehabilitation, however, is an ambiguous term which may refer to social reintegration or simply to the prevention of further offending (Blackburn, 1993; Halleck, 1987). In the former sense of the rehabilitation "ideal", the goal is to enable the individual to avoid further crime by increasing personal effectiveness. Individual welfare is as much a consideration as social utility, and services are directed to individual need. In this context, the service provider is as much the agent of the offender as of society, and the benefits to the individual provide an ethical justification for intervention (Blackburn, 1993).

If rehabilitation is construed simply as the prevention of reoffending, the ethical basis becomes questionable. Here, the goal is to restrict rather than enable, and this goal can be achieved by a variety of means, such as psychosurgery, drug administration or electronic tagging (Halleck, 1987). Moreover, there ceases to be any difference between rehabilitation and special deterrence, which also aims to prevent reoffending, but by means of intimidation. Rehabilitation in this narrow sense is justified solely by the protection of society, and neither individual benefit nor the avoidance of harm to the individual is a primary consideration.

Perhaps because of the fluctuating commitment of penal policy to the rehabilitation ideal, psychologists appear to have blurred this distinction. For example, it has become commonplace to define the target of intervention with offenders as "offending behaviour", even in forensic psychiatric settings. Recent practice has been influenced by the "principles of effective treatment" developed by Andrews (1995), which propose that the relevant targets are dynamic risk factors or "criminogenic needs". Dynamic risk factors are defined *empirically* as those personal and social characteristics of offenders which, when modified, are known to reduce the risk of further offending, although as Andrews acknowledges, very few variables have achieved this empirical status.

Andrews (1995) emphasises that application of the principles of effective intervention should take account of moral, ethical, legal and economic considerations and individual uniqueness. Nevertheless, a focus on changing "offending behaviour" raises a number of ethical concerns. Uncritical acceptance of the criminal law in dictating the goals of psychological intervention is the road to coercive practices disguised as treatment (Halleck, 1971). In apartheid South Africa, for example, "offending behaviour" included consenting sexual relations between people from different ethnic backgrounds. Defining the problems of offenders in terms of their offence also subordinates individual need to the goal of reducing recidivism, and defining programmes by offence category rather than psychological problem may deny some offenders treatment for their needs.

These issues are of particular concern in the case of mentally disordered offenders diverted to forensic psychiatric services. Because it is mental disorder rather than offending per se that justifies diversion, helping professionals in these services clearly have an obligation to ameliorate individual distress and dysfunction. This may be compromised when treatment programmes are "offence focused", and it has been argued that reduced recidivism is a necessary but not sufficient criterion for the effectiveness of intervention with this group (Blackburn, 1995). The goals of intervention should hence be as much "offender focused" as "offence focused".

Some behaviour therapists have argued that eliminating socially deviant behaviour in working with offenders should not be the primary goal in either penal or psychiatric settings. Davison and Stuart (1975), for example, distinguish between *minimal goals* to remove problematic behaviour and *optimal goals* to enhance social functioning. Minimal goals would include changing harmful behaviours, while optimal goals apply to all offenders. The constructional approach advocated by Goldiamond (1974) gives primacy to these optimal goals. Goldiamond argues that all interventions with offenders should focus on the construction or development of new social repertoires rather than simply the elimination of troublesome repertoires. A focus on goals that are in the interests of the offender also obliges therapists to question the moral desirability of changes which serve only the interests of institutional management or compliance.

Therapist Values and the Choice of Goals

To influence a person's values would be to deny their autonomy, and the APA *Ethical Principles* require that "psychologists respect the rights of others to hold values, attitudes, and opinions that differ from their own". Attempts to change values would therefore risk violating the professional code. This risk seems high when the goal of change is the avoidance of further criminal behaviour because moral and social values are clearly involved. For example, the dynamic risk factors identified by Andrews (1995) include antisocial values and beliefs for which "anticriminal sentiments" need to be substituted. In attempting to change offenders, therapists are hence imposing values that differ from those of their clients.

It is likely, however, that the imposition of therapist values is unavoidable in any psychological intervention. Although the techniques of intervention are arguably value-free, their implementation always entails values about the desired goal. Some therapists argue that in so far as all psychological treatment aims to influence the feelings, attitudes or lifestyles of clients, they are akin to propaganda, brainwashing and the educational indoctrination of values (Davison, 1991; Frank, 1973; Strupp, 1971). Frank (1973), for example, sees psychotherapy as a process of interpersonal persuasion in which therapist values, beliefs, and optimism serve to overcome demoralisation, instil hope, and provide a credible meaning of life for clients. Davison (1991) also believes that the imbalance of power in any therapeutic relationship means that decisions on goals are made ultimately by the therapist and reflect therapist values.

Empirical data support this characterisation of the therapy process, and more than a dozen studies have shown that the values of the individual therapist influence the course of therapy and the values of the client (Bergin, 1991; Tjelveit, 1986). In a survey of American mental health professionals, Jensen and Bergin (1988) found that they generally endorsed certain values as vital to the change process, and there was a high degree of consensus that mental health entails being a free agent, having a sense of identity and feelings of worth, being skilled in interpersonal communication, sensitivity, nurturance and trust, being genuine and honest, and having self-control and personal responsibility.

It is these mental health-related values which are commonly found to undergo change during therapy, although the adoption of therapist moral values has also been found (Tjelveit, 1986). This "conversion" by the therapist is not necessarily intentional, but it is unilateral and hence highlights the therapist's ethical responsibilities. Tjelveit argues that health value conversion does not present ethical problems and that therapists have an obligation to change values that may contribute to psychological problems. However, it may be difficult to divorce these from moral, religious or political values, for example when considering intimacy, self-control or sexual behaviour. Imposition of these latter values is ethically problematic because it reduces the client's autonomy. A particular danger is that therapists may communicate their personal values unintentionally, thereby reinforcing specific ethical positions.

These problems are amplified in motivating offenders to change. Miller (1994) suggests that motivational interviewing achieves its effects through facilitating internal processes of self-evaluation rather than through the imposition of someone else's values. However, all interventions in the criminal justice system require therapists to take a stand on values, and ethical neutrality is not possible. Therapists cannot reasonably argue that they do not make the rules and that the choice of goals is not theirs since attempts to change the offender in a particular direction imply acceptance of the moral legitimacy of the goal. Moreover, this entails personal value commitments on the part of therapists.

Interventions aimed at changing individual offenders may also reflect biased values which have social implications. At a time when homosexual behaviour was both illegal and regarded as psychopathological, some psychological interventions were directed to changing sexual orientation. Davison (1976) objected that this was ethically unacceptable, even when the client requested change, because the pressure for change came from society's prejudices. Treatment under these conditions not only condoned current prejudice but also impeded social change. Rappaport and colleagues (1980) raise similar objections to the treatment of juvenile offenders, arguing that psychological interventions focused on exclusively individual change simply aim to fit problem people into an inequitable society.

It is arguable whether these objections are sufficient to override the attempts of therapists to benefit individual offenders, but they nonetheless emphasise the need for therapists to become sensitive to the imposition of social values or norms on offenders. Tjelveit (1986) proposes that to minimise inappropriate value conversion, therapists need to be aware of their own values and make them explicit, and to recognise when conflicts of values may impede therapeutic relationships. This requires more attention to ethical issues, in both therapist training and supervision.

CONSENT AND COERCION IN CHANGING OFFENDERS

The requirement that clients should voluntarily consent to psychological treatment is universally recognised in professional codes of conduct. The BPS *Code of Conduct* states that psychologists should "normally obtain the consent of those to whom interventions are offered". This ethical standard stems from the principle of autonomy. Respecting this principle requires that the client's choice of whether or not to participate in the change process is made freely without external influences. Coercion in the form of threats or punishment to gain compliance raises ethical concerns not only because it may entail harm, but particularly because it interferes with free choice. However, manipulation through positive inducements raises the same ethical issues because it also undermines self-determination.

Motivating change in offenders may violate the ethical requirement for voluntary consent in three ways. First, offenders may not be in a position to give free consent. Second, by definition, ambivalent or reluctant clients have not given their consent to participate in treatment. Strategies for motivating change may hence be equivalent to compulsory treatment in which consent is overridden. Third, these strategies may entail direct attempts to manipulate choice.

Can Offenders Give Voluntary Consent?

The paradigm of voluntary participation is the traditional outpatient relationship, which is characterised by psychotherapists as "one between two freely consenting adults" (Strupp, 1971). It is frequently argued that these conditions cannot hold in prisons and secure hospitals (Feldman & Peay, 1982; Halleck, 1987; Monahan, 1980; Stolz et al., 1975). These are inherently coercive environments, and offenders are aware that cooperation with institutional regimes may favourably influence parole and release decisions. It has therefore been proposed that psychological treatment in prisons should be limited to those who voluntarily request it (Feldman & Peay, 1982; Monahan, 1980). Strict adherence to this would clearly rule out working with reluctant clients.

However, it was suggested earlier that choice is never wholly free, and this is particularly so in the choice to participate in therapy. People do not usually seek professional help for psychological problems unless they perceive pressures in their lives to change, whether from threats to relationships, jobs or social approval. Decisions to seek and accept therapy are therefore neither strictly voluntary nor free from coercion, even in the outpatient setting (Davison, 1976, 1991; Erwin, 1978). The argument that prisoners do not have the freedom of choice in therapy available to outpatients cannot, then, be sustained, and their residence in a coercive environment is not in itself a sufficient argument against offering them treatment.

This does not mean that therapists should acquiesce in institutional pressures on offenders to undergo treatment.

Compulsory Treatment of Offenders

Psychologists increasingly work with offenders whose treatment has been ordered by the courts. The BPS *Code of Conduct* notes that an exception to the requirement for voluntary consent is "when the intervention is made compulsory in accordance with the provisions and safeguards of the relevant legislation". However, the APA *Ethical Principles* recognise that psychologists' ethical responsibilities may conflict with legal requirements, and advise that the former should take precedence.

Empirical findings that those ordered by the courts to engage in psychological treatments may do as well as voluntary clients in terms of recidivism do not in themselves provide an ethical justification for compulsion. The most common defence is the utilitarian argument that compulsory treatment serves the general welfare of the community. Social utility, however, may conflict with fairness and the rights of the individual offender. For example, the indeterminate detention of "dangerous" offenders for public protection has to be balanced against the possible injustice of wrongful detention resulting from inherently fallible risk assessments. The utilitarian argument is persuasive only if there is a very high probability of future harmful behaviour by the individual.

Some mental health professionals believe that coerced treatment is never justified. Strupp (1971), for example, follows Szasz (1963) in arguing that "once the basic right 'to be let alone' is invaded, the state or its agents can similarly justify changing the behavior of any individual whose behavior is judged deviant, troublesome or obnoxious" (p. 161). Robinson (1974), in contrast, proposes that individuals who have physically harmed others "can lay no moral claim to the right not to be changed" because they have violated the right of the majority to live unmolested under the law. However, for illegal acts not involving physical harm, compulsory treatment is not ethically justified. Hate crimes, for example, however abhorrent to the majority, represent specific group ideologies, and "Behavioral and medical scientists have no role in arbitrating the competing claims between individuals and society in general" (p. 238).

Total rejection of compulsion does not seem a viable option, but unless therapists accept subservience to the coercive requirements of the state, a line must be drawn somewhere. Robinson's case for drawing the line at physical harm appears to be that those whose behaviour does not respect the rights of others to autonomy forfeit the right to be treated as autonomous agents. It could be argued that the line can be extended to crimes involving psychological harm, such as sexual crimes or "stalking", which also violate the autonomy of others. There are risks in this view, given ambiguities in the notion of "psychological harm", but it provides a possible justification for overriding the rights of the offender. It would not, however, justify coerced treatment of offenders whose behaviour merely annoys or causes a nuisance, such as car thieves or shoplifters.

Offenders required to undergo treatment by legal compulsion seem particularly likely to be among the reluctant clients for whom strategies for motivating change are deemed appropriate. The preceding argument suggests that an ethical justification for attempting change under such conditions is limited to the most harmful offenders. However, these considerations apply to any situation in which an offender has not consented to treatment. They therefore suggest limits to the justification for motivating the reluctant offender more generally.

Consent and Strategies for Motivating Change

Miller and Rollnick (1991) describe motivational interviewing as a set of nonauthoritarian strategies that are "more persuasive than coercive" and "more supportive than argumentative", and aim to increase the client's intrinsic motivation to change. They suggest that these strategies follow the requirement of voluntary consent, and that this applies equally to the legally coerced client whose personal control over outcomes should be emphasised by therapists. This claimed freedom of choice, however, does not appear to be consistent with the use of persuasive strategies, or "tipping the decisional balance", as Miller (1994) describes them. As has been emphasised, manipulation whether by persuasion or coercion raises ethical issues because it influences self-determination. In this respect, strategies which are more persuasive than coercive are not necessarily more ethical.

Motivational interviewing aims to avoid the perception on the part of the client of external pressure or coercion (Miller & Rollnick, 1991), and it might be argued that motivating change is simply a preliminary to eliciting voluntary consent. However, although giving advice, feedback and goal clarification are central procedures, more is involved than simply offering information and letting the client "take it or leave it". For example, strategies for motivating change include the creation of awareness of discrepancies between the consequences of changing and not changing. When the client is under the control of criminal justice agencies, the costs of not changing are almost invariably aversive. Similarly, "reframing" information offered by the client entails casting that information in a new light that is more likely to support change. Miller (1994) acknowledges that these strategies are manipulative in the sense of changing motivation and behaviour without the client's permission or awareness.

Motivational interviewing is not, however, exceptional in employing manipulation. It was noted earlier that all psychotherapies can be construed as forms of interpersonal influence involving manipulation and pressure (Frank, 1973). Motivational interviewing also draws on the social psychological principles developed in interviewing for research purposes, which raise similar ethical issues. Although voluntary participation is an ethical requirement in most human research, participation usually has no benefits for participants, who must somehow be persuaded to become involved. Gorden (1975) argues that the ethical dilemmas are partially dissolved by distinguishing between the "pure", the "persuaded" and the "coerced" volunteer, most "volunteers" actually being persuaded cooperators or at least nonresisters to gentle coercion. He suggests that strategies of persuasion are ethically defensible as long as any promises are kept and no one is harmed.

It would appear, then, that however much the therapist acknowledges the desirability of voluntary change, strategies to motivate offenders to change are inevitably manipulative and potentially coercive. It is doubtful whether this can be justified by appeal to nonmaleficence and fidelity alone, and some justification in terms of beneficence is necessary. Miller (1994), in fact, suggests that changes resulting from motivational interviewing would generally be viewed as benevolent. However, while the end can justify the means when the ends themselves are morally justifiable, in restricting the client's self-determination, therapists need to acknowledge that they are adopting a paternalistic role.

Informed Consent

Informed consent differs from voluntary consent since people may often volunteer with minimal information. Good practice demands that therapists should at the outset correct any unrealistic expectations the client may have about the nature of the therapeutic relationship and its possible outcome. The ethical requirement is that the client should be provided with enough information to make an informed decision about whether or not to participate in therapy. This determines the conditions which maximise voluntary consent.

Discussions of informed consent (American Psychological Association, 1992; Hare-Mustin et al., 1979; Margolin, 1982) recommend that the following types of information should be provided to clients before therapy is initiated: (a) an explanation of the treatment procedures and their purpose, (b) the role of the person providing therapy and his or her professional qualifications, (c) the benefits that can reasonably be expected, (d) any discomfort or risks that can be expected, (e) alternatives to treatment that might be of similar benefit, and (f) statements that the person can withdraw his or her consent and discontinue participation in therapy at any time.

Although awareness of the need for informed consent in psychological treatment has grown in recent years, consent procedures have not been accorded the emphasis they receive in research. One reason is that beyond certain basic items of information, such as the therapist's role and qualifications and the frequency and duration of therapy sessions, a standard form of information is unlikely to meet the needs of all types of clients, treatment methods or treatment settings. For example, therapists are rarely able to anticipate all of the outcomes for the client and others. Moreover, an explanation of some therapeutic procedures, such as the use of paradox, would limit their effectiveness. How much information should be provided, in what form, and at what point are therefore complex and controversial issues (Davison & Stuart, 1975; Hare-Mustin et al., 1979; Tjelveit, 1986; Widiger & Rorer, 1984).

Motivating offenders to change raises similar issues. Miller and Rollnick (1991) note that the initial session of motivational interviewing requires a structuring statement that should include reference to the roles of therapist and client, and a frank statement of limitations arising from dual agency when the client is legally coerced. Reference to helping the client explore alternative sources of help is also recommended. However, while this recognises the client's right to know the essentials of what is going on, the purpose is to hold the client rather than to present the maximal information needed for informed consent to accept or decline treatment.

In so far as motivational strategies are a prelude to treatment, it could be argued that eliciting informed consent is neither necessary nor reasonable at this stage, and that the purpose of intervention is to lead the client to the position where such consent is possible. However, as was indicated earlier, this is inevitably a manipulative process. This is not unique to motivational interviewing. Widiger and Rorer (1984) believe that informed consent is incompatible with many therapeutic techniques and that a compromise between universal standards and the demands of treatment effectiveness must be recognised.

Confidentiality

Whatever the limits on informed consent when employing strategies to change offenders, therapists have an obligation to provide information about any implications of the therapist's role as double agent, particularly the limits of confidentiality (Miller & Rollnick, 1991). The principle of autonomy recognises the client's right to privacy and to expect that personal disclosures made during therapy will be treated as confidential. The principle of fidelity also obliges therapists to be trustworthy and to divulge confidential information to others only with the client's consent. Questions of where professional loyalties lie often centre on concerns about confidentiality (Monahan, 1980).

Psychotherapists have traditionally adopted a deontological position, seeing the right to privacy as a moral absolute. Considerable dismay among therapists in the United States therefore followed the 1976 decision of the California Supreme Court in *Tarasoff v Regents of the University of California* that clinicians had a legal duty to warn third parties to whom their clients were a danger. It has subsequently been claimed that this resulted in defensive clinical practice and a reluctance of clinicians to work with dangerous offenders. However, guarantees of complete confidentiality in clinical practice have always misrepresented the facts (Hare-Mustin et al., 1979), and professional codes recognise exceptions to confidentiality when the safety or interests of either the client or others are threatened. Work in teams or multi-agency contexts also calls for an extended form of confidentiality, as does group treatment. Ethical dilemmas can be avoided by making explicit to the client from the outset what counts as private information and what kinds of information will be disclosed to others.

Nevertheless, the criminal justice system imposes strong pressures on therapists to violate confidentiality. Institutions, parole boards and review tribunals require information on the progress of offenders and may require written reports from those engaged in therapeutic change. Similarly, lawyers may seek evaluations and reports from therapists whose clients are involved in court proceedings. While therapists might reasonably be supposed to be in the best position to provide such information, both the legal system and mental health professionals have been slow to recognise the ethical conflicts involved in simultaneously adopting therapist and forensic roles (Strasburger et al., 1997). These roles require not only different skills, but also different levels of trust in relating to the client. Moreover, the principle of nonmaleficence does not apply in forensic settings, and clients may suffer significant psychological and material harm when confidential aspects of their lives are openly divulged (Strasburger et al., 1997). As far as possible, then, therapists working with offenders should decline requests for evaluations of their clients by others.

CONCLUSIONS

Motivating offenders to change inevitably entails compromises with the ethical principles that justify therapeutic intervention. Not only do therapists have to maintain a precarious balance between meeting the needs of their clients and imposing the goals of conformity demanded by the criminal justice system, they must also use methods that curtail the client's freedom of choice. However, unethical practice lies less in the failure to meet ethical aspirations than in the failure to recognise the aspirations that must be balanced.

Practitioners who undertake to change offenders also need to recognise that their own values and goals enter into the change process to influence outcomes. Davison (1991) has argued that we need to acknowledge that "therapists are purveyors of ethics, that they are contemporary society's secular priests, and that this heavy moral responsibility is inherent to the conduct of psychotherapy" (p. 147). This responsibility is increased when clients are the unwilling wards of a coercive system.

REFERENCES

American Psychological Association (1992). Ethical principles of psychologists and code of conduct. *American Psychologist*, **47**, 1597–1611.

Andrews, D. A. (1995). The psychology of criminal conduct and effective treatment. In J. McGuire (ed.) *What works: Reducing reoffending: Guidelines from Research and Practice* (pp. 35–62). Chichester: Wiley.

Appelbaum, P. S. (1997). Ethics in evolution: the incompatibility of clinical and forensic functions. *American Journal of Psychiatry*, **154**, 445–6.

Bandura, A. (1989). Human agency in social cognitive theory. *American Psychologist*, **44**, 1175–84.

Bergin, A. E. (1991). Values and religious issues in psychotherapy and mental health. *American Psychologist*, **46**, 394–403.

Bersoff, D. N. (ed.) (1999). *Ethical Conflicts in Psychology*, 2nd edn. Washington, DC: American Psychological Association.

Beauchamp, T. L., & Childress, J. F. (1979). *Principles of Biomedical Ethics.* Oxford: Oxford University Press.

Blackburn, R. (1993). *The Psychology of Criminal Conduct: Theory, Research and Practice.* Chichester: Wiley.

Blackburn, R. (1995). Mentally disordered offenders. In C. R. Hollin (ed.) *Working with Offenders: Psychological Practice in Offender Rehabilitation* (pp. 119–49). Chichester: Wiley.

Blackburn, R. (1996). What is forensic psychology? *Legal and Criminological Psychology*, **1**, 3–16.

British Psychological Society (2000). *Code of Conduct, Ethical Principles, and Guidelines.* Leicester: British Psychological Society.

Brodsky, S. L. (1980). Ethical issues for psychologists in corrections. In J. Monahan (ed.) *Who Is the Client? The Ethics of Psychological Intervention in the Criminal Justice System* (pp. 63–92). Washington, DC: American Psychological Association.

Davison, G. C. (1976). Homosexuality: the ethical challenge. *Journal of Consulting and Clinical Psychology*, **44**, 157–62.

Davison, G. C. (1991). Constructionism and morality in therapy for homosexuality. In J. C. Gonsiorek & J. D. Weinrich (eds) *Homosexuality: Research Issues for Public Policy* (pp. 137–48). Newbury Park, CA: Sage.

Davison, G. C., & Stuart, R. B. (1975). Behavior therapy and civil liberties. *American Psychologist*, **30**, 755–63.

Erwin, E. (1978). *Behavior Therapy: Scientific, Philosophical, and Moral Foundations.* Cambridge: Cambridge University Press.

Feldman, M. P., & Peay, J. (1982). Ethical and legal issues. In A. S. Bellak, M. Hersen & A. E. Kazdin (eds) *International Handbook of Behavior Modification* (pp. 231–61). New York: Plenum.

Francis, R. D. (1999). *Ethics for Psychologists.* Leicester: British Psychological Society.

Frank, J. D. (1973). *Persuasion and Healing*, 2nd edn. Baltimore, MD: Johns Hopkins University Press.

Goldiamond, I. (1974). Toward a constructional approach to social problems: ethical and constitutional issues raised by applied behavior analysis. *Behaviorism*, **2**, 1–84.

Gorden, R. L. (1975). *Interviewing: Strategy, Techniques, and Tactics.* Homewood, IL: Dorsey Press.

Halleck, S. L. (1971). *Psychiatry and the Dilemmas of Crime.* Berkeley, CA: University of California Press.

Halleck, S. L. (1987). *The Mentally Disordered Offender.* Washington, DC: American Psychiatric Press.

Hare, R. (1981). The philosophical basis of psychiatric ethics. In S. Bloch & P. Chodoff (eds) *Psychiatric Ethics* (pp. 58–75). Oxford: Oxford University Press.

Hare-Mustin, R. T., Marecek, J., Kaplan, A. G., & Liss-Levinson, N. (1979). Rights of clients, responsibilities of therapists. *American Psychologist*, **34**, 3–16.

Jensen, J. P., & Bergin, A. E. (1988). Mental health values of professional therapists: a national interdisciplinary survey. *Professional Psychology: Research and Practice*, **19**, 290–97.

Kazdin, A. E. (1975). *Behavior Modification in Applied Settings.* Homewood, IL: Dorsey Press.

Kendler, H. H. (1993). Psychology and the ethics of social policy. *American Psychologist*, **48**, 1046–53.

Kitchener, K. S. (1984). Intuition, critical evaluation and ethical principles: the foundation for ethical decisions in counseling psychology. *The Counseling Psychologist*, **12**, 43–56.

Kitchener, R. F. (1980). Ethical relativism and behavior therapy. *Journal of Consulting and Clinical Psychology*, **48**, 1–7.

Margolin, G. (1982). Ethical and legal considerations in marital and family therapy. *American Psychologist*, **37**, 788–801.

Miller, W. R. (1994). Motivational interviewing: III. On the ethics of motivational intervention. *Behavioural and Cognitive Psychotherapy*, **22**, 111–23.

Miller, W. R., & Rollnick, S. (1991). *Motivational Interviewing: Preparing People to Change Addictive Behaviour.* New York: Guilford Press.

Monahan, J. (ed.) (1980). *Who Is the Client? The Ethics of Psychological Intervention in the Criminal Justice System.* Washington, DC: American Psychological Association.

Plaud, J. J., & Vogeltanz, N. (1994). Psychology and the naturalistic ethics of social policy. *American Psychologist*, **49**, 967–8.

Rappaport, J. R., Lamiell, J. T., & Seidman, E. (1980). Ethical issues for psychologists in the juvenile justice system: know and tell. In J. Monahan (ed.) *Who Is the Client? The Ethics of Psychological Intervention in the Criminal Justice System* (pp. 93–125). Washington, DC: American Psychological Association.

Robinson, D. N. (1974). Harm, offense, and nuisance: first steps in the establishment of an ethics of treatment. *American Psychologist*, **29**, 233–8.

Skinner, B. F. (1953). *Science and Human Behaviour.* New York: Free Press.

Stolz, S. B., Wienckowski, L. A., & Brown, B. S. (1975). Behavior modification: a perspective on critical issues. *American Psychologist*, **30**, 1027–47.

Strasburger, L. H., Gutheil, T., & Brodsky, A. (1997). On wearing two hats: role conflict in serving as both psychotherapist and expert witness. *American Journal of Psychiatry*, **154**, 448–56.

Strupp, H. H. (1971). *Psychotherapy and the Modification of Abnormal Behavior: An Introduction to Theory and Research*. New York: McGraw-Hill.

Szasz, T. (1963). *Law, Liberty and Psychiatry*. New York: Macmillan.

Thelen, M. H., Rodriguez, M. D., & Sprengelmeyer, P. (1994). Psychologists' beliefs concerning confidentiality with suicide, homicide and child abuse. *American Journal of Psychotherapy*, **48**, 363–79.

Tjeltveit, A. C. (1986). The ethics of value conversion in psychotherapy: appropriate and inappropriate therapist influence on client values. *Clinical Psychology Review*, **6**, 515–37.

Waterman, A. S. (1989). On the uses of psychological theory and research in the process of ethical inquiry. *Psychological Bulletin*, **103**, 283–98.

Wexler, D. (1973).Token and taboo: behavior modification, token economies and the law. *California Law Review*, **61**, 81–109.

Widiger, T. A., & Rorer, L. G. (1984). The responsible psychotherapist. *American Psychologist*, **39**, 503–15.

Chapter 10

MOTIVATION FOR WHAT?
EFFECTIVE PROGRAMMES
FOR MOTIVATED OFFENDERS

JAMES McGUIRE

University of Liverpool, Liverpool, UK

The issue of motivation is a pivotal but often vexing one in almost all work with offenders. Clients referred to mental health, social welfare or other public services are generally assumed to be at least partially motivated to seek help, and therefore willing to participate in activities recommended by professionals. In criminal justice settings, the reverse is the case for those on the receiving end. Looked at objectively, the law acts upon them, usually against their will. While they are not wholly passive in that process, their typical perception of it is as an experience that is essentially coercive. Of course, there is a widespread feeling in society that this is exactly what should happen. Indeed many citizens would argue that society has a right if not an obligation to act in this manner towards those who have violated its laws.

To be sure, clients of mental health services, or who attend addictions units or related agencies, are far from uniformly engaged in the proceedings on offer. Individuals may attend clinics as a result of pressure from their doctors or from close relatives, while inwardly having no wish to be there. This can apply for example to children or adolescents brought to professionals by their parents, but it can also be found in the context of other types of relationship. Equally, individuals may act as a result of secondary motives such as a desire to be compensated for injuries they have sustained, and in a smaller proportion of cases, from attention-seeking or other emotional factors. Even where relatively straightforward medical treatment is involved, a sizeable proportion of supposedly motivated patients do not adhere to regimes prescribed by their physicians. This may apply even where the consequences of non-adherence could be significantly detrimental to an individual's health (Meichenbaum & Turk, 1987).

It has to be recognised, therefore, that all provision of help occurs within a context in which the individual's level of motivation is a function of many interrelated

Motivating Offenders to Change: A Guide to Enhancing Engagement in Therapy. Edited by M. McMurran.
© 2002 John Wiley & Sons, Ltd.

causes. This was pinpointed by Miller (1983) in his conceptual analysis of the balance of forces at work when someone with an alcohol problem seeks the help of a counsellor. Those insights led more or less directly to the development of motivational interventions and their wide application in the field of substance misuse, and more recently in other fields, as the chapters of this volume vividly illustrate.

COERCION, COMPULSION AND CONTROL

The hallmark of interventions in criminal justice, however, is that it is widely expected that some form of restraint must be inherent in them. The entire history of society's mission to deal with its wayward inhabitants is one of experimentation with various forms of constraint and control. In the distant past—and in the present in some countries—these forms of control were physical and even brutal. As famously argued by Foucault (1977), despite apparent continuity of the usage of such measures, over the past two centuries the focus of control has actually been upon the mind rather than the body of the offender. From leg-irons through imprisonment to electronic monitoring, the question of whether or not offenders are motivated to change has been a marginal one by comparison with the prime objective of controlling them.

The usage of coercion in any form raises fundamental questions about the nature of society itself. The manner in which society responds to crime and to the consequences that flow from criminal acts is central to many political debates. A pervasive question arising in such debates is that of how much coercion should be applied. No one expects that offenders will stop committing crimes simply because law-abiding persons ask them to. It is still commonly assumed that society will need to make them change, or impose personal costs if they do not. This underpins recurrent controversies over the existence of capital punishment, the legitimacy or otherwise of corporal punishment, the lengths of prison sentences, the use of custodial versus community penalties, and the acceptability of curfews and electronic tags.

It could be argued that the use of punishment, a central fixture of criminal justice in most societies, is predicated on the assumption that offenders will not change unless compelled to do so. Traditionally, arguments supporting the use of punitive sanctions in sentencing have been categorised in two broad camps, retributivist and consequentialist. The former defines punishment as an end in itself, and considers it an obligation that it be imposed. The punishment of wrong-doers is a signal of society's displeasure and is inherent in the process of keeping society intact. For the latter, punishment is designed to achieve an end, and to have an impact on wrong-doers of reducing the likelihood that they will offend again. This is an application of the philosophical ideas of utilitarianism to a perplexing social question. There are many other nuances within these broad definitions. All of this discussion raises philosophical arguments concerning the justifications for punishment that are beyond the scope of this chapter (see Walker, 1991 for more detailed exploration of such issues).

Paradoxically, however, it has become increasingly clear that even where strong elements of compulsion are contained within legal penalties, they are by no means guaranteed to deter offenders from reoffending, as might reasonably be expected.

There has been an increasing recognition in recent years that what matters in the application of deterrent sentences is the subjective perception of them by potential or would-be offenders. Research findings have suggested that offenders' judgements of the certainty, celerity and severity of penalties may play a crucial part in their estimates of whether or not a crime is "worth while" (Howe & Loftus, 1996). Experimental studies of whether deterrence can reliably achieve the objectives which the law attributes to it have seldom met with positive results (Sherman, 1988; Weisburd et al., 1990; see McGuire, 2002 for review and discussion). Overall, like everyone else most offenders have no desire to be incarcerated or otherwise controlled by the actions of criminal justice agencies. Yet there is little evidence that the motivational state of many offenders is very much influenced by the likelihood of official sanctions, at the crucial moment just preceding an offence.

In work with offenders, possibly more so than anywhere else, there is a sizeable gap between what the two parties to an encounter are attempting to do. Many prisoners adopt a coping strategy colloquially referred to as "sleeping" through their sentences. This implies that at some level while in prison individuals distance themselves from longer-term concerns, adjust to an acceptance of everyday discomforts, and disengage their thoughts from the realities of having lost freedom and contact with familiars. The result of not doing this may be an ongoing state of agitation while inside.

This is not to say that offenders do not have problems, or that they will not ask for help with them. But in many instances, the problems they nominate as of concern to them and those with which others are preoccupied do not coincide. A survey conducted some years ago in three English prisons supplied firm evidence of this. A sample of 250 prisoners was administered a questionnaire in which they were asked to record which problems they would face, and be most concerned about, on release. Only 17% of respondents listed reoffending as a problem (Priestley et al., 1984). The focus of these offenders' motivations was upon employment, family, monetary and other practical and personal problems. For the majority of them it appeared that the fact they had committed a crime and had been imprisoned as a result, though a powerful interference in their lives, was comparatively unimportant alongside other difficulties they perceived.

RESEARCH ON OFFENDER REHABILITATION

If sheer compulsion is not an effective means of encouraging offenders to change, what options remain for attempting the process of rehabilitation? A substantial volume of evidence now exists to show that rates of offending behaviour can be reduced among criminal recidivists. This runs counter to a widespread pessimism concerning the prospects of accomplishing this aim. Nevertheless, evidence supporting this position has been consolidated in a number of texts and disseminated through a variety of sources (Bernfeld et al., 2001; Gendreau, 1996; Harland, 1996; Hollin, 1999; McGuire, 1995, 2002; Palmer, 1992; Sherman et al., 1997).

As has happened in a number of fields, the process of consolidating knowledge and trying to draw conclusions from it has been greatly facilitated by the development of methods of systematic review. In particular, the growing use of

Table 10.1 Meta-analytic reviews of interventions with offenders (adapted from McGuire, 2002)

Author and date	Focus	Number of outcomes	Mean effect size
Garrett (1985)	Institutionalised young offenders	121	+0.18
Gensheimer et al. (1986)	Diversion schemes	51	+0.09
Mayer et al. (1986)	Social learning programmes	39	+0.36
Gottschalk et al. (1987a)	Community programmes for youths	101	+0.12
Gottschalk et al. (1987b)	Behavioural programmes	30	+0.20
Lösel & Koferl (1989)	Sociotherapeutic prisons (Germany)	18	+0.11
Whitehead & Lab (1989)	Diversion programmes	50	+0.13
Andrews et al. (1990)	Testing rehabilitation principles	154	+0.10
Izzo & Ross (1990)	Cognitive/non-cognitive comparison	46	2.5:1
Roberts & Camasso (1991)	Treatment of young offenders	46	+0.06–0.81
Lipsey (1992, 1995)	Comprehensive	397	+0.10
Nagayama Hall (1995)	Treatment of sex offenders	12	+0.12
Gendreau & Goggin (1996)	Intermediate punishment	138	0.00
Lipton et al. (1997)	Comprehensive	822	–
Lipsey & Wilson (1998)	Serious, persistent young offenders	200	+0.22/0.12
Alexander (1999)	Treatment of sex offenders	79	+0.10
Redondo et al. (1999)	European programmes	57	+0.15
Andrews & Dowden (1999)	Programmes for women offenders	24	–
Dowden & Andrews (1999)	Interventions with young offenders	229	+0.09
Dowden & Andrews (2000)	Reduction of violent recidivism	52	+0.07

meta-analysis as a method of integrating research findings has been a major influence. Since the mid-1980s, a series of 20 meta-analytic reviews has been published concerning the impact of different types of treatments on offender recidivism. Table 10.1 provides a list of these reviews, showing authors and dates of publication, their main focus, numbers of outcomes, and mean effect sizes. As can be seen from the table, some reviews had a narrow and selective focus, for example on diversion schemes for young offenders, or interventions addressed towards violent or sexual offending. The study by Gendreau and Goggin (1996) focused on the impact of intermediate punishments or "smart sentences", including tele-monitoring and "scared straight" programmes. Others have much broader coverage, and those by Lipsey (1992) and Lipton et al. (1997) were attempts to capture all of the available literature. In the latter case, this included published and unpublished studies on an international scale. Most studies report the mean effect size as a correlation coefficient (depicting the relationship between success and failure rates in experimental and control conditions). However, some did not report a mean effect size, in which case a range is given or the entry left blank. The review by Izzo and Ross (1990) was a study of the comparative effectiveness of programmes with and without cognitive-training elements, and the result is presented as an effect size ratio.

Among the meta-analyses summarised in Table 10.1, some primary studies (the original sources of data) have been incorporated in more than one review. Nevertheless, the total number of independent outcomes subsumed within the analyses cited in Table 10.1 is in the region of 2000. Most of these meta-analyses, as well as primary studies on which they are based, were conducted in North America. In most cases the interventions being evaluated were with younger offenders (predominantly in the age range 14–21), although there are also several that include studies of adults. It has been found that effect sizes for adult populations tend to be somewhat lower than those obtained with juvenile offender samples (Cleland et al., 1997). In most cases the follow-up period is relatively short: the mean is less than one year, though there are examples of studies with much longer follow-up than this. Also, the overwhelming majority of the results are based on studies of male offenders. While this reflects the general finding that most crimes are perpetrated by males, it nevertheless represents a serious omission and prohibits the generalisation of findings to women. A recent review by Andrews and Dowden (1999) was designed to remedy this deficiency, and explore whether similar patterns would emerge from studies with women offenders. While many studies report the inclusion in intervention programmes of members of different ethnic groups, the data are seldom analysed separately and hence have not been coded in meta-analyses.

Meta-analysis has of course been criticised on the grounds that its findings can only be as good as the quality of the original studies permits ("garbage in – garbage out"). The quality of design among studies of offender treatment varies considerably; however, in some reviews (e.g. Lipsey, 1992; Lipton et al., 1997) schemes have been developed for coding this in the analyses. Such a system has also been introduced in other studies using traditional narrative or tabulation approaches (e.g. Mackenzie 1997).

In terms of the conventions proposed by Cohen (1988) concerning the outcomes of meta-analysis, the average effects shown in Table 10.1 are not especially large. They surely contradict the assertion that "nothing works", but their relatively modest scale has allowed some commentators to dismiss the possibility that anything of value has been discovered (Logan et al., 1991; Simon, 1998). On the other hand, given the motivational dilemmas involved, we might well expect antisocial behaviour to be more resistant to change than some other types of problems, and effect sizes to be smaller as a result.

A question frequently asked, therefore, is whether these findings can have any real value or meaning for practitioners or policy makers. In response to this question, Rosenthal (1994) has drawn a useful distinction between *statistical* and *practical* significance. To judge whether these results are potentially useful, effect sizes can be compared with those obtained in other areas such as medical treatment or psychological therapy.

Effect sizes from outcome studies and reviews in those fields vary widely. To cite an example used by Rosenthal (1994), the drug aspirin has been shown to reduce the risk of a myocardial infarction (heart attack). The value of this is widely accepted: most laypersons are acquainted with it though rarely knowing its source. However, the effect size, at 0.034, represents a very small reduction in risk level. The practical significance of this small statistical effect was nevertheless sufficiently strong to lead to curtailment of experimental trials on the grounds that it was unethical to withhold aspirin from anyone at risk (Rosenthal, 1994; see McGuire, 2002 for a list of effect sizes for other interventions).

COMPARATIVE EFFECTIVENESS AND INTERVENTION GUIDELINES

Focusing on the average effect sizes of interventions with offenders is a distraction from a potentially more valuable exercise. This is to examine the patterns of differences in effect sizes obtained from different types of interventions, and here much has been learned that can subsequently be applied in practice.

Many researchers are now agreed that the results of these reviews make it possible to identify features of work with offenders that will make reductions in recidivism more likely (Gendreau, 1996; Hollin, 1999; McGuire, 2002). For the most part, these revolve around the development and provision of structured *programmes* for offenders. The word programme here can be used in several senses (McGuire, 2000a), but in its commonest meaning it refers to planned sessions of activity that involve offenders in learning new skills relevant to the process of avoiding criminal acts. For programmes to achieve their maximum benefits, there is a consensus that they should possess the following features:

1. The programmes and services which work best are founded on an explicit and well-articulated model of the causes of crime and criminal acts, which has conceptual clarity and is drawn from an empirically sound knowledge base in psychology, criminology and allied social sciences.
2. There is a recognition of the importance of assessment of risk of reoffending, based on criminal history and other variables, and of allocation of programme participants to different levels of supervision or service in accordance with this information.
3. It is essential to conduct assessments of dynamic risk factors (sometimes, perhaps misleadingly, called "criminogenic needs"); these include attitudes, criminal associates, skills deficits, substance abuse, or self-control problems known to be linked to offending behaviour, but which change over time.
4. More effective methods are ones that correspond to the active, focused and participatory learning and change styles encountered in many offenders, alongside an acknowledged need to adapt services to individual differences in this respect.
5. Effective interventions are characterised by clear objectives, and skilled and structured engagement by staff in tasks which are readily accepted as relevant to individual offenders' needs.

6. The largest and most consistent effects are obtained from application of a cognitive-behavioural approach, comprising a collection of theoretically inter-related methods which focus on the interplay between individuals' thoughts, feelings and behaviour at the time of an offence.
7. Delivery of such interventions should be undertaken by appropriately trained staff groups, who adhere to their appointed objectives, are provided the neces-sary resources, adopt suitable methods and undertake systematic evaluation of individuals' progress and of the outcomes of their services overall.

Several other patterns that emerge from these systematic reviews have both the-oretical and practical significance in other respects. First, some kinds of treatment have the effect of increasing recidivism. This set of findings might appear counter-intuitive to many people. There is a profound public belief that punishment will deter individuals from a course of action and the use of punitive sanctions is al-legedly a widely favoured response to offenders. Yet punitive, deterrence-based, criminal-sanctioning interventions perform by far the worst of the various treat-ments researched to date, and are usually associated with zero or negative effect sizes. Second, some reviews have found that on balance, community-based inter-ventions have larger effect sizes than those delivered in institutions (Andrews et al., 1990; Lipsey & Wilson, 1998; Redondo et al., 1999). When similar programmes were compared in their relative effects in institutional or community settings, the latter outperformed the former in terms of reduced recidivism in the ratio of approxi-mately 3.5 : 2. Poorly designed, inappropriate programmes or interventions will be unlikely to work regardless of the criminal justice setting. Well-designed services are most likely to achieve their maximum benefits when provided in a non-custodial setting.

As mentioned previously, attention to mean effect sizes in large-scale reviews is less informative than the study of patterns within groups of studies with similar features. The frequently cited meta-analysis by Andrews et al. (1990) demonstrated that when interventions with certain features thought to contribute to greater ef-fectiveness were clustered together, larger effect sizes were observed. Possession of those elements, as set out in the list given above, was associated with effect sizes (in terms of reduced recidivism) in excess of 50%. In primary studies of some in-terventions, such as Multi-Systemic Therapy, evaluations have yielded still larger effects, ranging as high as 70% (Edwards et al., 2001).

There has been a perception that, in summarising the findings of these reviews in the foregoing way, this somehow amounts to a claim that everything is now known that needs to be known about how to implement effective crime prevention with persistent offenders. That is hardly the position. The above findings represent only the clearest or most consistent trends emerging from the meta-analytic reviews. Numerous questions remain unanswered, and many issues still need to be clarified. Further research is essential if those goals are to be accomplished.

Similarly, while the outcomes to date support the use of certain approaches, it is possible that additional models or methods, not yet fully researched, could prove equally beneficial, if not more so. Conversely, much as one might prefer it to be otherwise, none of the foregoing amounts to a *guarantee* of a successful outcome. There are still too many variables operating in the occurrence of criminal offences that are not fully understood, and that are unlikely ever to be controllable. This applies similarly to the process of implementing programmes within agencies responsible for service delivery, an area which regrettably has often been overlooked (Gendreau et al., 1999). Nonetheless, there is widespread agreement that the current position is a considerable advance on the one that existed even a few years ago.

The findings of the "what works" research parallel those from a number of other areas which have led to the adoption of *evidence-based practice* in many applied disciplines. This has occurred almost simultaneously over the past decade in several fields, including education, medicine, psychological therapy and social work. In mental health, for example, reviewers such as Nathan and Gorman (1998) have identified pharmacological and psychological interventions most likely to contribute to the amelioration of specific problems and disorders. Recently, the Department of Health (2001) has issued a "treatment guideline" which specifies the most likely-to-succeed treatments for a range of difficulties in this field.

In several respects the process of change across all these fields has analogous features. From initial research indicating that interventions can be effective, studies progress to a stage where it is possible to be more specific concerning which types of intervention offer the strongest prospect for which type of problem. This can then be translated into a set of proposals for applying the findings in practice (Lipton et al., 2000). Broadly speaking, the development of effective programmes for work with offenders could be described as being on a cusp between these latter stages of consolidating research findings and establishing procedures that will maximise their relevance to practice.

RESEARCH AND PRACTICE: IMPLEMENTING PROGRAMMES

In the United Kingdom, with guidance from recent Home Office reviews (Goldblatt & Lewis, 1998; Vennard et al., 1997) senior managers and practitioners within the principal criminal justice agencies, including prison, probation and youth justice, have begun to take account of these findings. This may be indicative of an increasing trend towards application of evidence-based practice in criminal justice settings.

It should be remembered that, even when there was a widespread belief that "nothing works" to reduce rates of reoffending, a segment of practitioners, particularly in probation services, continued to pursue the agenda of providing rehabilitative programmes in offender work (Vanstone, 2000). From 1996 onwards, the provision of structured programmes designed to reduce offender recidivism became a "key performance indicator" in the prison service in England and Wales. A new centre for this activity was established in the form of the service's Offending Behaviour Programmes Unit. Though not necessarily owing their origins to this initiative, similar departures have since been made in criminal justice services in a number of countries. The process of adjudging programmes as suitable for use, and disseminating them throughout criminal justice agencies, has since been followed also in probation services, where pilot programmes originally designated as

Pathfinders are being gradually refined to meet research-based criteria. At the time of writing, a similar sequence of events appears likely to occur within the youth justice sector.

A particularly noteworthy development arising from this process has been the creation of the Home Office Joint Prison-Probation Accreditation Panel, an independent advisory body with the role of examining proposals for offender programmes as to their suitability for use in prison and probation settings. As part of its work, the Panel has developed a set of criteria for accreditation of programmes (Home Office Probation Unit, 2000). These were partly based on an earlier set of criteria developed by the prison service's General Accreditation Panel (HM Prison Service, 1997), but with some key additional elements. The criteria, now widely applied to structured criminal justice programmes in the UK, are as follows (adapted from McGuire, 2001):

1. *Model of change*. There should be a clear, evidence-based theoretical model which informs the design of the programme and explains how it is expected to have an impact on factors linked to offending behaviour.
2. *Dynamic risk factors*. Programme materials should identify factors linked to offending specified in the model, which if changed will lead to a reduction in risk of reoffending, and the programme contents should reflect these objectives.
3. *Range of targets*. Multi-modal programmes with a range of treatment targets have yielded the largest effect sizes in research reviews. Programme manuals specify an appropriate range of targets and the nature of their interrelationships.
4. *Effective methods*. The methods of change utilised in the programme should have empirical support concerning effectiveness and be coordinated in an appropriate way.
5. *Skills orientated*. Programmes targeting skills that will enable offenders to avoid criminal activities have yielded higher effect sizes in outcome studies. The skills targeted by the programme should have explicit links to risk of reoffending and its reduction.
6. *Intensity, sequencing, duration*. The overall amount of programming (numbers of contact hours), the mode of delivery of sessions, and total programme duration should be appropriate in the light of available evidence, the programme's objectives and contents, and the risk level of the targetted offender groups.
7. *Selection of offenders*. The population of offenders for whom the programme is designed should be explicitly and clearly specified. There should be agreed and realistic procedures for targetting and selection, and for exclusion of inappropriate referrals.
8. *Engagement and participation*. This criterion refers to the principle of responsivity. Information should be provided concerning how this will be addressed, and how offenders will be encouraged and motivated to take part in and adhere to the programme.
9. *Case management*. In prison settings, offenders are allocated a personal officer with responsibility for overseeing their individual sentence plans. On probation, they are supervised by a Case Manager. To be effective, programmes should be inter-linked with these processes, and guidelines provided for implementation within services.

10. *Ongoing monitoring.* In order to safeguard the integrity of a programme and the treatment methods used, procedures should be in place for collection of monitoring quality-of-delivery data, and systems established for review of this and for taking action on the basis of it.

11. *Evaluation.* Programme materials should include assessment and evaluation measures and a framework for evaluation of its overall delivery, and short- and long-term impact.

To date, several programmes have successfully satisfied this process and are currently being disseminated throughout different offender services. They include a number of "general offending" programmes designed to impart cognitive, problem-solving and social skills. There are also other more specialised interventions focused on violence, substance abuse, driving while intoxicated and sexual offending. Still more are in preparation, for example on domestic violence, or are in the process of being modified to meet accreditation standards. This development mirrors others that have been occurring elsewhere, most notably in Correctional Services of Canada.

This process and its sequelae have not been without their critics. One debate, which has also occurred in mental health, is that of "efficacy versus effectiveness" (see, for example, Persons & Silbersatz, 1998). This refers to the extent to which outcomes of controlled trials can be genuinely applicable in applied settings, where the composition of the target group is much more heterogeneous than in experimental research. Many evaluative studies in offender services, however, which fail to meet the criteria of high research-design quality, are in that position precisely because they reflect the daily realities of service delivery in criminal justice settings.

It is also feared that the stipulation of criteria for accreditation and quality control somehow compromises creativity and stultifies attempts to explore new areas and devise new initiatives; for example to address local patterns of offending or the needs of specific groups. It is difficult to see why the issuing of standards regarding work should in itself mean that there cannot also be innovation, but this argument remains to be fully tested. A third reservation sometimes expressed (Rex, 2001) concerns the dominance of cognitive-social-learning models, and cognitive-behavioural methods of working. However, this simply reflects the disproportionate quantity of outcome evidence that has emanated from that approach. It has not been claimed that such methods must be the only route to good outcomes, and it is odd to take advocates of such an approach to task for having adopted a systematic, evidence-based approach to their activities.

MOTIVATIONAL ENHANCEMENT IN OFFENDER PROGRAMMES

In community-based settings such as probation, a more concrete, fundamental obstacle continues to beset the widening usage of structured programmes. There is a major problem of attrition in respect of attendance. In current research designed to evaluate probation service *Pathfinder* programmes, a wide range of attendance and completion rates has been found (McGuire et al., 2001). While a few programmes have achieved completion rates approaching 80%, for many others the corresponding rates have been significantly lower. It is self-evident that potentially beneficial programmes can scarcely have an impact if those designated to participate in them simply fail to do so. The largest proportion of the dropout occurs prior to the programme's commencement. In other words, a sizeable number of those ordered by the courts to attend such services fail to arrive for the opening session. A smaller but still worrying proportion drops out during the programme sessions themselves, predominantly during the early stages. There is anecdotal, but nevertheless remarkably consistent feedback from probation units delivering these programmes to the effect that if offenders stay until approximately the sixth session, or roughly one-quarter of the typical structured programme, they are much more likely to remain until the end.

This pattern must be confirmed by much more systematic scrutiny of attendance and attrition rates and the patterns within them. However, there could be several explanations for such a finding. One may be that programmes are simply targetting the more highly motivated offenders to begin with, and the underlying process is one of self-selection. On a larger scale, one author has argued that this phenomenon is sufficient to explain all the positive findings to have emerged from the meta-analyses reviewed earlier (Simon, 1998). This does not of course undermine the value of programmes: it is by no means obvious that even individuals motivated to change will do so successfully without additional help.

As was seen earlier, one of the accreditation criteria applied by the Joint Prison-Probation Panel described above is that of *engagement and participation*. This entails a recognition of the dilemmas discussed at the beginning of this chapter, of inducing offenders to take part in activities which at the outset may make little sense, or may seem coercive, to them. In relation to this, progressively more use is being made of the model of motivational intervention with which this text is concerned.

An example may help to clarify how this can be applied in practice. One of the programmes accredited, initially entitled *Problem-Solving Training and Offence Behaviour* (McGuire, 1994), consisted in its original form of a series of 21 two-hour group sessions used as an "additional requirement" of a probation order. The methods deployed include social problem-solving training, focused first on general problems experienced by participants, and then on analysis of criminal acts they have committed. Problem-solving skills are then applied to more complex areas including self-management, social interaction and attitude change (McGuire & Hatcher, 2001). Preliminary evaluation of this programme has indicated that it secures change in a number of "dynamic risk factors" associated with subsequent offending behaviour.

Following scrutiny for the purposes of accreditation, the form of the programme was revised to incorporate a number of "motivational" elements (Rollnick & Miller, 1995) and other approaches to securing client engagement (Kanfer & Schefft, 1988). The current version, known as *ThinkFirst* (McGuire, 2000b) consists of three interconnected elements. The first is a series of four individual sessions provided by case managers for offenders on an individual basis. This is followed by a series of 22 group sessions. Finally, there is a further set of six individual sessions to consolidate learning and application to new situations. This is focused in particular

on the identification of risk factors for reoffending, and their management
individual offender.

Thus an attempt is made to apply motivational techniques to engage partic
as fully as possible in programme activities. This is applied on two levels.
staff are provided with supplementary training which is directed at devel(
techniques familiar in motivational interviews. One session is dedicated to a
cussion of potential obstacles to attendance, and probation staff approach th...
matters using "motivational interview" strategies. Case managers implementing
the programme are given training in specific motivational enhancement methods
and opportunities to practise the skills involved in their deployment.

Second, motivational issues are also addressed on a more explicit level within
the group-based sessions. Here, specific exercises are included which involve participants in some detailed analysis of their own capacity to change. This involves
a number of "force field" and decision-making activities in which the respective
costs and benefits of a life of crime are compared with those of "going straight".

CONCLUSION

The usage of motivational interventions was initially advocated and implemented
in the field of substance misuse, predominantly with reference to alcohol problems
(Miller, 1983; Miller et al., 1988). Subsequent studies showed how the use of "brief,
opportunistic interventions" incorporating motivational elements could increase
the likelihood that alcohol users, including those thought not ready to change,
would return for further appointments in substance-abuse services (Brown &
Miller, 1993; Heather et al., 1996). The model's applicability has been broadened,
for example to heroin use (van Bilsen & Whitehead, 1994) and other health-related
interventions (Rollnick et al., 1992). The potential applicability of the approach to
offenders was signalled by Garland and Dougher (1991) in work with sex offenders
and subsequently extended to a wider range of populations in this field.

Sadly, the number of evaluated motivational interventions to date is very low. Yet
these ideas have pervaded the thinking of many staff groups in criminal justice services and the motivational model, if perhaps not always accurately portrayed, has
become widespread. As the problem of compliance with correctional programmes
is virtually ubiquitous (see Bottoms, 2001), many criminal justice staff are constantly
preoccupied with attempts to resolve this problem.

It has been commented that the use of motivationally-based interventions, utili-
sing the techniques developed by Miller and others, poses ethical dilemmas
(Withers, 1995; see also Blackburn, this volume, Chapter 9). Much work with
offenders is suffused with parallel dilemmas. They emanate from the difficulty
of establishing a purportedly helping alliance within a wider context of restraint
and coercion (McGuire, 1997). It also remains unclear to what measure the law itself
can absorb the message that offenders can be enjoined to change through processes
that are not merely punitive (McGuire, 2000c). In attempting to resolve these conflicts, it may be that in criminal justice services, engaging those whose motivation
to change is in doubt does indeed pose an ethical dilemma. It can equally be argued,

on ethical grounds, that if as practitioners we are to expend effort intended to motivate change, it is incumbent upon us to offer effective programmes that are then likely to secure it.

REFERENCES

Alexander, M. A. (1999) Sexual offender treatment efficacy revisited. *Sexual Abuse: Journal of Research and Treatment*, **11**, 101–16.

Andrews, D. A. & Dowden, C. (1999) A meta-analytic investigation into effective correctional intervention for female offenders. *Forum on Corrections Research*, **11**, 18–20.

Andrews, D. A., Zinger, I., Hoge, R. D., Bonta, J., Gendreau, P. & Cullen, F. T. (1990) Does correctional treatment work? A clinically relevant and psychologically informed meta-analysis. *Criminology*, **28**, 369–404.

Bernfeld, G. A., Farrington, D. P. & Leschied, A. W. (eds) (2001) *Offender Rehabilitation in Practice: Implementing and Evaluating Effective Programs*. Chichester: Wiley.

Bottoms, A. (2001) Compliance and community penalties. In A. Bottoms, L. Gelsthorpe & S. Rex (eds) *Community Penalties: Change and Challenges*. Cullompton, Devon: Willan Publishing.

Brown, J. M. & Miller, W. R. (1993) Impact of motivational interviewing on participation and outcome in residential alcoholism treatment. *Psychology of Addictive Behaviors*, **7**, 211–18.

Cleland, C. M., Pearson, F. S., Lipton, D. S. & Yee, D. (1997) *Does age make a difference? A meta-analytic approach to reductions in criminal offending for juveniles and adults*. Paper presented at the Annual Meeting of the American Society of Criminology, San Diego, California.

Cohen, J. (1988) *Statistical Power Analysis for the Behavioural Sciences*. New York: Academic Press.

Department of Health (2001) *Treatment Choice in Psychological Therapies and Counselling: Evidence Based Clinical Practice Guideline*. Available at: *http://www.doh.gov.uk/mentalhealth/treatmentguideline/index.htm*

Dowden, C. & Andrews, D. A. (1999) What works in young offender treatment: a meta-analysis. *Forum on Corrections Research*, **11**, 21–4.

Dowden, C. & Andrews, D. A. (2000) Effective correctional treatment and violent reoffending: a meta-analysis. *Canadian Journal of Criminology*, October, 449–67.

Edwards, D. L., Schoenwald, S. K., Henggeler, S. W. & Strother, K. B. (2001) A multilevel perspective on the implementation of Multisystemic Therapy (MST): attempting dissemination with fidelity. In G. A. Bernfeld, D. P. Farrington & A. W. Leschied (eds) *Offender Rehabilitation in Practice: Implementing and Evaluating Effective Programs*. Chichester: Wiley.

Foucault, M. (1977) *Discipline and Punish: The Birth of the Prison*. Harmondsworth: Penguin.

Garland, R. J. & Dougher, M. J. (1991) Motivational intervention in the treatment of sex offenders. In W. R. Miller & S. Rollnick (eds) *Motivational Interviewing*. New York: Guilford Press.

Garrett, C. G. (1985) Effects of residential treatment on adjudicated delinquents: a meta-analysis. *Journal of Research in Crime and Delinquency*, **22**, 287–308.

Gendreau, P. (1996) Offender rehabilitation: what we know and what needs to be done. *Criminal Justice and Behavior*, **23**, 144–61.

Gendreau, P. & Goggin, C. (1996) Principles of effective correctional programming. *Forum on Corrections Research*, **8**, 38–41.

Gendreau, P., Goggin, C. & Smith, P. (1999) The forgotten issue in effective correctional treatment: program implementation. *International Journal of Offender Therapy and Comparative Criminology*, **43**, 180–87.

Gensheimer, L. K., Mayer, J. P., Gottschalk, R. & Davidson, W. S. (1986) Diverting youth from the juvenile justice system: a meta-analysis of intervention efficacy. In S. A. Apter & A. P. Goldstein (eds) *Youth Violence: Programs and Prospects*. Elmsford, NJ: Pergamon Press.

Goldblatt, P. & Lewis, C. (1998) *Reducing Offending: An Assessment of Research Evidence on Ways of Dealing with Offending Behaviour.* Home Office Research Study no. 187. London: Home Office.

Gottschalk, R., Davidson, W. S., Gensheimer, L. K. & Mayer, J. P. (1987a) Community-based interventions. In H. C. Quay (ed.) *Handbook of Juvenile Delinquency.* New York: Wiley.

Gottschalk, R., Davidson, W. S., Mayer, J. & Gensheimer, L. K. (1987b) Behavioral approaches with juvenile offenders: a meta-analysis of long-term treatment efficacy. In E. K. Morris & C. J. Braukmann (eds) *Behavioural Approaches to Crime and Delinquency.* New York: Plenum Press.

Harland, A. T. (ed.) (1996) *Choosing Correctional Options that Work: Defining the Demand and Evaluating the Supply.* Thousand Oaks, CA: Sage.

Heather, N., Rollnick, S., Bell, A. & Richmond, R. (1996) Effects of brief counselling among male heavy drinkers identified on general hospital wards. *Drug and Alcohol Review*, **15**, 29–38.

HM Prison Service (1997) *Criteria for Accrediting Programmes.* London: Offending Behaviour Programmes Unit, HM Prison Service.

Hollin, C. R. (1999) Treatment programmes for offenders: meta-analysis, "What Works", and beyond. *International Journal of Law and Psychiatry*, **22**, 361–71.

Home Office Probation Unit (2000) *What Works Initiative: Crime Reduction Programme. Joint Prison and Probation Accreditation Criteria.* London: Home Office.

Howe, E. S. & Loftus, T. C. (1996) Integration of certainty, severity and celerity information in judged deterrence value: further evidence and methodological equivalence. *Journal of Applied Social Psychology*, **26**, 226–42.

Izzo, R. L. & Ross, R. R. (1990) Meta-analysis of rehabilitation programmes for juvenile delinquents. *Criminal Justice and Behavior*, **17**, 134–42.

Kanfer, F. H. & Schefft, B. K. (1988) *Guiding the Process of Therapeutic Change.* Champaign, IL: Research Press.

Lipsey, M. W. (1992) Juvenile delinquency treatment: a meta-analytic inquiry into the variability of effects. In T. Cook, D. Cooper, H. Corday, H. Hartman, L. Hedges, R. Light, T. Louis & F. Mosteller (eds) *Meta-Analysis for Explanation: A Casebook.* New York: Russell Sage Foundation.

Lipsey, M. W. (1995) What do we learn.from 400 studies on the effectiveness of treatment with juvenile delinquents? In J. McGuire (ed.) *What Works: Reducing Re-offending: Guidelines from Research and Practice.* Chichester: Wiley.

Lipsey, M. W. & Wilson, D. B. (1993) The efficacy of psychological, educational, and behavioral treatment: confirmation from meta-analysis. *American Psychologist*, **48**, 1181–1209.

Lipsey, M. W. & Wilson, D. B. (1998) Effective intervention for serious juvenile offenders: a synthesis of research. In R. Loeber & D. P. Farrington (eds) *Serious and Violent Juvenile Offenders: Risk Factors and Successful Interventions.* Thousand Oaks, CA: Sage.

Lipton, D. S., Pearson, F. S., Cleland, C. & Lee, D. (1997) *Synthesizing correctional treatment outcomes: preliminary CDATE findings.* Paper presented at the 5th Annual National Institute of Justice Conference on Research and Evaluation in Criminal Justice, Washington, DC, July.

Lipton, D. S., Thornton, D., McGuire, J., Porporino, F. & Hollin, C. R. (2000) Program accreditation and correctional treatment. *Substance Use and Misuse*, **35**, 1705–34.

Logan, C. H., Gaes, G. G., Harer, M., Innes, C. A., Karacki, L. & Saylor, W. G. (1991) *Can Meta-analysis Save Correctional Rehabilitation?* Washington, DC: Federal Bureau of Prisons.

Lösel, F. & Köferl, P. (1989) Evaluation research on correctional treatment in West Germany: a meta-analysis. In H. Wegener, F. Lösel & J. Haisch (eds) *Criminal Behaviour and the Justice System: Psychological Perspectives.* New York: Springer-Verlag.

Mackenzie, D. L. (1997) Criminal justice and crime prevention. In L. W. Sherman, D. Gottfredson, D. L. Mackenzie, J. Eck, P. Reuter & S. Bushway (eds) *Preventing Crime: What Works, What Doesn't, What's Promising.* Washington, DC: Office of Justice Programs.

Mayer, J. P., Gensheimer, L. K., Davidson, W. S. & Gottschalk, R. (1986) Social learning treatment within juvenile justice: a meta-analysis of impact in the natural environment.

In S. A. Apter & A. P. Goldstein (eds) *Youth Violence: Programs and Prospects.* Elmsford, NJ: Pergamon Press.

McGuire, J. (1994) *Problem solving training and offence behaviour.* Manual and programme materials. Unpublished documents. University of Liverpool.

McGuire, J. (ed.) (1995) *What Works: Reducing Re-offending: Guidelines from Research and Practice.* Chichester: Wiley.

McGuire, J. (1997) Ethical dilemmas in forensic clinical psychology. *Legal and Criminological Psychology,* **2**, 177–92.

McGuire, J. (2000a) Defining correctional programs. *Forum on Corrections Research,* **12**, 5–9.

McGuire, J. (2000b) *ThinkFirst.* Manual and programme materials. London: Home Office.

McGuire, J. (2000c) Can the criminal law ever be therapeutic? *Behavioral Sciences and the Law,* **18**, 413–26.

McGuire, J. (2001) What works in correctional intervention? Evidence and practical implications. In G. A. Bernfeld, D. P. Farrington & A. W. Leschied (eds) *Offender Rehabilitation in Practice: Implementing and Evaluating Effective Programs.* Chichester: Wiley.

McGuire, J. (2002) Criminal sanctions versus psychological interventions in reduction of recidivism: a comparative empirically-based review. *Psychology, Crime and Law,* in press.

McGuire, J. & Hatcher, R. (2001) Offence-focused problem-solving: preliminary evaluation of a cognitive skills program. *Criminal Justice and Behavior,* **28**, 564–87.

McGuire, J., Hatcher, R., Hollin, C. R., Palmer, E., Bilby C. & Holmes, A. (2001) Offending behaviour programmes in England and Wales. Paper presented at the 10th European Congress on Psychology and Law, Calouste Gulbenkian Foundation, Lisbon.

Meichenbaum, D. & Turk, D. C. (1987) *Facilitating Treatment Adherence: A Practitioner's Guidebook.* New York: Plenum Press.

Miller, W. R. (1983) Motivational interviewing with problem drinkers. *Behavioural Psychotherapy,* **11**, 147–72.

Miller, W.R., Sovereign, R. G. & Krege, B. (1988) Motivational interviewing with problem drinkers: II. The drinker's check-up as a preventive intervention. *Behavioural Psychotherapy,* **16**, 251–68.

Nagayama Hall, G. C. (1995) Sexual offender recidivism revisited: a meta-analysis of recent treatment studies. *Journal of Consulting and Clinical Psychology,* **63**, 802–9.

Nathan, P. E. & Gorman, J. M. (eds) (1998) *A Guide to What Works.* New York, NY: Oxford University Press.

Palmer, T. (1992) *The Re-Emergence of Correctional Intervention.* Newbury Park, CA: Sage.

Persons, J. B. & Silbersatz, G. (1998) Are the results of randomized controlled trials useful to psychotherapists? *Journal of Consulting and Clinical Psychology,* **66**, 126–35.

Priestley, P., McGuire, J., Flegg, D., Welham, D., Hemsley, V. & Barnitt, R. (1984) *Social Skills in Prisons and the Community: Problem-Solving for Offenders.* London: Routledge.

Redondo, S., Sánchez-Meca, J. & Garrido, V. (1999) The influence of treatment programmes on the recidivism of juvenile and adult offenders: a European meta-analytic review. *Psychology, Crime & Law,* **5**, 251–78.

Rex, S. (2001) Beyond cognitive-behaviouralism? Reflections on the effectiveness literature. In A. Bottoms, L. Gelsthorpe & S. Rex (eds) *Community Penalties: Change and Challenges.* Cullompton, Devon: Willan Publishing.

Roberts, A. R. & Camasso, M. J. (1991) The effect of juvenile offender treatment programs on recidivism: a meta-analysis of 46 studies. *Notre Dame Journal of Law, Ethics and Public Policy,* **5**, 421–41.

Rollnick, S. & Miller, W. R. (1995) What is motivational interviewing? *Behavioural and Cognitive Psychotherapy,* **23**, 325–34.

Rollnick, S., Heather, N. & Bell, A. (1992) Negotiating behaviour change in medical settings: the development of brief motivational interviewing. *Journal of Mental Health,* **1**, 25–37.

Rosenthal, R. (1994) Parametric measures of effect size. In H. Cooper & L. V. Hedges (eds) *Handbook of Research Synthesis,* New York, NY: Russell Sage Foundation.

Sherman, L. W. (1988) Randomized experiments in criminal sanctions. In H. S. Bloom, D. S. Cordray & R. J. Light (eds) *Lessons from Selected Program and Policy Areas.* New Directions for Program Evaluation, no. 37. San Francisco, CA: Jossey-Bass.

Sherman, L., Gottfredson, D., McKenzie, D., Eck, J., Reuter, P. & Bushway, S. (1997) *Preventing Crime: What Works, What Doesn't, What's Promising*. Washington, DC: Office of Justice Programs.

Simon, L. M. J. (1998) Does criminal offender treatment work? *Applied and Preventive Psychology*, **7**, 137–59.

van Bilsen, H. P. J. G. & Whitehead. B. (1994) Learning controlled drugs use: a case study. *Behavioural and Cognitive Psychotherapy*, **22**, 87–95.

Vanstone, M. (2000) Cognitive-behavioural work with offenders in the UK: a history of influential endeavour. *Howard Journal*, **39**, 171–83.

Vennard, J., Sugg, D. & Hedderman, C. (1997) *Changing Offenders' Attitudes and Behaviour: What Works?* Home Office Research Study no. 171. London: HMSO.

Walker, N. (1991) *Why Punish? Theories of Punishment Re-assessed*. Oxford: Oxford University Press.

Weisburd, D., Sherman, L. & Petrosino, A. J. (1990) *Registry of Randomized Criminal Justice Experiments in Sanctions*. Unpublished report, Rutgers University, University of Maryland and Crime Control Institute.

Whitehead, J. T. & Lab, S. P. (1989) A meta-analysis of juvenile correctional treatment. *Journal of Research in Crime and Delinquency*, **26**, 276–95;

Withers, J. M. J. (1995) Motivational interviewing: a special ethical dilemma? *Behavioural and Cognitive Psychotherapy*, **23**, 335–9.

Chapter 11

OWNING YOUR OWN DATA:
THE MANAGEMENT OF DENIAL

D. Richard Laws

South Island Consulting, Victoria, British Columbia, Canada

Not everything that is faced can be changed; but nothing can be changed until
it is faced.

James Baldwin, *Notes of a Native Son*

WHAT IS DENIAL?

A common dictionary definition (*Encarta World English Dictionary*, 1999, p. 482)
states in part that denial is "a statement saying that something is not true or not
correct ... an inability or a refusal to admit that something exists ... [or] ... a state of
mind marked by a refusal or inability to recognize and deal with a serious personal
problem". That is not far from typical psychological definitions. For example, a
personality textbook (Frager & Fadiman, 1998, p. 126) states that "Denial is the
unwillingness to accept an event that disturbs the ego. Adults have a tendency to
'daydream' that certain events are not so, that they didn't really happen ... The
form of denial found most often in psychotherapy is the remarkable tendency
to remember events incorrectly". Denial, says this text (p. 130), excludes reality.
In this sense, denial is shown as one of the common defence mechanisms. More
recent contributions to the cognitive-behavioural literature take a more functional,
present-oriented position. For example, speaking of the two most common features
noted in this literature, Barbaree (1991, p. 2) has noted:

> Denial and minimization are the results of a psychological process involving
> distortion, mistaken attribution, rationalization, and selective attention and
> memory. The process serves to reduce the offenders' experiences of blame and
> responsibility for their offences ... Denial and minimization are both products
> of the same self-serving cognitive processes, but they differ in two ways. First,
> denial and minimization represent different degrees of the process. Whereas de-
> nial is extreme and categorical, minimization is graded. Second, denial usually

Motivating Offenders to Change: A Guide to Enhancing Engagement in Therapy. Edited by M. McMurran.
© 2002 John Wiley & Sons, Ltd.

concerns either the facts of the case or whether or not the offender has a problem that needs treatment. Minimization, on the other hand, concerns the extent of an offender's responsibility for the offence, the extent of their part in offending and the degree of harm their victims have suffered.

This seems to say that there is a dichotomy in denial. On the one hand there is categorical denial of culpability and, on the other, a graded continuum of minimization. For the purposes of this chapter I will consider denial to be distributed along a continuum from categorical denial to full admission. Between these poles lies a graded continuum containing various degrees of minimization and other self-protective statements.

WHY IS DENIAL A PROBLEM?

Denial is typically the first problem encounted by treatment providers who deal with criminal populations. While a small proportion of offenders will fully admit to their offending behaviour and acknowledge the need for treatment, the vast majority will not. Those already convicted may admit to offences that are supported by incontrovertible evidence but nothing more. Others will protest that it was a "bum rap" and that they had nothing to do with the crime. Others who have pleaded guilty may say that "My lawyer told me to do it", "I pleaded guilty to the lesser charge to avoid a harder fall" or "I did it to spare the victim". These statements hardly encompass the possibilities. Those offenders facing possible sanctions can, for the most part, be expected to be minimally forthcoming. This is what treatment providers face at the outset. It is discouraging, to be sure, and many consider various levels of denial to be an impenetrable wall.

There is a belief that denial is the main impediment to successful therapy. Therefore, many treatment programmes exclude offenders who deny at any level. This is not lost on offenders, who know that by denying they can escape the pain of having to divulge their actions, sexual preferences, attitudes and beliefs in treatment. As we shall see, there is no evidence to support the contention that denial militates against successful treatment. One could argue further that it is unethical and professionally irresponsible *not* to accept deniers in treatment.

ASSESSMENT OF DENIAL

Denial is typically assessed in a variety of ways. These include: (1) clinical interview, (2) psychometric classification, (3) typological classification, (4) penile plethysmography and (5) polygraphy.

Clinical Interview

This is the modality most frequently used and is the one most subject to error. I wish to state at the outset that this is not a job for the novice. Adequate clinical interview of offenders requires experience with criminal populations. Independent interviews of offenders should, ideally, not be conducted by persons with less that five years of interviewing experience. Postgraduate students in psychology, social work and criminology are frequently given this task, as are psychiatric residents. These persons need to be supervised by experienced clinicians. If the clinician cannot sit in on the interview they should be videotaped and reviewed periodically with the student in supervision sessions.

Many clinicians believe that the use of a structured interview form is too formal, cold, impersonal and damaging to establishment of rapport with the client. I have not found this to be the case. The problem with doing a forensic interview "freehand", so to speak, is that considerable skill is required to stay on task, making certain that the required questions are asked, and that the interviewer is not led into irrelevant areas by the client. I typically inform clients that I will be using an interview format because I feel that it is the best way to properly organize information so that the most accurate report possible may be written. The usual client response is one of indifference.

There are two excellent structured interview forms available. The first is the *Hare PCL-R: Interview and Information Schedule* (Hare, 1991). This form covers school adjustment, work history, career goals, finances, health, family life, sex/relationships, drug use, childhood, adolescent and adult antisocial behaviour, and a series of general questions. All of the questions are open-ended. Interviewers are encouraged to ask these questions in an informal style and to follow up any as needed. One may also add questions. (For example, it was necessary for me to add more detailed questions on sexual history and practices.) The general rule guiding PCL-R interviewing is: "Give the person a chance to lie". One is usually not disappointed. Although the PCL-R form may be completed as a file-only review, it is highly advisable to do a face-to-face interview, particularly with regard to the offender's interpersonal style. The other form is the *Manual for the Compilation of a Psychosocial History Suitable for Risk Appraisal* (Quinsey et al., 1998, pp. 253–67). The items in this form are keyed to the PCL-R but, being a psychosocial history, it is much broader. The questions are much more direct and precise in content.

The primary purpose of the structured interview approach is to obtain the offender's viewpoint *vis-à-vis* the known facts of the case. The extent to which his account is congruent with the known facts is used to determine the extent of his denial. Obviously, this match bears heavily upon conviction and sentencing but also provides guidelines for any subsequent treatment intervention.

Psychometric Classification

The use of psychological tests has generally taken two forms: (1) using tests to detect denial, and (2) using various psychometric approaches to categorize deniers. The following will provide a flavour of this approach.

Grossman and Cavanaugh (1990) hypothesized that "alleged" sex offenders who denied deviant activity would be motivated to appear more psychologically healthy than they were, and this tendency to fake-good would be more prominent in those facing charges. They administered the Minnesota Multiphasic Personality Inventory (MMPI) (Hathaway & McKinley, 1967) to 53 sex offenders and examined several validity scales. The hypotheses were supported. Denying offenders were more likely to minimize psychopathology. Those facing no charges showed significantly more psychopathology. Haywood and colleagues (1993) followed up this study by examining minimization or exaggeration (response bias) in a similar group of 59 offenders. Using the 16PF (Cattell et al., 1970) they determined that offenders who denied allegations of deviant behaviour were more likely to minimize personal problems than admitters. Admitters showed more exaggeration of problems. In a similar vein, Haywood and colleagues (1994) examined rationalizations and cognitive distortions in alleged child molesters. They compared fake-good and fake-bad profiles on the MMPI with seven validity scales of the Multiphasic Sex Inventory (MSI) (Nichols & Molinder, 1984). The Cognition scale (Abel et al., 1984) was used as a measure of cognitive distortions. Data indicated that five of the seven validity scales of the MSI were significantly related to two MMPI measures of minimization/exaggeration. MSI cognitive distortion scores were significantly related to similar scores on the Cognition scale. Admitters differed significantly from deniers on the MSI distortion scales.

Lanyon and Lutz (1984) also used the MMPI to assess defensiveness and denial in a group of primarily child molesters who were either indicted or convicted of a sexual offence. Persons known to be denying were compared to full admitters. They hypothesized that full or partial deniers would have higher defensiveness scores than admitters. They were able to best discriminate all deniers from admitters by the raw score index L + K − F. In a later study, Lanyon and colleagues (1991) found that all three MMPI deception scales (F − K, L − K, and L + K − F) discriminated between admitting and denying offenders. Readers unfamiliar with the MMPI (or MMPI-2) should be advised that the designations L, F, and K refer to the validity scales of that instrument. Pope and colleagues (1993, pp. 100–7) provide an overview of these scales. Elevations of the L scale suggest an individual who is unwilling to admit even minor flaws, who makes an unrealistic proclamation of virtue, or is attempting to deceive others about his or her motives or personal adjustment. Elevated F scale scores may suggest severe psychopathology, possible symptom exaggeration, faking of psychological problems or malingering. Elevated K scores suggest defensiveness or a great need to present oneself as very well adjusted. The assumption is that persons showing elevations on the validity scales are also dissimulating on the items in the test proper. The combination of these scales (e.g. L + K − F) represents the attempt to improve the discriminability of the validity scale scores.

Lanyon et al. (1991) also argued against using the MSI to assess honesty versus deception. They state (pp. 301–2): "A major difficulty in using this instrument . . . is that persons who report no sexually deviant behaviors or attitudes are automatically labeled as dishonest". The result of this is that the MSI is incapable of discriminating honest non-offenders from denying offenders.

A rather unique approach in this area was reported by Baldwin and Roys (1998). They examined data from the MMPI, the second edition of the MSI, the Abel–Becker Card Sort (Salter, 1988) and (uncommon in this type of research) penile plethysmography (PPG). Consistent with previous research, deniers displayed a fake-good pattern of responding and showed more defensiveness on the MMPI and MSI scales than admitters. They appeared more psychologically healthy on the MMPI clinical scales. Some differences were observed on the card sorting measure. Deniers reported less sexual arousal to descriptions of sexual contact with minor females, but both deniers and admitters reported attraction to adult females. The PPG results were inconclusive. Deniers and admitters both showed arousal to deviant sexual stimuli. This study appears to be a rather elaborate way of demonstrating a finding that, by 1998, was obvious.

Taking a different approach to the same issue, Birgisson (1996) administered the Eysenck Personality Questionnaire (EPQ) (Eysenck & Eysenck, 1975) and the Compliance Questionnaire (Gudjonsson, 1989) to 30 denying and 72 admitting sex offenders. On EPQ Neuroticism, deniers scored lower than admitters, and lower than the EPQ norm for males. Birgisson stated that this was consistent with previous MMPI work which showed deniers presenting as emotionally stable. Also consistent with MMPI research was the finding that EPQ Lie scores showed a fake-good profile. Deniers also showed lower Compliance scores than admitters. Birgisson (p. 124) states: "This...is consistent with the common clinical experience that deniers tend to stubbornly withstand persuasions and confrontations in therapy".

Psychometric approaches have also been used to categorize groups according to their demonstrated pattern of denial. Three studies illustrate this approach.

Nugent and Kroner (1996) examined denial and response styles. They administered the Balanced Inventory of Desirable Responding (BIDR) (Paulus, 1984), a measure of self-deception and impression management, and the Basic Personality Inventory (BPI) (Jackson, 1989), a measure of denial and social desirability, to 49 child molesters and 49 rapists. The authors reviewed the offenders' account of the offence compared to the official version. They established four categories of denial: (1) non-admitter (no offence occurred), (2) partial admitter (sexual contact but no offence), (3) partial admitter (only part of a sexual act) and (4) admitter (agrees with the official version). Categories 2 and 3 were collapsed for analysis. Results indicated that child molesters admitted more frequently. Child molesters tended to deny the amount of offending in which they engaged while rapists denied the amount of force used. The largest difference in response styles was on impression management. Child molesters appeared to be concerned about what others think about them, while rapists were less concerned about self-presentation.

Kennedy and Grubin (1992) interviewed 102 sex offenders in prison, 34 of whom were rapists, and the balance having offended against children. The offenders were asked to give their own account of the offences for which they had been convicted. The authors rated the offenders' accounts using a seven-part scale which included (1) offence (deny/admit), (2) responsibility (full/partial), (3) internal (disordered mental state), (4) external attribution (third parties), (5) preferences (sexual), (6) effect (on victim) and (7) social sanction (attitude toward sentence). Each of these elements was graded 0, 1 or 2. Cluster analysis was performed on the interview data. Full deniers were excluded from this analysis. Briefly, the analysis produced three groups: (1) *rationalizers*, who were most like to admit to a deviant preference, and least likely to blame a mental state, the victim or third parties, (2) *externalizers*, who were most likely to blame third parties or the victim, and to deny harm, and (3) *internalizers*, who were most likely to admit to the offence as charged and accept the sentence, admit victim harm, and blame a mental state and third parties. The authors argue that such a categorization might be useful in structuring treatment programmes.

A more ambitious effort may be seen in research under way by Jung (2000). Jung has developed an 18-level rating scale using 0, 1, 2 ratings similar in approach to Kennedy and Grubin (1992). The *Comprehensive Inventory of Denial–Sex Offender* (CID-SO) version focuses upon: (1) specific offence, (2) sex offending history, (3) guilt or shame over discovery, (4) focus on acceptable, nonsexual behaviours, (5) minimization—seriousness, (6) minimization—harm to victim, (7) blaming the victim, (8) internal attribution, (9) external attribution, (10) possibility of future offending, (11) intent/planning/premeditation, (12) deviant arousal/fantasies, (13) arousal [gratification, pleasure], (14) defensive/excessive hostility, (15) difficulty of change, (16) desire/expressed need of help, (17) false dissociation and (18) social sanction. Clearly, the Kennedy and Grubin categories are included but the CID-SO goes considerably further in attempting the dissection of the denial phenomenon. Presumably this developing instrument will be submitted to psychometric examination.

Rational Typologies

The construction of typologies for characterization of deniers has been quite common. These are referred to as "rational" typologies because they are, for the most part, common-sense constructions based on clinicians' and researchers' direct experience with offenders. Barbaree (1991) made a distinction between denial and minimization (see below). Most workers, however, view denial as distributed along a continuum from what is usually referred to as "absolute" or "categorical" denial to full admission. Following are some examples.

The sociologist C. Wright Mills (1940) wrote of the "vocabulary of motive" through which offenders attempt to disown their deviant behaviour and present themselves as normal individuals. A classic study by Scully and Marolla (1984) investigated the vocabulary of motive in convicted rapists. Their goal was to investigate *excuses* (admitting the act was bad but denying full responsibility) and *justifications* (accepting responsibility but denying that the act was wrong). They interviewed 114 men, all of whom were given an 89-page interview and 30 pages of open-ended questions. Interviews lasted from three to seven hours. In terms of justifying rape, they found five themes in deniers: (1) women as seductresses, (2) women mean "yes" when they say "no", (3) most women eventually relax and enjoy it, (4) nice girls don't get raped, and (5) only a minor wrongdoing. With respect to excuses, admitters attempted to explain how they were compelled to rape: (1) an appeal to use of alcohol and drugs, (2) an appeal to emotional problems and (3) presenting themselves as a "nice guy" who had made a mistake but was otherwise a decent fellow. Scully and Marolla note that their findings demonstrate a "cultural view of women as sexual commodities . . . the sexual objectification of women must be understood as an important factor contributing to an environment that trivializes, neutralizes, and, perhaps, facilitates rape" (p. 542). A similar approach to child molesters was reported by Pollock and Hashmall (1991).

There are numerous reports of rational typologies in the literature (see, for example, Happel & Auffrey, 1995; Hoke et al., 1989; Laflen & Sturm, 1994; Schlank & Shaw, 1996; Winn, 1996). Although each of these is distinct in its own right, all share common themes and items. There are three that are worth mentioning in detail.

As mentioned above, Barbaree (1991) distinguished between denial and minimization. His typology was based on the cited work of Scully and Marolla (1984) with rapists and Pollock and Hashmall (1991) with child molesters. Barbaree determined that there were three factors each for denial and minimization. For denial: (1) of any interaction, (2) that the interaction was sexual and (3) that the interaction was an offence. For minimization: (1) of responsibility (victim blame, external attributions, irresponsible internal attributions), (2) of extent (frequency, number of previous convictions, force used and intrusiveness) and (3) of harm (no long-term effects). Based on this work, Barbaree developed a *Denial and Minimization Checklist* for clinical use. Clearly, there are commonalities here with much of the research reported above. Barbaree's article is an oft-cited classic in the field and has been quite influential.

Equally influential has been Salter's (1988) typology. Jackson and Thomas-Peter (1994, p. 22) noted that Salter indicated that "different types of patterns of denial (admission with justification, denial of responsibility and minimization of the extent of the behaviour) are dependent upon the presence or absence of six basic components: (1) denial of the acts themselves, (2) denial of fantasy and planning, (3) denial of responsibility for the acts, (4) denial of the seriousness of the behaviour, (5) denial of internal guilt for the behaviour and (6) denial of the difficulty in changing abusive patterns. Salter's (1988) typology is unique in that the offender is not characterized in a categorical fashion (e.g. "partial admitter", "partial denier"). One or more of the above components may be present to provide a more individualized picture of denial. Salter's (1988) work is also oft-cited and influential.

More recently Marshall et al. (1999) have presented a conceptualization of denial and minimization based on their clinical work. This typology, in my opinion, encompasses all of the best features of previous work. It should be noted that this is a rational typology only and is not intended to be converted into a checklist such as Barbaree's (1991) or the developing categorization scheme related to treatment entry by Jung (2000). Table 11.1 shows the Marshall et al. (1999, p. 63) typology.

Is there a difference between sex offenders and other criminal offenders with respect to denial? I doubt very much that there are huge differences in denial among different types of offenders. Any person who has been apprehended in a criminal act and has something to lose in income, family, status or personal relationships has sufficient motivation to deny. There are only a handful of ways that one can squirm out from under an accusation or a irrefutable presentation of fact(s). Despite this, almost everyone tries. For example, if we reduce the list shown in Table 11.1, removing all items dealing specifically with sexual offending, we are left with the following (slightly modified):

Table 11.1 Features of denial and minimization

Complete denial
  False accusation
  • The police are out to get me
  • The victim hates me
  • The victim's mother is using it to deny access or get back at me
  Wrong person
  • It must have been someone else
  Memory loss
  • I'm not like that so I doubt that it happened
  • It could have happened but I can't remember
Partial denial
  Wasn't really sexual abuse
  • The victim consented
  • The victim enjoyed it
  • She/he was a prostitute or promiscuous
  • The victim said he/she was older
  • I was only massaging the victim
  • I was putting medicated cream on his/her genitals
  • It was only play
  • It was love
  • It was educational
  Denial of a problem
  • I did it but I am not a sex offender
  • I will never do it again
  • I don't have any interest in kids or forced sex
  • I don't have deviant fantasies
Minimizing the offence
  • The frequency was less than the victim claims
  • There was no coercion/force/threats
  • The intrusiveness was less than the victim claims
  • There are no other victims
Minimizing responsibility
  • The victim was seductive/provocative
  • The victim's parents were neglectful
  • I was intoxicated
  • I was severely stressed/emotionally disturbed
  • My partner wasn't satisfactory sexually
  • I have a high sex drive
  • The victim said no but really meant yes
Denying/minimizing harm
  • His/her friends or family tell me that the victim was not harmed
  • The victim's current problems were not caused by me
  • I was loving and affectionate so I couldn't have caused harm
  • I was not forceful so I couldn't have caused harm
Denying/minimizing planning
  • I acted on the spur of the moment
  • Things just unfolded
  • The victim initiated it
Denying/minimizing fantasizing
  • I do not think I have deviant fantasies
  • I did not think about abusing the victim prior to actually offending

Adapted by permission from Marshall et al. (1999, p. 63)

- The police are out to get me.
- The crime victim hates me.
- It must have been someone else.
- I'm not like that so I doubt that it happened.
- It could have happened but I can't remember.
- I did it but I am not a criminal.
- I will never do it again.
- The frequency was less than the charges state.
- There was no coercion/force/threats.
- There are no other crimes.
- I was intoxicated.
- I was severely stressed/emotionally disturbed.
- The crime victim's current problems were not caused by me.
- I acted on the spur of the moment.
- Things just unfolded.

Do these sound familiar? It seems to me that what works in one situation will likely work in another. Denial is denial, irrespective of offence category. Your intervention should be tailored to the type of denial you are facing.

Denial Revealed by Penile Plethysmography (PPG)

In the literature reviewed thus far only one study, that of Baldwin and Roys (1998) employed PPG, to no apparent effect. PPG is, and always has been, a highly controversial procedure. Briefly, it requires that the client attach an electronic sensor to the shaft of his penis. The assumption is that differential measures of penile diameter are related to "interest" or "preference" for various kinds of sexual activities. Typically, visual stimuli of males and females of various ages are presented to establish gender preference, and audiotaped descriptions of sexual activity are presented to establish interest or preference in violent or non-violent sexual activity. O'Donohue and Letourneau (1992, p. 125) have provided the basic rationale for the procedure:

> The underlying hypothesis for the use of penile tumescence measurement is known as the "sexual preference" hypothesis (Freund & Blanchard, 1981). This hypothesis states that "men who engage in sexually deviant acts are thought to prefer deviant behavior and their associated stimuli (over) those behavior and stimuli which are normalized and socially acceptable" (Murphy & Barbaree, 1986, p. 13). Arousal to deviant stimuli is taken to be an indication of a preference for deviant sexual acts, whether or not those acts were ever actually committed.

The author has had considerable experience with this procedure. Several points are worth noting. First, the equipment required is quite expensive. Second, it is highly labour intensive, assessments often taking two to three hours. Third, many subjects produce no response at all ("flat-liners"). Fourth, PPG profiles which suggest deviant sexual interest are not necessarily indicative of past or future offending. Fifth, it is not uncommon for supposedly normal clients to respond to deviant stimuli.

Sixth, clients who deny will simply say that they have no idea why they responded in the fashion that the record shows. In my experience, PPG is useful with clients who are full admitters and amenable to treatment. Confrontation with deniers (if they even agree to participate) is rarely successful. In their review O'Donohue and Letourneau (1992) note that there are problems with criterion responses (how much is enough for diagnosis?), a lack of procedural standardization for administering the procedure, problems with validity (predictive, content-related and construct) and response faking. These problems argue against the inclusion of PPG in sex offender assessments to determine denial. On the other hand, a recent meta-analysis by Hanson and Bussiere (1998) indicates that measures of deviant sexual arousal are related to sex offence recidivism.

Denial Revealed by Polygraphy

Although polygraphy, like PPG, has a controversial history with regard to the data being considered admissible evidence in court, it appears to be a useful tool that is here to stay. Green and Franklin (1999, p. 13–8) state that there are three uses for polygraphy in the management of sex offenders:

1. *Full disclosure polygraph examination.* The primary purpose of this examination is to obtain a full sexual history. There are two elements:
   a. disclosure of the kinds and frequencies of sexual acts or abuse involving himself and the present victim;
   b. disclosure of the entire number of victims and sexual acts he has perpetrated. It is the second element that most disturbs many professionals and laypersons because they believe that individuals should not be encouraged to incriminate themselves for crimes that have not been reported or prosecuted. However, persons who support polygraphy believe that obtaining a full history is essential to formulating an effective treatment and management plan.
2. *Maintenance polygraph examination.* These periodic examinations, occurring every six months or less, are intended to discover if the offender is in compliance with probation/parole or treatment conditions. Key elements of his offence cycle are often examined.
3. *Specific issue examination.* This examination focuses upon a particular crime or accusation and is less frequently used. This type of examination is the one most usually used by police examiners.

Green and Franklin (1999) state that there is a team approach to the offender consisting of a probation/parole officer, a treatment provider and a polygrapher. Offenders are given 60–90 days to make a full disclosure of their histories and are constantly reminded that they will undergo a polygraph examination. They state that their goal, whether it is a full disclosure or a maintenance examination, is for the offender to pass the examination. The data they offer are impressive. During the period 1993–1997, 136 examinations were conducted. Prior to the polygraph examination, offenders admitted to 653 offences; the examination revealed 37, 918 offences. In 1997, 33 sex offenders were convicted in Green and Franklin's jurisdiction. Prior to the polygraph examination, these 33 men admitted to 40 offences; the examination revealed 493 victims.

O'Connell (2000) reported somewhat more modest results. His research, like that of Green and Franklin (1999) showed that polygraph testing revealed more information on sexually deviant behaviour and lifetime sexual offending. Polygraphy revealed more than three times the number of offences than were previously known and increased reports of the number of different paraphilias. He also discovered that nearly half of sex offenders taking a full history disclosure examination attempted deception. Many of these deniers required as many as four additional examinations, disclosing more information with each successive test, to pass.

Like Green and Franklin (1999), O'Connell (2000) recommends periodic monitoring by polygraphy. He believes that monitoring examinations serve several purposes: (1) uncovering new problems, (2) encouraging compliance with supervision and treatment rules and (3) increasing self-disclosure in therapy.

In my experience, treatment providers who use polygraphy are almost fanatical in their support of the procedure. The problems with the procedure will persist. It is, like PPG, highly intrusive in its physiological measurement and it does force the offender essentially to testify against himself. This is what upsets persons with human and civil rights concerns. On the other hand, such limited data as we have strongly suggest that it is a powerful tool in combating denial.

TREATMENT OF DENIAL

There are three approaches to the treatment of denial: (1) community supervision, (2) pre-treatment programmes and (3) cognitive-behaviour therapy.

Supervision

Strate and colleagues (1996) believe that sex offenders can be safely managed in the community in the context of probation/parole. They argue that there should be several major changes in the criminal justice system. First, sex offenders should not be permitted to make no contest pleas or plead guilty to nonsexual offences. Further, they do not believe that conditional sentences should be allowed, nor should sex offenders be referred to diversion programmes as an alternative to filing of a criminal charge. Community supervison, they say, can be strengthed by working with a team composed of the probation/parole officer, the treatment provider and a polygraph examiner. Treatment and supervision requirements should be clearly communicated among prosecutors, defence lawyers and probation/parole agents. Finally, the probation/parole officers doing the actual supervision should have specialized training and job duties (i.e. they supervise only sex offenders).

Is supervision effective?

For over a decade the most popular treatment programme for sex offenders has been relapse prevention (RP). The basic RP procedures are thought to be applicable

to other disorders of impulse control such as compulsive (nondeviant) sexual behaviours, compulsive gambling, compulsive spending, smoking, problem drinking, shoplifting and interpersonal violence, and addictive behaviours such as alcohol or drug abuse (Laws, 1995). The original model has been succinctly described by
Pithers (1991). This model had two parts. The first, the Internal Self-Management
Dimension, taught the offender the nuts and bolts of RP, and the strategies and
procedures that could prevent him or her from relapsing to further offensive sexual behaviour. The second part, the External, Supervisory Dimension, involved
aggressive community supervision of the offender by probation/parole officers,
mental health professionals and selected collateral contacts in the community, a
sort of iron triangle of supervision. Cumming and McGrath (2000) expanded this
to what they called a "supervision diamond" by adding a polygraph examiner.
Clearly the offender is tightly hemmed in by such supervisory control. Is this aggressive approach effective? Does it markedly decrease reoffence rates? Marshall
et al. (1999) believe that it does not. They state that:

> making treatment... overly elaborate, and coupling that with extensive post-
> release supervision, sends a message to our clients that we may not wish them
> to accept. Such elaborate procedures indicate to our clients that we believe that
> their problems are so extensive as to be all but insurmountable, and that we do
> not believe that they can manage their lives on their own (p. 139).

As evidence for this claim they cite the outcome data of the classical bigger-better
study of sex offender treatment, California's Sex Offender Treatment and Evaluation Project (SOTEP) (Marques et al., 2000). This programme ran from 1985 to 1995
in a secure facility with intensive follow-up in the community. SOTEP elaborated
upon but was built upon both of the dimensions described by Pithers (1991). It
contained all of the knick-knackery of RP and then some and so served as a perfect model for Marshall et al.'s hypothesis that too much intricate treatment and
too intensive post-treatment supervision will almost certainly ensure failure of the
clientele. If this hypothesis is true, they said, two results should follow: (1) treated
clients should do no better than matched untreated clients, and (2) after post-
incarceration supervision is terminated (in this case, after 1 year) recidivism rates
of treated subjects should increase. Survival rates provided by the project director
for 4+ years post-treatment confirmed the hypothesis of Marshall et al. Marshall
et al. consider these data to be a powerful indictment of super-intensive community supervision. The purpose of treatment and supervision, they say, should be
to empower clients, not infantalize them by implicitly or explicitly suggesting that
they cannot manage without someone to watch over them.

Pre-treatment Programmes

A correctionally-oriented programme was reported by Happel and Auffrey (1995).
Their goal is to interrupt the "dance of denial" prior to an offender entering their
treatment programme at the Muskegon Treatment Facility (MTF) in Michigan. To
accomplish this they created the MTF Therapy Review Board, a rather Inquisition-
like panel which interviews offenders prior to their entering treatment. Three

psychologists interview the inmate, taking what appear to be "good cop-bad cop" roles to break resistance. For example, one psychologist may convey positive regard and understanding, while another displays confrontation and challenge. Happel and Auffrey (1995, pp. 13–14) state that this badgering creates "a state of cognitive dissonance . . . [so that] . . . sex offenders start to realize that telling the truth is essential if they are to benefit from treatment . . . [and that] . . . the Review Board process promotes confession and catharsis". This conclusion seems doubtful.

Kear-Colwell and Pollock (1997) argue strongly against a confrontational approach to piercing the wall of denial. Confrontation, they say, seeks an admission of guilt, a squaring of the known facts of the case with the offender's account, and an admission that they have a problem that needs changing. They recommend the adoption of the Prochaska and DiClemente (1982) stages of change model. These stages are: (1) precontemplation, (2) contemplation, (3) preparation, (4) action and (5) maintenance. This is not dissimilar to the continuum of denial described above. The individual moves from a stage of denying the problem, to considering that a problem may exist, to preparing to do something about it, to taking direct action to change behaviour and keep it changed. The motivational approach advanced by Miller and Rollnick (1991) exemplifies the practical application of this model to treatment. Garland and Dougher (1991) recommend use of the motivational approach as a pre-treatment strategy to engage offenders, particularly motivational interviewing and the careful presentation of assessment results.

Brake and Shannon (1997) have offered an explicit model of a pre-treatment programme. They properly note that few offenders are complete admitters or complete deniers and argue that provisions should be made to accept them into treatment. They also offer a classification scheme with four "levels" of denial and twelve "types" of denial. The levels are: (1) weak avoidance, (2) projections/moderate avoidance, (3) projections/strong avoidance and (4) primitive denial/severe denial. The persons falling into levels 1 and 2 present the least intractable forms of denial but all are considered for treatment. Brake and Shannon have developed a pre-treatment programme whose goal is to "lessen denial about the instant offense. Once this has been accomplished, the offender is referred to an offense-specific treatment program" (pp. 5–6). The pre-treatment programme is presented in six stages, each stage having a series of interventions intended to lessen denial:

1. Stage 1: *Containment*. Accept the fact of denial, respect the offender, allow him to save face.
2. Stage 2: *Symptom relief*. Acknowlege discomfort, describe hope.
3. Stage 3: *Reframe denial*. Explain denial, reframe sexual arousal.
4. Stage 4: *Reframe accountability*. No blaming of others, invite personal choice and responsibility, reinforce positive change.
5. Stage 5: *Model empathy*. Talk about family, acknowledge offender victimization, use role reversal.
6. Stage 6: *Successive approximation of confrontation*. Request permission for confrontation, confront by successive approximation, suggest polygraph.

The preceding is an extremely skeletal presentation of this program. There are 21 sessions in all, each conducted in a one-to-one format in an attempt to match the upcoming treatment intervention to the level of denial presented. The reader should compare this approach to that of Jenkins (1990), who also employs "invitations to responsibility". The Brake and Shannon (1997) approach is, I think, a rather good one but obviously most appropriate to a residential or long-term community programme. Although they argue for a one-to-one approach, I think that this might be presented more effectively as a "pre-group group" to involve all participants in the denial problem. A rolling group would likely be the least labour intensive approach.

Cognitive-Behaviour Therapy

One of the earliest reports of treatment of deniers described a brief intervention (seven $1\frac{1}{2}$-hour sessions) (O'Donohue & Letourneau, 1993). With regard to denial, programme components included: (1) cognitive restructuring of beliefs about adult–child sexual contact, (2) education about sex offender therapy and (3) possible consequences of continued denial. A follow-up measure was sent to therapists of clients who received continuing treatment subsequent to the group. Although the total number of participants was small (n = 17), the authors reported that 11 (65%) changed from denier to admitter status at post-treatment.

A somewhat less successful approach was reported by Schlank and Shaw (1996). They conducted a 16-session group for 10 clients who had failed to be admitted to treatment programmes due to denial. The programme components included (1) a segment on the nature of denial, (2) victim empathy and (3) relapse prevention (RP). A unique feature of the programme was requiring the clients to apply RP to a behaviour that they were willing to change (e.g. smoking marijuana). They were then asked to apply the model to a mythical client who might be guilty of the offence for which the participant had been accused. However, only five of the ten clients admitted to their offences.

Possibly the most successful practitioners of the cognitive-behavioural approach to denial have been Jenkins (1990) and Marshall (1994; Marshall et al., 1999, 2001).

Jenkins (1990) has reported extensively, albeit subjectively, on his therapeutic approach called "invitations to responsibility". His approach seems to me to be an amalgam of individual and group psychotherapy, family therapy and cognitive-behavioural therapy. This is a slow and measured treatment that gradually "invites" the offender to assume responsibility for his actions and take the major lead in altering his deviant behaviour. It is very labour intensive. Jenkins has reported that the typical length of treatment is three years, although he admits that most of the important work is done in the first year.

Marshall (1994) reported on the institutional treatment of 81 offenders, 15 rapists and 66 child molesters. This was a brief treatment, approximately 12 weeks in length, intended to deal with denial and minimization. This programme was somewhat similar to the approach described by Brake and Shannon (1997) although not heavily structured. It was conducted as a rolling group. Marshall's programme focused upon acceptance of the client but not the offence(s), invitations to take responsibility for his actions, and encouraging disclosure. In this he was aided by the older members of the group. Pre-treatment, the percentages in each category were: (1) deniers (31%), (2) minimizers (32%) and (3) full admitters (37%). Post-treatment these percentages changed dramatically: (1) deniers (2%), (2) minimizers (11%) and (3) full admitters (86%).

Marshall et al. (1999) eschew the popular use of psychoeducational approaches to sex offenders, favouring instead what they call "psychotherapeutic process". Upon examination, however, this approach appears to be a psychotherapy-like version of cognitive-behavioural therapy. In Marshall et al.'s 1999 report it appears that denial is not treated as a unique entity but rather is subsumed under the more general area of cognitive distortions. Denial is dealt with in the context of each participant making a disclosure of his version of the offence(s). Marshall et al. (1999, p. 70) state:

> These individual disclosures are typically repeated over several sessions and extensive discussions ensue regarding the offender's interpretation of the victim's behaviour, his own behaviour, and his expressed or implied attitudes and beliefs . . . the offender's interpretations and beliefs are challenged and restructured by the group . . . these challenges and restructuring go on throughout the program as evidence of distortions continues to emerge.

In their 1999 volume, Marshall et al. do not provide data specific to overcoming denial. Rather, they simply consider it part of the baggage that offenders carry, and treat it as one element in an array of personal problems.

In their most recent work (Marshall et al., 2001), they report a unique approach to overcoming denial. In discussions with deniers they realized that the main obstacle to getting them into a treatment programme was the clients' fear that the therapists would challenge their claim of innocence. "Accordingly," say Marshall et al.:

> we decided that we would issue a promise . . . to not discuss their offense much less challenge their denial . . . We believe this is critical to securing their cooperation . . . Within this context we indicate to the participants that our goals are to help them identify problems in their lives that put them in a position to be successfully accused of sexual offending or that generated sufficient animosity in others that someone accused them of an offense they claim not to have committed. We suggest to them that there must have been something about their behavior, attitudes or feelings that put them in a position to be accused and convicted of a sexual offense, and that we need, therefore, to identify these issues and help them learn to change (p. 208).

This is an extremely clever approach to denial. By making a simple promise and keeping it, the therapists engage the clients in a programme they say they do not need, for a problem they say they do not have, to prevent another offence that they say they did not commit in the first place.

CONCLUSIONS

It is difficult to summarize information from a literature of such complexity. However, if one is going to do something about denial and attempt to engage offenders in treatment, decisions must be made. For assessment of denial, a competent clinical interview must be performed first. In my view, the best formats are the *PCL-R: Interview and Information Schedule* (Hare, 1991) and the *Psychosocial History* (Quinsey et al., 1998). Psychometric investigations have produced little of clinical value. The studies of who is and who is not a sex offender are really elaborations of the obvious. The psychometric studies producing typologies (Jung, 2000; Kennedy & Grubin, 1992) may be promising approaches. The rational typologies have assisted clinicians in appreciating the dimensionality of denial. There are many to choose from; I have suggested that the Marshall et al. (1999) typology probably illumines the problem best. PPG should be avoided. It is expensive, highly intrusive and too often provides uninterpretable results. Whether one likes it or not, it appears that polygraphy is now part of the sex offender treatment landscape. Such data as we have look very promising indeed. Pre-treatment programmes to lessen denial are more a popular idea than a reality. It seems a useful tool rather than having to waste time in formal treatment dealing with severe levels of denial. If one is operating a psychoeducational programme (as many therapists will be) then the Brake and Shannon model (1997) would be the one of choice. Finally, most clinicians do not have experience that comes even close to the skills of Marshall and his colleagues or of Jenkins. I would recommend, therefore, that one adopt elements of the many cognitive-behavioural programmes reported in the literature. I would further recommend that the stages of change approach (Prochaska & DiClemente, 1982) and the related motivational approach (Garland & Dougher, 1991; Miller & Rollnick, 1991) be incorporated in that treatment.

The literature is clear that denial may be overcome by a variety of means. It is less clear, but very intriguing, that perhaps attempts to overcome it are simply not necessary.

AUTHOR'S NOTE

The editor of this volume has requested all authors to be aware that the book is about "offenders of all types" and that "authors who specialise in one kind of offender ... [should] ... aim to extend their case". For the past 30 years, with few exceptions, I have worked with all varieties of sexual offenders. These were all male, mainly adults, educated and uneducated, single, married and divorced, engaging in a broad range of occupations, and who exhibited a broad range of criminal as well as deviant sexual behaviour. Despite the heterogeneity of their sexual predilections, the common thread that ran through all the cases was the display of virtually the same types of denial mechanisms. While I am unable to extend this experience to accommodate other types of offenders, I hope that my readers will note the similarities in their respective clienteles.

REFERENCES

Abel, G.G., Becker, J.V., & Cunningham-Rather, J. (1984). Complications, consent and cognitions in sex between children and adults. *International Journal of Law and Psychiatry, 7,* 89–103.

Baldwin, K., & Roys, D.T. (1998). Factors associated with denial in a sample of alleged adult sexual offenders. *Sexual Abuse: A Journal of Research and Treatment*, **10**, 211–26.

Barbaree, H.E. (1991). Denial and minimization among sex offenders: assessment and treatment outcome. *Forum on Corrections Research*, **3**, 30–3.

Birgisson, G.H. (1996). Differences of personality, defensiveness, and compliance between admitting and denying male sex offenders. *Journal of Interpersonal Violence*, **11**, 118–25.

Brake, S.C., & Shannon, D. (1997). Using pretreatment to increase admission in sex offenders. In B.D. Schwartz & H. Cellini (eds) *The Sex Offender: New Insights, Treatment Innovations, and Legal Developments* (pp. 1-5–5-16). Kingston, NJ: Civic Research Institute.

Cattell, R., Eber, H.W., & Tatsuoka, M.M. (1970). *Handbook for the 16PF*. Champaign, IL: Institute for Personality and Ability Testing.

Cumming, G.F., & McGrath, R.J. (2000). External supervision: how can it increase the effectiveness of relapse prevention? In D.R. Laws, S.M. Hudson, & T. Ward (eds) *Remaking Relapse Prevention with Sex Offenders* (pp. 236–53). Thousand Oaks, CA: Sage.

Encarta World English Dictionary (1999). New York: St Martin's Press.

Eysenck, H.J., & Eysenck, S.B.G. (1975). *Manual of the Eysenck Personality Questionnaire (Junior and Adult)*. San Diego, CA: Educational and Industrial Testing Service.

Frager, R., & Fadiman, J. (1998). *Personality and Personal Growth, 4th edn*. New York: Longman.

Freund, K., & Blanchard, R. (1981). Assessment of sexual dysfunction and deviation. In M. Hersen and A.S. Bellack (eds) *Behavioral Assessment: A Practical Handbook*, 2nd edn (pp. 427–55). New York: Pergamon.

Garland, R.J., & Dougher, M.J. (1991). Motivational intervention in the treatment of sex offenders. In W.R. Miller and S. Rollnick (eds) *Motivational Interviewing: Preparing People to Change Addictive Behavior* (pp. 303–19). New York: Guilford.

Green, P., & Franklin, B. (1999). The sex offender, the polygraph, and community corrections. In B.K. Schwartz (ed.) *The Sex Offender: Theoretical Advances, Treating Special Populations, and Legal Developments* (pp. 13-1–13-10). Kingston, NJ: Civic Research Institute.

Grossman, L.S., & Cavanaugh, J.L., Jr (1990) Psychopathology and denial in alleged sex offenders. *Journal of Nervous and Mental Disease*, **178**, 739–44.

Gudjonsson, G.H. (1989). Compliance in interrogative situations: a new scale. *Personality and Individual Differences*, **5**, 53–8.

Hanson, R.K., & Bussiere, M.T. (1998), Predicting relapse: a meta-analysis of sexual offender recidivism studies. *Journal of Consulting and Clinical Psychology*, **66**, 348–62.

Happel, R.M., & Auffrey, J.J. (1995). Sex offender assessment: interrupting the dance of denial. *American Journal of Forensic Psychology*, **13**, 5–22.

Hare, R.D. (1991). *The Hare PCL-R: Interview and Information Schedule*. Toronto, ON: Multi-Health Systems, Inc.

Hathaway, S.R., & McKinley, J.C. (1967). *MMPI Manual*. New York: Psychological Corporation.

Haywood, T.W., & Grossman, L.S. (1994). Denial of deviant sexual arousal and psychopathology in child molesters. *Behavior Therapy*, **25**, 327–40.

Haywood, T.W., Grossman, L.S., & Hardy, D.W. (1993). Denial and social desirability in clinical evaluations of alleged sex offenders. *Journal of Nervous and Mental Disease*, **181**, 183–8.

Haywood, T.W., Grossman, L.S., Kravitz, H.M., & Wasyliw, O.E. (1994). Profiling psychological distortion in alleged child molesters. *Psychological Reports*, **75**, 915–27.

Hoke, S.L., Sykes, C., & Winn, M. (1989). Systemic/strategic interventions targeting denial in the incestuous family. *Journal of Strategic and Systemic Therapies*, **8**, 44–51.

Jackson, C., & Thomas-Peter, B.A. (1994). Denial in sex offenders: workers' perceptions. *Criminal Behaviour and Mental Health*, **4**, 21–32.

Jackson, D.N. (1989). *Basic Personality Inventory Manual*. London, ON: Sigma Assessment Systems.

Jenkins, A. (1990). *Invitations to Responsibility: The Therapeutic Management of Men who are Violent and Abusive*. Adelaide: Dulwich Centre.

Jung, S. (2000). Comprehensive Inventory of Denial–Sex Offender version. Unpublished research instrument. Victoria, BC: Forensic Psychiatric Services Commission.

Kear-Colwell, J., & Pollock, P. (1997). Motivation or confrontation: which approach to the child sex offender? *Criminal Justice and Behavior*, **24**, 20–33.

Kennedy, H.G., & Grubin, D.H. (1992). Patterns of denial in sex offenders. *Psychological Medicine*, **22**, 191–6.

Laflen, B., & Sturm, W.R. (1994). Understanding and working with denial in sexual offenders. *Journal of Child Sexual Abuse*, **3**(4), 19–36.

Lanyon, R.I., & Lutz, R.W. (1984). MMPI discrimination of defensive and nondefensive felony sex offenders. *Journal of Consulting and Clinical Psychology*, **52**, 841–3.

Lanyon, R.I., Dannenbaum, S.E., & Brown, A.R. (1991). Detection of deliberate denial in child abusers. *Journal of Interpersonal Violence*, **6**, 301–9.

Laws, D.R. (1995). A theory of relapse prevention. In W. O'Donohue & L. Krasner (eds) *Theories of Behavior Therapy* (pp. 445–73). Washington, DC: American Psychological Association.

Marques, J.K., Nelson, C., Alarcon, J-M, & Day, D.M. (2000). Preventing relapse in sex offenders: what we learned from SOTEP's experimental treatment program. In D.R. Laws, S.M. Hudson, & T. Ward (eds) *Remaking Relapse Prevention with Sex Offenders* (pp. 321–40). Thousand Oaks, CA: Sage.

Marshall, W.L. (1994). Treatment effects on denial and minimization in incarcerated sex offenders. *Behaviour Research and Therapy*, **32**, 559–64.

Marshall, W.L., Anderson, D., & Fernandez, Y. (1999). *Cognitive Behavioural Treatment of Sexual Offenders*. Chichester: Wiley.

Marshall, W.L., Thornton, D., Marshall, L.E., Fernandez, Y.M., & Mann, R. (2001). Treatment of sexual offenders who are in categorical denial. *Sexual Abuse: A Journal of Research and Treatment*. **13**, 205–16.

Miller, W.R., & Rollnick, S., (1991). *Motivational Interviewing: Preparing People to Change Addictive Behavior*. New York: Guilford.

Mills, C.W. (1940). Situated actions and vocabularies of motive. *American Sociological Review*, **5**(6), 904–13.

Murphy, W.D., & Barbaree, H.E. (1986). Assessment of sexual offenders by measures of erectile response: psychometric properties and decision making. Manuscript prepared for the National Institute of Mental Health, Order 86MO50650051D.

Nichols, H.R., & Molinder, I. (1984). *Manual for the Multiphasic Sex Inventory*. Tacoma, WA: Author.

Nugent, P.M., & Kroner, D.G. (1996). Denial, response styles, and admittance of offenses among child molesters and rapists. *Journal of Interpersonal Violence*, **11**, 475–86.

O'Connell, M.A. (2000). Polygraphy: assessment and community monitoring. In D.R. Laws, S.M. Hudson, & T. Ward (eds) *Remaking Relapse Prevention: A Sourcebook* (pp. 285–302). Thousand Oaks, CA: Sage.

O'Donohue, W., & Letourneau, E. (1992). The psychometric properties of the penile tumescence assessment of child molesters. *Journal of Psychopathology and Behavioral Assessment*, **14**, 123–74.

O'Donohue, W., & Letourneau, E. (1993). A brief group treatment for the modification of denial in child sexual abusers: outcome and follow-up. *Child Abuse and Neglect*, **17**, 299–304.

Paulus, D.L. (1984). Two-component models of socially desirable responding. *Journal of Personality and Social Psychology*, **46**, 598–609.

Pithers, W.D. (1991). Relapse prevention with sexual aggressors. *Forum on Corrections Research*, **3**, 20–3.

Pollock, N.L., & Hashmall, J.M. (1991). The excuses of child molesters. *Behavioral Sciences and the Law*, **9**, 53–9.

Pope, H.S., Butcher, J.N., & Seelen, J. (1993). *The MMPI, MMPI-2, & MMPI-A in Court*. Washington, DC: American Psychological Association.

Prochaska, J.O., & DiClemente, C.C. (1982). Transtheoretical therapy: toward a more integrative model of change. *Psychotherapy: Theory, Research, and Practice*, **19**, 176–288.

Quinsey, V.L., Harris, G.T., Rice, M.E., & Cormier, C.A. (1998). *Violent Offenders: Appraising and Managing Risk*. Washington, DC: American Psychological Association.

Salter, A. (1988). *Treating Child Sex Offenders and Victims: A Practical Guide*. Newbury Park, CA: Sage.

Schlank, A.M., & Shaw, R. (1996). Treating sex offenders who deny their guilt: a pilot study. *Sexual Abuse: A Journal of Research and Treatment*, **8**, 17–23.

Scully, D., & Marolla, J. (1984). Convicted rapists' vocabulary of motive: excuses and justifications. *Social Problems*, **31**, 530–44.

Strate, D.C., Jones, l., Pullen, S., & English, K. (1996). Criminal justice policies and sex offender denial. In K. English, S. Pullen, & L. Jones (eds) *Managing Adult Sex Offenders on Probation and Parole: A Containment Approach* (pp. 4-3–4-18). Lexington, NY: American Probation and Parole Association.

Winn, M.E. (1996). The strategic and systemic management of denial in the cognitive/behavioral treatment of sexual offenders. *Sexual Abuse: A Journal of Research and Treatment*, **8**, 25–36.

Chapter 12

MOTIVATING THE UNMOTIVATED: PSYCHOPATHY, TREATMENT, AND CHANGE

James F. Hemphill and Stephen D. Hart*
Simon Fraser University, British Columbia, Canada

Conventional wisdom holds that psychopathic offenders are "untreatable," unmotivated, and unlikely to change their behavior—particularly criminal behavior—even when provided with high-quality, intensive treatment resources (Fotheringham, 1957; Gray & Hutchison, 1964; Reid & Gacono, 2000). In this chapter, we critically examine both this conclusion and the evidence upon which it is based. We begin by discussing the nature of psychopathy, its assessment and diagnosis, and the association between psychopathy and criminal conduct. Next, we briefly review the existing literature on treatment, summarizing and expanding upon key points made in excellent reviews in recent years (see especially Blackburn, 1993a, b; Dolan & Coid, 1993; Lösel, 1998; Wong & Hare, in press). In particular, we discuss the limitations of existing research, key research findings, and other research trends. In the final section, we speculate about the treatment-relevant motivational deficits that characterize psychopathy, and some possible motivational strengths, and make some recommendations for the development of new treatment programs.

THE NATURE OF PSYCHOPATHY

Assessment and Diagnosis

In major diagnostic systems such as the fourth edition of the *Diagnostic and Statistical Manual of Mental Disorders* (DSM-IV; American Psychiatric Association, 1994) and

---

* Correspondence should be addressed to Professor Stephen D. Hart.

Motivating Offenders to Change: A Guide to Enhancing Engagement in Therapy. Edited by M. McMurran.
© 2002 John Wiley & Sons, Ltd.

the tenth edition of the *International Classification of Diseases and Causes of Death* (ICD-10; World Health Organization, 1992), personality disorder is defined as a disturbance in relating to one's self, others, and the environment that is chronic in nature, typically evident by childhood or adolescence and persisting into middle or late adulthood. Symptoms of personality disorder are rigid, inflexible, and maladaptive personality traits—tendencies to act, think, perceive, and feel in certain ways that are stable across time, across situations, and in interactions with different people. What distinguishes psychopathy from other personality disorders is its specific symptom pattern. Interpersonally, psychopathic individuals are arrogant, superficial, deceitful, and manipulative; affectively, their emotions are shallow and labile, they are unable to form strong emotional bonds with others, and they are lacking in empathy, anxiety, and guilt; behaviorally, they are irresponsible, impulsive, sensation seeking, and prone to delinquency and criminality (Arieti, 1963; Cleckley, 1941; Hare, 1970, 1993; Karpman, 1961; McCord & McCord, 1964).

What we now recognize as personality disorder was first identified and described by psychiatrists working with adults who were hospitalized or were in conflict with the law. The majority of patients suffered from "total insanity," illnesses that appeared to result in a general disintegration or deterioration of mental functions (Berrios, 1996), but some cases were characterized by rather specific disturbances of emotion and volition, demonstrating that mental disorder could exist even when reasoning was intact. The terms used to refer to such conditions included *manie sans délire, monomanie*, moral insanity, and *folie lucide* (Millon, 1981; Pichot, 1978). The understanding of these conditions was refined over time, eventually leading to the modern clinical concept of personality disorder in the first half of the twentieth century.

There are different approaches to the assessment and diagnosis of psychopathy. Despite strong parallels at a conceptual level, at an operational level various diagnostic criteria sets for psychopathic, antisocial, dissocial, and sociopathic personality disorder definitely are not equivalent. Perhaps the biggest difference is that diagnostic criteria for psychopathic or dissocial personality disorder typically include a broad range of interpersonal, affective, and behavioral symptoms. In contrast, diagnostic criteria for antisocial or sociopathic personality disorder tend to focus more narrowly on overt delinquent and criminal behavior. The differences between these two diagnostic traditions are discussed at length elsewhere (Hare et al., 1991; Hart & Hare, 1997; Hemphill & Hart, in press; Lilienfeld, 1994; Widiger & Corbitt, 1995). Perhaps the most important consequence of the focus on delinquent and criminal behavior in diagnostic criteria sets for antisocial or sociopathic personality disorder is that they lack specificity (i.e. misconduct can be a manifestation of other forms of disorders as well), and this can lead to over-diagnosis in forensic settings and under-diagnosis in other settings (see especially American Psychiatric Association, 1994, p. 647).

Much of the research on psychopathy in adulthood has used multi-item symptom construct rating scales such as the original or revised Psychopathy Checklist (PCL and PCL-R; Hare, 1980, 1991) or the Screening Version of the PCL-R (PCL:SV; Hart et al., 1995). These tests require trained observers to rate the severity of personality disorder symptoms based on all available clinical data (e.g. interview with the respondent, review of case history information, interviews with collateral

Table 12.1   PCL-R criteria for psychopathy

Item

1. Glibness/superficial charm
2. Grandiose sense of self-worth
3. Need for stimulation/proneness to boredom
4. Pathological lying
5. Conning/manipulative
6. Lack of remorse or guilt
7. Shallow affect
8. Callous/lack of empathy
9. Parasitic lifestyle
10. Poor behavioral controls
11. Promiscuous sexual behavior
12. Early behavioral problems
13. Lack of realistic, long-term goals
14. Impulsivity
15. Irresponsibility
16. Failure to accept responsibility for own actions
17. Many short-term marital relationships
18. Juvenile delinquency
19. Revocation of conditional release
20. Criminal versatility

Source: Hare (1991).

informants). The PCL and PCL-R were designed for use in adult male forensic populations, with some items being scored entirely or primarily on the basis of criminal records. The PCL-R comprises 20 items scored on a 3-point scale (0 = item doesn't apply, 1 = item applies somewhat, 2 = item definitely applies). Table 12.1 lists the PCL-R items, which are defined in detail in the test manual. Total scores can range from 0 to 40; scores of 30 or higher are considered diagnostic of psychopathy. The PCL:SV is a 12-item scale derived from the PCL-R. It was designed for use in adult populations, regardless of gender, psychiatric status, or criminal history. Table 12.2 lists the PCL:SV items, which are defined in detail in the test manual. Scoring of the PCL:SV requires less information, and less detailed information, than does the PCL-R; further, the PCL:SV can be scored even when the person does not have a criminal record or when the complete record is not available. Items are scored on

Table 12.2   PCL:SV criteria for psychopathy

Part 1	Part 2
1. Superficial	7. Impulsive
2. Grandiose	8. Poor behavioral controls
3. Deceitful	9. Lacks goals
4. Lacks remorse	10. Irresponsible
5. Lacks empathy	11. Adolescent antisocial behavior
6. Doesn't accept responsibility	12. Adult antisocial behavior

Source: Hart et al. (1995).

the same 3-point scale used for the PCL-R. Total scores can range from 0 to 24; scores of 12 or higher indicate "possible psychopathy," and scores of 18 or higher indicate "definite psychopathy."

As is true for all personality disorders, it is useful to conceptualize psychopathy in dimensional terms. Although it is common to say that people either do or do not suffer from psychopathy, most nosological systems (such as the DSM-IV and ICD-10) and psychological tests (such as the PCL-R and PCL:SV) explicitly recognize that this distinction is, to some extent, an arbitrary one and that people within each group differ with respect to the nature and severity of psychopathic symptomatology they exhibit.

Consistent with the dimensional perspective, factor analytic research indicates that psychopathic symptoms have a hierarchical three-factor structure (Cooke & Michie, 2001). The first factor reflects an arrogant and deceitful interpersonal style, comprising symptoms such as grandiosity, superficiality, lying, and manipulativeness. The second factor reflects deficient affective experience, comprising symptoms such as shallow but labile affect, lack of empathy, and lack of remorse. The third factor reflects an impulsive and irresponsible behavioral style, comprising symptoms such as pathological sensation-seeking and failure to plan for the future. The three factors are highly correlated and together form an overarching general factor, namely, psychopathy. This factor structure is robust, evident across assessment procedures and cultures.[1]

Psychopathy as measured by the PCL-R and PCL:SV also has an established pattern of comorbidity with other mental disorders. With respect to acute mental disorders, psychopathy tends to be positively associated with substance use disorders, particularly drug abuse disorders (e.g. Hemphill et al., 1994; Smith & Newman, 1990). In contrast, psychopathy tends to be negatively associated with schizophrenic and other psychotic disorders, major depressive disorders, and anxiety disorders (e.g. Hart & Hare, 1989; Rice & Harris, 1995). No clear pattern of comorbidity has been established with organic mental disorders, bipolar mood disorders, and other acute mental disorders. With respect to personality disorders, psychopathy is positively associated with borderline, narcissistic, and histrionic (i.e. DSM-IV Cluster B or "dramatic-erratic-emotional") personality disorders, negatively associated with avoidant, dependent, and obsessive-compulsive (i.e. DSM-IV Cluster C or "anxious-fearful") personality disorders, and has no clear pattern of comorbidity with schizoid, schizotypal, or paranoid (i.e. DSM-IV Cluster A or "odd-eccentric") personality disorders (Blackburn, 1998, 2000; Hare, 1991; Nedopil et al., 1998).

An important point to be made here is that it is problematic to describe a person in any meaningful way simply as "psychopathic" or "not psychopathic." Individuals differ with respect to which psychopathic symptoms they exhibit at any given time, as well as the developmental course of the symptoms, how they are manifested, and their severity. In addition, individuals will differ with respect to other

---

[1] In addition to the 2-factor (Hare et al., 1990) and the 3-factor (Cooke & Michie, 2001) solutions previously identified, Hare (personal communication, March 22, 2002), has conducted analyses of extensive data sets and has found that a 4-factor solution adequately represents the items in the PCL-R. The first three factors are identical to those found by Cooke and Michie, and the fourth factor reflects general antisocial behavior and is composed of the following five PCL-R items: Poor behavioral controls, Early behavioral problems, Juvenile delinquency, Revocation of conditional release, and Criminal versatility.

personality traits they exhibit, the presence of any comorbid mental disorders, and even things such as intellectual abilities. Psychopathy can be a useful concept for helping to describe and forecast some aspects of a person's psychosocial adjustment although, like all psychiatric diagnoses, it is a rather crude or general concept. Often more useful—information can be obtained by conceptualizing psychopathy in dimensional terms, but this information will always be limited in important ways. When evaluating offenders, making a DSM-IV diagnosis of antisocial personality disorder or administering the PCL-R does not obviate the need for a comprehensive assessment of psychological functioning or criminogenic risks and needs.

Psychopathy and Criminal Conduct

The mechanisms underlying the association between psychopathy and crime are not entirely clear but, to the extent that one accepts criminal behavior as deliberate and purposeful in nature, it seems quite plausible that psychopathic symptomatology exerts a powerful influence over an individual's decision-making with respect to crime. Various symptoms of psychopathy may have a distinctive, perhaps even independent, impact on decision-making (Hart & Hare, 1996).

The symptom facet *arrogant and deceitful interpersonal style* comprises a number of specific characteristics, notably grandiosity. The grandiosity observed in psychopathic offenders is a kind of pathological dominance, a preoccupation with seeking and exerting status, control, and influence over others. Psychopathic offenders relate to other people primarily as status objects rather than as love or attachment objects (Harpur et al., 1994; Hart & Hare, 1994). The status needs of psychopathic offenders can be gratified through crime. Committing crimes—and especially violent crimes—in overt defiance of authority allows psychopathic offenders to feel superior to victims, criminal peers, and (possibly) police. Crime may net concrete rewards such as money or material goods, which may enhance status. Also, preoccupation with status can lead to suspiciousness and a tendency to misperceive maleficent motives underlying the behavior of others (e.g. Kernberg, 1998). Psychopathic offenders are (hyper-)sensitive to challenges to their status and may respond aggressively in defense (Blackburn, 1993b; Blair et al., 1995; Hart & Hare, 1996; Serin, 1991).

The symptom facet *deficient affective experience* comprises characteristics such as shallow but labile affect (Hare, 1991, 1998a). Psychopathic offenders tend not to experience strong or persistent mood states. They certainly experience affects, but these may change rapidly over time. Thus, psychopathic offenders often are perceived as emotionally volatile and may respond to rather mundane frustrations with disproportionate anger and even criminal violence. Another characteristic included in this symptom facet is lack of empathy. Lack of empathy is the tendency to be uncaring of others, or the tendency not to appreciate others' feelings, especially the impact of one's own behavior on them. Lack of empathy may result in an increased likelihood of violent or criminal behavior because psychopathic offenders have weak affectional bonds with others and may be unable to consider or appreciate the harm they cause victims. Put simply, deficient empathy negates some of the psychological costs or consequences of crime for psychopathic offenders (Blair, 1995; Blair et al., 1995; Hare, 1996).

The symptom facet *impulsive and irresponsible behavioral style* comprises characteristics such as sensation-seeking, a pathological preference for activities that are arousing and, conversely, intolerance of boredom and routine. The impulsivity of psychopathic offenders is a tendency to act without forethought (Hare, 1991; Hart & Dempster, 1997). Both of these characteristics result in a failure to form and implement behavioral plans without considering alternative courses of action or the consequences of the plans—specifically, over-focusing on potential rewards and under-focusing on potential costs (Hart & Dempster, 1997; Newman & Wallace, 1993; Wallace et al., 1999).

Whatever the causal mechanisms, empirical research indicates that psychopathic symptoms have a robust association with criminal conduct. This association has been observed in both retrospective and prospective research using the PCL-R and PCL:SV in a variety of different populations in North America and Europe, including adult male and female offenders, mentally disordered offenders, female offenders, young offenders, sexual offenders, and civil psychiatric patients (for reviews, see Hare, 1998b, 1999; Hare et al., 2000; Hart & Hare, 1997). In general, psychopathic symptoms are associated with early age at onset of criminality, persistence of offending, diversity of offending, and increased risk for violence in institutions and the community. The crimes committed by psychopathic offenders frequently are opportunistic, instrumental, or sadistic in nature. Although measures of psychopathy such as the PCL-R were designed to facilitate research on psychopathy, they have emerged as potent predictors of criminal conduct (for reviews, see Dolan & Doyle, 2000; Hemphill et al., 1998; Salekin et al., 1996). In fact, the predictive power of the PCL-R and PCL:SV is significant even after controlling for past offenses (e.g. by removing variance accounted for by measures of criminality or by eliminating items related to criminal history), often approaching or even surpassing that of actuarial instruments designed solely to predict recidivism.

PSYCHOPATHY AND OFFENDER TREATMENT

Limitations of the Existing Research

Much has been written about the treatment of psychopathy. One can find interesting and valuable review papers devoted to the topic (Blackburn, 1990, 1993a, 1993b; Doren et al., 1993; Garrido et al., 1996; Lösel, 1998; Meloy, 1995; Wong & Hare, in press), and even entire books, (Dolan & Coid, 1993; Doren, 1987). Unfortunately, far more has been written about the subject than actually is known about it. Although scores of potentially relevant articles have been published in the past 50 years, there is no body of scientifically sound research on the treatment of psychopathic offenders. Not a single study reported in the scientific literature meets minimal criteria for methodological adequacy accepted in the field of psychotherapy outcome evaluation (Chambless & Ollendick, 2001; Hodgins & Müller-Isberner, 2000), and only a handful meet more liberal criteria of adequacy (Wong & Hare, in press).

Previous reviews have identified common methodological weaknesses in the existing research on the treatment of psychopathy. We can summarize these as follows. First, the studies suffered from a *lack of adequate control groups*. Many studies did not include any kind of control group at all, and sample sizes tended to be reasonably small. Some studies included no-treatment or comparative treatment ("treatment as usual") control groups, but did not randomly assign offenders to these groups. A few studies attempted to offset the absence of random assignment by matching treated and control offenders post hoc on selected variables, but these groups were not equivalent with respect to other potentially important variables. The bottom line is that not a single study used a true experimental design, one in which treatment and control groups were formed prior to treatment using random assignment and in which group equivalence with respect to theoretically important variables was evaluated. Second, the studies were hampered by a *failure to control for heterogeneity within treatment groups*. The studies ignored between-subject differences in the nature and severity of psychopathic symptomatology. The studies also ignored comorbid psychopathology, both acute mental disorder and personality disorders, and other criminogenic risk and need factors, such as employment status, marital status, and so forth. As all these factors appear to have important and potentially independent links with criminal behavior, the failure to assess and control them may have obscured important findings. Third, the studies have used *inconsistent concepts and measures of psychopathy*. Some studies relied entirely on medico-legal definitions of psychopathy, others used self-report inventories, and some made retrospective clinical assessments based on institutional records. Very few have used standardized and validated tests, such as the PCL-R or PCL:SV, administered according to the recommended procedures. As a consequence, it is very difficult to compare the findings from various studies. Fourth, in most studies there was a *lack of attention to developmental factors*. Some research has examined the treatment of psychopathy-related traits in children or adolescents but—as is the case with all personality disorders—there is no good evidence that psychopathy *per se* exists prior to adulthood, let alone that it can be measured reliably in a manner comparable to psychopathy in adulthood. Even studies of adults have over-focused on the treatment of offenders in early adulthood, typically ignoring developmental changes associated with middle or late adulthood. Fifth, the studies typically had *inadequate definition and implementation of treatment*. The vast majority focused on treatments that have never been described or manualized, so it is impossible to know precisely which therapeutic interventions were used. Similarly, most studies did not take proper steps to ensure and evaluate treatment integrity; studies have paid little attention to therapeutic process variables that might have shed light on mechanisms of change. Sixth, the studies are characterized by *severely restricted outcome criteria*. Most focused exclusively on post-treatment antisocial behavior, either substance use, institutional infractions, or criminal recidivism. None examined changes in primary psychopathic symptomatology over time; in fact, in most studies there was no direct contact with offenders at follow-up except via official records. Even those investigators who prospectively followed psychopathic offenders via criminal records tended to have reasonably short follow-up periods.

But there is an even greater problem that pervades this literature: Most researchers are unclear about the goal or target of the programs they evaluated, whether the programs were designed for the treatment of psychopathy or treatment despite psychopathy. Logically, programs designed to treat psychopathy are those intended to alleviate the disorder, that is, to render the affected individual asymptomatic. Such programs should be targeted specifically at primary symptoms of psychopathy; that is, the therapeutic activities should be beneficial to people with the disorder, but benign or possibly even noxious to people without the disorder. The success of such programs should be measurable directly in terms of the breadth and magnitude of symptom reduction versus no treatment or another active treatment. Because antisocial behavior may be a consequence of psychopathy, not a primary symptom, any post-treatment reduction in criminality should be considered an unintended and indirect benefit. In contrast, programs designed to treat despite psychopathy are those intended to encourage desistence of criminality in offenders who happen to suffer from psychopathy. Psychopathy here should be considered an individual difference variable that moderates or mediates treatment response, rather than a treatment target. The success of such programs should be measurable solely in terms of reduction in recidivism rate versus no treatment or another active treatment. Any reduction in psychopathic symptomatology should be considered an unintended and indirect benefit.

Using these definitions and descriptions, it appears that virtually all the research to date is of the latter type, that is, treatment despite psychopathy. This makes good sense in many respects. There is no good evidence that treatment of any type leads to important changes in personality disorder symptomatology of any type (Chambless & Ollendick, 2001). On the other hand, effecting change with respect to specific problem behaviors or symptoms—that is, behavioral or symptomatic management—is a much more reasonable and feasible goal for treatment (Doren, 1987; Lösel, 1998; Wong & Hare, in press). For example, evidence is accumulating that it may be quite possible to reduce impulsivity in patients suffering from various personality disorders using pharmacotherapy (von Knorring & Ekselius, 1998) or to reduce self-harmful behavior in patients with borderline personality disorder using dialectical behavior therapy (Chambless & Ollendick, 2001).

Key Research Findings

Notwithstanding the limitations in existing research, it is possible to draw some inferences about the treatment of psychopathy from recent studies (Alterman et al., 1998; Cooke, 1997; Hare et al., 2000; Harris et al., 1991; Hemphill, 1992; Hicks et al., 2000; Hill et al., 1996; Hobson et al., 2000; Hughes et al., 1997; Mulloy et al., 1996; Ogloff et al., 1990; Reiss et al., 1996, 1999, 2000; Rice et al., 1992; Seto & Barbaree, 1999; Shine & Hobson, 2000; Yates & Nicholaichuk, 1998).

Three conclusions about the research to date can be drawn with considerable confidence. First, the most consistently replicated and robust finding is that *psychopathic offenders engage in more disruptive behavior during treatment than do non-psychopathic offenders*. For example, Ogloff et al. (1990) found that psychopathic offenders received lower scores on motivation/effort during treatment and on degree of treatment improvement than did non-psychopathic offenders; both of these variables were coded from clinical and institutional files. In the study by Rice et al. (1992), psychopathic offenders received more placements in seclusion for violent or disruptive behavior, more negative entries in the clinical records for disruptive or countertherapeutic behavior, and more referrals to an institutional disciplinary subprogram, than did non-psychopathic offenders. Rogers and colleagues (Hicks et al., 2000; Hill et al., 1996) found that psychopathic offenders who received a variety of interventions were given significantly more disciplinary infractions for

disruptive and violent institutional behaviors than were non-psychopathic offenders, and Hill et al. (1996) found a positive association between PCL:SV scores
and treatment noncompliance among civilly committed patients. In the study by
Alterman et al. (1998), There was a positive association between PCL-R scores and
cocaine or benzodiazepine use, assessed via toxicology analyses of urine samples,
among patients who participated in a methadone treatment program. Hughes et
al. (1997) found that higher PCL-R scores were associated with lower scores on a
global measure of clinical change. Seto and Barbaree (1999) assessed a set of variables associated with in-session treatment performance and treatment change rated
by research assistants from clinical notes and treatment reports, and another set
rated jointly by the clinical director and group therapist; these investigators found
that offenders with higher PCL-R scores received scores that reflected poorer treatment ratings. Reiss et al. (1999; see also Reiss et al., 1996) coded existing medical
records for a variety of behaviors in a high-security hospital in the UK. During
the last two years in the institution, proportionately more psychopathic offenders
were placed in seclusion or special care than were non-psychopathic offenders, and
proportionately fewer psychopathic offenders received ratings of good social functioning than did non-psychopathic offenders; the two PCL-R groups did not differ
on ratings of problematic sexual behavior or violent behaviors in the institution.
Reiss et al. (1999) conducted additional analyses to compare ratings during the first
two years after admission with those during the two years preceding discharge.
Non-psychopathic offenders seemed to improve across time on ratings of social
functioning and on placements in seclusion or special care; psychopathic offenders
did not demonstrate these improvements. Hobson et al. (2000) found that offenders
with higher PCL-R scores received ratings by therapy staff reflecting poorer adjustment during and between therapeutic activities. Finally, in the study by Hare et al.
(2000), psychopathic offenders were more likely than non-psychopathic offenders
to be put in segregation. Taken together, these findings indicate that psychopathic
offenders are more disruptive in institutional settings than are non-psychopathic
offenders and that the special security risks associated with psychopathy must be
taken into account by those who design institutional treatment programs.

Second, *psychopathic offenders are less likely than non-psychopathic offenders to remain
in treatment*. For example, Mulloy et al. (1996) and Ogloff et al. (1990) found that
psychopathic offenders had significantly shorter lengths of stay in a therapeutic
community, in part because they were more likely to be ejected due to misbehav-
ior. Alterman et al. (1998) found that higher PCL-R scores were associated with
uncompleted treatment, and Seto and Barbaree (1999) found that sexual offenders
who dropped out of correctional treatment received higher scores on the PCL-R.
Finally, Hare et al. (2000) found that psychopathic offenders were less likely than
non-psychopathic offenders to complete educational and vocational programs and
were more likely than non-psychopathic offenders to be fired from a prison job.
To maximize treatment response in psychopathic offenders, it is important to find
some way to ensure that they receive a full course of therapy. Programs that institute
a rule whereby dishonesty results in automatic ejection are dooming psychopathic
offenders to failure, giving them a perfect opportunity to escape treatment.

Third, *psychopathic offenders are convicted at a higher and faster rate than are non-
psychopathic offenders for post-treatment criminality and violence identified from official
records*. This is one of the clearest findings from prospective (Hemphill, 1992; Seto &

Barbaree, 1999) and retrospective (Harris et al., 1991; Rice et al., 1992) follow-up studies (but cf. Hare et al., 2000; Reiss et al., 2000), although this is hardly surprising given that psychopathic offenders generally had higher rates of criminality and violence *before* treatment (Hemphill et al., 1998). Also, this finding does not rule out the possibility that treatment actually reduced risk of criminality among psychopathic offenders from what it might otherwise have been. These points must be kept in mind when interpreting the results of program evaluations to avoid reaching unfounded and unduly pessimistic conclusions regarding the efficacy of treatment (or lack thereof).

Just as investigators should be cautious about concluding that treatment is not effective with psychopathic offenders, so too should they be cautious about concluding that treatment is effective. For example, Hughes et al. (1997) found that most patients who participated in treatment received positive scores on a global measure designed to index change. There are two reasons why findings from this study should be interpreted cautiously as evidence that psychopathic patients benefitted from treatment. First, all patients with PCL-R scores greater than 30 were not admitted to the treatment program. If psychopathy is conceptualized as a taxon (Harris et al., 1994), and if a score of 30 on the PCL-R is the cutoff used to identify this taxon (Hare, 1991), then few if any psychopathic patients were included in this study. Second, it appears that the measure of global change was primarily rated from in-therapy progress based largely on information provided by treatment staff. As we discuss below, positive ratings of performance in treatment may be unrelated—or even negatively related—to behavioral measures of antisocial behavior (Rice et al., 1992; Seto & Barbaree, 1999).

Perhaps the most important conclusion that can be drawn from our review of the literature is *there is no good evidence that psychopathy can be treated reliably and effectively, but neither is there any good evidence that psychopathy is untreatable* (Blackburn, 1993a, 1993b; Lösel, 1998; Wong & Hare, in press). There is simply an absence of good evidence. Consequently, it would be wrong to deny psychopathic offenders access to treatment programs on the grounds that they are untreatable. It would, however, be reasonable to institute a policy of differential treatment for psychopathic offenders in which they are assigned to programs with more structure or less emphasis on emotional and interpersonal processes. It also would be wrong to stop designing, implementing, or evaluating treatment programs for psychopathic offenders. It is quite possible that some existing programs are efficacious in behavioral or symptomatic management, but that we have not conducted the appropriate research to uncover evidence of success. It is not necessary to conduct large-scale comparative outcome evaluations at this point; given the severe lack of data, single-case, case series, and small-sample evaluation designs all would be appropriate.

Other Research Trends

Two other trends are apparent in the research findings, although they must be considered tentative findings given the limited data upon which they are based. The first research trend is that some forms of treatment may have an adverse impact on psychopathic offenders. One study found that treated psychopathic offenders were reconvicted and/or rehospitalized at higher rates for violence following participation in a therapeutic community than were untreated psychopathic offenders (Rice et al., 1992). Another study found that, among offenders with high scores on the interpersonal/affective facet of psychopathy, offenders who had participated in educational and vocational training programs were subsequently convicted of general offences at a higher rate than were offenders who had not participated (Hare et al., 2000, see figure 3, p. 638). Both studies used quasi-experimental designs, however, making it impossible to conclude that treatment *per se* (as opposed to selection or other factors) made offenders "worse." There are also other reasons to temper the conclusion that treatment makes psychopathic offenders worse: Rice et al. (1992) evaluated a treatment program that operated from 1968 to 1978 and "would not meet current ethical standards" (Harris et al., 1991, p. 628); therefore, the results may not generalize to contemporary treatment programs. The study by Hare et al. (2000) failed to find differences in reconviction rates following treatment between psychopathy groups that were formed on the basis of total PCL-R scores, which is the score that clinicians commonly interpret in clinical practice. Much more research that is methodologically sound clearly is needed to determine the robustness of the findings and the extent to which different treatment outcomes are associated with different intervention programs; it seems reasonable to assume that not all treatment programs will have deleterious effects among psychopathic offenders.

The second research trend, which is more strongly supported by empirical data, is the finding that the interpersonal/affective facet of psychopathy seems to be more strongly associated with treatment behaviors and treatment outcome—particularly adverse behaviors—than is the social deviance facet of psychopathy (Hare et al., 2000; Hobson et al., 2000; Hughes et al., 1997). This pattern of findings suggests that (a) researchers should routinely analyze and separately report results for the different PCL-R factors because these different facets of psychopathy may have important interpretive value for evaluating treatment outcome, (b) investigators should be cautious when evaluating treatment efficacy based largely or solely on ratings derived from direct interpersonal interactions with psychopathic offenders, and (c) those who design treatment programs should recognize the unique interpersonal/affective features of psychopathy and should incorporate these into their treatment plans. This last point is later discussed throughout the section entitled "Working Around Motivational Deficits"; we now briefly discuss and expand upon the first two points.

Researchers who conduct treatment outcome studies might supplement their analyses using PCL-R factor scores in addition to those analyses conducted using PCL-R total scores. This conclusion is based on the assumption that psychopathic offenders may use their interpersonal/affective skills to their advantage to convince treatment staff that they have successfully benefited from treatment and are deserving of important benefits. For example, the interpersonal/affective features—particularly the interpersonal features—of psychopathy are expected to have a stronger association with behaviors such as early release following treatment and release directly into the community (e.g. Reiss et al., 1999) than are the social deviance features of psychopathy. Investigators should be aware that there currently are two ways of computing factor scores, one based on a two-factor solution (Hare et al., 1990), and another based on a more recently identified three-factor solution (Cooke & Michie, 2001). Both of the currently published studies that have directly examined the association between the different facets of psychopathy and behaviors following treatment (Hare et al., 2000; Hobson et al., 2000) have computed PCL-R factor scores using the two-factor solution. At present it seems conceptually and practically useful for researchers to conduct the analyses separately for both sets of factor scores.

Other research, in addition to the studies that have found a differential association between each of the PCL-R factors and behavior following treatment, suggests that investigators should be cautious when evaluating treatment efficacy based solely upon ratings of treatment performance derived from clinical judgments of in-session treatment behaviors (Hughes et al., 1997). This is because these ratings may not actually be associated—or may be inversely associated—with behavioral indices of treatment success. The study by Rice et al. (1992) found that only those variables related to patient *behaviors* in treatment—and not those related to staff judgments of patient performance in treatment—were consistently associated with subsequent reconvictions and/or rehospitalizations. That staff may be unduly influenced by the interpersonal/affective characteristics of psychopathy is suggested by the findings that, despite having a history of poor institutional performance, (a) psychopathic offenders and non-psychopathic offenders received similar staff recommendations that they be released from the forensic psychiatric institution, and (b) the two PCL-R groups also were equally likely to become group leaders. This latter privilege was reserved in part for those patients who had performed well in the treatment program (Rice et al., 1992, pp. 401–2). Further, the study by Seto and Barbaree (1999) paradoxically found that, among sex offenders who had elevated psychopathic characteristics, offenders who received ratings of *positive* treatment performance were convicted of any offence at almost three times the rate, and of a violent offence at more than five times the rate, than were other offenders.

MOTIVATIONAL DEFICITS

What are the Motivational Deficits of Psychopathic Offenders?

Past reviews have not focused specifically on cataloging the treatment-related motivational deficits associated with psychopathy, although all touch on the issue to some extent. Any discussion of the issue is hampered by the lack of a generally accepted model of motivation for change that sets out factors that may be necessary or sufficient to ensure treatment participation and response. Motivation for therapy is a multifaceted concept whose parameters frequently are imprecisely defined. In the discussion below we draw on conceptual and empirical frameworks identified by several sets of investigators (Prochaska et al., 1992; Rosenbaum & Horowitz, 1983) concerning motivation for therapy in clinical settings. We relate the defining clinical characteristics of psychopathic offenders (Cleckley, 1976; Hare, 1991; McCord & McCord, 1964), and clinical observations, with these motivational deficits to illustrate key motivational problems facing psychopathic offenders.

There appears to be some general consensus in these various writings that, for change to occur in treatment programs, the following conditions are important:

1. *The offender acknowledges personal problems and freely participates in treatment.* Treatment participation ideally occurs under conditions where offenders admit having personal problems that are to form the focus of the therapeutic interventions. This aspect of motivation often is so central to treatment that individuals who fail to acknowledge personal problems may be initially encouraged or required to participate in interventions aimed at enhancing readiness to change rather than being allowed to enter an intensive intervention program (Harris et al., 1991; Prochaska, 1991; Prochaska et al., 1992). Psychopathic offenders frequently find little wrong with themselves and with their behaviors and often only become involved in treatment because they are directed or mandated to do so by family, friends, the courts, or other junctures of the criminal justice system. This may lead psychopathic offenders to feel coerced into entering treatment that is ostensibly "voluntary," a situation that is associated with treatment resistance (Farabee et al., 1993; Hird et al., 1997).

2. *The offender is interested in changing.* Even if individuals admit to having personal problems, they are not always interested in changing these behaviors. Psychopathic offenders may recognize the interpersonal, financial, and legal problems that their behaviors cause them but they may nonetheless be unmotivated to change these behaviors. Psychopathic offenders may, in fact, define themselves by these very behaviors that clinicians want to change. Rather than perceive these behaviors in negative terms they may instead perceive them in positive terms. Antisocial and criminal acts may be viewed by psychopathic offenders as "exciting" and "challenging" behaviors that psychopathic offenders believe others would engage in if they were not so frightened, reserved, and inhibited.

3. *The offender views his or her problems as psychologically-based and believes that psychological interventions are potentially beneficial.* For contemporary psychological interventions to be maximally effective, offenders who acknowledge personal problems and who are interested in changing must also believe that their problems are psychologically based and that psychological interventions are potentially beneficial. (Individuals who believe that their problems are psychological in nature view their problems as the result of cognitive and emotional responses to past and present experiences; Rosenbaum & Horowitz, 1983.) Offenders who believe that psychological interventions are not effective in general, or who believe that their problems are not psychologically based (e.g. are caused by biological factors or by others) in particular, are expected to receive minimal benefit from psychological interventions. Given that psychopathic offenders typically have little psychological insight, and do not recognize personal problems and the impact that their behaviors have on others, it seems unlikely that they will initially view psychological interventions as potentially beneficial to them.

4. *The offender recognizes his or her contributions to personal problems.* Individuals who blame their problems on adverse situations or on others will be difficult to change using contemporary psychological interventions. Psychological

approaches focus on promoting a sense of personal responsibility and self-efficacy to promote change (Bandura, 1977), and contemporary correctional treatment programs are no different. Relapse prevention interventions, for example, attempt to reduce antisocial behavior (a) by helping offenders become aware of factors that place them at risk to reoffend, and (b) by providing skills to manage these factors (Hemphill & Hart, 2001). One of the defining features of psychopathy is the failure to accept personal responsibility for one's actions (Hare, 1991). This means that psychopathic offenders will be a particularly challenging group to change.

5. *The offender establishes a positive relationship with a therapist and is willing to accept help.* Regardless of the type of therapy, individuals typically are expected to discuss and explore personally revealing and sensitive information in therapy that they may not have openly discussed before. This requires that a positive relationship be established with the therapist that is characterized by trust, confidence in the therapist's intent to help, and cooperation (Elliott, 1985; Hill et al., 1988; Mahrer & Nadler, 1986). Unfortunately, psychopathy is associated with a broad range of interpersonal and affective deficits. Characteristics of superficiality, grandiosity, pathological lying, manipulativeness, and shallow emotional experiences, coupled with suspiciousness and dishonest interactions with the therapist and others (e.g. Kernberg, 1998), clearly hinder the ability to easily establish a positive therapeutic alliance. Psychopathic offenders might further resist help if they perceive a power differential between the therapist and themselves and view therapy as an affront to their attempt to seek and exert status and influence.

6. *The offender strives for autonomy and independence.* A major goal of many contemporary interventions is to have individuals become autonomous and independent, rather than to heavily rely upon others. This does not mean that the goal of therapy is to have patients altogether eschew reasonable support by others. Rather, it means that patients are encouraged for the most part to be self-sufficient and are discouraged from unduly depending upon others. Excessive reliance on others, particularly if the support is not reciprocated in kind, is frequently considered taking advantage of the goodwill of others. For the most part, psychopathic offenders do not want to be self-sufficient. In fact, they require considerable interpersonal involvement so that they can manipulate and use others to have their needs met. Once family, friends, and relatives tire of being used and refuse to provide further assistance, pychopaths move on to find support from other unsuspecting Good Samaritans.

7. *The offender has clear and realistic treatment goals.* Treatment goals should be realistic and compatible with what the therapy reasonably can accomplish; they also should be carefully thought out, elaborated, and clear (Rosenbaum & Horowitz, 1983). Treatment length in clinical settings often is fairly short, and it is important to keep this in mind when identifying treatment goals. For example, of the eight exclusively inpatient programs for sex offenders in Canada described by Wormith and Hanson (1992) in a survey of treatment programs, the median treatment offered is 13 to 14 hours per week (range: 2 to 33) for 4 to 5 months in length (range: 4 to 9 months). Psychopathic offenders often blame their problems on society and on others who they perceive to be overly sensitive, unaccepting, and rigid. Put another way, and as mentioned

earlier, psychopathic offenders do not see their contributions to their personal problems. A corollary of this is the goals that psychopathic offenders identify for treatment are not necessarily consistent with the goals that eventually will form the basis of treatment. Psychological interventions typically require that patients view their symptoms as psychologically based and that they believe therapy will provide an opportunity for self-exploration and understanding.

8. *The offender is self-reflective and has psychological insight into his or her behaviors.* Therapists do not, of course, expect client reports to be completely free of subjectivity, bias, or distortions, because these factors characterize "normal" responses in nonclinical settings (e.g. Wiggins, 1973). Nonetheless, for positive therapeutic change to occur, many interventions require that patients have the capacity to be introspective, self-aware, and willing to explore problems from a psychological perspective. Evidence suggests that some offenders are less introspective than others (Zamble & Quinsey, 1997) and some do not clearly distinguish among factors associated with clinical change (Hemphill & Howell, 2000). Psychopathy is not associated with any specific intellectual or cognitive deficits that might cause problems with the ability to *intellectually* explore one's condition, but it is associated with affective deficits that may limit the ability to *emotionally* explore one's condition.

9. *The offender experiences marked emotional distress, guilt, or shame regarding his or her problems.* Patients often enter therapy and continue to work on psychological problems because they are motivated to reduce or eliminate feelings of anxiety and distress. Offenders incarcerated in forensic settings often report experiencing marked emotional distress and anxiety early in their correctional terms (e.g. MacKenzie & Goodstein, 1985; Zamble, 1992; Zamble & Porporino, 1990), and mounting psychological problems upon release have been linked to relapse in the community (Zamble & Quinsey, 1997). Nonetheless, it is not uncommon for offenders to voluntarily participate in therapy for reasons other than marked psychological distress or anxiety. Many offenders agree to participate in treatment to increase their chances of securing early release or to obtain noncustodial dispositions. That psychopathy is associated with profound affective deficits, including shallow affect, lack of empathy, and lack of remorse or guilt (Hare, 1991, 1998a), suggests psychopathic offenders will not be propelled to enter and actively participate in treatment in order to alleviate feelings of emotional distress but instead will participate in therapy for other reasons.

10. *The offender exerts considerable effort to maintain treatment changes.* Many correctional programs have as basic tenets the assumption that offenders who have successfully mastered certain skills in treatment (a) will recognize situations when these skills should be applied, and (b) will actually apply them outside of therapeutic contexts. For these assumptions to hold, offenders clearly must be motivated on an ongoing basis to implement and maintain therapeutic gains. Many offenders are reconvicted within one year following release from correctional facilities into the community (e.g. Hart et al., 1988; Hemphill, 1998; Leschied et al., 1988; Visher et al., 1991; Zamble & Quinsey, 1997). This means that psychopathic offenders who are unmotivated, or only partially motivated, to change are at great risk to relapse very quickly.

In summary, then, a number of characteristics that define psychopathy are associated with treatment-related motivational deficits; these characteristics include lack of insight, lack of distress, lack of attachment, lack of trust, lack of honesty, lack of responsibility, and lack of impulse control. It is little wonder that therapists are so pessimistic about the ability to effectively treat psychopathic offenders (Fotheringham, 1957; Gray & Hutchison, 1964; Reid & Gacono, 2000).

Working Around Motivational Deficits

When working with psychopathic offenders, a little therapeutic pessimism can be a good thing, helping to guard against naïve acceptance by therapists of their clients' self-reports of behavioral change (e.g. Doren, 1987; Seto & Barbaree, 1999). Therapeutic nihilism, on the other hand, is both unhelpful and unfounded. Nonetheless, it seems reasonable to conclude that therapy will be most effective and efficient in exacting long-lasting change if therapeutic strategies take into account disorder-specific strengths and deficits. In the previous section we focused on the motivational deficits of psychopathic offenders. But what about motivational *strengths*? Do psychopathic offenders have any, and might these strengths help us identify alternatives to the usual interventions?

We suggest at least four strengths. The first is *status orientation*. Psychopathy is associated with a strong need to feel superior to other people (Harpur et al., 1994; Hart & Hare, 1994). This means that psychopathic offenders "need" other people, although as status objects rather than as love objects. After all, one cannot feel superior unless someone else is inferior; one cannot be high status unless someone else is low status. It also means that psychopathic offenders are likely to experience discomfort not when affection or approval is withheld from them but when they are denied status or feelings of superiority. The second strength is a *strong desire for and tolerance of novelty*. Psychopathic offenders seem to find unfamiliar situations interesting rather than stressful. This means that it is not usually too difficult to convince psychopathic offenders to try something new, like a new job or new peer relationship or a new way of thinking. Indeed, they are likely to find access to new activities or situations intrinsically rewarding. It also means that psychopathic offenders are likely to experience difficulties or even distress not when they initiate behavioral change but when they attempt to maintain it. The third strength is that many psychopathic offenders possess *good interpersonal skills*. Psychopathic offenders can be articulate, engaging, interpersonally charming, and persuasive (Cleckley, 1976; Hare, 1991; McCord & McCord, 1964). Good interpersonal skills can be beneficial both for participating in psychological therapies and for initiating and implementing intervention strategies outside of therapy. The fourth strength of psychopathic offenders is that they like to be *in control* rather than to take direction. This is an important strength because, as we have seen, many correctional programs emphasize personal responsibility and autonomy as primary goals for therapy.

We conclude with a number of suggestions or recommendations for treatment based on our speculations about the motivational deficits and strengths of psychopathic offenders. In our view, to enhance the motivation of psychopathic offenders, treatment programs should:

1. *Formally assess motivation to participate in treatment.* Interventions are unlikely to be effective in the long-term if psychopathic offenders demonstrate little motivation to change. Mandating treatment may initially cause psychopathic offenders to perfunctorily participate in treatment—or to focus on actively treating *other* offenders in treatment settings with group formats—but may not result in lasting change for psychopathic offenders outside therapeutic settings. Psychopathic offenders who are not motivated to change may either be expelled by treatment staff or may drop out of treatment themselves (Ogloff et al., 1990). Treating unmotivated offenders who prematurely drop out of treatment and who deny opportunities to other more motivated offenders clearly is a waste of limited treatment resources. Alternatively, unmotivated psychopathic offenders may complete treatment programs but choose not to apply what they have learned outside therapeutic contexts. These scenarios suggest that it would be beneficial to formally assess the motivation of psychopathic patients before enrolling them in treatment (see Simpson & Joe, 1993). Psychopathic offenders who are considered for treatment need not demonstrate motivation across every dimension of motivation, but they should demonstrate motivation other than the sole desire to secure early release or obtain noncustodial dispositions. In addition to examining the various dimensions of motivation delineated in the previous section, motivation for treatment should also include an examination of the purported reasons that psychopathic offenders have entered treatment, their participation in and benefit derived from previous treatment programs, their current commitment to change, and so forth. Psychopathic offenders deemed to be clinically unmotivated for treatment might first participate in a group designed to facilitate motivation, enhance readiness to change, and recognize personal behaviors that are problematic; only reasonably motivated psychopathic offenders could be considered for more intensive correctional treatment. The important point here is that psychopathic offenders who participate in intensive treatment programs should view themselves as active and willing treatment participants.

2. *Highlight criminal lifestyle as low status.* If psychopathic offenders view their antisocial behaviors in positive terms, then two important goals of therapy are to help them redefine these antisocial behaviors as socially undesirable and to replace these behaviors with prosocial behaviors. Psychopathic offenders who perceive their antisocial behaviors as low status will more likely want to change than will psychopathic offenders who perceive their antisocial behaviors as high status. Further, prosocial behaviors that capitalize on the considerable strengths of psychopathic offenders can help them achieve higher status via socially legitimate means. In terms of vocational choices, psychopathic offenders can be encouraged to select jobs that involve strong interpersonal skills, a persuasive demeanor, and a desire for excitement. It is, of course, important for therapists and other correctional staff to monitor the progress of psychopathic offenders to determine that they use their strengths for prosocial ends rather than for antisocial ends by simply expanding their repertoire of antisocial behaviors and potential pool of victims. In terms of recreational choices, psychopathic offenders can be encouraged to select activities that involve excitement and novelty.

3. *Help psychopathic offenders understand the rationale behind psychological interventions.* Even though the contributions of psychological functioning to behavioral problems are not always readily apparent to some individuals, the basic principles behind psychological interventions can be readily taught to and understood by individuals in therapy. Patients do not need to be presented with all of the complexities and nuances of psychological interventions and theories to understand the basic tenets of psychological therapies. By providing a few concrete examples, patients quickly recognize the role that thoughts and feelings play in the development and maintenance of problematic behaviors. Ensuring early in therapy that patients understand and accept the basic principles behind psychological interventions is important for laying a solid foundation for subsequent interventions. Two challenges unique to psychopathic offenders must be considered when teaching them the rationale underlying psychological interventions. First, psychopathic offenders are impulsive (Hare, 1991; Hart & Dempster, 1997), meaning that they act without carefully deliberating the pros and cons of their behaviors. Second, psychopathic offenders appear to have an information-processing deficit that impairs their ability to naturally and effectively regulate their psychological functioning (Wallace et al., 1999). Both of these factors suggest that more time and effort will need to be spent helping psychopathic offenders recognize and identify the often subtle and fleeting psychological processes that precede their behaviors.

4. *Explore personal contributions to problems.* Many offenders initially involved in treatment frequently have a poor understanding of their personal contributions to criminal behaviors. They report that their antisocial and/or criminal behaviors occurred with little warning (Zamble & Quinsey, 1997, p. 54) and that there was little they could do to stop these events. More careful consideration of the events leading up to their antisocial behaviors and the commonalities among their offences, however, often reveal consistent patterns of behaviors that follow a reasonably predictable course (Hemphill & Hart, 2001; Howell & Enns, 1995; Marlatt & Gordon, 1980, 1985). These findings suggest that offenders underestimate their personal contributions to antisocial behaviors. Given that psychopathic offenders like to maintain control over others and over situations, they may find interventions that emphasize personal control to be particularly empowering. In keeping with this emphasis on personal control and self-management skills, which presumably will increase generalizability of treatment gains to non-institutional settings, an important intervention strategy for psychopathic offenders will be to have them avoid altogether situations that place them at high risk to commit antisocial and/or criminal behaviors.

5. *Establish a positive therapeutic alliance with the therapist.* Establishing the therapist as an authoritative expert might not be counter-therapeutic for treating some patients, but this approach likely will alienate psychopathic offenders and damage the therapeutic alliance. This is because psychopathic offenders strive to exert control and dominance over others. When working with psychopathic offenders, therapists should emphasize their role as treatment facilitators who are interested in helping psychopathic offenders maximize their potential while

remaining free of criminal activities. Therapists may initially spend a good deal of time working with psychopathic offenders to establish a positive therapeutic alliance and to work with, rather than against, the clinically challenging interpersonal, affective, and behavioral characteristics of psychopathic offenders. Therapists should be forthright and honest with psychopathic offenders from the outset of therapy, while being sensitive to the clinical characteristics of psychopathy. There is a delicate balance that therapists must strike between being honest in therapy and not setting up an overly dominant therapeutic relationship. As a basic condition of conducting therapy with psychopathic offenders, for example, some therapists routinely plan to compare statements made by psychopathic offenders in treatment with those available from collateral sources. Therapists do this because of the tendency of psychopathic offenders to lie, deny, and minimize their involvement in antisocial and criminal activities (Cleckley, 1976; Hare, 1991; McCord & McCord, 1964). Before commencing therapy, therapists should inform their patients of this practice, delicately indicate the reasons for it, and obtain informed consent from psychopathic offenders to consult collateral records. This may help reduce the adverse impact on the therapeutic alliance because psychopathic offenders already are suspicious and distrustful of others (Kernberg, 1998). Nonetheless, any loss of status or novelty should be temporary and limited in nature.

6. *Emphasize self-sufficiency.* "Parasitic lifestyle" is the term that Hare (1991, see PCL-R Item 9) uses to refer to the persistent financial dependence and reliance that psychopathic offenders have on others. Some of these "parasitic" behaviors may be illegal in nature (e.g. pimping, engaging in criminal behaviors, cheating social assistance), whereas others may not (e.g. manipulating friends and family for financial support). Regardless of whether psychopathic offenders engage in behaviors that are illegal or not, they may be willing to participate in treatment to avoid or reduce further problems with family, friends, relatives, or the criminal justice system. Psychopathic offenders have considerable social, interpersonal, and cognitive skills that, if harnessed for prosocial means, could serve them exceedingly well; psychopathic offenders are articulate, personable, assertive, and persuasive. This contrasts with many other offenders, who lack basic skills that first need to be taught before the skills can be implemented (Zamble & Porporino, 1990; Zamble & Quinsey, 1997). Put another way, psychopathic offenders possess important social and cognitive skills but lack motivation or direction to use these skills in prosocial ways, whereas other offenders lack social skills but possess the motivation to change. The desire of psychopathic offenders to avoid current and future legal and social difficulties may be important for helping them initiate prosocial ways to financially support themselves.

7. *Manage antisocial behaviors rather than change personality characteristics.* As previously mentioned, there frequently are important constraints in terms of treatment length, hours of therapeutic contact, and correctional resources. Considering these constraints, it seems more reasonable for therapists and clients to focus on managing socially inappropriate behaviors rather than to focus on attempting to change pervasive and long-standing maladaptive personality characteristics (Harpur & Hare, 1994).

8. *Teach offenders strategies to change their behaviors.* Thoughts, feelings, and behaviors all serve as important targets for therapy. In terms of interventions designed to target maladaptive cognitions, psychopathic offenders might be taught to identify thoughts that initiate or maintain antisocial behaviors. Believing that others are malicious and have harmful intentions may cause psychopathic offenders to misinterpret benign situations as threatening and to act in a manner consistent with this misperception. In the following section we argue that interventions designed to modify maladaptive feelings may not be particularly fruitful for treating psychopathic offenders. In terms of interventions designed to target maladaptive behaviors, psychopathic offenders might be taught to plan ahead and to reflect. Impulsivity, or thinking before acting, is a defining characteristic of psychopathy (Hare, 1991; Hart & Dempster, 1997) that has two important clinical implications for treatment. First, treatment programs can teach psychopathic offenders to plan ahead by formulating short- and long-term goals, identifying realistic ways of achieving these goals, selecting the best way or ways of achieving these goals, and monitoring in an ongoing fashion the success of the behavioral plans. It seems reasonable to conclude that psychopathic offenders will more successfully achieve important goals if they are encouraged to map out and monitor broad plans for action. Second, treatment programs can teach psychopathic offenders to routinely pause, reflect, and monitor their behaviors. Laboratory research has demonstrated that information-processing deficits among psychopathic offenders may be partially overcome, at least with respect to specific tasks, when they are required to pause (Newman et al., 1987). This finding suggests that psychopathic offenders can effectively process cues in their environment when they are required to reflect on their behavior.

9. *Focus on cognitive strengths rather than affective deficits.* Treatment programs for psychopathic offenders have two basic approaches for dealing with deficits: they can either attempt to improve the deficits (Lowenstein, 1996), or they can largely ignore the deficits and instead work with existing strengths (Templeman & Wollersheim, 1979). Which of these two approaches might be successfully used with psychopathic offenders? The lack of a conceptually rich and empirically supported theory of the development of affect in normal individuals means that there is little evidence on which to base interventions designed to remediate abnormal affective experiences among psychopathic offenders. Further, several investigators have argued that psychopathic offenders are unlikely to benefit from correctional programs aimed at reducing intrapsychic turmoil and at developing self-esteem, empathy, and conscience (Rice et al., 1992; Wong & Hare, in press). Taken together, these findings suggest that structured cognitive-behavioral interventions will offer the most promise for treating psychopathic offenders (see Andrews et al., 1990; Templeman & Wollersheim, 1979).

10. *Develop strategies to maintain behavioral change.* Motivation needs to be high upon release into the community and sustained for long periods of time to prevent relapse and to consolidate previous treatment gains. Individuals who are motivated to change make considerable sacrifices, and are committed, to

maintain change (Rosenbaum & Horowitz, 1983). Psychopathic offenders must constantly be vigilant to implement newly acquired skills taught in therapy. This is particularly true when the skills are not completely mastered in applied settings and have not been fully incorporated into behavioral repertoires. Whenever possible, close supervision and continued follow-up treatment in the community are important for maintaining motivation, preventing relapse, and generalizing treatment gains in therapy to real-life situations, particularly during the period of time shortly after release. Regardless of the interventions employed, psychopathic offenders should be aware that they are particularly vulnerable to relapse and must continue to sustain their efforts to avoid relapse. Nonetheless, relapse is often the rule and not the exception (Prochaska et al., 1992); relapse consequently should be considered a normal part of the treatment process with psychopathic offenders and positive treatment gains should be emphasized.

SUMMARY

Psychopathic offenders pose a high risk for criminal and violent behavior, even compared to other serious and persistent offenders. Psychopathic offenders present a major challenge to treatment providers because of the complex nature of the disorder itself, its comorbidity with other forms of mental disorder, and its association with other criminogenic risks and needs.

Unfortunately, the scientific literature on the treatment of psychopathy is hampered by serious methodological problems and provides little guidance concerning what is or is not effective. These problems include the failure to distinguish between treatments that target psychopathy versus those that treat psychopathy as a moderating or mediating factor; lack of adequate control groups; failure to control for heterogeneity within treatment groups; inconsistent concepts and measures of psychopathy; lack of attention to developmental factors; inadequate definition and implementation of treatment; and reliance on severely restricted outcome criteria and short follow-up periods.

The major conclusion of our review, echoing that of past commentators, is that there is no good evidence that psychopathy can be treated reliably and effectively, but neither is there any good evidence that psychopathy is untreatable. The existing literature supports the view that, compared to non-psychopathic controls, psychopathic offenders engaged in more disruptive behavior during treatment, were less likely to remain in treatment, and committed more post-treatment criminality and violence. It is important to emphasize that these findings do not mean that psychopathic offenders are untreatable.

Psychopathic symptoms appear to cause a number of treatment-relevant motivational deficits, including lack of insight, lack of distress, lack of attachment, lack of trust, lack of honesty, lack of responsibility, and lack of impulse control. But psychopathic offenders may also have important motivational strengths that may help them in therapy, including a strong status orientation, a strong desire for and tolerance of novelty, good interpersonal skills, and the strong desire to be in control.

In our view, treatment programs for psychopathic offenders should formally assess motivation to participate in treatment, highlight the view that leading a criminal lifestyle is low status, help psychopathic offenders understand the rationale behind psychological interventions and explore their contributions to personal problems, establish a positive therapeutic alliance with the therapist that is perceived by psychopathic offenders as non-threatening, emphasize self-sufficiency, attempt to manage antisocial behaviors rather than to change personality characteristics, teach psychopathic offenders a variety of therapeutic strategies to change their behaviors and maintain positive changes, and focus on cognitive strengths rather than on affective deficits.

In conclusion, there is little support for the conventional wisdom that psychopathic offenders are untreatable. At this point in time, therapeutic nihilism concerning the treatment of psychopathy is unhelpful and unfounded; therapeutic pessimism is natural and potentially helpful; and a little therapeutic creativity and optimism can be of great assistance. Treatment providers should devote attention to developing interventions that take into account the unique motivational strengths and deficits of psychopathic offenders, and researchers should devote attention to conducting methodologically adequate evaluation studies. We hope that we will live to see the day when the outcome studies on the treatment of psychopathy outnumber the pessimistic reviews.

REFERENCES

Alterman, A. I., Rutherford, M. J., Cacciola, J. S., McKay, J. R., & Boardman, C. R. (1998). Prediction of 7 months methadone maintenance treatment response by four measures of antisociality. *Drug and Alcohol Dependence*, **49**, 217–23.

American Psychiatric Association (1994). *Diagnostic and Statistical Manual of Mental Disorders*, 4th edn. Washington, DC: APA.

Andrews, D. A., Zinger, I., Hoge, R. D., Bonta, J., Gendreau, P., & Cullen, F. T. (1990). Does correctional treatment work? A clinically relevant and psychologically informed meta-analysis. *Criminology*, **28**, 369–404.

Arieti, S. (1963). Psychopathic personality: some views on its psychopathology and psychodynamics. *Comprehensive Psychiatry*, **4**, 301–12.

Bandura, A. (1977). Self-efficacy: toward a unifying theory of behavioral change. *Psychological Review*, **84**, 191–215.

Berrios, G. E. (1996). *The History of Mental Symptoms: Descriptive Psychopathology Since the Nineteenth Century*. Cambridge: Cambridge University Press.

Blackburn, R. (1990). Treatment of the psychopathic offender. *Issues in Criminological and Legal Psychology*, **16**, 54–66.

Blackburn, R. (1993a). Clinical programmes with psychopaths. In C. R. Hollin & K. Howells (eds) *Clinical Approaches to the Mentally Disordered Offender* (pp. 179–208). Chichester: Wiley.

Blackburn, R. (1993b). *The Psychology of Criminal Conduct: Theory, Research and Practice*. Chichester: Wiley.

Blackburn, R. (1998). Psychopathy and personality disorder: implications of interpersonal theory. In D. J. Cooke, A. E. Forth, & R. D. Hare (eds) *Psychopathy: Theory, Research and Implications for Society* (pp. 269–301). Dordrecht: Kluwer.

Blackburn, R. (2000). Treatment or incapacitation? Implications of research on personality disorders for the management of dangerous offenders. *Legal and Criminological Psychology*, **5**, 1–21.

Blair, R. (1995). A cognitive developmental approach to morality: investigating the psychopath. *Cognition*, **57**, 1–29.

Blair, R., Jones, L., Clark, F., & Smith, M. (1995). Is the psychopath morally insane? *Personality and Individual Differences*, **19**, 741–52.

Chambless, D. L., & Ollendick, T. H. (2001). Empirically supported psychological interventions: Controversies and evidence. *Annual Review of Psychology*, **52**, 685–716.

Cleckley, H. (1941). *The Mask of Sanity*. St Louis, MO: Mosby.

Cleckley, H. (1976). *The Mask of Sanity*, 5th edn. St Louis, MO: Mosby.

Cooke, D. J. (1997). The Barlinnie Special Unit: the rise and fall of a therapeutic experiment. In E. Cullen, L. Jones, & R. Woodward (eds) *Therapeutic Communities for Offenders* (pp. 101–120). Chichester: Wiley.

Cooke, D. J., & Michie, C. (2001). Refining the construct of psychopathy: towards a hierarchical model. *Psychological Assessment*, **13**, 171–88.

Dolan, B., & Coid, J. (1993). *Psychopathic and Antisocial Personality Disorders: Treatment and Research Issues*. London: Gaskell.

Dolan, M., & Doyle, M. (2000). Violence risk prediction: clinical and actuarial measures and the role of the Psychopathy Checklist. *British Journal of Psychiatry*, **177**, 303–11.

Doren, D. M. (1987). *Understanding and Treating the Psychopath*. New York: Wiley.

Doren, D. M., Miller, R., & Maier, G. J. (1993). Predicting threatening psychopathic patient behavior in an inpatient milieu. *International Journal of Offender Therapy and Comparative Criminology*, **37**, 221–9.

Elliott, R. (1985). Helpful and nonhelpful events in brief counseling interviews: an empirical taxonomy. *Journal of Counseling Psychology*, **32**, 307–22.

Farabee, D., Nelson, R., & Spence, R. (1993). Psychosocial profiles of criminal justice- and noncriminal justice-referred substance abusers in treatment. *Criminal Justice and Behavior*, **20**, 336–46.

Fotheringham, J. B. (1957). Psychopathic personality: a review. *Canadian Psychiatric Association Journal*, **2**, 52–75.

Garrido, V., Esteban, C., & Molero, C. (1996). The effectiveness in the treatment of psychopathy: a meta-analysis. In D. J. Cooke, A. E. Forth, J. Newman, & R. D. Hare (eds) *International Perspectives on Psychopathy* (pp. 57–9). Leicester: British Psychological Society.

Gray, K. G., & Hutchison, H. C. (1964). The psychopathic personality: a survey of Canadian psychiatrists' opinions. *Canadian Psychiatric Association Journal*, **9**, 452–61.

Hare, R. D. (1970). *Psychopathy: Theory and Research*. New York: Wiley.

Hare, R. D. (1980). A research scale for the assessment of psychopathy in criminal populations. *Personality and Individual Differences*, **1**, 111–19.

Hare, R. D. (1991). *The Hare Psychopathy Checklist-Revised*. Toronto: Multi Health Systems.

Hare, R. D. (1993). *Without Conscience: The Disturbing World of the Psychopaths Among Us*. New York: Pocket Books.

Hare, R. D. (1996). Psychopathy: a clinical construct whose time has come. *Criminal Justice and Behavior*, **23**, 25–54.

Hare, R. D. (1998a). Psychopathy, affect and behavior. In D. J. Cooke, A. E. Forth, & R. D. Hare (eds) *Psychopathy: Theory, Research and Implications for Society* (pp. 105–37). Dordrecht: Kluwer.

Hare, R. D. (1998b). Psychopaths and their nature: implications for the mental health and criminal justice systems. In T. Millon, E. Simonsen, M. Birket-Smith, & R. D. Davis (eds) *Psychopathy: Antisocial, Criminal, and Violent Behavior* (pp. 188–212). New York: Guilford.

Hare, R. D. (1999). Psychopathy as a risk factor for violence. *Psychiatric Quarterly*, **70**, 181–97.

Hare, R. D., Clark, D., Grann, M., & Thornton, D. (2000). Psychopathy and the predictive validity of the PCL-R: an international perspective. *Behavioral Sciences and the Law*, **18**, 623–45.

Hare, R. D., Harpur, T. J., Hakstian, A. R., Forth, A. E., Hart, S. D., & Newman, J. P. (1990). The Revised Psychopathy Checklist: reliability and factor structure. *Psychological Assessment*, **2**, 338–41.

Hare, R. D., Hart, S. D., & Harpur, T. J. (1991). Psychopathy and the DSM-IV criteria for antisocial personality disorder. *Journal of Abnormal Psychology*, **100**, 391–8.

Harpur, T. J., & Hare, R. D. (1994). Assessment of psychopathy as a function of age. *Journal of Abnormal Psychology*, **103**, 604–9.

Harpur, T. J., Hart, S. D., & Hare, R. D. (1994). Personality of the psychopath. In P. T. Costa, Jr, & T. A. Widiger (eds) *Personality Disorders and the Five-Factor Model of Personality* (pp. 149–73). Washington, DC: American Psychological Association.

Harris, G. T., Rice, M. E., & Cormier, C. A. (1991). Psychopathy and violent recidivism. *Law and Human Behavior*, **15**, 625–37.

Harris, G. T., Rice, M. E., & Quinsey, V. L. (1994). Psychopathy as a taxon: evidence that psychopaths are a discrete class. *Journal of Consulting and Clinical Psychology*, **62**, 387–97.

Hart, S. D., & Dempster, R. J. (1997). Impulsivity and psychopathy. In C. D. Webster & M. A. Jackson (eds) *Impulsivity: Theory, Assessment, and Treatment* (pp. 212–32). New York: Guilford.

Hart, S. D., Cox, D. N., & Hare, R. D. (1995). *The Hare Psychopathy Checklist: Screening Version (PCL:SV)*. Toronto: Multi Health Systems.

Hart, S. D., & Hare, R. D. (1989). Discriminant validity of the Psychopathy Checklist in a forensic psychiatric population. *Psychological Assessment: A Journal of Consulting and Clinical Psychology*, **1**, 211–18.

Hart, S. D., & Hare, R. D. (1994). Psychopathy and the Big 5: Correlations between observers' ratings of normal and pathological personality. *Journal of Personality Disorders*, **8**, 32–40.

Hart, S. D., & Hare, R. D. (1996). Psychopathy and risk assessment. *Current Opinion in Psychiatry*, **9**, 380–3.

Hart, S. D., & Hare, R. D. (1997). Psychopathy: assessment and association with criminal conduct. In D. M. Stoff, J. Breiling, & J. D. Maser (eds) *Handbook of Antisocial Behavior* (pp. 22–35). New York: Wiley.

Hart, S. D., Kropp, P. R., & Hare, R. D. (1988). Performance of male psychopaths following conditional release from prison. *Journal of Consulting and Clinical Psychology*, **56**, 227–32.

Hemphill, J. F. (1992). Recidivism of criminal psychopaths after therapeutic community treatment. Master's thesis, University of Saskatchewan, Saskatoon, Saskatchewan, Canada.

Hemphill, J. F. (1998). Psychopathy, criminal history, and recidivism. Doctoral dissertation, University of British Columbia, Vancouver, British Columbia, Canada.

Hemphill, J. F., & Hart, S. D. (2001). The assessment and treatment of offenders and inmates: general considerations. In R. A. Schuller & J. R. P. Ogloff (eds) *An Introduction to Psychology and Law: Canadian Perspectives* (pp. 217–47). Toronto: University of Toronto Press.

Hemphill, J. F., & Hart, S. D. (in press). Forensic and clinical issues in the assessment of psychopathy. In A. M. Goldstein (ed.) *Forensic Psychology (Comprehensive Handbook of Psychology, vol. 11)*. New York: Wiley.

Hemphill, J. F., Hare, R. D., & Wong, S. (1998). Psychopathy and recidivism: a review. *Legal and Criminological Psychology*, **3**, 139–70.

Hemphill, J. F., Hart, S. D., & Hare, R. D. (1994). Psychopathy and substance use. *Journal of Personality Disorders*, **8**, 169–80.

Hemphill, J. F., & Howell, A. J. (2000). Adolescent offenders and stages of change. *Psychological Assessment*, **12**, 371–81.

Hicks, M. M., Rogers, R., & Cashel, M. (2000). Predictions of violent and total infractions among institutionalised male juvenile offenders. *Journal of the American Academy of Psychiatry and Law*, **28**, 183–90.

Hill, C. E., Helms, J. E., Tichenor, V., Spiegel, S. B., O'Grady, K. E., & Perry, E. S. (1988). Effects of therapist response modes in brief psychotherapy. *Journal of Counseling Psychology*, **35**, 222–33.

Hill, C. D., Rogers, R., & Bickford, M. E. (1996). Predicting aggressive and socially disruptive behavior in a maximum security forensic psychiatric hospital. *Journal of Forensic Sciences*, **41**, 56–9.

Hird, J. A., Williams, P. J., & Markham, D. M. H. (1997). Survey of attendance at a community-based anger control group treatment programme with reference to source of referral, age of client and external motivating features. *Journal of Mental Health*, **6**, 47–54.

Hobson, J., Shine, J., & Roberts, R. (2000). How do psychopaths behave in a prison therapeutic community? *Psychology, Crime & Law*, **6**, 139–54.

Hodgins, S., & Müller-Isberner, R. (eds) (2000). *Violence, Crime, and Mentally Disordered Offenders: Concepts and Methods for Effective Treatment and Prevention*. Chichester: Wiley.

Howell, A. J., & Enns, R. A. (1995). A high risk recognition program for adolescents in conflict with the law. *Canadian Psychology*, **36**, 149–61.

Hughes, G., Hogue, T., Hollin, C., & Champion, H. (1997). First-stage evaluation of a treatment programme for personality disordered offenders. *Journal of Forensic Psychiatry*, **8**, 515–27.

Karpman, B. (1961). The structure of neuroses: with special differentials between neurosis, psychosis, homosexuality, alcoholism, psychopathy and criminality. *Archives of Criminal Psychodynamics*, **4**, 599–646.

Kernberg, O. F. (1998). The psychotherapeutic management of psychopathic, narcissistic, and paranoid transferences. In T. Millon, E. Simonsen, M. Birket-Smith, & R. D. Davis (eds) *Psychopathy: Antisocial, Criminal, and Violent Behavior* (pp. 372–92). New York: Guilford.

Leschied, A. W., Austin, G. W., & Jaffe, P. G. (1988). Impact of the Young Offenders Act on recidivism rates of special needs youth: clinical and policy implications. *Canadian Journal of Behavioral Science*, **20**, 322–31.

Lilienfeld, S. O. (1994). Conceptual problems in the assessment of psychopathy. *Clinical Psychology Review*, **14**, 17–38.

Lowenstein, L. F. (1996). The diagnosis and treatment of young psychopaths: part two. *Criminologist*, **20**, 207–17.

Lösel, F. (1998). Treatment and management of psychopaths. In D. J. Cooke, A. E. Forth, & R. D. Hare (eds) *Psychopathy: Theory, Research and Implications for Society* (pp. 303–54). Dordrecht: Kluwer.

MacKenzie, D. L., & Goodstein, L. (1985). Long-term incarceration impacts and characteristics of long-term offenders: an empirical analysis. *Criminal Justice and Behavior*, **12**, 395–414.

Mahrer, A. R., & Nadler, W. P. (1986). Good moments in psychotherapy: a preliminary review, a list, and some promising research avenues. *Journal of Consulting and Clinical Psychology*, **54**, 10–15.

Marlatt, G. A., & Gordon, J. R. (1980). Determinants of relapse: implications for the maintenance of change. In P. O. Davidson & S. M. Davidson (eds) *Behavioral Medicine: Changing Health Lifestyles* (pp. 410–52). New York: Brunner/Mazel.

Marlatt, G. A., & Gordon, J. R. (eds) (1985). *Relapse Prevention: Maintenance Strategies in the Treatment of Addictive Behaviors*. New York: Guilford.

McCord, W., & McCord, J. (1964). *The Psychopath: An Essay on the Criminal Mind*. Princeton, NJ: Van Nostrand.

Meloy, J. R. (1995). Antisocial personality disorder. In G. Gabbard (ed.) *Treatment of Psychiatric Disorders*, 2nd edn (pp. 2273–90). Washington, DC: American Psychiatric Press.

Millon, T. (1981). *Disorders of Personality: DSM-III, Axis II*. New York: Wiley.

Mulloy, R., Smiley, W. C., Dawda, D., & Hart, S. D. (1996). Psychopathy and cognitive-behavioral treatment success in personality disordered offenders. Paper presented at the Annual Meeting of the American Psychological Association, August, Toronto, Ontario.

Nedopil, N., Hollweg, M., Hartmann, J., & Jaser, R. (1998). Comorbidity of psychopathy with major mental disorders. In D. J. Cooke, A. E. Forth, & R. D. Hare (eds) *Psychopathy: Theory, Research and Implications for Society* (pp. 257–68). Dordrecht: Kluwer.

Newman, J. P., Patterson, C. M., & Kosson, D. S. (1987). Response perseveration in psychopaths. *Journal of Abnormal Psychology*, **96**, 145–8.

Newman, J. P., & Wallace, J. F. (1993). Psychopathy and cognition. In K. S. Dobson & P. C. Kendall (eds) (1993). *Psychopathology and Cognition* (pp. 293–349). San Diego, CA: Academic Press.

Ogloff, J. R. P., Wong, S., & Greenwood, A. (1990). Treating criminal psychopaths in a therapeutic community program. *Behavioral Sciences and the Law*, **8**, 181–90.

Pichot, P. (1978). Psychopathic behavior: a historical overview. In R. D. Hare & D. Schalling (eds) *Psychopathic Behavior: Approaches to Research* (pp. 55–70). Chichester: Wiley.

Prochaska, J. O. (1991). Prescribing to the stage and level of phobic patients. *Psychotherapy*, **28**, 463–8.

Prochaska, J. O., DiClemente, C. C., & Norcross, J. C. (1992). In search of how people change: applications to addictive behaviors. *American Psychologist*, **47**, 1102–14.

Reid, W. H., & Gacono, C. (2000). Treatment of antisocial personality, psychopathy, and other characterologic antisocial syndromes. *Behavioral Sciences and the Law*, **18**, 647–62.

Reiss, D., Grubin, D., & Meux, C. (1996). Young "psychopaths" in special hospital: treatment and outcome. *British Journal of Psychiatry*, **168**, 99–104.

Reiss, D., Grubin, D., & Meux, C. (1999). Institutional performance of male "psychopaths" in a high-security hospital. *Journal of Forensic Psychiatry*, **10**, 290–9.

Reiss, D., Meux, C., & Grubin, D. (2000). The effect of psychopathy on outcome in high security patients. *Journal of the American Academy of Psychiatry and Law*, **28**, 309–14.

Rice, M. E., & Harris, G. T. (1995). Psychopathy, schizophrenia, alcohol abuse, and violent recidivism. *International Journal of Law and Psychiatry*, **18**, 333–42.

Rice, M. E., Harris, G. T., & Cormier, C. A. (1992). An evaluation of a maximum security therapeutic community for psychopaths and other mentally disordered offenders. *Law and Human Behavior*, **16**, 399–412.

Rosenbaum, R. L., & Horowitz, M. J. (1983). Motivation for psychotherapy: a factorial and conceptual analysis. *Psychotherapy: Theory, Research and Practice*, **20**, 346–54.

Salekin, R., Rogers, R., & Sewell, K. (1996). A review and meta-analysis of the Psychopathy Checklist and Psychopathy Checklist-Revised: predictive validity of dangerousness. *Clinical Psychology: Science and Practice*, **3**, 203–15.

Serin, R. C. (1991). Psychopathy and violence in criminals. *Journal of Interpersonal Violence*, **6**, 423–31.

Seto, M. C., & Barbaree, H. E. (1999). Psychopathy, treatment behavior, and sex offender recidivism. *Journal of Interpersonal Violence*, **14**, 1235–48.

Shine, J. H., & Hobson, J. A. (2000). Institutional behavior and time in treatment amongst psychopaths admitted to a prison-based therapeutic community. *Medicine, Science and the Law*, **40**, 327–35.

Simpson, D. D., & Joe, G. W. (1993). Motivation as a predictor of early dropout from drug abuse and treatment. *Psychotherapy*, **30**, 357–68.

Smith, S. S., & Newman, J. P. (1990). Alcohol and drug abuse-dependence disorders in psychopathic and nonpsychopathic criminal offenders. *Journal of Abnormal Psychology*, **99**, 430–9.

Templeman, T. L., & Wollersheim, J. P. (1979). A cognitive-behavioral approach to the treatment of psychopathy. *Psychotherapy: Theory, Research and Practice*, **16**, 132–9.

Visher, C. A., Lattimore, P. K., & Linster, R. L. (1991). Predicting the recidivism of serious youthful offenders using survival models. *Criminology*, **29**, 329–66.

von Knorring, L., & Ekselius, L. (1998). Psychopharmacological treatment and impulsivity. In T. Millon, E. Simonsen, M. Birket-Smith, & R. D. Davis (eds) *Psychopathy: Antisocial, Criminal, and Violent Behavior* (pp. 359–71). New York: Guilford.

Wallace, J. F., Vitale, J. E., & Newman, J. P. (1999). Response modulation deficits: implications for the diagnosis and treatment of psychopathy. *Journal of Cognitive Psychotherapy*, **13**, 55–70.

Widiger, T. A., & Corbitt, E. M. (1995). Antisocial personality disorder in *DSM-IV*. In J. Livesley (ed.) *DSM-IV Personality Disorders* (pp. 127–34). New York: Guilford.

Wiggins, J. S. (1973). *Personality and Prediction: Principles of Personality Assessment*. Reading, MA: Addison-Wesley.

Wong, S., & Hare, R. D. (in press). *Program Guidelines for the Institutional Treatment of Violent Psychopaths*. Toronto, Canada: Multi Health Systems.

World Health Organization (1992). *ICD-10: International Statistical Classification of Diseases and Related Health Problems*, 10th rev. Geneva: WHO.

Wormith, J. S., & Hanson, R. K. (1992). The treatment of sexual offenders in Canada: an update. *Canadian Psychology*, **33**, 180–98.

Yates, P., & Nicholaichuk, T. (1998). The relationship between criminal career profile, psychopathy, and treatment outcome in the Clearwater sexual offender program [Abstract]. *Canadian Psychology*, **39** (2a), 97.

Zamble, E. (1992). Behavior and adaptation in long-term prison inmates: descriptive longitudinal results. *Criminal Justice and Behavior*, **19**, 409–25.

Zamble, E., & Porporino, F. (1990). Coping, imprisonment, and rehabilitation: some data and their implications. *Criminal Justice and Behavior*, **17**, 53–70.

Zamble, E., & Quinsey, V. L. (1997). *The Criminal Recidivism Process*. New York: Cambridge University Press.

Chapter 13

MOTIVATING MENTALLY DISORDERED OFFENDERS

JOHN E. HODGE* AND STANLEY J. RENWICK†
* Rampton Hospital, Retford, UK
† Duchess of Kent Hospital, Catterick Garrison, UK

INTRODUCTION

It has long been recognised that, despite its common usage, the term "mentally disordered offender" is fraught with conceptual and operational difficulties (Blackburn, 1993; Hollin & Howells, 1993a). Such problems have been described in terms of the challenges this poses legislators and service providers in respect of appropriately addressing the management requirements of this population (Baker, 1993; Coid & Kahtan, 2000; Prins, 1993). This occurs (at least in part) because of the potential collision of a number of distinct social and psychological domains. Hence, the individual's behaviour and actions require to be understood in terms of mental illness, psychological dysfunction, character, social and cultural mores, and legal prescription. Less clearly articulated, however, are the profound problems these difficulties pose for therapeutic intervention with such patients. Most especially, we believe, there has been a remarkable lack of consideration given to the complex interplay of factors underpinning such patients' motivation for engagement and participation in the treatment process. This disregard of motivational matters occurs despite the fact that, at the individual patient level, these factors often bear heavily on clinical decision-making regarding crucial issues such as continuing detention and perceived dangerousness. It is therefore our contention that detailed examination of motivational issues in this population is long overdue.

In order to clarify the conceptual conundrum posed by such patients, it is appropriate to identify the defining markers of the target population. In part, this might appear tautological, merely specifying those individuals convicted of offences that are also deemed to be suffering from a mental disorder. While this would comfortably address the majority of individuals one would wish to describe as mentally disordered offenders (i.e. patients in secure hospitals and psychiatric units, and

Motivating Offenders to Change: A Guide to Enhancing Engagement in Therapy. Edited by M. McMurran.
© 2002 John Wiley & Sons, Ltd.

those cared for by community forensic mental health services), it does not necessarily clarify the status of the significant number of those resident within the penal system who experience mental health problems (Taylor, 1986), nor indeed those treated within criminal justice community offender programmes. Were this not problematic enough, it is also clear that this population is not homogeneous with respect to the nature of their mental disorders. That is, any population of mentally disordered offenders will probably consist of patients with primary diagnoses from either DSM Axis I or II, namely major mental illness, personality disorder or learning disabilities, each with their own unique features and challenges. Indeed, the picture is further clouded by the high levels of comorbid difficulties evidenced in these patients (Blackburn et al., 1990, 2002; Coid, 1992; Mbatia & Tyrer, 1988; Quayle et al., 1998.). Such clinical complexity inevitably serves to impact on likely therapeutic intervention and outcome (Hollin & Howells, 1993b; Linehan, 1993) and hence must be taken into consideration when examining issues regarding therapeutic motivation.

Furthermore, and self-evidently, the treatment and management of such patients has to take into account the reality of their offender status. That is, for many such patients, their freedom is constrained and controlled, and there is an overtly criminal justice component to the manner in which they are managed. This, we will argue, is played out on a number of different levels, from environmental circumstances and resources, through (anti-)therapeutic climate and culture, and political and legal elements, to case management. Within the therapeutic contract, this can be evidenced in the competition between (often incompatible) treatment goals. Hence, alleviation of presenting symptomatology and enhancement of psychological well-being will jostle with risk and harm reduction as primary objectives for intervention. This can all too readily send very mixed and confusing messages to the patient. It can lead to some (or all) of an individual's problem behaviour being seen, for example, as arising as a result of his or her illness symptomatology. As such, alleviation of the symptomatology is expected to lead to resolution of the problem behaviour. In contrast, similar behaviours may be viewed as being within the conscious control of the individual, the person therefore being deemed responsible for the consequences, with psychological/psychiatric issues merely considered in respect of mitigation. Further, not only can issues of rehabilitation and punishment co-exist uncomfortably in respect of the same patient, but also for the same behaviours across individuals, clinicians often oscillating in their analyses of causation. Thus, in some cases, members of the clinical team view the patient's behaviour as stemming from social or psychological causes, while at other times the patient's diagnosis may be the overriding factor in causal attribution. This can impact not only on the way therapy is sanctioned and delivered, but also the climate and environment in which the individual resides during care and treatment. Obviously, there is a need to factor these issues into the intervention and outcome analysis. Sadly, despite increasing interest in issues such as outcome, there is little to indicate sensitivity to such confounding factors (Rice & Harris, 1997).

The above serves to highlight one of the main themes of this chapter, namely that any attempt at an understanding of motivation and its influence on intervention must consider not only intrinsic but also extrinsic and contextual factors. Indeed, it is the all too pervasive failure to recognise and respond to the equal importance of both of these domains (and their interaction), which we believe has led to the traditional therapeutic nihilism that has surrounded this population.

CONTEXTUAL INFLUENCES ON MOTIVATION

One of the most striking aspects of the majority of "forensic" facilities within which therapeutic efforts are undertaken is the extent to which such facilities have not apparently been designed with the facilitation of clinical activity in mind. Most obviously, this is manifest in the overt and pervasive signs of security and containment. Locks on doors, bars on windows, and razor wire perimeter fencing—all serve notice of the primary function of such institutions. Without question, such strictures are essential, not only to protect the public, but also to protect staff and patients. There can be little doubt that there is nothing more undermining of patient motivation and engagement than a perceived sense of the inherent lack of safety in the environment in which they reside. The difficulty is often that rehabilitation and security are rarely seen as complementary; rather, they compete for prominence in the minds of practitioners and the executive.

That security systems and procedures can be so deeply intrusive into the day to day world of the patient can, to a degree, be seen as an accident of history. Many hospitals and prison facilities were designed and built by previous generations, either with alternative functions or certainly differing clinical and service priorities in mind. However understandable, this does not obviate the difficulties thereby created for those attempting to develop and sustain a positive therapeutic milieu. Though rarely expressed, we believe that it is reasonable to conclude that there must be limits to the extent to which environments can be seen to be supportive and sustaining of therapeutic commitment. That is, there must be some environments in which psychotherapeutic activity is irrevocably compromised by the immediate circumstances. For example, how realistic is it to expect the patient to be able to establish therapeutic engagement when contact takes place in accommodation designed for other purposes, such as storerooms, dining rooms, and cells? What signal does this send the participant about the value placed on such endeavours by the host institution? How reasonable is it to expect progress in the development of, say, prosocial behaviours, when the prevailing institutional climate is likely to negate any efforts at behavioural expression and repertoire development?

Such problems may be seen to be exacerbated by old and inadequate accommodation; however, it would be naïve to assume that shiny new facilities in themselves would resolve the potential problems. Our experience is that even greenfield facilities can be blighted by a failure to place therapeutic requirements before cost constraints or aesthetic niceties. Hence, for example, units may be designed with few or no dedicated interview or treatment facilities. Further, even when these facilities are planned, it is remarkable how in reality they can be reconfigured for other, more mundane functions (such as storerooms).

Were this not problematic enough, it can be argued that the tension between treatment and security is dynamic, with prominence oscillating between the two functions at each other's expense. Hence, the price of therapeutic development is often seen to be the relaxation of prevailing security arrangements, and any tightening of security is usually at the cost of therapy. Partly, this can be seen to have arisen as a consequence of the attitude of "forensic" services towards risk. That is, they have a tendency to operate from the perspective of risk aversion and avoidance rather that management. Thus, compromises in security are seen to reflect organisational failure rather than unfortunate, but inherent, sequelae of dealing with mentally disordered offenders or indeed any detained populations. Obviously, serious breaches of security are highly problematic, and have to be addressed accordingly. However, what is all too regularly evident is the extent to which services respond to relatively minor infractions in a manner clearly out of proportion to the prevailing circumstance. This can be very clearly seen at the individual patient level, in the degree to which relatively minor incidents can be used as evidence of serious and global risk, with all the attendant implications for short- to medium-term decision-making regarding disposal.

It would be all too easy to level responsibility for the array of challenges high-lighted above at the door of unit clinical and operational managers, but rarely if ever do forensic practitioners themselves advance concerns about the conditions within which they are expected to deliver their service. Even when such structural problems are acknowledged (Department of Health, 1992), there is—certainly in the UK—precious little evidence to indicate that statutory authorities move quickly either to radically transform or, if necessary, close the offending institution. It is the height of arrogance (or perhaps ignorance) to assume that such lack of action is not lost on those patients who have the misfortune to be detained in these institutions. Even in such a context, it is unlikely that poor therapeutic progress will, on a day-to-day case management basis, be attributed to the institution and not to the individual patient.

We would propose that there are two fundamental processes maintaining this state of affairs. The first is the dominance of retributive justice considerations in the management of mentally disordered offenders. Second, there is the pervasive influence of a traditional medical model of care, maintained by the legal framework within which services are provided.

As identified earlier, therapeutic objectives for such patients have the twin aims of improving psychological status and risk reduction. In practice these often collide, leaving the patient (and indeed the therapist) in a somewhat confused and helpless position. On the one hand, much is made within the medico-legal system of issues of treatability underpinning decision-making regarding both initial and continuing detention issues, yet at the same time, rarely are inpatient and community discharge issues managed in a manner wholly determined by the prevailing care needs of the individual.

Though barely acknowledged, there can be little doubt that in the management of mentally disordered offenders there is consideration of appropriate retributive justice requirements. This is often not overtly specified, possibly because it comprises a complex amalgam of judgements concerning index offence severity, culpability, and illness status (Blackburn, 1993). The effects of this can be felt well beneath the level of executive decision making, often being manifest in the manner in which the patient is managed on a day-to-day basis. That is, it can become very easy for practitioners to develop a judgemental mind set regarding the apportioning of re-sources and opportunities, interfering with their ability to act in an advocacy role on behalf of all of their patients. Not surprisingly, patients are often very sensitive to such attitudes.

That such issues are manifest in practice is evident from the stream of Inquiries that have been initiated concerning facilities treating the mentally disordered offender (Coid & Kahtan, 2000). That there is little apparent evidence of learning the lessons of history is therefore something of a mystery. Certainly, many of the apparent solutions that have been advanced (e.g. reducing institutional size) do not appear to address the underlying issues. What has yet to be subject to consideration are the potential difficulties inherent in providing rehabilitation from within an implicit illness model of offending (Taylor et al., 1993). Indeed, the majority of issues raised above can be seen to flow directly from the dominance of this paradigm. It is arguably the traditionalist medical reliance on pharmacotherapy as the main agent of clinical change that has ensured the maintenance of many of the environmental impediments to patient motivation and engagement. Fundamentally, this paradigm requires little of the client other than to be the passive recipient of the allotted medication, and little of the environment other than to have him or her available at medication time. Hence, from this perspective, it is perfectly appropriate to view the immediate care task as that of safe custody and containment. Equally, for the patient, the paradigm serves to absolve him/herself from active participation within the change process, past responsibility and future opportunity being a function of changing illness status. Thus, impediments to broader therapeutic efforts are seen, within this model, to have little relevance to outcome.

Despite being operationally and administratively attractive, there is only limited support for the illness model of offending (Monahan et al., 2001). Few mentally disordered offenders offend directly as a result of their illness. Equally, there is little clinical evidence that pharmacotherapy alone is sufficient to produce a resolution of the individual's presenting and continuing dangerousness. This is evidenced by the difficulties posed to the system by the relatively few patients whose illness is subject to relatively quick remission following detention. What clinical experience graphically highlights is the pervasive need of mentally disordered offenders for psychological interventions targeted at the constellation of issues pertinent to their presenting problems and the requirement to provide optimal conditions within which this can be delivered.

The above analysis has served to identify the array of extrinsic and contextual factors powerfully influencing patient engagement and motivation within mentally disordered offender settings. That many mentally disordered offenders are subject to severe restriction of their freedom is self-evident. The length and degree of such restriction is inherently bound up in the severity of their offending. Services unambiguously signal the need for the mentally disordered offender to demonstrate engagement in treatment and improvement in conduct before progress can occur. However, as suggested, an array of additional overt and covert variables intrude into this equation. The relative scarcity of skilled therapists, the priority often paid to security, and the poor quality of the therapeutic environment all serve to influence the message the patient receives about his or her circumstances. Considered from this perspective, it is somewhat unrealistic to expect that such patients will be drawn to engage and maintain motivation for contact in a manner (broadly) equivalent to that found in other, more standard, settings.

It is, in our opinion, incumbent upon practitioners and managers to address the types of issues highlighted above in order to optimise patient motivation. This requires that responsibility be accepted at executive level for the provision of an appropriately therapeutic landscape within which practitioners can strive at individual patient level to establish and maintain commitment to psychological and behavioural change. The implications of such challenges for the development of future services will be examined later. Before this can be addressed, it is essential that intra-psychic factors pertinent to the motivational analysis be examined.

INTRINSIC FACTORS INFLUENCING MOTIVATION

The complexity of the task facing a therapist wishing to engage any offender in treatment is considerable. Two issues in particular make the task more daunting. First, offenders often come to therapy with limited intra- and interpersonal resources with which to address the challenges posed by the therapist and the therapy (Renwick et al., 1997). They may have limited awareness of their inner world, either emotionally or cognitively, and little experience of positive self-control and mastery of their environment (except for some when offending, and then only briefly).

Problems in the interpersonal domain may surface as a result of the little or no experience the individual may have had in establishing and maintaining successful relationships. Such problems often find first expression in chaotic and dysfunctional family relationships in childhood, which form the basis of many of the difficulties experienced in later life. As a result, such patients are likely to be particularly sensitive to issues of trust, rejection and threat to identity. This certainly does not provide the ideal platform from which to draw the cooperative and collaborative interaction essential to the development of a positive therapeutic relationship. Similarly, the social and moral perspective that the offender brings to their offending behaviour may be quite distinct from that adopted by the medico-legal setting in which they find themselves residing, or indeed society in general. This may arise as a consequence of the individual having allegiance to a particular social grouping or subculture that adopts a very different and distinct set of social and moral rules and values. Whether arising from personal experience of victimisation from early childhood or the inculcation of deviant attitudes and values, this means that offenders may not naturally acknowledge that their behaviour is morally wrong, socially unacceptable, or indeed problematic.

When the offender is mentally disordered, the situation is further confounded by illness factors. Mental disorder can affect and distort an individual's beliefs, attitudes, mood, and capacity for rational and analytic thought. Even when treated or in remission, the residue of the disorder can limit a client's insight into the nature of their offences or their confidence in their ability for self-control. Alternatively, since there is often a link between stress and relapse in mental disorder (Davison & Neale, 2001), effective progress in therapy, which is often stressful, can trigger a relapse in the mental disorder, making further progress at that time unlikely.

Seriously violent crimes committed in the context of a mental disorder can, when the mental disorder is successfully treated, result in trauma (Kruppa et al., 1995) or bereavement reactions (Fraser, 1988; Kleve, 1995). Such a traumatic reaction may well be manifest in symptoms of intrusion and avoidance, which will cloud the clinical presentation. The latter, for example, might find expression in patients actively seeking to avoid talking or indeed thinking about their past actions, denying responsibility or indeed slipping back into psychotic justification for their actions.

Clients bring all these elements with them when attempts are made to engage them in a change process. Often these issues go unrecognised by therapists and clinical teams. Lack of recognition of the difficulties clients have in forming social relationships, the discomfort of recounting or revisiting their experiences, or the lack of confidence in believing they can control their behaviour make it easy to come to the conclusion that clients are being "resistant" or "difficult" when in fact they are struggling to come to terms with what is to them a completely novel experience—engaging in therapy. Similarly, a lack of appreciation of a client's cultural background may result in a therapist or clinical team adopting an inappropriately punitive attitude when the client has difficulty in embracing more generally acceptable social values.

Similarly, a lack of acknowledgement of trauma or bereavement issues and their consequences can create all manner of difficulties in the development of effective therapeutic relationships and on the client's motivation to change and willingness to engage with staff. Trauma reactions can be misdiagnosed as "psychosis", endogenous mood swings or as evidence of denial. Similarly, bereavement reactions often attract a diagnosis of "depression". These misdiagnoses usually result in medication, which may interfere with the client's progress through these problems, while the intense anger, which can accompany trauma or bereavement, becomes seen as part of the client's pathology.

Clearly it is inappropriate and frankly dangerous to adopt too simplistic assumptions about motivation in mentally disordered offenders. The clinical challenges they present in developing and supporting their motivation for change are among the most complex likely to face any practitioner in any field of health or social care.

From the outset it is important to establish that, for mentally disordered offenders, engagement in treatment is not necessarily the same thing as being motivated to change. Indeed, for offenders with high levels of psychopathy, engagement in treatment may lead to higher rates of recidivism (Hare et al., 2000), perhaps because the treatments themselves offer opportunities to engage in and reinforce psychopathic cognitions and behaviours. For other mentally disordered offenders, engagement in treatment may almost become a form of institutionalisation— a behavioural requirement unrelated to any real understanding of the need for personal change. This was illustrated some years ago by one of our patients who had recently been transferred from another institution. When, after some serious confrontations between him and others on the ward, we were discussing his need for anger treatment, he very angrily responded that he had already had three courses on anger management and did not need any more treatment!

At the same time, lack of engagement in treatment does not necessarily mean lack of motivation to change (DiClemente, 1999). In some cases, treatment options may be limited, for example to groupwork, because of resource limitations, staff preferences or institutional policy. Patients may display resistance to some aspect of the treatment *method* on offer, despite being otherwise highly motivated to change. The factors underlying such resistance can be quite subtle, as illustrated by a recent patient who had been working well with treatment for a range of problems, but who quite suddenly became unresponsive when we began to address issues of childhood sexual abuse that he himself had identified as a major treatment target. Eventually, it emerged that males had perpetrated most of his sexual abuse, and, as a result, he believed that any males appearing to offer help would later insist on sexual favours in return. Although he desperately wanted help to come to terms with his abuse, he was unable to engage with a male therapist. When a female therapist was introduced for this part of his treatment, he quickly was able to re-engage. Unfortunately it is uncommon (and not always possible) for treatment method to be addressed as a major factor in treatment plans, yet it is often critical when dealing with such damaged people.

This client also demonstrates another facet about motivation to change that is often disregarded. Clients with complex disorders may display quite different motivation for different aspects of their problems. "Motivation to change" is often treated as if it is some global trait or characteristic of the individual. Little acknowledgement is given to the reality that clients can be highly motivated to address some of their problems while, *at the same time* be resistant to working on others (DiClemente, 1999; Rollnick et al., 1999). This can best be conceptualised within Prochaska and DiClemente's (1986) stages of change model by acknowledging that clients with multiple problems can be in different stages for each problem. Within the motivational interviewing approach developed by Miller (Miller, 1983; Miller & Rollnick, 1991), this phenomenon is addressed by adopting a general strategy of starting with problems the client is prepared to acknowledge, before steering him or her towards other, less agreeable topics. In some cases the starting point can seem a very long way from the core issues. However, this strategy can be particularly important for mentally disordered offenders, especially where the client is unable to acknowledge either their mental disorder or their offence.

The combination of mental disorder and offending can create unique and complex issues for helping clients resolve motivational problems. A common problem is that of clients who commit serious crimes within the context of a delusional belief system. If the delusional system is treatment resistant, then the client can maintain a rationalisation of the offence consistent with his delusional beliefs. At the same time, attempts to challenge or modify the client's delusional beliefs will undermine the client's rationalisation of the offence and will inevitably meet resistance as the client begins to understand the seriousness of his actions.

Similar problems arise with clients who have firmly held beliefs even though these may not reach delusional intensity. Many personality disordered clients hold firm beliefs that they use to justify their criminal behaviour. While not delusional, many of these beliefs can seriously undermine their motivation to engage fully in treatment or rehabilitation. If, as a result of personal experience in formative years, a person believes the world is a hostile place and that others are out to get him or her, it may be very difficult indeed to become persuaded that there are viable or safe alternatives for self-protection to pre-emptive acts of violence. Clients such as these may be conceptualised as remaining in Prochaska and DiClemente's (1986) precontemplation stage.

At the same time, these are often very vulnerable individuals whose fixed beliefs deny them the opportunity of positive attachments with others. Their beliefs are central to the rationalisation or justification of their offending, and their loss would render them even more vulnerable. Any motivational work aimed at addressing these beliefs is likely to fail. A more productive approach may be to *focus on reducing the client's general vulnerability*, both by persisting in developing a positive therapeutic relationship while acknowledging and validating other problems that the client advances. There is some evidence to support both of these strategies in mentally disordered populations.

Current evidence suggests that whatever the type of psychological therapy, the most consistent factor in predicting therapeutic success is the quality of the therapeutic relationship (Martin et al., 2000). People with mental disorders in general and mentally disordered offenders in particular often have fundamental problems in developing and sustaining relationships with others. Indeed, for those with personality disorders, many of the defining characteristics of the disorders lie within the domain of poor interpersonal functioning, while it has long been recognised that people with major mental illness such as schizophrenia have considerable difficulties with relationships. Nevertheless, research supports the idea that the relationship or therapeutic alliance is crucial. Frank and Gunderson (1990) have shown that where schizophrenic patients and their therapists are able to develop good alliances, there is better compliance with medication, less dropout, and better outcome. However, less than half their patient–therapist pairs were able to achieve an effective therapeutic relationship. Gehrs and Goering (1994) showed that the *perception* of a good relationship by patient and therapist was predictive of a good outcome, yet there is a consensus that this is very difficult to achieve with psychotic patients.

Achieving therapeutic relationships with severely mentally disordered offenders is complex, time-consuming and resource-intensive. There is little guidance from the literature at present on how such a relationship is to be achieved. There is some evidence that the Rogerian concept of *congruence* may be particularly important with more disturbed clients (Mearns & Thorne, 1988). Congruence refers to the genuineness of the therapist and their ability to work with the client without putting up a professional front. This seems very similar to the concept of genuineness advanced by Truax and Carkhuff (1967), who argued that warmth, genuineness and empathy were the basis of the therapeutic alliance. That these can be difficult to achieve and maintain with mentally disordered offenders does not invalidate them as the basis for working with these clients.

In a review of psychotherapy research, Roth and Fonagy (1996) identified therapist experience as important to the development of a therapeutic alliance, and a better predictor of outcome in more disturbed clients than professional training. More experienced therapists lost fewer clients to dropout, and seemed to cope better when the client's attitude to therapy was predominantly negative and hostile. However, the review offered little help in understanding the process of developing an effective relationship.

One strategy that can contribute to effective relationships is the use of *validation*. Validation is an approach advocated by Linehan (1993) as a core strategy of dialectic behaviour therapy, a therapeutic approach designed to help women with borderline personality disorder who self-harm. Linehan (1993) describes validation as an acceptance strategy that "communicates to the patient in a non-ambiguous way that her behaviour makes sense and is understandable in the current context" (Linehan, 1993, p. 221). This is achieved in three steps. *Active observation* establishes what has happened or is happening to the patient. *Reflection* is where the therapist reflects the patient's own feelings, thoughts, assumptions and behaviours. This has the effect of constantly communicating to the patient they are being listened to and at the same time checking the therapist's understanding of what is taking place. Finally the therapist provides *direct validation* by looking for and reflecting the validity of the client's response. Where the response is dysfunctional, it is usual that some element of the client's behaviour is appropriate to the context in which it occurs and can be validated.

CONCLUSIONS AND THE WAY FORWARD

In this chapter, we have attempted to challenge the prevalent fundamentally nihilistic view of efforts to engage and motivate the mentally disordered offender. While advocating the acceptance of a more realistic perspective on the challenges facing the therapist, and indeed patient, it would not be our intention to offer a gloomy scenario. Rather, it is proposed that with this patient population, especially, the issue of motivation has to be considered as multi-layered and addressed accordingly. In particular we have sought to emphasise that the motivational issue resides not only with the individual offender, nor indeed with the patient–therapist axis, but also wih the immediate clinical context and prevailing therapeutic climate. It is, in our opinion, only when such factors are in alignment that motivational conditions are likely to be optimised and positive outcome can be expected. More crucially, as has been argued, any dissonance between the different elements is likely to serve as a major impediment to therapeutic success. While this should seem self-evident, it is clear that, historically, rarely, if ever, has such an holistic approach to patient motivation and therapeutic efforts with the mentally disordered offender been advanced.

As suggested previously, one area where such problems are played out in inpatient settings has been in the competing demands of therapy and security. We have attempted to argue that this traditional conflict has not been helpful and indeed is often very destructive both for patient and institution. It is our view that this need not be the case. Security and therapy can and should be synergistic. This can be described simplistically in terms of positive patient motivation and therapeutic progress being the best form of security. Equally, however, creative and dynamic security systems and procedures can permit the development and application of powerful therapeutic opportunities. It has been argued above that this requires a transformation of the all too pervasive culture of risk avoidance, and the factoring of therapy and motivational issues into the overall security equation.

It has similarly been proposed that an equivalent tension occurs at the level of the individual mentally disordered offender patient between management of therapeutic progress and retributive justice requirements. This we believe is especially corrosive because the latter remains covert and hence unclear. The ensuing tensions serve to confuse and undermine patient and therapist alike. Thus, in our view, the making explicit of such justice requirements, thus permitting their operationalisation, would actually constitute a progressive rather than a regressive step. This would permit clinical status to act as the primary driver, especially during the crucial latter stages of a patient's treatment.

No matter how important the above may prove, the effects are only likely to be felt in an environment and culture conducive to motivation and therapy. Much has been made of the extent to which such issues remain largely ignored by practitioners and policy makers. This we believe need not continue to be the case. For some time, efforts have been made to operationalise ward culture and climate, and evaluate it more systematically in mainstream psychiatric settings (Moos, 1974). There is no reason why forensic services for mentally disordered offenders should be exempt from similar examination. This might provide powerful leverage for environmental and cultural change.

Given the significant implications for patients of perceived failure to engage or progress, it would appear fair to demand that forensic services achieve appropriate environmental and cultural standards. In other words, institutions and services should be held accountable when independent scrutiny indicates that practices and procedures have fallen below predetermined acceptable levels. History suggests that advisory systems manifestly fail to deliver such an agenda. We would argue, however, that advisory systems suffer from a lack of appropriate concepts and standards to properly scrutinise and evaluate the pertinent factors described in this chapter. The development of more appropriate standards together with regular scrutiny might help instil a more dynamic culture of service delivery; that is, one which is truly patient and outcome orientated. Resolution of this would, without doubt, deliver a contextual canvas on which the intrinsic factors pertinent to therapeutic motivations could be meaningfully addressed and progressed. Within this context, active consideration of the individual's motivational circumstances would lie at the heart of therapeutic efforts.

Such resolutions can only be achieved if managers and policy makers are made aware of the importance of environment and procedures in achieving effective therapeutic change. If treatment and rehabilitation are the primary objectives (and in health care systems they should be) then the context must reflect this. This can only be achieved by psychologically minded clinicians making themselves heard and demonstrating the need for policy, environmental design and security systems to reflect this. Without this, there will be little pressure on current systems to change and the complacent attitude will prevail that motivation for change is entirely the responsibility of the client or patient.

Unfortunately, as we have indicated, even many psychologically minded clinicians disregard the importance of context and environment in their work and either "make do" or adopt treatment approaches where issues of motivation are embedded within narrow theoretical models of change. It is imperative that such clinicians become aware of the broader psychological factors impacting on their work, and that we thereby enlist their support to develop pressure for change.

Such change is unlikely to occur quickly. While advocating that the pressure at executive and policy level must be developed and maintained, we have also tried to illustrate that there are still strategies that clinicians can adopt with current patients to impact on their motivation. We believe that much more direct and independent attention needs to be paid to patient motivation in any care programme approach with this population. It is our view that therapeutic endeavours with mentally disordered offenders have tended to consider motivational issues from within the perspective of the specific intervention adopted, that is, in post hoc fashion, as part of the treatment approach directed towards either the illness or the offending behaviour. It is arguably because of this that existent approaches to the management of motivation are essentially drawn from "mainstream" clinical theorising.

We believe that mentally disordered offenders constitute a very distinct clinical population, within which issues of motivation require particular consideration. Indeed, it is our view that it is in the operationalisation of patients' motivation that the clinical conundrum is reconcilable. The functional analysis of the individual's motivation is the matrix that synthesises illness, personality, offending, and cultural features in order to make sense of the individual and their circumstances. This is, in our view, the most appropriate platform from which to determine treatment and continuing care needs.

This focus on motivation remains equally salient throughout the course of therapy (see Prochaska & Levesque, this volume, Chapter 4), irrespective of the particular clinical goal at the time (e.g. inappropriate sexual behaviour, anger dysregulation). It highlights the need for identification of the functionality for the individual of much of their offending behaviour and, consequently, the barriers and levers to change. Similarly, initial motivational and engagement difficulties may be evaluated not only in terms of being forensic markers, but also in respect of the limited resources, history of damage, and cultural values that individuals bring to therapeutic contact. Hence, recognition can be given to the likelihood of fluctuations in motivation during the therapeutic process. This emphasises the potential need to return to explicit motivational work during difficult periods. All the above must take place within the context of a close and trusting therapeutic alliance with the patient.

In conclusion, it is our view that mentally disordered offenders are seriously disadvantaged by the complexities of the issues involved in motivating them to change, and by the environment in which this motivational work is required to take place. It has been argued here that such complexities have, to date, been little understood and rarely addressed. Rather, there has been a tendency for services and practitioners to draw on limited conceptualisations of patient motivation from "mainstream" therapeutic practice. Arguments advanced above aim to present the alternative perspective that working with mentally disordered offenders requires a unique multi-layered approach to motivation. This proposes that optimising patient motivation requires practitioners to strategically address contextual issues while developing a more tactical approach to therapeutic work with the individual client.

REFERENCES

Baker, E. (1993). The social and legal framework. In K. Howells & C.R. Hollin (eds) *Clinical Approaches to the Mentally Disordered Offender*. Chichester: Wiley.

Blackburn, R. (1993). *The Psychology of Criminal Conduct: Theory, Research and Practice*. Chichester: Wiley.

Blackburn, R., Crellin, M.C., Morgan, E.M. & Tulloch, R.M.B. (1990). Prevalence of personality disorders in a Special Hospital population. *Journal of Forensic Psychiatry*, **1**, 43–52.

Blackburn, R., Logan, C., Donnelly J. & Renwick, S. (2002). Personality disorders, psychopathy and other mental disorders: comorbidity among patients at English and Scottish high security hospitals. Submitted for publication.

Coid, J. (1992). DSM-III Diagnosis in Criminal Psychopaths: a way forward. *Criminal Behaviour and Mental Health*, **2**, 78–79.

Coid, J. & Kahtan, N. (2000). Are Special Hospitals needed? *Journal of Forensic Psychiatry*, **11**, 17–35.

Davison, G.C. & Neale, G.M. (2001) *Abnormal Psychology*, 8th edn. New York: Wiley.

Department of Health (1992). *Report of the Committee of Inquiry into complaints about Ashworth Hospital*, vols I & II. London: HMSO.

DiClemente, C.C. (1999). Motivation for change: implications for substance abuse treatment. *Psychological Science*, **10**, 209–13.

Frank, A.F. & Gunderson, J.G. (1990). The role of the therapeutic alliance in the treatment of schizophrenia. *Archives of General Psychiatry*, **47**, 228–36.

Fraser, K.A. (1988) Bereavement in those who have killed. *Medicine, Science and the Law*, **28**, 127–30.

Gehrs, M. & Goering, P. (1994). The relationship between the working alliance and rehabilitation outcomes of schizophrenia.*Psychosocial Rehabilitation Journal*, **18**, 43–54.

Hare, R. D., Clark, D., Grann, M. & Thornton, D. (2000). Psychopathy and the predictive validity of the PCL-R: an international perspective. *Behavioral Sciences and the Law*, **18**, 623–45.

Hollin, C.R. & Howells, K. (1993a). The mentally disordered offender: a clinical approach. In K. Howells & C.R. Hollin (eds) *Clinical Approaches to the Mentally Disordered Offender*. Chichester: Wiley.

Hollin, C.R. & Howells, K. (1993b). A clinical approach to the mentally disordered offender: prognosis. In K. Howells & C.R. Hollin (eds) *Clinical Approaches to the Mentally Disordered Offender*. Chichester: Wiley.

Kleve, L. (1995). How brief is a killer's grief? A case illustration. *Clinical Psychology Forum*, **76**, 23–7.

Kruppa, I., Hickey, N. & Hubbard, C. (1995). The prevalence of post traumatic stress disorder in a special hospital population of legal psychopaths. *Psychology, Crime and Law*, **2**, 131–41.

Linehan, M.M. (1993). *Cognitive-Behavioural Treatment of Borderline Personality. Disorder*.New York: Guilford Press.

Martin, D.J., Garske, J.P. & Davis, M.K. (2000). Relation of the therapeutic alliance with outcome and other variables: a meta-analytic review. *Journal of Consulting and Clinical Psychology*, **68**, 438–50.

Mbatia, J. & Tyrer, P. (1988). Personality status of dangerous patients in a special hospital. In P. Tyrer (ed.) *Personality Disorders: Diagnosis, Management and Course*. London: Wright/Butterworth Scientific.

Mearns, D. & Thorne, B. 1988). *Person-Centred Counselling in Action*. Thousand Oaks, CA: Sage

Miller, W.R. (1983). Motivational interviewing with problem drinkers. *Behavioural Psychotherapy*, **11**, 147–72.

Miller, W.R. & Rollnick, S. (1991). *Motivational Interviewing: Preparing People to Change Addictive Behaviour*. New York: Guilford Press.

Monahan, J., Steadman, H.J., Silver, E., Appelbaum, P.S., Robbins, P.C., Mulvey, E.P., Roth, L.H., Grisso, T. & Banks, S. (2001). *Rethinking Risk Assessment: The MacArthur Study of Mental Disorder and Violence*. Oxford: Oxford University Press.

Moos, R.H. (1974). *Evaluating Treatment Environments: A Social Ecological Approach*. New York: Wiley.

Prins, H. (1993). Service provision and facilities for the mentally disordered offender. In K. Howells & C.R. Hollin (eds) *Clinical Approaches to the Mentally Disordered Offender*. Chichester: Wiley.

Prochaska, J.O. & DiClemente, C.C. (1986). Toward a comprehensive model of change. In W.R. Miller & N. Heather (eds) *Treating Addictive Behaviours: Processes of Change* (pp. 3–27). New York: Plenum Press.

Quayle, M., Clark, F., Renwick, S.J., Hodge, J. & Spencer, T. (1998). Alcohol and secure hospital patients: I. An examination of the nature and prevalence of alcohol problems in secure hospital patients. *Psychology, Crime and Law*, **4**, 27–41.

Renwick, S.J., Black, L., Ramm, M. & Novaco, R. (1997). Anger treatment with forensic hospital patients. *Legal and Criminological Psychology*, **2**, 103–16.

Rice, M. & Harris, G. (1997). The treatment of mentally disordered offenders. *Psychology, Public Policy and Law*, **3** (1), 126.

Rollnick, S., Mason, P. & Butler, C. (1999) *Health Behaviour Change: A Guide for Practitioners*. London: Churchill Livingstone.

Roth, A. & Fonagy, P. (1996). *What Works for Whom?* New York: Guilford Press.

Taylor, P. (1986). Psychiatric disorder in London's life-sentenced offenders. *British Journal of Criminology*, **26**, 63–78.

Taylor, P. J., Mullen, P. & Wessely, S. (1993). Psychosis, violence and crime. In J. Gunn & P. J. Taylor (eds) *Forensic Psychiatry: Clinical, Legal, and Ethical Issues* (pp. 329–71). Oxford: Butterworth Heineman.

Truax, C.B. & Carkhuff, R.R. (1967). *Towards Effective Counselling and Psychotherapy*. Chicago, IL: Aldine.

Chapter 14

DOES PUNISHMENT MOTIVATE OFFENDERS TO CHANGE?

CLIVE R. HOLLIN

Centre for Applied Psychology, University of Leicester, UK

Like fish and chips, salt and pepper, and Lennon and McCartney, the words "crime" and "punishment" are forever linked in the collective associative lexicon. It is likely that this association dates from the earliest times, and certainly since records have been kept, in that society's standard response to wrongdoing was to administer punishment. It is also clear from the historical record that, until comparatively recently, on those occasions when punishment was meted out the punitive measures were inevitably harsh and severe in the extreme. As Siegel (1986) notes, at various times in history the legal punishment for committing a crime has included flogging, branding, amputation, stoning and deportation. In addition, there were many variations of administration of the death penalty, including burning, beheading and hanging. Similarly, when incarceration was used, prison regimes were cruel in the extreme: Thomas (1998) describes the tread-wheels, oakum sheds, and crack-labour that broke the spirits of prisoners in Victorian Britain.

Lilly and colleagues (1995) make the point that the severity of such punitive measures did not come about by chance. Throughout history, the consequences of crime for the offender have mirrored society's favoured explanation for crime. As Lilly et al. suggest, many early societies held the belief that an individual who committed a crime was possessed by demons. It follows that the harsh punishment was directed not at the person but at the evil spirit, often with religious intent. Similarly, rituals like trial by ordeal or submerging in water were based on the belief that God would not let an innocent person suffer: for the accused to die was a clear sign of their guilt. Of course, the sharp distinction between the spiritual and the political could become blurred. Thus, a punishment delivered in the name of God might, as if by coincidence, serve some local political purpose.

It is only comparatively recently that there has been a major shift away from spiritualistic explanations of crime and their associated forms of punishment. This shift in thinking came about through the advent of classical theory, a theoretical

Motivating Offenders to Change: A Guide to Enhancing Engagement in Therapy. Edited by M. McMurran.
© 2002 John Wiley & Sons, Ltd.

development generally ascribed (Roshier, 1989; Russell, 1961; Siegel, 1986; Tierney, 1996) to the influence of two key figures, the Italian nobleman and economist Cesare Beccaria (1738–94), and the British philosopher Jeremy Bentham (1748–1832). The basic underpinning of classical theory lies in the concept of free will: that each individual is free to choose what he or she wishes to do. Yet further, classical theory takes the view that our actions are guided by hedonism; that is, we will always want to act in ways that avoid pain and bring pleasure. Thus, according to classical theory the criminal is someone who, when the occasion arises, acts of their own free will to estimate the net gain or loss from their committing a crime. If the gains are perceived as outweighing the loss then crime follows and *vice versa*. As these theoretical assumptions about human action apply equally to everyone, so it must be assumed that we are all equally likely to commit a crime (and hence we are all equal before the law).

Thus, as Lilly et al. wryly suggest, classical theory offers a model of the criminal as a calculator, an individual surveying the balance sheet of life before making rational choices about obeying or breaking the law. The contemporary human scientist might ask, "Where does free will originate?" or "How does free will cause human action?". Indeed, the nature of free will and rational choice are deep philosophical issues (Honderich, 1993; Skinner, 1971), but "The classical answer is that they are simply there; they are taken as given. They are part of the conception of human rationality which . . . is one of the starting assumptions of classical criminology" (Roshier, 1989, p. 72).

Thus, accepting Lilley et al.'s metaphor of the criminal as a calculator with free will, the significant impact of classical theory was to redefine the role and function of law and punishment. Adopting a utilitarian stance, classical theory maintains that laws should protect the community. It follows that the function of punishment is to prevent harm to the community. Thus, following classical theory, the administration of punishment should therefore act to prevent further crimes.

The topic of punishment is one that continues to generate a great deal of theoretical debate among philosophers and criminologists (e.g. Honderich, 1976; von Hirsch, 1993; Walker, 1991). It is clear that the issues have become a great deal more complex than the original utilitarian approaches to crime and punishment. However, to address the question posed in the title to this chapter, the focus here remains with a line of thought that can be traced directly to classical theory. If punishment is to prevent and reduce crime, then the suggested mechanism by which this effect takes place is one by which fear of punishment *deters* the individual from deciding to offend.

DETERRENCE

The conceptual underpinning of the notion of deterrence flows directly from classical theory. Criminology texts divide deterrence into two types, *general deterrence* and *special deterrence*. The former refers to the society-wide effects of punitive sanctions: thus, deterrence theory suggests that members of society will obey the law because they fear the consequences that they perceive will follow their lawbreaking. The latter, special deterrence, speaks to the effects of sentencing on the individual offender. If the aversive quality of the punishment outweighs the advantages gained from criminal acts, then, the theory maintains, the individual will be deterred from committing further crimes. However, with respect to special deterrence it is important to note that the theory does not suggest that the punishment has to be extreme or severe.

Beccaria's utilitarian view of crime and punishment led to the concept of proportionality between offence and sanction. The thinking behind the idea of proportionality is plain. If two crimes are punished equally then there is no scope for deterring people from the most serious crime. For example, if theft and murder were both punished by the death penalty, then thieves would have nothing to fear that would deter them from killing their victims. Thus, according to this view of crime and criminal sanctions, the punishment must fit the crime.

One of the appealing aspects of deterrence from a research standpoint is that in principle its effects should be measurable. If a new sanction is brought into place specifically to impact on certain crimes or specific groups of offenders, then it should be possible to measure its effects in terms of general reductions in the crime rate. Similarly, if punishment does motivate offenders not to reoffend, then evidence for this should be seen in studies that have evaluated punitive measures.

The most obvious example of general deterrence is seen in the debate about the effectiveness of the death penalty. The death penalty is widely used around the globe as a punishment for serious offences, typically murder and other serious violent crimes or crimes against the state (Hood, 1996). The death penalty is said to serve two functions: first, to punish the offender for their crime; second to deter others from committing similar crimes. At first glance, it may seem a relatively simple research task to investigate the general deterrent effect of the death penalty. There are legal administrations that have had the death penalty and then abolished it, resulting in a natural pre–post experimental paradigm. If the level of serious crimes, such as murder, were suppressed by the deterrent effect of the death penalty then a rise in frequency of serious crime after abolition would be predicted. However, in reality there are many confounds operating—such as changes in sentencing policy, population variations over time, and shifts in crime detection—that make it difficult to disentangle fluctuations in the crime figures (Peterson & Bailey, 1991).

Acknowledging the research difficulties, Walker (1991) discusses the situation in New Zealand where changes in legislation between 1924 and 1962 meant that the death penalty was applied, abolished, reinstated, in abeyance, and finally abolished once more. Walker notes that the changes were well publicised, as were cases where the death penalty was applied. The murder rate in New Zealand did fluctuate over the period, as might be expected, but "The fluctuations bore no discernible relationship to the status of the death penalty: one cannot tell from them when it was in force and when it was not" (Walker, p. 16).

Again with respect to the death penalty, Hood (1996) offers a comprehensive analysis of the question of deterrence. (It should be noted that the extant research focuses on the deterrent effect of the death penalty specifically for murder. Hood notes that there are no empirical studies of the effect of the death penalty on other crimes such as drug offences and politically motivated crime.) Hood's careful analysis leads him to an interesting position. Hood argues that those in favour of abolition would wish to see evidence that the death penalty has a significant deterrent effect. On the other hand, those in favour of the death penalty would seek to be assured that there was no significantly increased risk to the public before sparing the lives of criminals. Hood concludes that "The balance of evidence, looked at in this way, favours the abolitionist position" (p. 212). It is worth noting that commentators such as Walker and Hood are careful not to state that deterrence does not work; rather, they suggest that the evidence as it stands fails to support the arguments in favour of general deterrence.

What is the position with deterrence other than as considered through research concerning the death penalty? There are three lines of evidence that can be used to inform the debate on deterrence: first, studies of the effects of different types of sanctions applied within the criminal justice system; second, the findings of individual studies of specific projects aimed at deterring offenders; third, the findings of the meta-analyses regarding intervention with offenders.

The Effects of Sanctions

Any contemporary criminal justice system has a range of sanctions at its disposal, ranging from cautions and fines to loss of liberty or even execution. If punishment motivates offenders to desist from offending—that is, if punishment deters future offending—then we might expect to see a reduction in offending after the administration of punitive sanctions through sentencing. Of course, there is a substantial knowledge base concerning the effects of sentencing. For example, many countries publish statistics revealing rates of recidivism after periods of imprisonment; there are studies of the effects of probation orders; and similar studies of rates of reoffending after the imposition of a fine. In making sense of such evidence it is difficult to compare outcomes across different sentence types as it is unlikely that those offenders sentenced to, say, a period on probation will have the same offence characteristics as those given long prison sentences. A solution to this problem is, within sentence types, to compare actual and predicted rates of offending. The continual development of statistically sophisticated prediction instruments, such as the Offender Group Reconviction Scales (Copas & Marshall, 1998), allows strong comparisons to be made between actual and expected rates of reconviction.

Research reported by Lloyd and colleagues (1994) provides a good example of a study concerned with reconviction rates following different types of sanctions. Lloyd et al. compared the effects of four types of sanction imposed by the courts: these sanctions were community service orders, a probation order, a probation order with additional requirements, and imprisonment. With substantial numbers of offenders within each sentence type, Lloyd et al. reported an analysis of actual and expected rates of reconviction for the four sentences. There were two findings of immediate note: first, there were no substantial differences between actual and predicted reconviction rates *within* the four types of sentence; second, the overall rate of *actual* reconviction across the four types of sentence was remarkably similar (clustered around 50%). Thus, for offenders sentenced to a particular sanction the actual rate of reoffending appeared to be unaffected by the penalty. Similarly, the closeness of the figures across sentences suggests that different sentences were not having a different effect in terms of reducing reoffending.

In commenting on the Lloyd et al. study, McGuire (1995) makes the observation that: "On the basis of these figures, it [sentence type] has little or no impact on the subsequent behaviour of offenders, whatever its severity. Sentences of the court, on the individual level at least, do not appear to have any clear-cut deterrent effect" (p. 16).

It is possible that nested within the average figures are cases of offenders where the sentence has had a deterrent effect. However, a different type of study to that conducted by Lloyd et al. would be needed in order to discover whether such an effect was present. Nonetheless, there are sufficient studies in the literature to call into question the magnitude of the deterrent effect of criminal sanctions. This is not to say that sanctions cannot have a deterrent effect, rather that the evidence in favour of such a position is far from conclusive. McGuire's (in press) review of the evidence reaches a similar conclusion: stating that while deterrence may work for some offenders, McGuire suggests that it is questionable whether the effect is sufficiently robust to be the foundation for a policy on sanctions within the criminal justice system. With a focus specifically on deterrence and violent crime, Berkowitz's (1993) review of theory and research again reaches a similar conclusion.

The Findings of Specific Projects

Another approach to the question of the effects of punishment on the offender is to consider specific initiatives intended to achieve a deterrent effect. There are many such initiatives, including programmes such as "Scared Straight", "Shock Probation", "Short, Sharp, Shock", "Jailhouse Shock", and "Shock Incarceration for Women". While there are several individual evaluations of such initiatives (e.g. Thornton et al., 1984), it is the question of the effectiveness of boot camps that has sustained a protracted and substantial body of research (Cowles & Castellano, 1995; Cronin, 1994; MacKenzie & Hebert, 1996).

Boot camps

Even the most cursory glance at the literature shows that the term "boot camp" is used in a variety of ways. While there is not a widely accepted definition of a "boot camp", Cronin (1994) gives a good, concise description: "Characterized by a strong emphasis on military structure, drill, and discipline, these programs [boot camps] offer a new twist on the use of residential programs for convicted criminals" (p. 1).

Why this emphasis on structure, drill and discipline? The rationale would appear to be that such experiences will, in some way, motivate the offender to desist from a life of crime. Whether this motivation is the product of deterrence, modifying some aspect of the offender's psychological functioning (self-esteem and self-respect are terms often used in this context), or some other unspecified mechanism remains a moot point.

In seeking to evaluate the effectiveness of boot camps, the immediate problem is the variation in regimes subsumed under the term "boot camp". A search of the Internet revealed a large number of web sites (mainly American) advertising "boot camp" facilities, principally aimed at problem children and delinquent teenagers (e.g., http://www.kci.org/publication/bootcamp/prerelease.htm). It is certainly the case that while the central ethos may be similar, different boot camps run different regimes. Clearly, there are difficult research issues to resolve in investigating the effectiveness of boot camps.

However, regardless of the problems faced by researchers, it is apparent that there are high expectations of the effects of boot camps. As MacKenzie and Souryal (1995a, p. 2) note:

> The public and policy makers appear to expect boot camps to accomplish spectacular results. Boot camps provide a short term of incarceration in a strict military environment with a rigid daily schedule of hard labor, drill and ceremony, and physical training. There is obviously a hope that this tough punishment will deter offenders from continuing their criminal activities.

Clearly the harsh approach advocated by proponents of boot camps will raise moral and philosophical objections (Mathlas & Mathews, 1991; Morash & Rucker, 1990; Schrest, 1989): however, the pressing issue here looks to the outcome evidence. There is a body of research that gives an indication of the effectiveness of boot camps in terms of both process and effect on recidivism.

Process measures

In a typical study, MacKenzie and Shaw (1990) compared adjustment and attitude change in inmates sentenced either to traditional incarceration or to a boot camp. They found that compared to their traditional peers, the boot camp inmates were more positive about their experience of imprisonment, were more positive about their future, and held more prosocial attitudes. Burton and colleagues (1993) reported the same pattern of findings, noting that the experience of boot camp "*Did positively change probationers' attitudes* [their italics] in crucial areas, which may potentially shape the likelihood of future criminality" (p. 51). Indeed, MacKenzie and Souryal (1995b) list a range of positive process outcomes, including inmates being drug free and physically healthy, inmates believing the programme has helped them, and an overall positive impact on the families of offenders.

However, as MacKenzie and Souryal (1994, p. 20) note, the finding that boot camp inmates become less antisocial during incarceration may be a selection effect:

> It is important to remember that these offenders were different from the general prison population. By and large, they were convicted of nonviolent crimes and had less serious criminal histories. In fact, in several States, it is likely that many of the offenders would have received probation if the boot camp had not been in operation. As a consequence, their prison experience may have been very different from that of a more "typical" offender.

Recidivism

A string of studies has looked at the impact of boot camp regimes on recidivism (MacKenzie & Shaw, 1993; MacKenzie et al., 1995), as well as adjustment during community supervision (MacKenzie & Brame, 1995). The picture emerging from these studies is not a simple one: the findings show some fluctuation in outcome according to variables such as the location of the boot camp regime, the actual measure of reoffending, and the offender's situation after release.

MacKenzie et al. (1995) reported a study of the effectiveness of boot camps in reducing recidivism in eight American states. They found that in four states there was no impact of boot camps on recidivism, in one state there was an *increase* in recidivism after the boot camp, and in three states there were mixed findings regarding recidivism. The mixed findings were a consequence of the measure of reoffending: in one state the rate for new crime revocations went down, but they had more technical violations; in three states the boot camps were associated with fewer revocations, fewer new crimes, and fewer technical revocations than dropouts from the programme but not from controls. Further, it is possible that success is related to the intensity of supervision after release (MacKenzie & Brame, 1995). Nor can it be assumed that all boot camp regimes are similar, leaving the possibility that these differences are related to varying outcome. As MacKenzie et al. (1995) note, the more successful boot camp programmes, in terms of reducing recidivism, "devoted a comparatively large amount of time to therapeutic activities" (p. 353). MacKenzie et al. (1995, pp. 353–4) offer the conclusion that:

> It is hardly surprising in our research that offenders were positively affected by their experience in the boot camps that had components characteristic of effective treatment programs but that the recidivism of boot camp releasees was actually higher than for the comparative groups in the camp that emphasized physical activity and military deportment without any therapeutic programming. Certainly, there is little past research to suggest that the physical exercise, military atmosphere, and hard labor aspects of these programs would successfully change the behavior of the offenders if, at the same time, the criminogenic needs of the offenders are not being addressed.

This conclusion is also implicit in McKenzie's (2000) review of the effectiveness on rehabilitation. Using a three-way classification of the outcome evidence, based on "what works", "what doesn't work", and "what's promising", McKenzie (2000, p. 32) lists the following regimes under "what doesn't work":

> Correctional programs that increase control and surveillance in the community;
> Programs emphasizing structure, discipline and challenge (boot camps using old-style military models, juvenile wilderness programs);
> Programs emphasizing specific deterrence (shock probation and Scared Straight).

A third line of evidence regarding the effects of punishment comes from a recent line of research applying meta-analysis to the literature on the effects of interventions with offenders.

The Meta-Analyses

Dating from Garrett's (1985) study, there have been a number of meta-analytic studies of offender treatment (Andrews et al., 1990; Lipsey, 1992; Redondo et al., 1999), with several syntheses also available (Gendreau, 1996; Lipsey, 1995; Lösel, 1995a, b, 1996; McGuire & Priestley, 1995). The main impact of these meta-analyses has been to give fresh impetus to interventions with offenders based on the foundations of treatment and rehabilitation (Hollin, 1999). However, several of the meta-analyses also considered the impact of interventions based on deterrence and punishment. Lipsey (1995, p. 74) summarises this aspect of the findings of the meta-analyses:

> Some particular attention should be given to the few treatment categories associated with negative effects. Most notable are the deterrence approaches such as shock incarceration. Despite their popularity, the available studies indicate that they actually result in delinquency increases rather than decreases.

Indeed, Lipsey (1995) expresses the view that the extant evidence raises "grave doubts about the effectiveness of these forms of treatment" (p. 74). Lipsey's conclusion is in accord with the other lines of evidence discussed above, so that it becomes difficult to resist the view that a consistent effect of deterrence is difficult to find. It appears that attempts to motivate offenders to stop offending through punishment are not having the intended effect. Surely this finding flies in the face of common sense: why should punishment actually make matters worse?

An answer to this question might be found in basic research in the behavioural sciences. The situation can be viewed as one in which offending is a form of human behaviour, and the aim of the criminal justice system is to produce conditions that lead to the reduction in the frequency of offending. What does behavioural research tell us of the optimum conditions for reducing behaviour?

REDUCING BEHAVIOUR: A BEHAVIOURAL PERSPECTIVE

One aspect of the experimental study of behaviour, as typified by the work of B. F. Skinner (Skinner, 1938, 1974), was a concern with understanding the conditions associated with a decrease in the frequency of a given behaviour. In the technical sense used in behaviour analysis, the term *punishment* refers to a situation (or in the language of behaviour analysis, a *contingency*) in which the consequences of a behaviour produce a decrease in its frequency. As will be discussed, the experimental work gave rise to a number of defining characteristics of effective punishment; i.e. the characteristics of a contingency in which behaviour decreases in frequency over time (Axlerod & Apsche, 1983). These behavioural principles have been applied in various settings to decrease behaviours such as self-harm and aggression (Martin & Pear, 1999).

Now, if the aim of punishment in the criminal justice system is to decrease the frequency of offending, and if experimental and applied behaviour analysis has revealed something of the nature of effective punishment, then how do the two compare? Table 14.1 shows what behaviour analysis has revealed about the conditions that produce a decrease in behaviour.

If these conditions are applied to the functioning of the criminal justice system what conclusions can be drawn?

1. Temporal Proximity

The consequences of a behaviour have the greatest effect in terms of changing the frequency of a behaviour when they occur close to the behaviour. If the

Table 14.1 Effective punishment

1. The punishing consequence of the behaviour should immediately follow the behaviour.
2. The punishing consequence of the behaviour should be inevitable, i.e. the punishing consequence should follow *every* occurrence of the behaviour.
3. The punishing consequence of the behaviour should be intense.
4. Choose an effective punishment.
5. Punishment is most effective when another form of behaviour is available that provides an alternative means by which to produce a different set of consequences.

consequences of a behaviour are delayed then their impact is lessened significantly. For example, one of the reasons it is difficult to stop young people smoking is because the long-term effects of smoking, particularly ill-health, are perceived as being a long way off. Indeed, they are so far off that they might never happen! On the other hand, the short-term gains from smoking, such as physiological change and peer group approval, are so close to the behaviour as to have maximum effect.

With regard to criminal behaviour, as Jeffrey (1965) observed in the formulation of Differential Reinforcement Theory, the same principle applies with respect to the temporal contiguity of the consequences of offending. When the offender is apprehended the process of justice means a delay of months between behaviour and the punishing consequences imposed by the courts. It is not difficult to see that for some criminals the punishment for offending is so distant, while the rewards for crime are so close, that the balance favours short-term gains.

2. Inevitability

If the punishing consequences of a behaviour are inevitable then that behaviour rapidly decreases in frequency. For example, if when attempting a spot of DIY, every time I touch a wire I get an electric shock then I'll rapidly learn not to touch that wire (and probably any others in the vicinity). It is not hard to imagine that if *every* time an offender committed a crime they were apprehended and convicted, then their offending would diminish rapidly. However, it is clear that in the real world this is not the case: victim and offender surveys consistently show that a great many crimes go unreported and hence undetected (Coleman & Moynihan, 1996). This under-reporting of crime is not limited to minor offences: for example, Groth and colleagues (1982) reported that sex offenders admitted to an average of five undetected crimes, with a range of up to 250 undetected rapes. With some exceptions, notably domestic homicide, it is likely that for most offenders punishment is far from inevitable.

3. Intensity

Not only must the punishing consequences of a behaviour be immediate and inevitable, to have maximum effect they must be of maximum intensity. The reason for this initial maximum intensity lies in the behavioural phenomenon of *desensitisation*. If there is a gradual exposure to an aversive situation or event it is possible to become adapted to the stimulus so that it no longer has a punishing effect. This process of adaptation is captured in the long-standing clinical technique of systematic desensitisation (Wolpe, 1958). Systematic desensitisation is frequently used with phobias, in which gradual exposure to a feared event or object is used to help the person cope with and even eliminate their fear.

The functioning of the criminal justice system might appear as if it is designed to desensitise offenders to the effects of punishment. Like the arachnophobe being gradually introduced to the sight and touch of the spider until it no longer holds fear, the offender may work their way through the hierarchy of receiving a caution, paying a fine, being sentenced to community service, complying with a probation order, experiencing short periods of custody, and ultimately a long custodial sentence. With such repeated exposure to these layers of punishment it is not surprising that, in the main, sanctions fail to have the desired effect.

4. Effective Punishers

As with beauty, reward and punishment are in the eye of the beholder. Within behavioural analysis, a punishment contingency is defined as one in which, *for the individual concerned*, the consequences of a behaviour lead to a reduction in the frequency of that behaviour. The emphasis on the individual is critically important in understanding behaviour change. Thus, for some people praise might well function as a reward, increasing the frequency of the behaviour that produces the praise. However, for other people, perhaps particularly adolescents, praise can function as a punisher, decreasing the frequency of the behaviour that produced the praise (Brophy, 1981).

In this light, it is possible to re-examine the assumption that the consequences of crime as delivered by the criminal justice system are, indeed, punishing in that they deliver an aversive penalty to the offender. To people who have never experienced prison the thought of a prison sentence may be distinctly unpleasant. While it is true that prisons are places of misery and unhappiness, any one who has ever worked in a prison will know that not all offenders find the experience either aversive or unpleasant.

5. Other Options

In behavioural terms, the delivery of effective punishment will, by definition, decrease the frequency of a behaviour. However, in order to avoid punishment in the short- and long-term, the individual must have available an alternative behaviour. In the absence of an appropriate alternative behaviour, the individual will repeat the behaviour in the future, resulting in a cycle of behaviour and punishment. Punishment is not constructive in the sense that it shows the individual what to do differently to avoid punishment, nor does it establish new behaviours that might gain the same outcome by legitimate means, it simply suppresses the immediate occurrence of a behaviour. Indeed, after delivery of punishment the next incidence of the behaviour may be more furtive or risky in order to avoid detection.

The Side-Effects of Punishment

It is tempting to think that punishment eliminates unwanted behaviour. However, both experimental and applied studies of behaviour show that punishment acts to *suppress* behaviour (Martin & Pear, 1999). When the punishment is discontinued it is often the case that the behaviour will revert to its original levels or even return at a higher level. This observation is entirely in line with the reconviction data after criminal sanctions: for example, after a period of imprisonment many offenders continue to offend, sometimes committing more serious offences.

The process of suppression of behaviour, i.e. the delivery of punishing consequences, is not a neutral event. Punishment raises strong emotions in the punished. For example, when people are punished they may well resent the imposition of the punishment, and may be frustrated in that their goals are being denied, and that they find themselves in an environment (e.g. arrest, court, probation office and custody) that makes them unhappy. Such personal states and environmental circumstances are prime setting conditions for aggression and violence (Berkowitz, 1993). In this light it is not surprising that those concerned with the administration of punishment—police officers, probation staff, prison staff—are deeply concerned about the incidence of assault experienced in the line of duty.

The administration of punishment can precipitate health problems for the punished individual. Surveys of prison populations have found a significantly higher incidence of mental disorder among prison populations than among the general population (Gunn et al., 1978). While there are several possible explanations for this increased rate in morbidity, there is a strong case to be made for the aversive nature of imprisonment acting as a stress that precipitates poor mental heath. Further, it is known that the rate of suicide in prisons is uncomfortably high (Dooley, 1990).

The act of the administration of punishment also serves to model retribution and vengeance as an appropriate response to misdemeanour. It is known that modelling is of immense importance in explaining human behaviour (Bandura, 1977), in that people may act in the way they perceive others acting towards themselves. If society elects to solve the problem of crime by the administration of punishment, then it is not surprising that punished offenders solve the relationship and financial problems in their lives in ways that inflict harm and punishment on other people. For example, Dobash and colleagues (2000) in their study of violent men, reported that the sources of argument that culminated in domestic violence towards women included money, trivial issues in domestic life, and jealousy.

CONCLUSION

The administration of punishment by the criminal justice system is a complex social act. The key point to focus on with respect to the administration of punishment is the outcome to be achieved. If the desired outcome is retribution for breaking the law, then the appropriate (whatever that may be) punitive measures will achieve that outcome. If the desired outcome is incapacitation for the purposes of public protection then, once again, inflicting the appropriate punishment (i.e. loss of liberty) will achieve this end. It is clear that in such instances there is an obvious link between punishment and its desired effect. Whether society wishes to administer punishment for these purposes is open to debate (Honderich, 1976; Walker, 1991), but it is apparent that punishment can serve these twin ends of retribution and incapacitation.

It is when punishment is advocated as a means of bringing about change in behaviour that the link between the administration of punishment and its intended outcome becomes significantly more uncertain. The notion that punishment can motivate changes in behaviour is the foundation of deterrence theory. The examination of the evidence with regard to *general* deterrence suggested that there is very little consistent support for the proposition that punishing offenders inhibits the antisocial behaviour of other members of society. Why should this be? An explanation can be found by considering the basic theoretical underpinnings of the notion of general deterrence. It will be recalled that the analogy was drawn that classical theory sees human action, including criminal behaviour, in terms of a calculator with free will (Lilly et al., 1995). Thus, we are seen as obeying the law (or not) because on balance the disadvantages of crime (i.e. punishment) outweigh its advantages. Indeed, it is the case that offenders may at times make rational decisions about offending (Cornish & Clarke, 1986). However, it is also evident that human action is more complex than the computations of a calculator: we obey the law, for example, because we believe in a legitimate social order, or because the law codifies moral beliefs in right and wrong, or for political reasons (Tyler, 1990).

Moving from general to *specific* deterrence, it is also doubtful whether punishment motivates long-term behaviour change at the individual level. Again, it is possible to see flaws in the "criminal as calculator" model in accounting for the offender's behaviour. Without denying that offenders may at times make rational decisions, it is also the case that at the point of committing a crime the offender may not be functioning at his or her optimum psychological or emotional state (Zamble & Quinsey, 1997). Further, it is also evident that decisions, including rational decisions, are the product of an individual's learning history. Any theoretical attempt to understand individual actions, including criminal acts, must account for a history of complex interactions between social and individual factors (Gresswell & Hollin, 1992).

If punishment demonstrably fails to motivate offenders to change, what are the alternatives in terms of changing offenders? A radical proposal lies in a monumental restructuring of the criminal justice system, moving its theoretical base into the 21st century and developing policies and practices based on contemporary knowledge about human behaviour. At a more prosaic level, it is clear that there is nothing constructive about punishment yet there are practical alternatives that can reduce crime (Hollin, 2001). The general unwillingness to adopt such alternatives as standard practice in the criminal justice system arguably lies in the (understandable) political reluctance to be seen to be delivering expensive specialist services to offenders. The current trend towards an analysis of the economic advantages of effective, evidence-based crime prevention services (Welsh et al., 2001), rather than advantages for the offenders, may be an approach that makes the shift from punishment to effective practice one that is more viable in the future.

REFERENCES

Andrews, D. A., Zinger, I., Hoge, R. D., Bonta, J., Gendreau, P., & Cullen, F. T. (1990). Does correctional treatment work? A clinically relevant and informed meta-analysis. *Criminology*, **28**, 369–404.

Axlerod, S. & Apsche, J. (eds). (1983). *The Effects of Punishment on Human Behaviour*. New York: Academic Press.

Bandura, A. (1977). *Social Learning Theory*. Englewood Cliffs, NJ: Prentice Hall.

Berkowitz, L. (1993). *Aggression: Its Causes, Consequences, and Control*. New York: McGraw-Hill.

Brophy, J. (1981). Teacher praise: a functional analysis. *Review of Educational Research*, **51**, 5–32.

Burton, V. S., Marquart, J. W., Cuvelier, S. J., Alarid, L. F., & Hunter, R. J. (1993). A study of attitudinal change among boot camp participants. *Federal Probation*, **57**, 46–52.

Coleman, C. & Moynihan, J. (1996). *Understanding Crime Data: Haunted by the Dark Figure*. Buckingham: Open University Press.

Copas, J. & Marshall, P. (1998). The offender group reconviction scale: a statistical reconviction score for use by probation officers. *Applied Statistics*, **47**, 159–71.

Cornish, D. B. & Clarke, R. V. G. (eds) (1986). *The Reasoning Criminal: Rational Choice Perspectives on Offending*. New York: Springer-Verlag.

Cowles, E. L. & Castellano, T. C. (1995). *"Boot Camp" Drug Treatment and Aftercare Intervention: An Evaluation Review*. Washington, DC: National Institute of Justice.

Cronin, R. C. (1994). *Boot Camps for Adult and Juvenile Offenders: Overview and Update*. Washington, DC: National Institute of Justice.

Dobash, R. E., Dobash, R. P., Cavanagh, K. & Lewis, R. (2000). *Changing Violent Men*. Thousand Oaks, CA: Sage.

Dooley, E. (1990). Prison suicide in England and Wales 1972–1987. *British Journal of Psychiatry*, **156**, 40–5.

Garrett, C. J. (1985). Effects of residential treatment of adjudicated delinquents: a meta-analysis. *Journal of Research in Crime and Delinquency*, **22**, 287–308.

Gendreau, P. (1996). Offender rehabilitation: what we know and what needs to be done. *Criminal Justice and Behavior*, **23**, 144–61.

Gresswell, D. M. & Hollin, C. R. (1992). Towards a new methodology for making sense of case material: an illustrative case involving attempted multiple murder. *Criminal Behaviour and Mental Health*, **2**, 329–41.

Groth, A. N., Longo, R. E. & McFadin, J. B. (1982). Undetected recidivism among rapists and child molesters. *Crime and Delinquency*, **3**, 450–8.

Gunn, J., Robertson, G., Dell, S. & Way, C. (1978). *Psychiatric Aspects of Imprisonment*. London: Academic Press.

Hollin, C. R. (1999). Treatment programmes for offenders: meta-analysis, "what works", and beyond. *International Journal of Law and Psychiatry*, **22**, 361–72.

Hollin, C. R. (Ed). (2001). *Handbook of Offender Assessment and Treatment*. Chichester: Wiley.

Honderich, T. (1976). *Punishment: The Supposed Justifications*, rev. edn. Harmondsworth: Penguin.

Honderich, T. (1993). *How Free Are You? The Determinism Problem*. Oxford: Oxford University Press.

Hood, R. (1996). *The Death Penalty: A World-Wide Perspective*, rev. edn. Oxford: Clarendon Press.

Jeffery, C. R. (1965). Criminal behavior and learning theory. *Journal of Criminal Law, Criminology, and Police Science*, **56**, 294–300.

Lilly, J. R., Cullen, F. T. & Ball, R. A. (1995). *Criminological Theory: Context and Consequence*, 2nd edn. Thousand Oaks, CA: Sage.

Lipsey, M. W. (1992). Juvenile delinquency treatment: a meta-analytic inquiry into the variability of effects. In T. D. Cook, H. Cooper, D. S. Cordray, H. Hartmann, L. V. Hedges, R. J. 22 Light, T. A. Louis & F. Mosteller (eds) *Meta-Analysis for Explanation: A Casebook*. New York: Russell Sage Foundation.

Lipsey, M. W. (1995). What do we learn from 400 studies on the effectiveness of treatment with juvenile delinquents? In J. McGuire (ed.) *What Works: Reducing Reoffending*. Chichester: Wiley.

Lloyd, C., Mair, G. & Hough, M. (1994). *Explaining Reconviction Rates: A Critical Analysis*. London: HMSO.

Lösel, F. (1995a). The efficacy of correctional treatment: a review and synthesis of meta-evaluations. In J. McGuire (ed.) *What Works: Reducing Reoffending*. Chichester: Wiley.

Lösel, F. (1995b). Increasing consensus in the evaluation of offender rehabilitation? Lessons from recent research syntheses. *Psychology, Crime, & Law*, **2**, 19–39.

Lösel, F. (1996). Working with young offenders: the impact of the meta-analyses. In C.R. Hollin & K. Howells (eds) *Clinical Approaches to Working with Young Offenders*. Chichester: Wiley.

MacKenzie, D. L. (2000). *Sentencing and Corrections in the 21st Century: Setting the Stage for the Future*. Report submitted to the National Institute of Justice, Office of Justice Program, US Department of Justice.

MacKenzie, D. L. & Brame, R. (1995). Shock incarceration and positive adjustment during community supervision. *Journal of Quantitative Criminology*, **11**, 111–42.

MacKenzie, D. L. & E. E. Hebert (eds) (1996). *Correctional Boot Camps: A Tough Intermediate Sanction*. Washington, DC: National Institute of Justice.

MacKenzie, D. L. & Shaw, J. W. (1990). Inmate adjustment and change during shock incarceration: the impact of correctional boot camp programs. *Justice Quarterly*, **7**, 125–50.

MacKenzie, D. L. & Shaw, J. W. (1993). The impact of shock incarceration on technical violations and new criminal activities. *Justice Quarterly*, **10**, 463–87.

MacKenzie, D. L. & Souryal, C. (1994). *Multisite Evaluation of Shock Incarceration*. Washington, DC: US Department of Justice.

MacKenzie, D. L. & Souryal, C. (1995a). A "Machiavellian" perspective on the development of boot camp prisons: a debate, unpublished symposium presentation.

MacKenzie, D. L. & Souryal, C. (1995b). Inmates' attitude change during incarceration: a comparison of boot camp with traditional prison. *Justice Quarterly*, **12**, 501–30.

MacKenzie, D. L., Brame, R., McDowall, D., & Souryal, C. (1995). Boot camp prisons and recidivism in eight states. *Criminology*, **33**, 327–57.

McGuire, J. (1995). The death of deterrence. In J. McGuire & B. Rowson (eds) *Does Punishment Work? Proceedings of a Conference*. London: Institute for the Study and Treatment of Delinquency.

McGuire, J. (in press). Criminal sanctions versus psychologically-based interventions with offenders: a comparative empirical analysis. *Psychology Crime & Law*.

McGuire, J. & Priestley, P. (1995). Reviewing "what works": past, present and future. In J. McGuire (ed.) *What Works: Reducing Reoffending*. Chichester: Wiley.

Martin, G. & Pear, J. (1999). *Behavior Modification: What It Is and How to Do It* 6th ed. Upper Saddle River, NJ: Prentice Hall.

Mathlas, R. E. S. & Mathews, J. W. (1991). The boot camp program for offenders: does the shoe fit? *International Journal of Offender Therapy and Comparative Criminology*, **35**, 322–7.

Morash, M. & Rucker, L. (1990). A critical look at the idea of boot camp as a correctional reform. *Crime and Delinquency*, **36**, 204–22.

Peterson, R. D. & Bailey, W. C. (1991). Felony, murder and capital punishment: an examination of the deterrence question. *Criminology*, **29**, 367–95.

Redondo, S., Sánchez-Meca, J. & Garrido, V. (1999). The influence of treatment programmes on the recidivism of juvenile and adult offenders: an European meta-analytic review. *Psychology, Crime, & Law*, **5**, 251–78.

Roshier, B. (1989). *Controlling Crime: The Classical Perspective in Criminology*. Milton Keynes: Open University Press.

Russell, B. (1961). *A History of Western Philosophy*, 2nd edn. London: Allen & Unwin.

Schrest, D. K. (1989). Prison "boot camps" do not measure up. *Federal Probation*, **53**, 15–20.

Skinner, B. F. (1938). *The Behavior of Organisms*. New York: Appleton-Century-Crofts.

Skinner, B. F. (1971). *Beyond Freedom and Dignity*. New York: Knopf.

Skinner, B. F. (1974). *About Behaviorism*. New York: Knopf.

Siegel, L. J. (1986). *Criminology*, 2nd edn. St Paul, MN: West.

Thomas, D. (1998). *The Victorian Underworld*. London: John Murray.

Thornton, D., Curran, L., Grayson, D. & Holloway, V. (1984). *Tougher Regimes in Detention Centres: Report of an Evaluation by the Young Offender Psychology Unit*. London: HMSO.

Tierney, J. (1996). *Criminology: Theory and Context*. London: Prentice Hall.

Tyler, T. R. (1990). *Why People Obey the Law*. New Haven, CT: Yale University Press.

von Hirsch, A. (1993). *Censure and Sanctions*. Oxford: Clarendon Press.

Walker, N. (1991). *Why Punish?* Oxford: Oxford University Press.

Welsh, B. C., Farrington, D. P. & Sherman, L. W. (2001). *Costs and Benefits of Preventing Crime*. Boulder, CO: Westview Press.

Wolpe, J. (1958). *Psychotherapy by Reciprocal Inhibition*. Stanford, CA: Stanford University Press.

Zamble, E. & Quinsey, V. L. (1997). *The Criminal Recidivism Process*. Cambridge: Cambridge University Press.

Chapter 15

FUTURE DIRECTIONS

MARY MCMURRAN

School of Psychology, Cardiff University, Cardiff, UK

INTRODUCTION

Contributors to this book have provided us with a clear understanding of how offenders' motivation to change may be construed and assessed, useful detail of how offenders' motivation to change may be enhanced, and a careful analysis of the ethics of motivating offenders to change. In relation to both theory and practice, it seems that knowledge of the understanding and treatment of addictions has a considerable amount to offer to the understanding and treatment of offending (Hodge et al., 1997). Here again, we have benefited from the knowledge and experience of addictions specialists, added to that of experts who work with offenders. Drawn together in one text, this material will surely prove a valuable resource for professionals who treat offenders. Yet, readers of this book will almost certainly identify gaps and shortcomings in the current state of theory, practice and evidence that should spur them to expand existing knowledge. What might those newly enthused professionals and researchers consider tackling?

THEORY

Therapeutic strategies that are derived from the study of addictions have provided a starting point for designing motivational interventions with offenders. Nevertheless, we should not apply methods designed in any other field to offenders without rigorous theory testing and outcome evaluation. Theoretical enrichment of our understanding of motivation to change offending is a priority.

In developing motivational interventions, the stages of change model (formally known as the transtheoretical model; TTM) has had enormous impact in the addictions field, with the development of stage-appropriate interventions. Does the stages of change pathway apply to offenders? It has been pointed out that the

---

Motivating Offenders to Change: A Guide to Enhancing Engagement in Therapy. Edited by M. McMurran.
© 2002 John Wiley & Sons, Ltd.

stages of change model derives largely from research on smoking, and may not be generalisable to alcohol and drug use (Sutton, 2001), let alone offending behaviour. There have been questions raised about the measurement and validity of the stages, and there is also controversy regarding whether a person should be allocated to a single stage or whether a profile of the person's scores over all the stages is more meaningful (Carbonari & DiClemente, 2000). Sutton (2001) has called for a rethink on the stages of change model as applied to substance use, and this surely should alert us to the need to examine more closely its applicability to offenders.

What factors affect motivation to change in offenders? It may help to know about the individual's motivations for engaging in offending in the first place. It is probable that a coherent and theoretically integrative motivational model for offending would help develop effective interventions, yet this is still an underdeveloped area. Cox and Klinger (1988), for example, described a motivational model of alcohol use, from which they went on to derive a schedule for the assessment of motivation and procedures of motivational counselling (Cox & Klinger, 2002). They outlined a route map, which, depending upon the nature of various features, leads to a decision either to drink or not drink. Factors affecting the decision include historical factors (e.g. personality, environment and drinking reinforcement history), current factors (e.g. positive and negative incentives, situational factors), mediating cognitive events and expected effects (enhancement or reduction of positive or negative affect). This route leads to approach or avoidance—drink or not drink.

Four types of motive have been derived from this model: (1) enhancement (internal positive reinforcement), (2) social (external positive reinforcement), (3) coping (internal negative reinforcement), and (4) conformity (external negative reinforcement). These motives are associated with different contextual antecedents and drinking outcomes (Cooper, 1994), and different personality types (Stewart & Devine, 2000). Targeting people's particular motives for drinking and taking personality characteristics into account may enhance the effectiveness of motivational interventions.

Such a model could be adapted for motivation to offend, and research conducted into its validity with offenders. Motivational pathways that echo the work of Cox and Klinger (1988) have recently begun to emerge in the offender literature. Polaschek and colleagues (2001) have developed a model of the behaviour chain leading to rape. Based on evidence from rapists, the authors trace a motivational pathway that includes background factors, goal formation, approach, preparation, offence and post-offence phases. An outline of this model is presented in Table 15.1. Within each of the phases a set of features pertains, with the specific characteristics being variable, depending on the people involved and their circumstances. This explains the flexibility of goals and variations in behaviour as the chain progresses. For example, a combination of angry mood and victim resistance may lead to different behaviours from circumstances where the mood is depressed and the victim compliant. While the principal purpose of this model is to classify offenders, it clearly has much to offer the development of interventions, including those aimed at motivating people to change. The motivational phase of models such as this could be expanded, and it may be useful to illustrate pathways in relation to other types of offending.

Table 15.1   Rape offence chain model

Phase	Features
Background	Background factors Coping style Mood
Goal formation	Establish goals Planning
Approach	Encounter victim Communicate intent Victim response Evaluation of progress towards goal Establish secondary goals Approach strategy selection
Preparation	Decide to commence sexual activity Appraise potential of situation Prepare for assault
Offence	Sexual assault Victim response Offender evaluation
Post-offence	Situation management Evaluation of situation Affective response Behavioural response Long-term response

Source: Adapted from Polaschek et al. (2001).

ASSESSMENT

There is no substitute in clinical practice for a comprehensive and multifactorial assessment of motivation, such as that described by Lawrence Jones in Chapter 3. Nonetheless, it is also important to standardise assessments of motivation, so that one person's "very motivated" or "not motivated" is the same as the next person's, and so that change over time may be measured. The problem of the measurement of motivation has been addressed in therapy generally, and most particularly in the study of addictions, with the development of a number of questionnaires. The University of Rhode Island Stages of Change Questionnaire (URICA) (McConnaughy et al., 1983, 1989) is problem non-specific and measures stage of change in therapy generally. The Stages of Change Readiness and Treatment Eagerness Scale (SOCRATES) (Miller & Tonigan, 1996) is a motivational measure specific to drinking. The Readiness to Change Questionnaire (RTC) (Rollnick et al., 1992) is a short derivative of the URICA and is drink-specific. Its close relation, the Readiness to Change Questionnaire–Treatment Version (RCQ [TV]) (Heather et al., 1999) is designed for people in treatment.

The existence of such a range of questionnaires measuring motivation to change drinking is testament to their usefulness. It is likely that such questionnaires would similarly be of value in assessing offenders, and the development of questionnaires for offending and offenders will involve considerable psychometric examination. We should not assume that what works for addictions would also work for offending. For example, we tried to adapt the RTC to measure motivation to change offending behaviour (McMurran et al., 1998). The words "my drinking" were changed to "my offending" to form the Readiness to Change Offending Questionnaire (RCOQ). This was examined on a population of personality disordered secure psychiatric hospital patients, with each patient's psychiatrist and key nurse rating the patient's stage of change. This produced discouraging results, with poor internal consistency of the new questionnaire's subscales, and no concurrent validity with staff ratings of motivation to change.

There are at least two possible reasons why adapting stage of change assessments from addictions to offending is not straightforward. First, assessment may be limited by the lower frequency of offence behaviour. Drinking and drug use may occur several times a day, whereas even the most dedicated criminal is probably less active. Measuring commitment to changing a behaviour that is very frequent may mean that it is possible to develop a more sensitive measure compared with the measurement of changing a behaviour that is relatively infrequent. This may be especially true when dealing with some serious offenders, as in our study (McMurran et al., 1998), where people may have offended only once in their lives, with that one offence being serious enough to warrant detention. Measures of motivation to change need to be examined on a range of offender types. Second, drinking is a reasonably well-defined behaviour, whereas offending includes a wide range of activities—violence, sexual offending, acquisitive offending, and so on—and many offenders are versatile in their criminality. It may be unclear to what "my offending" is referring.

The message is that care must be taken in adopting or adapting questionnaires from other fields. We cannot be sure that they will work with offenders, and psychometric checks need to be conducted. Assessments should be derived from theory, and if new models of offenders' motivation should be drawn up, we may see new assessment tools.

TREATMENT

The theory section above indicates that investigations into offenders' motivations may help to develop effective new treatment approaches. How treatments are delivered is another matter. DiClemente (1999), in his précis of motivational issues in relation to substance abuse treatment, identified several issues that warrant examination in relation to the treatment of offending. One issue with obvious relevance to offenders is that intrinsic motivation appears to produce better long-term outcomes than extrinsic motivation. It may be helpful, nonetheless, in some cases to "encourage" treatment attendance, although there are ethical implications with this, as addressed by Ron Blackburn in Chapter 9. The aim in compulsory treatment may be to enhance intrinsic motivation, and, in working with offenders, it is important to understand how extrinsic and intrinsic motivations interact. There is much work to be done here to investigate the effectiveness of court-mandated treatments, and treatments that are more or less obligatory before the prisons' parole board will consider release. The impact of motivational enhancement treatments under these conditions needs to be examined.

The issue of "responsivity" in offender treatments (Andrews et al., 1990) is that treatments should be delivered in a style that suits the needs and abilities of the client. Responsivity is broadly taken to include matching the intervention with the client's gender, culture, cognitive abilities and learning style. Apart from the actual content of treatments that suit them to the clients, there are a number of stylistic features that require further examination. Some clients may fare better in groups, whereas others may do better in individual sessions; some may do well in mixed gender or mixed culture groups, whereas others may not; and some may respond to active teaching methods, whereas others may prefer to be more studious and contemplative. While these notions seem reasonable, they are not well supported by empirical evidence. The facets of responsivity are under-explored, and there is considerable work to be done to examine what styles of intervention suit which clients.

Another variable in motivating offenders to change that requires attention is the influence of therapist characteristics, again something shared with offender treatments more generally, as well as addictions treatments (Carroll, 2001). Who is an effective therapist and what does he or she do that makes him or her effective? As Carroll points out, researching therapists is no easy task—patients are rarely randomised to therapists, the "therapist sample size" is small, and we assume therapists can adapt equally well to the delivery of all types of treatment. Nonetheless, it is important to investigate therapist attributes that may affect a client's motivation. Basic aspects that are easy to measure are type and level of qualifications, training and extent of experience. More difficult to measure, but nonetheless very important, are personal qualities such as patience, extraversion, toughness and psychological-mindedness. One should not assume that there is a right kind of personality for working with offenders, but rather that certain therapist qualities may suit certain clients.

EVALUATION

Evaluation inevitably recalls the question: "What works best with whom under what conditions?". In this case, what motivational interventions effect most change, in what kind of offenders, and where, by whom, and when are these interventions best conducted?

First, we need to be clear about what we expect motivational interventions to do. Are we aiming to motivate people to change their behaviour or to engage in treatment? Motivational interventions alone can certainly effect change in addictions. In Project MATCH, for example, a four-session motivational enhancement therapy for changing drinking worked as well as more intensive therapies (Project MATCH Research Group, 1997). Indeed, some commentators believe that the assessment phase prior to treatment may have been an active ingredient. It may well be that intensive intervention is not always necessary for drinkers. The same is probably true for offenders, yet in offender treatment these days resources are being ploughed primarily into intensive treatments for high-risk offenders, with little support given for brief interventions, despite the fact that they may work, at least with some people.

Most accredited offender treatment programmes these days contain a motivational component; indeed, this is usually a requirement for accreditation. It may be worth while to design and evaluate a motivational enhancement module, alone and in conjunction with other treatment components, to see what works best and in which combinations. A dismantling approach to examine which components of treatment are most effective and in what combination is one way to streamline and improve treatments.

As with all treatment research, and to paraphrase Farrington (2001), we need high-quality experimental and quasi-experimental evaluations of the effectiveness of motivational enhancement programmes. Valid and reliable measures need to be used, and these should include both observations of behaviour and indicators of change, usually psychometric tests. Change needs to be assessed as the intervention progresses to check that movements are in the desired direction. Criterion measures should be relevant to the goal of treatment. Where motivation is concerned, this may be primarily to measure subsequent treatment attendance and participation, although the effect of the motivational component on the final outcome is also important. In addition, we would do well to examine the cost–benefit ratio for our interventions.

CONCLUSION

Contributions to this book provide models for understanding motivation to change, and indicate some of the variety of motivational enhancement intervention approaches—cognitive-behavioural, drama-based and psychodynamic. They cover some of the venues in which motivational interventions are applied—prisons, hospitals, and the community—and address some specific problems that might be encountered in working with offenders. These chapters contain academic, empirical and practical information. They will, it is hoped, inspire the enterprise that is required to address the developmental issues outlined above.

REFERENCES

Andrews, D.A., Zinger, I., Hoge, R.D., Bonta, J., Gendreau, P. & Cullen, F.T. (1990). Does correctional treatment work? A clinically relevant and psychologically informed meta-analysis. *Criminology*, **28**, 369–404.
Carbonari, J.P. & DiClemente, C.C. (2000). Using transtheoretical model profiles to differentiate levels of alcohol abstinence success. *Journal of Consulting and Clinical Psychology*, **68**, 810–17.
Carroll, K.M. (2001). Constrained, confounded, and confused: why we really know so little about therapists in treatment outcome research. *Addiction*, **96**, 203–6.
Cooper, M.L. (1994). Motivations for alcohol use among adolescents: development and validation of a four-factor model. *Psychological Assessment*, **6**, 117–28.
Cox, W.M. & Klinger, E. (1988). A motivational model of alcohol use. *Journal of Abnormal Psychology*, **97**, 168–80.
Cox, W.M. & Klinger, E. (eds) (2002). *A Handbook of Motivational Counseling: Motivating People for Change* Chichester: Wiley.
DiClemente, C.C. (1999). Motivation for change: implications for substance abuse treatment. *Psychological Science*, **10**, 209–13.
Farrington, D.P. (2001). Crime prevention. *The Psychologist*, **14**, 182–3.

Heather, N., Luce, A., Peck, D., Dunbar, B. & James, I. (1999). Development of a treatment version of the readiness to change questionnaire. *Addiction Research*, **7**, 63–83.

Hodge, J.E., McMurran, M. & Hollin, C.R. (eds) (1997). *Addicted to Crime?* Chichester: Wiley.

McConnaughy, E.A., Prochaska, J.O. & Velicer, W.F. (1983). Stages of change in psychotherapy: Measurement and sample profiles. *Psychotherapy: Theory, Research, and Practice*, **20**, 368–75.

McConnaughy, E.A., DiClemente, C.C., Prochaska, J.O. & Velicer, W.F. (1989). Stages of change in psychotherapy: a follow-up report. *Psychotherapy: Theory, Research, and Practice*, **26**, 494–503.

Miller, W.R. & Tonigan, J.S. (1996). Assessing drinkers' motivation for change: the Stages of Change Readiness and Treatment Eagerness Scale (SOCRATES). *Psychology of Addictive Behaviors*, **10**, 81–9.

McMurran, M., Tyler, P., Hogue, T., Cooper, K., Dunseath, W. & McDaid, D. (1998). Measuring motivation to change in offenders. *Psychology, Crime and Law*, **4**, 43–50.

Polaschek, D.L.L., Ward, T., Hudson, S.M. & Siegert, R.J. (2001). Developing a descriptive model of the offence chains of New Zealand rapists: taxonomic implications. In D.P. Farrington, C.R. Hollin & M. McMurran (eds) *Sex and Violence: The Psychology of Crime and Risk Assessment*. London: Routledge.

Project MATCH Research Group (1997). Project MATCH secondary a priori hypotheses. *Addiction*, **92**, 1671–98.

Rollnick, S., Heather, N., Gold, R. & Hall, W. (1992). Development of a short "readiness to change" questionnaire for use in brief opportunistic interventions among excessive drinkers. *British Journal of Addiction*, **87**, 743–54.

Stewart, S.H. & Devine, H. (2000). Relations between personality and drinking motives in young adults. *Personality and Individual Differences*, **29**, 495–511.

Sutton, S. (2001). Back to the drawing board? A review of applications of the transtheoretical model to substance use. *Addiction*, **96**, 175–86.

INDEX

Index compiled by Annette Musker